MW01006470

BISON
BOOKS

# A Yaqui Life

The Personal Chronicle of a Yaqui Indian

by
ROSALIO MOISÉS, JANE HOLDEN KELLEY,
and WILLIAM CURRY HOLDEN

Introduction by
JANE HOLDEN KELLEY

UNIVERSITY OF NEBRASKA PRESS
LINCOLN                    LONDON

First Bison Book printing of second edition: 1991
Most recent printing of second edition indicated by the last digit below:
10      9      8      7      6      5      4      3

Library of Congress Cataloging in Publication Data
Moisés, Rosalio, 1896–1969.
A Yaqui life.
Previous ed. (c1971) published under title: The tall candle.
1. Moisés, Rosalio, 1896–1969.  2. Yaqui Indians—Biography.  I. Kel-
ley, Jane Holden, 1928–   joint author.   II. Holden, William Curry,
1896–   joint author.   III. Title.
[E99.Y3M6 1977]   970'.004'97[B]   76–56789
ISBN 0-8032-8175-7 (pbk.)

This book was originally published under the title *The Tall Candle: The Personal Chronicle of a Yaqui Indian.*

Rosalio Moisés died in May, 1969, in Tucson, Arizona. We deeply regret that his candle went out before he held this book in his hand. It was his wish that it be dedicated *a la tribu Yaqui.*

J. H. K.
W. C. H.

# Contents

A section of illustrations follows page 164.

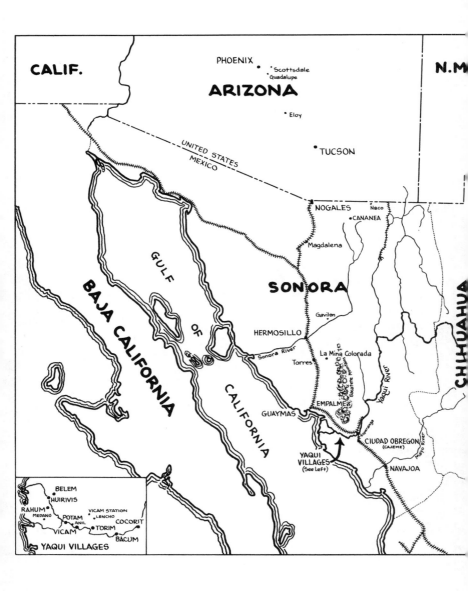

# Introduction

By Jane Holden Kelley

WILLIAM CURRY HOLDEN first met Rosalio Moisés in 1934, and their destinies were curiously intertwined from that date. One was a trained historian and part-time anthropologist, the other a gifted observer of life around him with the remarkable facility of memory that one often finds among groups who rely on oral rather than written history. This book is a culmination of their mutual influence on each other and on me. It is not a Yaqui ethnography. Rather, it is the story of one Yaqui whose lifetime coincided with a vital era in Yaqui history. I have chosen to call it a personal chronicle both because of the strong historical awareness that forms an integral part of Rosalio's world and because of the rather disjointed, episodic character of the narrative, which lacks the smooth flow of a story line pursuing a well-ordered theme. The title comes from a belief deeply held by Rosalio that every person on earth has a candle in heaven and, except in cases of accidental death, one lives until his candle burns down.

It is not my purpose in this Introduction to provide a full Yaqui history and cultural description, but only as much background as the reader needs to understand Rosalio's story. The first two sections, "The Setting" and "A Historical Sketch," are simply capsule versions of the materials that are more ably and amply presented in the books listed in the Selected Bibliography. Indeed, for the reader who is acquainted with the works of Edward Spicer and Ralph Beals, these first two sections are superfluous. People and events described in this personal chronicle are tied into generalized Yaqui history in a third section of the Introduction, which concludes with an ethnographic description. The latter has two purposes. In the main, it is meant to provide background for the reader; in addition, some ethnographic details emerge from Rosalio's story that have not previously been recorded for the Yaquis, and they are hereby added to the ethnographic record.

The Yaquis are perhaps the best-known aboriginal group in north-western Mexico. Their name carries connotations of bravery, fierceness, religious fanaticism, and a single-minded pursuit of tribal autonomy to people even beyond the Mexican border. Their story reflects a deep commitment to a way of life and embodies the tragic consequences of a society under incredible strain.

When first encountered by the Spaniards, the Yaquis were a substantial horticultural tribe scattered in rancherias, or small settlements, over the Yaqui Valley in the southern part of the modern Mexican state of Sonora. Linguistically, culturally, and physically they were closely related to the Mayo tribe that occupied the river valley to the south. The Yaquis, Mayos, and other tribes spoke dialects of the Cahita language of the Uto-Aztecan language stock.

Traditionally there are said to be eight villages (*ocho pueblos*). These are actually the result of the Jesuit consolidation of the dispersed population from eighty-odd rancherias into eight mission towns in the seventeenth century. To the Yaquis, however, their locations and boundaries were established by divine fiat, and supernatural sanctions for their existence are many. From west to east the eight villages are Belem, Huirivis, Rahum, Potam, Vicam, Torim, Bacum, and Cocorit.

Throughout the centuries, indeed to the present day, the land of the Yaquis has been of utmost importance to Yaqui culture. God gave these lands to the Yaquis, according to deep-seated beliefs, and a more final authority cannot be found in the Yaqui world-view.

Perhaps no other group of aboriginal Americans have protected their land more tenaciously or more consistently. In spite of long years of bloody wars and periods of systematic deportation and extermination, the Yaquis still live on Yaqui land. Within the past century and a half, this persecution has acted to reinforce group identity, emphasizing the separateness of the Yaquis from the surrounding populations. Now that overt persecution has ended, Yaqui culture and tribal unity are under more subtle change-producing pressures, and yet the basic framework of Yaqui culture seems remarkably persistent.

## The Setting

The upper tributaries of the Yaqui River head in southern Arizona, north-central and northeastern Sonora, and the Sierre Madre Occidental of Chihuahua. The main course of the river is southward across much of the state of Sonora. In its lower reaches, it cuts through the low but rugged frontal range to find its way to the Gulf of California across the coastal plain. The latter portion of the river was unstable in the past and many old channels exist. It is here that the Yaqui villages are located, where the rich alluvial valley soil is suitable for intensive cultivation.

Yaqui territory includes not only the rich valley lands, but also broad areas on each side of the river and the adjacent Sierra Madre, which have been of particular importance. Hunting parties have long used the mountains, and they became a refuge during times of war and trouble. The phrase "Sierra Yaquis" recurs again and again in Rosalio's narrative, referring to those individuals who fled their villages to seek comparative safety in the mountains.

The lower part of the Yaqui Valley is virtually frost free. It supports a subtropical thorn thicket vegetation, while the upper river and lands bordering the lower valley on the north are a part of the Sonoran desert. Marked differences exist between the valley vegetation and that of the adjacent lands or mesas. Mesquite is the single most dominant type of vegetation in both the valley and elsewhere. Mesquite trees grow to a height of forty feet, and scrubby mesquite forms the main ingredient of the dense brush, or thorn thicket, that makes travel almost impossible except along paths or across cleared areas. Few plants, not excluding the wild flowers, lack a spiny armoring. A great variety of cacti, cottonwoods, palo verde, jito, and other plants are interspersed among the mesquite. Dense canebrakes are found in the valley.

Although the region may technically be called subtropical, the flora belongs to the desert because of the annual distribution of rainfall. Two rainy seasons occur, separated by hot, dry intervals. The main rainy season comes in the summer from late June to September, usually in the form of violent thunderstorms. In December and January, actual rainfall along the coastal strip is slight; however, enough rain falls in the mountains containing the headwaters of the main rivers to cause flooding of the lowlands, allowing two crops a year to be harvested in this frost-free zone. The summer heat with temperatures in excess of 125°F. has been a subject of much interest and concern to all who live in the region. Rosalio makes several references to it.

Yaqui agriculture has been intimately tied to the natural flooding cycle of the river. The construction of a large dam, which diverted the lion's share of water away from Yaqui lands to the new, non-Yaqui irrigation district around Obregon, seriously crippled Yaqui agricultural production for a number of years, including those years described in this book when Rosalio was living in the Yaqui villages.

Aside from utilizing the natural richness of the valley lands and the favorable climate for intensive agriculture, other aspects of the natural environment are of benefit to the Yaquis. The abundant wildlife was hunted regularly in the past. The special religious significance of the deer to the Cahita and other Uto-Aztecan-speaking tribes of northwestern Mexico predates the arrival of the Spanish. Invested with a wealth of supernatural beliefs and ritual, deer hunting occupied a role of ongoing importance in the supernatural and psychological areas of the world of Yaqui men. Game provided a dietary source of protein fairly regularly and created an important secondary food source when crops failed. Hunting of less desirable game, such as wood rats, was regarded by most as a final resort to avert starvation. As Rosalio puts it, one could judge how hungry the people of Torim were by how close the big wood rats could be found to the village. In periods of food shortages, the wood rat population was cleaned out in increasingly larger concentric circles around each village or rancheria.

Some wild plant products were favorites, harvested in times of plenty as well as in times of famine. Other plants, considered starvation fare, were not relished. The carrizo cane has long been exploited for making a variety of objects. The early Spanish name for Cahita territory was Petatlan (*petate*-land, or place of mats), suggesting that the common modern house type utilizing carrizo cane mats for walls is indeed an aboriginal trait. Many of the native woods are used for implements and containers, and the omnipresent mesquite has gained a new importance in the modern cash economy because of the great commercial demand for fence posts, crossties, charcoal, and firewood.

## A Historical Sketch

Relatively few years elapsed between the initial landing of the Spaniards in Veracruz (1519) and their appearance in northwest Mexico. The earliest contacts between Yaquis and Spaniards were brief, involved few Spaniards, and caused no serious disruption of Yaqui life. A battle occurred on October 5, 1533, between the Yaquis and Diego de Guzmán, who was on a slave raid. For the Yaquis this was an omen of things to come rather than an event of major consequence. Alvar Núñez Cabeza de Vaca and his companions are known to have crossed Cahita country in a trek from their Florida shipwreck of 1528 to the west coast of Mexico. Another Spaniard, Francisco de Ibarra, lived peacefully among the Yaqui for a time in 1564 while prospecting for silver.

The real conquest of Sonora, in the early seventeenth century, fell to Don Diego Martínez de Hurdaide, a Spanish captain who took part in three expeditions against the Yaquis. The Yaquis carried the field in each of the three engagements. After seriously crippling the Spanish forces in northwestern Mexico, the Yaquis, however, did not assume the offensive. Within a year, they sued for peace, which Hurdaide bestowed with due ceremony on April 15, 1610.

Within a decade the Jesuits Andrés Pérez de Ribas and Tomás Basilio, along with some Christianized Tehuecos Indians, entered Yaqui territory without military escort. The chronicle of Pérez de Ribas is the classic source on the aboriginal culture of the Yaquis and the changes effected in their lives during the early mission period. Yaqui acceptance of the mission system was rapid and wholehearted. In 1623 they had mellowed sufficiently to allow Hurdaide to enter their territory with a small military escort. They accepted civil officials appointed by Hurdaide from among their own numbers. For the next two or three generations, the entire Yaqui country was peaceful. Consolidation of the population from the eighty dispersed rancherias into eight mission towns proceeded smoothly. A large part of the success of this early missionizing must be attributed to the caliber of the Jesuits assigned there, to the absence of corollary military force, and to the fact that Yaqui culture and population remained healthy, vigorous, and productive.

With the discovery of a fabulous silver mine at Alamos in 1684 large numbers of Spaniards with nonreligious motives were attracted to the area for the first time. Their gradual encroachment culminated in the first Yaqui-Mayo revolt, in 1740. In the following years individual Yaquis began to move outside the Yaqui Valley, becoming valued workers in the mines and elsewhere.

The Jesuits were expelled from the New World in 1767, primarily because of European-based political maneuverings. When the Jesuits were suddenly removed from their numerous New World missions, a vacuum was left. The Franciscans who took over the Yaqui missions encountered none of the success of their predecessors. For the next several generations, stress and distrust were evident between the Yaquis and the Spanish, although no major flare-up occurred. As Spicer remarks, "After 120 years the typical Spanish frontier situation had finally developed in the Yaqui-Mayo country."[1]

In a sense, the chain of modern events may be said to have begun in

[1] Edward Spicer, *Cycles of Conquest* (Tucson: University of Arizona Press, 1962), pp. 52-53.

1825, just after the wars of Mexican independence. A crisis was precipitated in Yaqui country when Mexican government soldiers attempted for the first time to collect taxes from the Yaquis. Juan Banderas, who emerged as the Yaqui leader, made alliances with the Mayos, Pimas, and Opatas. Their combined force was able to successfully sweep the region clean of Mexicans. As on the earlier occasion cited above, however, their military advantage was not pursued beyond the immediate objective. Mexican forces were allowed to retrench and ultimately inflicted a defeat on the Indian alliance. In 1827, Banderas made a treaty with the Mexicans and was placed on the government payroll, but a few years later he was up in arms again. On this occasion he was captured and shot at Arizpe, the Sonoran capital of that day, along with his second in command, an Opata Indian named Dolores Gutiérrez.

The lines between Yaqui-Mexican positions in the Banderas rebellion were not as clearly drawn as one might surmise. While most of the Yaquis supported Banderas, some two hundred Yaqui men fought with the Mexicans. This sort of factionalism was to become a familiar theme in Yaqui history from 1825 to 1927; Yaquis were to be found on all sides of most issues. Furthermore, an influential group of Mexicans sided with the Yaquis in the first Banderas uprising.

Banderas' execution briefly removed a capable leader, but fighting erupted again within a year. Even before Banderas' execution, Yaqui leadership had divided into two significant groups: those who accepted the Mexican presence as a permanent fact of life; and those who refused to admit a higher authority than the tribe itself. The former group was led by Juan Ignacio Jusacamea of Torim pueblo until his death about 1840. The latter group lacked a known leader after Banderas was removed.

From 1830 to 1859, Governor Manuel Gándara was the main political force in Sonora. Like most Mexican politicans of the middle decades of the nineteenth century, his main problem was to sustain his own position against rivals. The Yaquis and the Mayos were not molested most of the time, although Gándara could and did inspire them to take up arms against his political enemies from time to time. In Gándara's final struggle with General Pesqueira from 1857 to 1862, the Yaquis were almost constantly involved in military action against the Pesqueira faction. General Pesqueira, victorious in his struggle with Gándara, finally invaded the Yaqui-Mayo heartland in 1862. A believer in enforced "peace," Pesqueira and his assistant, Colonel García Morales, began a relentless campaign in which many Yaqui leaders were captured and shot and Yaqui property was ruthlessly destroyed. The highlight of General García

Morales's campaign was the burning of 450 Yaquis in the Bacum church.

The French invasion of Guaymas in 1865 brought relief from years of oppression, and therefore found favor among some Yaquis. A Yaqui leader who had fought with Gándara, Mateo Marquin (or José María Barquin), gave active support to the French cause. However, the French were defeated and driven from Sonora in 1866, again leaving the Yaquis, or at least some of them, on the losing side.

An uneasy peace followed General Morales's pacification campaign. The new state constitution of 1874 contained the proviso that Yaquis who lived in the pueblos (i.e., under Mexican control) could enjoy the privileges of citizenship, while those who lived outside the towns were not to receive those rights. That same year, Governor Pesqueira appointed the Yaqui José María Leyva (Cajeme) as *alcalde mayor* of the Yaqui and Mayo towns. Cajeme, who had fought with Pesqueira against the French and therefore did not enjoy the support of a large number of the Yaquis, became the dominant figure in Yaqui affairs until 1887.

When old General Pesqueira appointed his son, José Pesqueira, as his successor in 1875, rebellion broke out anew in the Yaqui and Mayo country. Cajeme, leading Yaqui and Mayo soldiers against the younger General Pesqueira, was defeated at Pitahaya. A new round of military subjugation of the rebellious Indians ensued. Strangely enough, Cajeme was not removed from office.

The Pesqueira dictatorship was effectively challenged by the Torres family, who took over the key position in Sonoran politics in 1879 when General Luis E. Torres was elected governor. Thus began a new Sonoran dynasty that lasted until 1910. The governorship did not remain in the hands of the Torres family, but was their patrimony to pass around within their political clique.

Governor Torres and his aides conceived a new format for dealing with the Yaquis and the Mayos. Noting that the previous pacification attempts had solved little, they asked the support of the federal government in establishing military garrisons within Yaqui-Mayo country. The soldiers would "protect" the Indians and serve as "civilizing examples." By this time, of course, the other tribes in the state had been effectively brought under control and attention could be focused on the two recalcitrant tribes who still controlled the richest agricultural land in the state. The Mexican government declined the proposition, and garrisons were not established at this time.

The last Mayo uprising had its beginnings at the battle of Capetemaya in 1882. Agustin Ortiz, brother of Governor Carlos Ortiz (a Torres puppet), reacted to a rumor that Cajeme was attending a conference with Mayo leaders in order to plan a new rebellion. Wishing to nip such a plan in the bud, Ortiz attacked the conference and was defeated. Shortly thereafter a prominent Mayo leader, José Zarapero, was captured and shot. Cajeme appointed Jesús Moroyoqui as his successor. During the two years of the rebellion, Cajeme did not muster Yaqui troops to the defense of the Mayos as he probably could have done. The backbone of the Mayo rebellion was broken by 1884, although resistance continued until 1887, the year Jesús Moroyoqui and Cajeme were killed.

In the early 1880s Cajeme had tried to consolidate his authority within the Yaqui tribe. The tribe was quite willing to let him cope with outsiders and military matters, but feeling ran against him when he overreached the authority deemed proper by Yaqui standards and preempted civil powers as well.

Many Yaquis disagreed with Cajeme's policies; by and large his critics left the valley. The year 1885 saw an attempt made on Cajeme's life by one of his own estranged officers, and a counterdemand from Cajeme that the culprits be punished, backed by the holding of some Mexican boats for ransom. The Mexicans replied by dispatching a force under the command of General José Guillermo Carbó. Yaqui troops successfully defended the fortress of Anil, but otherwise met defeat. Cajeme offered peace if all Mexican forces withdrew, but the Mexicans refused. The Potam Peace Conference of 1885 produced a document never signed by the principals and hostilities resumed. The fortress of Anil finally fell to Mexican hands, and bitter fighting continued in 1886. The Yaqui plight seemed hopeless after the staggering defeat at Buatachive, where two hundred Yaquis died and two thousand were taken prisoner. Smallpox swept through the valley. Ultimately a peace treaty was signed at Torim, the town that became the administrative center for General Lorenzo Torres. Small garrisons were built at Cocorit and at the port of Medano.

Some four thousand Yaquis were settled under Mexican control in the eight pueblos at this time. Thousands of others, probably the majority of the tribe, sought work outside of the Yaqui Valley. A small group of Yaquis, Cajeme among them, remained in the Bacatete Mountains outside of Mexican control, raiding and harrassing both the Mexicans and the Yaquis who had capitulated to Mexican demands.

Cajeme was taken prisoner, held captive for some time, and executed in 1887 in the belief, or at least in the hope, that his removal would stop Yaqui rebellion. As in the case of Juan Banderas, the hope was not realized.

As Juan Banderas aroused in his adversaries a reluctant admiration for his talented and gifted leadership, so did Cajeme. Within a month of Cajeme's death renewed fighting broke out. Well-organized Yaquis operated out of their mountain strongholds, raiding and retreating as mobile guerrilla units. Juan Maldonado, known as Tetabiate, took over as chief of the mountain bands, providing a critical focal point of military leadership.

In the valley, General Torres again proceeded to distribute land to those Yaquis who had capitulated and to the Mexicans. His own family took over extensive property in the conservative town of Torim, building a substantial house there. In 1887, the Scientific Commission surveyed tribal lands, under military escort, and two years later an irrigation canal laid out by the survey was completed. An effort made in 1890 to attract the dispersed Yaquis back to their homeland was not successful; not a single individual rose to the offered inducements.

After a long correspondence between Tetabiate and Colonel Francisco Peinado about peace, in which Tetabiate's demands sounded a good deal like those of Banderas and Cajeme before him, Tetabiate descended from the mountains with his entire band, including women and children. The Peace of Ortiz was signed by him and two of his men in 1897. Tetabiate was placed on the government payroll. Land distribution continued.

War was resumed with renewed vigor in 1899, with Tetabiate again leading a remnant of the militants. The Mexicans, for their part, were determined to end Yaqui insurrection once and for all. Military measures were taken to seal off the offending mountains that offered such a convenient and safe harbor to the rebels. In addition, a new program of resettling recalcitrant Indians was begun. A large intelligence network thrived on information obtained from informers about Yaqui activities.

Mexican soldiers carried the battle into the heart of the Bacatete Mountains in 1899. As troops penetrated the Sierra, the thousands of Sierra Yaquis who normally were dispersed throughout the rough country were driven into a few sanctuaries. On January 18, 1900, several military detachments converged upon the Yaqui stronghold at Mazocoba. A pitched battle began at 10:00 A.M. and was ended only when darkness descended. The military report of General Torres estimates that some four hundred Yaquis were killed, not counting those that "precipitated themselves" into the canyons below.[2] Approximately one thousand women

[2] Fortunato Hernández, *Las razas indígenas de Sonora y las guerras del Yaqui* (Mexico: J. de Elizalde, 1902), pp. 172 ff.

and children were taken prisoner. Of these, the "major part" died on the march from Mazocoba to Tetacombiate. Finally, some 864 prisoners were confined in the Guásimas *cuartel*. In contrast, the official figures for the Mexican losses cite 18 dead and 62 wounded. This battle is well chronicled in Sonoran history and in Yaqui oral folk history as the Massacre of Mazocoba. Yaqui versions of the massacre place the casualty figures much higher than do the military records, and in at least some versions, the massacre is seen as the result of unwarranted shooting of unarmed Yaquis. It seems clear that the Yaquis were virtually unarmed, as General Torres reports that "thirty-five fire-arms of all classes" were taken from the Yaquis.[3] Tetabiate was present but escaped. Hernández hints that his escape may have left others holding the bag. Another Yaqui leader, Pablo Ruiz Opodepe, was killed. General Torres says that this man was recognized by the rebels as their supreme leader and that he was, without doubt, the spirit (*alma*) of the revolution.[4]

In 1901, Tetabiate was killed by a Mexican detachment under the command of his own former lieutenant, Major Loreto Villa, who received a second-class Cross of Military Merit for this action. The Bacatete Mountains were virtually cleared of Yaquis, but small groups fought on wherever they could.

Rafael Izábal (also spelled Yzábal or Isábal), one of the Torres family puppets, became governor in 1903. His name seems to arouse a more intense feeling and hatred among the Yaquis than does the name of any other official. Spicer notes that Izábal is vividly remembered as the "evil spirit" of the deportation period.[5] Perhaps Izábal's religious views compounded the injuries he directly inflicted upon the Yaquis by his vigorous policies of deportation and execution. An anachronism for the Díaz period, he was one of the few officials who early gave expression to strong sentiments of anticlericalism such as later gained official sanction when Calles became president of Mexico.

Under Governor Izábal, many Yaquis were deported to the haciendas of Yucatán or Oaxaca. Others were killed. Arizona became a sanctuary. The trickle of refugees that began in 1887 became a flood in the years after 1903 as more and more Yaquis fled across the border. The Arizona Yaquis viewed themselves as refugees from their rightful land and not as permanent settlers in a new country.

[3] Ibid., p. 174.
[4] Ibid.
[5] Edward Spicer, "Potam, a Yaqui Village in Sonora," *American Anthropological Association Memoir* 77 (1954), p. 32.

The year 1910 was monumental in the history of the Mexican republic. The social revolution unleashed at that time swept Porfirio Díaz (president since 1876) from power. Díaz's henchmen over the country were toppled. In Sonora this meant the end of the Torres dynasty.

The role of the Yaquis during the ensuing revolutionary years is difficult to summarize, and in many ways the revolution was peripheral to central Yaqui concerns. Initially, however, the valley Yaquis sided with the establishment against the revolutionaries. The role of the tribe as a political force often differed from roles played by individuals in regard to the network of personal relationships and attitudes maintained by members of the tribe. Those who had become government informers or joined the federal army had a vested interest on the side of Díaz's regime and the Torres establishment. Some of them had, in effect, become "Mexicans," but their identity as Yaquis was well known to other Yaquis. As the revolutionary movement became factionalized, Yaquis fought with various revolutionary armies.

Valley Yaquis offered to make peace with the revolutionaries, advancing the old demand that they be given their land and all non-Yaquis be removed. Obregón, leader of the revolutionary army, responded adversely to this demand, sending in young General Lázaro Cárdenas, later to be president of Mexico, to use forceful persuasion. Many, believing Obregón would return their lands, had joined the Obregón forces and marched triumphantly to Mexico City at the conclusion of the revolution. Adolfo de la Huerta became governor of Sonora in 1919. Reassignment of Yaqui lands to non-Yaquis was renewed, culminating in the 1926 hostilities. The match that ignited the powder keg this time was an incident involving Obregón, who was stumping the country in his second presidential campaign, and the Yaqui General Luis Matuz, who had fought with Obregón in the revolution. Matuz detained Obregón at Vicam Switch to discuss the eternal problem of Yaqui land and its distribution. Mexican soldiers, believing Obregón to be held prisoner, came to liberate him, and the fat was in the fire again. Yaquis fled to the mountains and Arizona by the hundreds. The battle of Cerro del Gallo (Hill of the Rooster) was the last major battle of the Yaqui wars. Open hostility ended in 1927.

In 1927, Mexican military garrisons were placed in every Yaqui village for the first time. The old practice of putting Yaquis on the Mexican payroll was continued on a greatly expanded scale. Since 1927 two garrisons, one Yaqui and one Mexican, have been stationed in each town, each within plain view of the other. One is manned by Yaquis in civilian clothes. The more imposing Mexican garrison is staffed with uniformed men, not a few of whom are Yaquis or Mayos in the regular army. The paymaster of the Yaqui zone and some of the higher-ranking officers of the "real" army have often been "Mexicanized Yaquis" who still have relatives among the Yaqui population and whose life and family history are locally well known. In the years since 1927, Yaqui attempts to preserve the land intact for their own use have been largely unsuccessful. Most of the vast, rich lands south of the river are in the hands of Mexicans and Americans. A sort of "reservation" now exists that includes the land north of the river and the Bacatete Mountains.

While this book is an expression of one Yaqui's view of his world, and therefore inevitably one-sided in regard to the Mexican-Yaqui conflict, one must keep in mind the problems faced by the Mexicans in the creation of a republic. A large, militant minority that controlled rich agricultural land was bound to create a knotty issue for the established government. The Yaqui campaigns must have been viewed as a hardship assignment for soldiers conforming to traditional military tactics of marching in columns against a highly mobile enemy who scattered and faded into the landscape in time-honored guerrilla fashion. It is generally agreed that the Yaquis held the advantage of terrain. Their intimate knowledge of the Sonoran mountains and their ability to live off the land or to merge into a peaceful work force on a hacienda undoubtedly bestowed certain military advantages on the Yaquis and rendered the Mexican soldier's duty onerous in the extreme. In fact, military duty in the Yaqui wars was often used by the Ministry of War as a punishment for insubordination or other military offenses. The Mexicans were trying to incorporate native groups into the national mainstream, rather than isolating them on reservations or exterminating them, as has been the fate of so many aboriginal groups elsewhere.

### The Place of This Personal Chronicle in History

Many of the characters belonging to Rosalio's grandparents' generation took part in Yaqui affairs of the mid-nineteenth century. One woman that Rosalio knew well, and from whom he absorbed many stories, was reportedly born about 1810. Certainly his grandparents and their contemporaries were alive during the Pesqueira regime, but we know nothing about their attitudes and actions.

The French invasion of Guaymas in 1865 is documented history. An interesting problem is presented by the importance of French individuals in a number of Rosalio's stories that are set before the 1865 invasion. His grandmother, María Daumier Valencia Palos, claimed a French father and used a French name. She was born well before the French invasion, and yet Rosalio is specific about the fact that the French father was one of a number of Frenchmen who landed in Guaymas and settled briefly in Torim. As an added complication, María Daumier Valencia Palos claimed that Arturo Frias, twenty years her junior, shared the same French father. María Daumier Valencia Palos said it was a French priest who performed her marriage in Torim. Old Augustina Valencia, reportedly born about 1810, told a story of pre-1850 flights to the mountains in which a French priest accompanied the Yaqui band, shared their misfortunes, and was captured with them. It is clear that French priests and other Frenchmen were more highly regarded by the Yaquis of Rosalio's family than were Mexicans or Spaniards. Quite possibly the stories are true and individual Frenchmen were repeatedly associated with the Yaquis. On the other hand, it is possible that a French name was assumed by the grandmother because of admiration for the French, and this amiable fiction was fostered by the light-colored skin that was one of the most striking characteristics of the grandmother and some of her descendants.

With the Cajeme era, during the 1880s, it becomes possible to faintly sketch certain of the characters in this chronicle onto the historical backdrop. Rosalio's paternal grandparents were pro-Cajeme, and Abelardo Cochemea, the grandfather, was proud to have fought at Cajeme's side. María Daumier Valencia Palos often repeated stories of Cajeme's exploits, stressing that Cajeme had the Yaquis' best interests at heart. The Cochemea family did not think so highly of Cajeme's successor, Tetabiate, which offers a contrast to Spicer's appraisal of Tetabiate as the great hero of this epoch of Yaqui history.[6]

By the late 1880s or early 1890s, Rosalio's family was among the large number of refugees who removed themselves from the Yaqui villages. Abelardo Cochemea apparently left the Yaqui valley after Cajeme's capture, following his son, Miguel Palos, to the Colorada Mine (La Mina Colorada), where they and many of their friends and relatives sat on the sideline of events in the Yaqui country until 1900. For some Yaquis, such as Rosalio Moisés's immediate family at the Colorada Mine, the period from the late 1800s to 1900 was relatively calm and peaceful. Contacts with the mountain and valley Yaquis were clearly maintained. The Colorada Mine itself was a temporarily secure haven in which Yaqui men

[6] Ibid., p. 31.

were recognized as skilled miners. It was into this apparent security that Rosalio Moisés was born in 1896, and his memories or impression of the life there are warm and happy. The Massacre of Mazocoba was the first major, stark tragedy that impinged upon his life. In its aftermath, he was thrust into the harsh realities of what it meant to be a Yaqui in Sonora at the turn of the century. His family left the Colorada Mine in 1900, his father working as a miner at two other mines before he gave up and joined the mountain Yaquis. Rosalio, in the care of his grandparents, went to the state capital of Hermosillo, which was used as a collecting center for Yaquis being readied for execution or deportation. Eventually, Rosalio's grandfather was among the deported. Rosalio frequently witnessed the execution of friends and relatives, and on more than one occasion he helped carry bodies away for burial.

Rosalio's father crossed to Arizona in 1904, followed in 1905 by Rosalio and remaining members of the household headed by his remarkable grandmother. Thereafter, until 1932, Rosalio and his immediate family were peripheral to what was happening in Sonora, except that his father led military expeditions in 1912 during the Orozquista revolt and in 1914 during the Constitutional revolution in the belief that the time was ripe, in the midst of revolutionary crisis, to push the Mexicans from Yaqui lands. Each time he became discouraged after a few months and returned to Arizona to bide his time. While physically removed from the action, the Yaquis in Arizona were well aware of events in Sonora as a result of a steady stream of people and provisions that went between the two states.

An interesting and little-known sidelight to the Mexican revolutionary picture is that military forces in northwest Mexico were often moved by rail across the international boundary into Tucson, Arizona, with the permission of the United States government. They were then trans-shipped east on the Southern Pacific back into Mexico. This was necessitated by the lack of east-west rail lines in northwest Mexico. Troop movements from Hermosillo and its environs to, say, Naco or Cananea were either on foot, horseback, or via this devious train route. During our interviews, Rosalio kept referring to so-and-so who jumped a troop train in Tucson. This seemed to me to be self-apparent nonsense, but he stuck to his story so consistently that I checked with Dr. Michael Meyer of the University of Nebraska, an expert on this time and place, and he verified the fact that Mexican troops were shipped through Tucson at this time.

In a way, the Mexican Revolution was peripheral to central Yaqui concerns. Many individual Yaquis were swept along in its wake, however.

Into Rosalio's world in Arizona there came men who had ridden with Pancho Villa, men who had fought against Pancho Villa, the hated Yaqui traitors who had been informers for Izábal and who later fought for the federal forces in the revolution, Yaquis who fought for Madero and Obregón, men who jumped troop trains in Tucson, and countless Yaquis from the Sierra who fought in no Mexican army.

One of the consequences of a situation such as prevailed for the Yaquis in Sonora during the Díaz period and during the currents and counter-currents of revolution is that people who take on a new political role cannot easily shed the network of personal relations they maintained earlier if they remain in the vicinity. In following the stories of individuals in Rosalio's chronicle, one finds a few who are portrayed as totally evil, such as Governor Izábal and one particular Yaqui traitor, or *torocoyori*. Other *torocoyoris*, however, did not completely step outside their earlier kin and friendship relations when they became traitors, but continued to function in both old and new roles to varying degrees. This is illustrated by the story of the *torocoyori* Juan González.

Among the many Yaquis at the Colorada Mine in the late 1890s were Rosalio's family and the brothers Juan and José González. When the community was torn apart by the repercussions of the Massacre of Mazocoba, Rosalio's mother left with José González; Juan González went to Hermosillo to become a government informant; and Rosalio's father eventually joined the Sierra Yaquis. Rosalio, with his grandmother and other family members, moved to Hermosillo. This meant that Juan González, now a *torocoyori*, and María Daumier Valencia Palos lived in the same town from 1900 to 1905 and that they had a well-established personal relationship, probably kin-based, that predated Juan González's assumption of the *torocoyori* role. Further crosscurrents are introduced by the fact that María's son, Miguel Palos, became a Sierra Yaqui and that son's wife ran off with Juan's brother. Presumably because of the latter factor, Juan, in his role of *torocoyori*, openly vowed to kill Miguel Palos. It is, I think, a fair appraisal of María Daumier Valencia Palos's attitude to say that she was devoted to her one son, and probably no one ever meant more to her. Yet in spite of the fact that Juan González had every intention of killing her son, she maintained cordial relations with him as long as she lived in Hermosillo. For his part, Juan González did not cease identifying as a Yaqui or interacting with them. While he was known and hated for his enthusiastic and active role in having many Yaquis deported and killed, and while he personally rode in many Yaqui hunts in the Altar region, he nonetheless consistently supplied María Daumier Valencia Palos with information about Mexican troop movements, military plans to poison the mountain waterholes, and other military plans, knowing full well that she was in constant touch with the Sierra Yaquis and that this military information would be swiftly dispatched to the Sierra.

Judging from Rosalio's appraisal of individuals who were operating as *torocoyoris*, every individual was held responsible for his own actions, but closely associated family members bore no stigma for his actions. To an amazing degree, parents, wives, consorts, and children of *torocoyoris* were fully accepted, even when receiving support from or living with the traitor. For example, the wife of a notorious *torocoyori* was living in Arizona. Her husband sent her money from Hermosillo that he earned as a government informer, and it was this money that supported her and her children. She was highly regarded by the Arizona Yaquis, and in fact, Rosalio's father, a rather well known Sierra Yaqui, had a long-term affair with this woman.

Rosalio's personal chronicle thus touches upon many of the dramatic events of Yaqui and Sonoran history at the turn of the century, in the revolutionary period, and through the last Yaqui uprising of 1926, although he was not on hand for a single battle. These facts of history as lived by the Yaquis were of passionate interest to Rosalio, and have been retold so often that they now have the luster of an old, often polished piece of silver. The bulk of this personal chronicle deals, however, not with the Yaqui wars, but with growing to manhood in Arizona, being drawn to the Yaqui villages like a moth to a candle, struggling to live in his homeland, and his deciding, after eighteen years, that hunger and repeated tragedy was too high a price to pay for living on Yaqui soil.

## About the Yaquis

My purpose here is, first, to give basic background that will serve as a guide to certain aspects of Yaqui culture that Rosalio has assumed his audience would understand, and second, to extract certain information about little-known Yaqui ways from Rosalio's narrative.

### Yaqui Religion and Beliefs about the Supernatural

Long ago, the Surem lived along the Yaqui River on one of the now abandoned channels south of the modern river. These people were short statured like Filipinos. For many thousands of years they did not know how to farm, but lived by hunting animals, gathering wild potatoes, fishing, and collecting shellfish and shrimp along the coast. They had no religion, no government. One day in Surem country a dead mesquite tree or dry pole (*palo seco*) began to go tap-tap-tap like a telegraph set, but no one could understand what it was saying. They went to ask the wise man, Mapoli, who lived to the north near Guaymas Bay, if he could help them. He said his daughter could tell them what it meant. She was a *sirena* who lived in the sea. She told the Surem and her father that white men coming from the east would bring them seeds to plant and cows and horses, and that they would baptize all the children. The tapping tree told of many wonderful things that were to happen. Many of the Surem were afraid. They fought among themselves. Some, who moved away to the north to settle along the present course of the Yaqui River, became the Yaqui tribe. The other Surem have disappeared, and their river died. The Yaqui settled into the eight pueblos. These pueblo names are very, very old. Afterwards the Spaniards came and baptized everyone, and then the Yaquis had a religion.

This is Rosalio Moisés's version of the widely known Yaqui origin myth. Other versions are given by Spicer.[7] The Spaniards are here cast in the role of culture heroes who supplied everything of value to the Yaquis. When I have suggested to Rosalio that the Yaquis were good farmers with a complex government, military system, and religion of their own before the Spaniards came, he has completely rejected the idea.

Biblical stories are placed geographically in the Yaqui area, giving a close personal touch to Christian teachings. Rosalio reports that some believe Jesus Christ was born in the local pueblo of Belem, whose name is Spanish for Bethlehem. The story of the Tower of Babel, also referred to by Rosalio as the Tower of Babylonia, refers to native Indian languages of Sonora. As Rosalio tells that story, all the Indians once spoke the same language, and everyone could talk freely with everyone else. They began building the Tower of Babylonia so they could reach heaven. When the tower got up so high, God destroyed the top of it and told all the people not to work on the tower any more. The next morning when everyone woke up, no one could understand anybody else, and everyone got mad because they could not understand one another any more. That is how we came to have so many languages. This story was a source of great amusement to Rosalio.

Modern Yaqui religion is the end product of the fusion of aboriginal with Spanish and Mexican Catholic systems. A Catholic calendar of saints' days and religious observances provides the cogs which move the annual religious cycle forward under the auspices of the ceremonial societies. One must remember that Yaqui Catholicism has developed in comparative isolation from the Catholicism of surrounding Mexican

[7] Edward Spicer, *Pascua, a Yaqui Village in Arizona* (Chicago: University of Chicago Press, 1940), p. 240; also "Potam," p. 121.

groups. Not since the Jesuit days have there been really strong ties to contemporary Mexican-Catholic culture.

Five men's and two women's ceremonial societies form the core of organized religious activity: the *maestros* (male altar society), the *matachines*, the *fariseos* (Pharisees), the *caballeros*, the *coyotes*, and the women's societies, which are described in detail by Spicer.[8] Brief descriptions are given here inasmuch as Rosalio makes frequent reference to the societal membership of characters mentioned in this book, and in fact, society affiliation is one of the criteria that he used consistently in delimiting personalities. *Pascolas* and deer dancers are secular and not organized into societies, but, as in the case of society membership, these dance roles were always mentioned by Rosalio as an identifying characteristic.

The *maestros* are lay priests in the eyes of the Yaquis, although not now encouraged and in some cases not even recognized by the official Catholic bureaucracy. They care for the people in the absence of a priest. At times in the Rio Yaqui, the differences between Yaqui Catholicism and Mexican (Sonoran) Catholicism have been so deep that the Yaquis refused ordained priests, feeling that their own *maestros* met their needs more effectively. The *maestros* coordinate the ceremonial duties of the other men's societies, notifying society leaders of impending ceremonies and reminding them of their duties. They are required to commit passages of liturgy and standard prayers to memory, must have the ability to read other appropriate passages and give sermons and admonitions, and must be able to conduct any ceremony in the extensive Yaqui repertoire. Their offices are required at many private ceremonies, such as marriages and funerals. The *maestros* within each village are organized by age. The eldest, called the *maestro mayor* or, in Yaqui, *maito jo'owe*, is regarded as the leader. The sacristans, subordinate to the *maestros*, have charge of the care and preparation of certain ritual articles.

The *matachines* are costumed dancers and musicians who perform at funerals, on Sundays during the spring and summer, and at various other ceremonies. The Virgin Mary is their patroness.

Inasmuch as Rosalio was a *fariseo*, this is the society about which there is the most information in his personal chronicle. The *fariseo* society is active only during the long Easter season. For about three months they are the dominant group, appearing at virtually every ceremony and assuming extensive functions beyond the realm of religious ritual. The *fariseos* consist of two groups, the masked and the unmasked.

[8] Spicer, *Pascua*, pp. 117–145; and Edward Spicer, *Perspectives in American Indian Culture Change* (Chicago: University of Chicago Press, 1961), pp. 59–63.

Jesus Christ is the patron of the *fariseos*. Rosalio did not seem to differentiate between *fariseos* and *caballeros* as sharply as Spicer does. He often describes the *caballeros* as the *fariseos* with swords. While the unmasked *fariseos* are regarded as the Soldiers of Rome, the persecutors of Christ, the *caballeros* take the role of the good, pro-Christian soldiers. *Fariseos* and *caballeros* engage in symbolic battles on Holy Saturday at the climax of the Easter celebration. During Holy Week these two societies actually take over most of the civil, legal, police, and religious roles of the village.

From Rosalio's several accounts of dancing as a *fariseo*, there emerges a composite picture of *fariseo* activities as well as several vivid descriptions of the physical hardships involved in wearing a goatskin mask lacking adequate ventilation and holding a Yaqui rosary in the teeth while undergoing strenuous activity for a long, sleepless period.

The *fariseo* and *caballero* societies among the Yaquis, as among many other groups in Sonora and Sinaloa (the Mayos, for example, have *fariseos*) are a direct outgrowth of the Jesuit teaching technique whereby religious stories were acted out. The Passion Play has proved eminently suitable for dramatic presentation among many groups in the world, and among the Yaquis it is called La Fiesta de Gloria.

The *coyote* ceremonial society consists of dance groups composed of only three members: a captain and two subordinates. The *coyote* society has lost much of its significance in recent time, especially among the Arizona Yaquis. In the last century, it was a vital, important organization. The main character in this narrative who was an active *coyote* is Rosalio's father, a *coyote* captain. Rosalio maintained that the *coyote* dancing society was the core of the military society.

The two women's ceremonial groups are the altar women, in charge of the female saints and the church altar, and the *cantoras*, or chanters, who accompany the *maestros* in chanting prayers and liturgy.

Membership in the ceremonial societies most often comes as a result of a *manda* or *promesa* (promise) made by an ill person or his parents to the effect that if the sick person is spared, he will become a member of the *matachines*, *fariseos*, or some other society. People may also assume membership after a vision or revelation, or more prosaically and less frequently one may simply become an apprentice, learning the required ritualistic behavior. Membership in a society is usually, although not always, for life.

*Pascolas* and deer dancers are also important to the ceremonial observances of the Yaquis. These dancers are more secular and lack the formal organization of the ceremonial societies. Their songs, dances, and other activities are apparently non-Catholic in origin, combining current secular jokes and caricatures with animal motifs which are probably a survival of pre-Catholic elements. Although women were never official *pascola* dancers, Rosalio mentions upon two occasions the unusual point that his paternal grandmother was allowed to dance as a *pascola* after asking permission of the performing *pascolas*. Her *pascola* burlesques were apparently enormously successful.

Each existing pueblo carries out its own ceremonial cycle which is not identical with those of the other villages. Different feast days are emphasized at different places. The local patron saint always rates a major fiesta. The Easter ceremony is a major ceremony in every Yaqui pueblo. Arrangements for most fiestas are made by the *fiesteros*, best described in Spicer;[9] Rosalio tells something of the arrangements made for a Día de San Juan fiesta at Vicam. Aside from the scheduled calendar of ceremonial activity, a great many private observances are held which involve various members of the ceremonial societies, and perhaps the *pascolas* and deer dancers. Funerals, marriages, confirmation by the rosary, baptisms, feasts put on as the result of a *promesa,* and other events require ceremonial action.

As a whole, the Yaquis are a deeply religious people. Ritual activities so permeate the lives of many that outsiders often accuse them of being fanatics. For those people deeply involved, a tremendous amount of time is tied up in ritual duties. The task of acquiring the various sorts of knowledge necessary to fulfill one's role as a *maestro, fariseo,* and so on, is no small chore.

Not all Yaquis share this deep religiosity. Rosalio's paternal grandfather seems to have been neutral on religious matters and Rosalio's mother, Cecelia, was an out-and-out disbeliever who, when younger, attended church and religious fiestas; later in her life she apparently gave up these formalities. Rosalio noted that the fact that Cecelia was part Tarahumara may account for her lack of religious feeling. Interestingly enough, the family of one of the villages in which Rosalio lived that is most noted for their nonreligious attitudes are Tarahumara-derived relatives of Cecelia. However, there are no rumors of non-Yaqui ancestry for Rosalio's grandfather. In his case, Rosalio rather attributed his lack of interest in religious matters to a general antisocial temperament.

Rosalio Moisés did not categorize himself as a Catholic, not even as a Yaqui Catholic, although he participated in Yaqui religious observances

[9] Spicer, "Potam," pp. 72–75.

whenever possible. During his extensive roaming he encountered many other religions. The Salvation Army particularly impressed him because no one fights with anyone else, whereas he repeatedly saw people of Catholic or Yaqui Catholic persuasion fight within their own families. Because Jesus Christ appeared to him in a vision and saved him when he was desperately ill, Rosalio regarded Christ as his personal patron; his *promesa* to belong to the *fariseo* society was made because Jesus is the *fariseo* patron. He also felt an affinity for the Protestant Church of Christ because of the name. In Lubbock, Texas, he pointed out the First Church of Christ as "his church," although I doubt that he ever entered its portals.

A wide range of beliefs about the supernatural, beyond the Catholic beliefs and ritual, are derived from both aboriginal and Mexican-Spanish sources. Supernatural animals and spirits, and myths about these things, have a place in Yaqui beliefs, although knowledge about those beliefs is not universally shared. Attitudes vary from acceptance through neutrality and academic interest to rejection. Some of these beliefs may be found in Spicer and in Beals,[10] but little of this class of data has been published as yet.

Several categories of individuals specialize in dealing with these aspects of the supernatural world: witches, wise men (*sabios*), and curers (*curanderos*) exercise their powers for good and evil. A multiplicity of shades and gradations of these various specialties exist. The delineation of the many ways in which these roles for manipulating the supernatural world are envisioned by the Yaquis would require a separate treatise based on a great deal more data than I possess. Rosalio made the following descriptive distinctions, to name but a few. One can be *poco hechicero* (just a little bit of a witch); the reputed witchcraft may be limited to one case; it may be a popular belief that an individual is a chronic witch; a witch may accept payment for performing witchcraft, or he may only practice for personal reasons. Curers may specialize in antiwitchcraft, in which case they will be deemed to be something of a witch themselves, or they may deal more in less supernatural forms of curing. Some individuals who do not fully qualify for the exalted position of *sabio* fulfill the role of fortuneteller. Many witches and curers are regarded as being somewhat

[10] Ibid., pp. 114 ff.; Ralph Beals, "The Aboriginal Culture of the Cahita Indians," *Ibero-Americana* 19 (1943), pp. 57–70; Ralph Beals, "The Comparative Ethnology of Northern Mexico Before 1750," *Ibero-Americana* 2 (1932), pp. 124–131; Ralph Beals, "The Contemporary Culture of the Cahita Indians," *Bureau of American Ethnology Bulletin* 142 (1945), pp. 190–201.

"wise," but it is my impression that the great *sabios*, always few in number, were less likely to combine the roles of curer and/or witch with their role of seer and wise man. Rosalio only saw one of the great *sabios* in his lifetime, a man called José María Nóteme. His grandmother told him that in the old days there were more. From Rosalio's description, this aged and venerated individual acted as a prophet but not as a curer, and certainly no taint of anything as base as witchcraft was associated with him in Rosalio's mind.

Categories of causes of illness and death cannot be well delimited with the scattered information herein available. Rosalio did allow for natural illness and death. Cyclic epidemics of rabies, smallpox, cholera, and other named diseases are cited. He himself suffered from malaria. Malnutrition, many childhood and childbirth problems, common diarrhea, accidents, and other categories are basically "natural." Rosalio cites several examples of curing used for this category of ailments. What is not clear to me is the extent to which "natural" ailments were acquired because of bad omens, bad luck, and other rationales that could be viewed as directly or indirectly supernatural. Medical doctors could treat the "natural" ailments, but certain categories of illness were believed by Rosalio to be totally beyond the reach of even the most gifted doctors. A bad fright that "causes the guts to rise" is one such malady. A fright administered by the Yaquis is believed to have been responsible for the death of the hated Governor Izábal. Supernatural fright caused by a ghost climbing upon one's shoulders could result in the guts rising. This may lead rapidly to death, or with proper treatment by a *curandero*, recovery is possible. *Chictura* is a condition of disorientation, a sudden loss of one's way in a well-known locale. It can affect more than one person at the same time, and procedures exist for correction of this condition. Quite a number of deaths mentioned in the narrative are attributed to supernatural reasons such as witchcraft and ghost sickness. Death from *tristiza*, or sadness, is another common diagnosis.

The intimately related and intertwined mechanics of witchcraft and curing appear in incident after incident in Rosalio's narrative. Many tantalizing questions arise from this wealth of information for which we find no answers. For example, how many people believed to be witches actually considered themselves witches? Rosalio said that it was widely believed among Arizona Yaquis that he was a witch because so many of his enemies there had died. He publicly uttered remarks, which he called "prayers," against various people, such as his mother-in-law. The rather immediate demise of his mother-in-law was the first of several manifestations that his "prayers" were answered, and this is undoubtedly the reason for his Arizona reputation. On the other hand, he says that no one in the Yaqui villages ever suspected him of witchcraft. The claims that he was a witch amused rather than scared him, perhaps because he was safely removed from Arizona most of the time. He believed that he had latent curing abilities and that in time he might have become a good *curandero* like his grandmother. That is to say, he had an inclination toward the less supernatural varieties of curing, with an emphasis on herbal and other remedies.

Some of the various techniques described by Rosalio as being used by witches seem to derive from European witchcraft. He mentioned the use of dolls into which pins are stuck, stinging herbs rubbed, and so forth; the gathering of dirt from a footprint and the subsequent burying in the graveyard of this dirt wrapped with thorns in a cloth; and the grinding up of human bones to place in food. Divining a witch's identity by dropping an egg in water, reciting Catholic prayers, and waiting for the witch's image to appear, a technique attributed to at least two *curanderos*, is certainly European-derived, as is watching the inclination of a candle flame for an indication of the direction from which supernatural trouble is coming. Shamanistic curing through the sucking of foreign objects from the body and a number of herbal remedies may be native to aboriginal American Indian culture.

One is tempted to see unusual affluence as a factor that opens the door to charges of witchcraft. It may be noted that many, although by no means all, accused witches were fairly well off, or had been at some time.

That Rosalio is not aberrant in his preoccupation with the subject of witchcraft is indicated by a story that received wide newspaper coverage about 1953. A Yaqui woman living in Guadalupe, Arizona, was believed by a Mexican rancher to have bewitched his wife. The Mexican asked the Yaqui witch to stop. When his wife died, he shot the witch. He told this story to the judges and was apparently freed.

The interpretation of the meaning of signs and an evaluation of these signs in terms of good and bad luck was something that occupied Rosalio almost perpetually. Few events and happenings were left uninterpreted. Some of the more portentious signs are cited in his narrative; for example, when snakes, frogs, and other animals climb trees, a bad flood is coming; buzzards circling a house calling a name means that that individual will die; black baby chicks are bad luck; a black baby chick that tries to crow like a rooster is double bad luck; if *fariseo padrinos* or *madrinas* fall down while running with their *fariseo ahijado*, they will die before the following

Easter; if one casts one's shadow upon a wall at sunrise and the shadow has no head, death will follow.

The way in which almost every event is evaluated in terms of good and bad luck does not come clearly through the narrative. This aspect emerged most clearly from watching Rosalio in his day-to-day activities and in chatting about immediate events, as opposed to the times when he was telling me what to put in the book. In effect, he kept an invisible scorecard for every day's activities, and the most minute happening would be tallied. Omens were ranked. The low-level daily tally that added up to a good-luck day or a bad-luck day was subsumed under more important omens, like those listed above. Most important were visions and dreams that foretold the future. He has been given many visions in his life, the most important of which was his trip to heaven where he met Jesus Christ.

I have tried unsuccessfully to trace the origin of the particularly striking belief alluded to in the title of this book, that each person has a candle burning in heaven and that one lives until his candle burns down. The belief apparently has a wide northern Mexican distribution, as Fidél Zúniga Sánchez of northern Nuevo León tells me his mother often told him of his candle in heaven.

During our final joint reading of the manuscript in July, 1968, Rosalio asked if I knew who Billy Graham was. He said he had heard Billy Graham prophesy that the world would end in six years. He felt strongly that this information was wrong, inasmuch as he himself had had religious experiences in which he talked to Jesus Christ and was shown the future. Innumerable other signs about what the future held for him personally and for the world were also known to him. He believed that in the not too distant future a large-scale world disaster would occur, as foretold by Yaqui *sabios* long ago, but that some people would survive.

Aside from his trip to heaven, he had many dreams that contained omens and glimpses of future events. A dream that recurred much more often than his personal chronicle details was that he was flying; as he got older, he flew lower. When the flying dreams first came to him, he saw tall buildings, big cities, and other things distant in time and space such as he had never seen at that time. The flying dream was an omen of good luck. It was also considered to be good luck if one dreamed he was killed. On several occasions he dreamed that people he knew were on a boat and the boat was leaving; this foretold their death. He once dreamed that his sister was on a ship but he was able to get her off, and as a consequence she did not die, in spite of having been told she had cancer. Rosalio believed he saved his sister in this supernatural struggle. He dreamed that white men were going to visit Torim; after he had met the white men, he then dreamed of the arrival of specific individuals. He also dreamed of the murder of Simon Arenas. The dreams just described were unsolicited, as it were. On many occasions he went to bed with the intention of having a dream that would give him certain information about a particular subject. He told me that these dreams always came about 3:00 A.M. Many dreams were interpreted backwards. A dream showing his watermelon patch in good condition meant the crop would be poor, for example.

Rosalio described several magical aids, some of which have not been previously recorded. A *chone* is a scalp, or a doll to which a scalp is attached, that has supernatural powers. Magical cigarettes made from native tobacco (*macucho*) can be sent through the air to spy on people and they can be used to harm people. Both of these potent devices should be used only by witches strong enough to cope with their power. A witching *olla*, or pot, was described as having been used by two Yaqui witches; however, it is the Papagos that Rosalio believed to be the real experts with this concoction.

*El justo juez* is a book of recitations cited by Rosalio a number of times as a powerful supernatural agent. Correct recitation is an arduous task, and complete recitation two or three times is required for really strong protection. Once the recitation has been correctly performed, one can, for example, walk out of jails unseen. Rosalio once had a copy of this book but found it too risky, as incorrect recitation backfires. He preferred a mail-order book called *El oculto talisman* which had much shorter recitations.

Rosalio's grandmother María Daumier Valencia Palos and old Augustina Valencia seem to be the main sources from which various myths and stories passed to Rosalio. *Sierpas* are giant animals that live in canyons, caves, and elsewhere. Several localities in the Yaqui territory are known as the habitations of famous *sierpas* in the past, and Rosalio has visited some of those places. By and large the *sierpas* are supposed to reside in their subterranean lairs, feeding on whatever can be sucked in, growing larger and larger until one day they go to the sea, where they then stay. All *sierpas* are believed to be people who once did something wrong, like marrying a near relative. The most famous *sierpa* story concerns a giant rattlesnake *sierpa* at Cenyoa-Baam which was slain by an *argolito*. The latter is a little man from another world who streaks through the air with a long rope trailing behind him. One wonders if the *argolito* story derives from meteors, for which the Spanish word is *aerolito*. Beals mentions a version of this snake story and its relationship with a dwarf who kills it, the latter being called a *suawáka*.[11]

The *coludo*, yet another supernatural creature, looks rather like a coyote but is distinguished by an unusually long tail, large stand-up ears, and seven toes. Rosalio personally examined a pelt of one killed at Chumaiumpaaku, and saw a live one on another occasion. *Coludos* are said to be a sign of buried treasure.

Ghosts and other apparitions were seen and heard by Rosalio on many occasions. Some of them are well known, such as the *llorona*, believed by Rosalio to be one individual who wanders from place to place, although he is aware that other people believe there are multiple *lloronas*. The *yoeta* of Santeagueño, near Corasepe rancheria, is believed to represent a Mexican cowboy, not a Yaqui, whose yips are frequently heard. The ghost of Babu-u, another well-known manifestation, climbed upon the shoulders of a former governor of Torim, causing his "guts to rise" and his death. More usually, the ghost of Babu-u was merely seen and did no harm.

A few instances of hunting lore and hunting magic were related by Rosalio. Some individuals were regarded as having an unspecified control over game, as in the case of the two men who were lucky because deer stood still with heads in full view. Certain rabbits and deer are bad like witches and can cause harm to the hunter unless he is adept at distinguishing good from evil.

After the publication of the fascinating book by Carlos Casteñada about the highly complex drug culture practiced by the Yaqui Don Juan, I was again in Texas and asked Rosalio if he knew anything about this sort of thing, or if he knew of any Yaqui who controlled drugs in the manner of Don Juan. He was totally unfamiliar with this aspect of drug culture. When I said that Don Juan had been deported and thus spent a great deal of time away from the Yaqui villages, Rosalio was decisive in his opinion that this knowledge had been acquired from Mexican sources.

*Civil, Military, and Legal Organization*

The governmental aspects of Yaqui culture are of only peripheral importance to Rosalio's personal chronicle and their superficial treatment here is due to this. The tradition of eight Yaqui villages is deeply ingrained, in spite of the fact that other towns and settlements exist and some of the traditional eight are not now functioning entities. Vicam Switch, or Vicam Station, on the railroad now overshadows old Vicam.

[11] Beals, "Contemporary Culture," p. 199.

Offshoot villages have formed on some village lands. Some of the traditional villages have become so depleted that their political and religious structure is headquartered in another village. Spicer describes the current situation in which Huirivis village organization is now based at Potam because the Huirivis lands lack sufficient water to support the village population. Mexican encroachment south of the river has caused new Yaqui towns to be located north of the river, replacing those on the south. Thus, Bataconsica has effectively replaced old Bacum, and Torokova is the new town of old Cocorit residents.[12]

The older Yaqui settlement pattern of a fairly dispersed population based in rancherias has not been eliminated. Perhaps it would be more realistic to say that we do not know whether or not it was ever eliminated, or whether it has become reestablished. Rancherias do exist at the present time, and there is some reason to believe that the names and locations of certain of the rancherias are old. Both Rosalio's paternal grandparents were born at the Corasepe rancheria a short distance north of Torim on Torim pueblo lands, and distant relatives lived there until recently.

Each village is now, and has always been, an autonomous civil unit. This is not to say that in both prehistoric and historic time tribal action was impossible. When the Yaquis met Hurdaide in battle, the whole tribe must have been mobilized. More recently, Cajeme, Tetabiate, and others have commanded people from all villages. But this sort of tribal unity is limited to military matters and is considered to be of limited duration.

Three organizational units constitute the framework of civil authority within each village: the five governors and their assistants, the *pueblo mayor* group, and the military organization. The governors are designated as first, second, third, and fourth governors. The fifth governor is called the *chicotero*, the person who punishes by whipping, or *alawasin*, perhaps best translated as sheriff.[13] The governors are chosen annually at a general meeting and installed in early January. Some variation in procedure evidently exists between the different villages. Spicer reports that in Potam, governors were installed on January 5.[14] In Torim the 1953 installation was on January 6, the Día de los Reyes, and informants there said that this is customary. The governors' symbols of office, silver-tipped wooden staves, are extremely important in the ritual of civil affairs. The first governor, who exercises the most authority, has the duty of presiding with all due protocol at the many official gatherings that occur in the

[12] Spicer, "Potam," pp. 15, 16.
[13] Ibid., p. 65.
[14] Ibid., pp. 64–65.

Yaqui *guardia*. The *chicotero* has duties beyond the official punishing of convicted individuals; he passes out the governors' staves of office at meetings and gathers them up when the meeting has been concluded.

The *pueblo mayor* theoretically holds office for life, although provisions exist for removing a person from that position. He is regarded as the spokesman for the people of the pueblo. A number of other individuals hold the title of *pueblo*, and we were told in Torim that outgoing governors join this body.

According to Rosalio, the military organization centers in the *coyote* society, whose membership largely consists of men who made a *manda* or *promesa* to the Virgin of Guadalupe during an illness. While there can be a number of captains in a village at any one time, one is designated the main village captain. The position of village captain in Torim is regarded as a lifetime post, but the captain can be removed by concerted village action. Spicer emphasizes the ritual and military functions of the society.[15] Our informants in Torim emphasized the civil authority of the main village captain, crediting him with the responsibility for maintaining law and order within the village and for channeling citizens' complaints to the governors or to the *pueblo mayor*. The captain shares the duty of maintaining law and order in Torim with a commandant, who theoretically also holds his position for life, and who has authority outside the village center in the rural parts of the village lands.

The relative importance of the various positions varies to some extent with the personalities involved. The role of captain in Torim has been important as a key political post; the last two or three incumbents have been in a position to help make important decisions about political and economic matters. Two captains of Torim have been removed from office in the last thirty years because of flagrant abuse of their office for personal gains. One sold a truck given to the peublo by the Mexican government for about two hundred dollars, with which he bought cattle. He was tried, officially whipped by the *chicotero*, and removed from office, but was allowed to keep his herd. Since the office is relatively permanent, the person holding it can consolidate his political power over a period of time in a way that the first governor cannot.

The Yaqui military organization forms the core from which an army of adult Yaqui men could be rapidly assembled under conditions of war. Actual field leadership does not necessarily rest upon members of the *coyote* society, according to Rosalio, but depends more on leadership performance.

[15] Ibid., pp. 67 ff.

The Yaquis have a well-codified legal system. According to Yaqui ideals, all individuals living in the pueblos should be completely under the jurisdiction of Yaqui law. In practice, Mexican authorities are now sometimes involved, especially in the more serious cases.

People who are disturbing the peace or people against whom a formal charge is lodged are taken into custody and held at the *guardia* until appropriate action can be taken. If the charges are serious, a trial is held. Spicer describes a trial at Potam.[16] Rosalio describes a murder trial that occurred in Vicam in 1926, a witch's trial at Cocorit in 1935, and what might be called a mistrial or a trumped-up trial in Torim in 1946.

It is convenient to describe each of the ceremonial societies and the various civil and military positions as separate entities, although none operate independently. A set of checks, balances, and intertwined relationships exists. The *maestros* have a major voice in the selection of the governors. The first governor works closely with the village captain and commandant. The *fariseo* and *caballero* societies actually take over most of the village authority during the Easter season. The frequently held meetings are public, and elders, older women, church officials, and members of the men's ceremonial societies often have an opportunity to speak. Theoretically, all decisions are arrived at democratically.

Permeating all formalized aspects of the religious, civil, legal, and military systems is a great deal of ritual, ceremony, and protocol. The various symbols of identification and authority such as the flags and staves of office are an important part of all proceedings. The order in which people are recognized at meetings is closely prescribed. The content of the opening and closing speeches by the governor is highly patterned. Behavior at trials must conform to certain rules, and seating arrangements at trials and meetings are highly stylized.

Contemporary Yaqui society is under a tremendous strain. The old pressures is to assimilate with Mexican culture still actively conflict with a massive conservatism to maintain the Yaqui ways. This conflict is no longer manifested in war and flight, but in more subtle ways. One important consequence, aside from "creeping acculturation," is a deepening of factionalism, crosscutting and dividing the society. A not uncommon pattern has been for a "good Yaqui" who perhaps fought bravely for the Yaqui cause to succumb gradually to the temptations of cooperating with the Mexican authorities, or, after accepting a political office, making deals to his own advantage. In describing this process in regard to one individual, Rosalio Moisés says, "He was a good *coyote* soldier. He fought in the Sierra

[16] Spicer, "Potam," pp. 98–100.

and still carries the scars. Now he is just a coyote for money." A great deal of mutual distrust exists. Rank and file Yaquis distrust the Yaqui officials, as is made amply clear by Rosalio's description of the years he was in the Yaqui villages. It is generally felt to be unwise to leave anyone alone with outsiders. Some of our informants in 1952 went to extraordinary lengths to secure private interviews so they could talk freely.

*The Social Framework*

Little has been reported of Yaqui child training or other facets of the life cycle, except as they are observed ritually at baptism, confirmation, and so forth. A few details on this subject emerge from Rosalio's life story, although I hesitate to say how generally these remarks apply to Yaqui child-training practices. Small children seem to be treated permissively. Once when Rosalio was visiting in our home and one of our younger children poured a sack of sugar on the floor, Rosalio told about the time his youngest daughter emptied all the flour they possessed for food into the dirt. When asked how he responded to her behavior, he said that they did not punish her because she did not know what she did, and strongly intimated that I should not punish my child. He spoke disapprovingly of parents who spank their children, and said his annual visits to a particular relative are always unpleasant because he had to watch children being spanked.

In Rosalio's earliest years at the Colorada Mine (1896–1900), much of the daily routine of child care was left to older children. Many of the families living there were related in some way, and so perhaps there were certain elements of kin-based obligations in the caretaking responsibilities. His chief, or at least favorite, caretaker was Chepa Moreno, the daughter of his paternal grandfather's half-brother. Her importance to Rosalio was reinforced by their subsequent relationship. While they did not live in the same town after Chepa and her family were deported to Yucatán, they corresponded and visited regularly.

I received the impression from talking with Rosalio that the adults paid little attention to the children, who were pretty much left on their own. If adults were needed, or if adults interceded in children's affairs, a wide range of men and women were available. Thus, while Rosalio's father never took him to the company store, something considered to be a great treat by the children at Colorada, Rosalio was taken to the store by another man, a distant relative. His own mother, his paternal grandmother, and possibly his father's sister, all of whom lived in an extended household unit, were rather interchangeable as authority figures.

Men did not take an active part in child training. Rosalio was never picked up or held by any of the men in the family, and when he was taken to the company store by Rujelio Moreno, he was carried face down under one arm "like a stick of firewood." As an adult and father, Rosalio remembered that he once held his oldest son, but he never picked up or showed any physical affection for any of his other children. While this is not strictly true (we have a photograph of him holding his youngest daughter when she was a baby), it represents his feeling about the ideal behavior of a man toward small children.

The stable extended family that formed the matrix through which his young life moved at the Colorada Mine was thoroughly disrupted by the Massacre of Mazocoba in 1900 when both his parents left the family unit and he moved into a far different socioeconomic position in Hermosillo. Warm personal security evaporated. Degrading experiences became commonplace.

Child training among older children was far from permissive among the Yaquis at the turn of the century. There was a conscious intent to instill self-discipline, stamina, the ability to withstand hardships, and similar personality qualities in Yaqui youth by measures which might seem harsh to us in the latter part of the twentieth century. Rosalio mentioned that a fairly standard punishment for older boys who disobeyed their parents was to tie them to a fence post with their feet a foot or so off the ground and build a small grass fire under their feet.

The timing of the move from Colorada to Hermosillo coincided with his change in status from a permissively treated small child to a more harshly treated older child. Other circumstances such as the dissolution of the family unit and their worsening social position undoubtedly hastened his transition from one status of childhood to the next. Rosalio was thrust from a permissive sort of child training under the care of a favorite cousin into the harsh discipline meted out by his grandmother. His reaction to these several changes in his life was distinctly negative. He evoked a clear, vibrant hatred toward his grandmother for her behavior during this period when she treated him "like a slave." He was still bitter at the age of seventy-two about being given the thinnest blanket, having to run more errands than other children in the family, and so on. And yet by Yaqui standards, his training was relatively mild. He was, for example, never tied to a post with his feet blistering over a smoldering fire. He remembered that older women constantly admonished his grandmother to be more strict with him.

Rosalio had a certain admiration for his father's military prowess, coupled with a total disinterest in becoming a Yaqui soldier when he was old enough. It is likely that his father was equally ambivalent toward him, as Rosalio reported that Miguel Palos frequently told him, "You don't belong to this family." Although boys as young as Rosalio accompanied Miguel Palos on two military expeditions that he led from Arizona in 1912 and 1914, Rosalio was never tempted, saying, "Why should I walk three hundred miles?" nor was he asked to go along.

The Yaqui have traditionally expected both males and females to be chaste before marriage. Girls usually married at twelve to sixteen years, boys at a slightly older age. Premarital chastity was rigorously enforced in the past, with harsh punishment for deviation. This is still an ideal, but the practice is no longer as strictly enforced.

If premarital chastity is expected, the same cannot be said for the post-marital state. Spicer points out that many of his informants in Pascua were living with individuals to whom they were not formally married, either in the church or in a civil ceremony.[17] As I traced individual life histories, the ease with which alliances were shifted became abundantly clear. Rosalio distinguished between people married in the church, those married in a civil ceremony, and those who were merely living together (*se juntaron*, as he said). From the information at my disposal, it seems that a constant affiliation with the first official spouse is a rarity. On the other hand, some of the couples living together without legal sanction may stay together for most of their adult life, until parted by death.

The first marriage ceremony ritually marks the passage into adulthood, and it is not deemed necessary to go through other marriage ceremonies with other partners. The importance of the first marriage is reflected in the burial customs. A person who has officially married is given an adult funeral when he dies, whereas an unmarried individual is given a child's funeral with *pascola* dancers, even though he may be forty-five years old and the parent of ten children. In some cases, couples who have actually lived together for most of their adult life will marry in their old age at the Virgin del Camino fiesta on July 1. Rosalio found this behavior amusing and unnecessary. Among contemporary Yaquis, especially those in the United States, legal considerations such as social security benefits are causing couples to marry who probably would not otherwise bother. Elopement occurs infrequently. Rosalio told of a couple who eloped from the Colorada Mine because their parents objected to their marriage on the grounds that they were close kin.

A number of men in each village are known to have plural "wives" in

[17] Spicer, *Pascua*, pp. 77–79.

the sociological rather than the legal sense. As a rule, these men are the more affluent citizens who can afford such a luxury. The residential patterns accompanying this polygyny include multiple wives residing in the same household (with the oldest wife as the least favored by the husband but most powerful in terms of running the household), multiple wives residing in separate houses within a household compound or complex, and individual wives scattered in their own houses throughout the village or villages. In the latter instance, there may be little contact between the various women. In some cases, the addition of wives to a household is instigated by the older wife. More usually, the man takes the initiative. Rosalio knew of at least one case in which a woman had plural "husbands." He regarded the possession of plural wives as normal and faintly amusing, while plural husbands were seen as mildly deviant. Examples of a man marrying sisters (together or sequentially) and of a woman marrying her deceased husband's brother were related by Rosalio, as were examples of a man living with a woman and her daughter; there are cases where a man lived with them consecutively, as well as a case in which the man lived with mother and daughter at the same time. These relationships are further complicated in actual practice by multiple relationships on the part of the plural "spouses." For instance, a former governor of Torim had a number of "wives" that he visited fairly regularly and openly. He actually maintained a cycle of shifting residence from woman to woman. Some of these wives also lived regularly with another man or other men.

Incest is not approved by the Yaquis, but it is apparently tolerated by the contemporary society, according to information supplied by Rosalio. Instances of both mother-son (rare) and father-daughter (more common) incest were described, although he did not mention brother-sister incest. The *sierpa*, or serpent, myths, in which a person is turned into a *sierpa* because of having committed incest, are evidence for stricter sanctions against these acts in the past.

Rosalio's information about the variation in mating practices is generally confirmed by Robert Ravicz, who accompanied my father to the Yaqui villages in 1953. Ravicz was especially interested in this topic, and he told me that he had encountered examples of virtually every mating pattern with which he was familiar. When his data are published, this aspect of contemporary Yaqui social organization will be elucidated. It is not known whether these widely varying Yaqui mating patterns have any great time depth, reflect the disintegration of Yaqui society in the late nineteenth century, or are a more recent phenomenon.

It is my opinion that the flexibility attending the establishment of family units was one of the survival mechanisms that allowed strong cultural continuity in the midst of the pressures facing the Yaquis at the turn of the century. Rosalio's aunt may be taken as an example. She always resided in or adjacent to her mother's household throughout her adult life. Her first and legal husband was killed about 1900 by Mexicans. She formed at least four other alliances; two were affairs conducted outside of her residence. The last two alliances involved, in one case, adding a man to her mother's extended family residence and, in the case of the last alliance, the establishment of a separate nuclear residence. Her four children were fathered by four men. In spite of shifting mates, she and her children were always part of a Yaqui family matrix that usually included one or more adult males working for provisions or wages, as well as the core of adult women who contributed continuity and stability. The adult male was sometimes a husband or a consort, and from 1900 to 1904, the role of provider was filled by her father, Abelardo. Only during the last year of their stay in Hermosillo, after Abelardo had been deported, was there no fully adult male in the extended household to act as breadwinner. Even here, a young man attached himself to the household in a platonic arrangement that involved his supplying some funds to the household, and the grandmother María had a "good friend" who later escorted the entire family across the border, thereafter becoming an integral part of the household in Arizona. Women of virtually every age entered into new household arrangements with men, as is seen in the case of Rosalio's grandmother María. Rosalio would not say, and he may not have known, if his grandmother had sexual relations with Crecensio Murillo, and indeed he strongly indicated that it did not matter. The important point was that Crecensio was an adult male who offered escort protection on the trip to Arizona and who contributed wages to the household in Arizona.

The fact that individuals, especially the men, were so interchangeable in fulfilling basic family roles contributed markedly to the preservation of family cores. Family flexibility also was able to adjust to the loss of adult females, as was the case when Rosalio's mother left him. The role of adult male was, however, the role most frequently vacated; it was not unusual for a woman to bury two or three husbands and consorts. I should hasten to add that not all new alliances were formed because of the death of one of the members. Rosalio mentions even more instances of people who merely stopped living with one person and started living with another than he does of the dissolution of a "marriage" because of the death of one of the members. More often than not the parting was simple, unemotional, and matter-of-fact. Such emotions as Rosalio and his wife, Loreta, displayed seem to be quite rare. In general, emotional shallowness characterizes the "marital" relationship, as it does most other interpersonal relationships for the Yaquis of Rosalio's generation, and probably also of the generation or two before his.

In Rosalio's own case, his first sexual experience was with Loreta, his first wife. This marriage was arranged by the families. He knew her by sight, but was not personally acquainted with her before they met on their wedding day. After several tempestuous years, they effected a dramatic separation; Rosalio then married a girl in California in a civil ceremony. In subsequent years while living in the Yaqui River villages, he lived with at least four other women, fathering children by two of them. Since neither of the latter women by whom he had children had ever been officially married, *pascolas* are said to have danced at their funerals.

Men usually claim children they have fathered, and a rather accurate tally of "real" as opposed to sociological fatherhood seems to be general knowledge within a community. Most adults have had children by two, three, four, or five different individuals, who in turn have had children by other men or women.

The residence of children shows a great deal of variation, depending on circumstances. The preferred place of residence is with the biological parents. It is common for children, especially very young ones, to go with the mother when parents separate, but children may live apart from their mother. Rosalio's mother left Miguel Palos for another man, taking only her baby with her. The older children, including Rosalio, were cared for by Miguel Palos's mother. Children are primarily supported and cared for by the members of the household in which they reside. Absent parents usually maintain contact and make contributions to the household when possible. Rosalio actually resided with his own children for only brief periods of time, and he never lived in the household to which one of his daughters belongs. Nevertheless, he acknowledged all of his children and was acknowledged by them as their father. He contributed money or gifts periodically and was in regular contact with all his surviving children.

If for some reason the children cannot live with a parent, a wide range of relatives and ritual kin may care for the children. The household unit seems to be extremely flexible, and able to accommodate peripheral people for extended periods of time. This is illustrated in Rosalio's early life story, as his grandmother with her dominant personality formed a residential focal point around which many individuals clustered. Interestingly enough, Rosalio would not fully respond to a question about who was living in his household at a given time. Only key family members were cited. In tracing other individuals' stories, it turns out that other relatives and even unrelated people were actually part of the extended household at different times. The sociological household was at some times physically contained in one house; at other times the adjacent ramada sheltered more individuals who ate and slept in the household; and at still other times, two or more houses with their ramadas might function as a single household. The latter type of household was established in Colorada, Tucson, and Sasco, with María Daumier Valencia Palos and her son, Miguel Palos, occupying one house, while María's daughter, Camilda, occupied a nearby house. The occupants of both houses ate together and otherwise functioned as a single unit.

Few people live alone in Yaqui communities. A man is needed to supply some form of income and a woman is needed to cook. As long as he lived in Yaqui communities, or even in situations where other Yaquis were present, as in section houses on the railroad, Rosalio always belonged to a household to which he contributed income, and in which there was a woman who cooked. Perhaps the most atypical feature of Rosalio's later life was that after 1952 he lived alone at least nine or ten months a year, without a woman to cook for him, "batching" in west Texas. One of the results of his having been bewitched in 1967 was that he could eat food cooked by another person, but food he prepared for himself was bitter. He therefore ate fairly regularly with my grandmother, in effect establishing the more typical Yaqui household arrangement on a more regular basis than previously, although he had eaten with the family sporadically over the years. Throughout his life story, he specified where he lived and with whom he ate, and repeatedly gave the menu, thereby emphasizing the central importance of these household relationships in his life, as well as pointing up the importance of food and his love of detail.

Rosalio knew some Yaqui kinship terms, but used the Spanish nomenclature in conversations with me. One of the great difficulties in using the original version of Rosalio's autobiography (see below, p. li) was the cavalier use of the terms "cousin," "niece," "nephew," "aunt," and "uncle." When the individuals to whom the terms were applied were actually traced, the relationships were often vague. The terms had more of an age-grading significance. Someone roughly his age would be a cousin; an older person, or a person who was of the parental generation, was an aunt or an uncle. Younger people tended to be called nieces and nephews. Beals notes that the native kinship system emphasized age and sex distinctions.[18]

Rosalio was an amazingly rich source of genealogical information. Beyond the substantial number of individuals whose relationship is definitely known, the exact relationship of a larger group of "relatives" cannot be traced. He believed that his grandmother knew the genealogical details for many of them, but he merely accepted them as distantly related, applying to them the terms "aunt," "uncle," "cousin," and so forth.

Ritual kinship is as important as actual genealogical relationships, especially from a short-range point of view. Ritual godparents are selected for baptism, confirmation, marriage, membership in a religious society, funerals, and other occasions. For the specific occasion, the reciprocal obligations between a family and the *compadres* are fairly specific and their interaction patterned. Genealogical relatives may be and often are chosen as *compadres*. The ritual kinships so established are often extended far beyond the immediate occasion. The strength of this bond is variable and may well involve reciprocal behavior for a lifetime. Furthermore, a sort of kin relationship may be set up through *compadres* to other individuals and families.

Some individuals accept the role of *padrino* or *madrina* more often than others. Rosalio's paternal grandmother was almost a professional *madrina*, so many times did she serve in that capacity. Other individuals consistently refuse to accept invitations to act in this role. The actual responsibilities of a *compadre* and the expenditures involved vary according to the situation and resources. Spicer describes this institution for Pascua Village,[19] and many instances are to be found in the pages of this book.

The use of personal names is not narrowly fixed among the Yaquis. Rosalio used a number of names during his lifetime. Most of them were family-derived, but upon at least three occasions he made up names on the spur of the moment. He was given the name Rosalio Moisés Valenzuela at birth. In honor of his baptismal *padrino*, Javier Aldamea, he was officially baptized as Javier. Many people who knew him as a child called him Lio or Rosa Lingo. He used the familial names of Valenzuela, Palos, and Hurtado. The Spanish name Valenzuela was chosen by Rosalio's father as a small boy in preference to the Yaqui name, Cochemea or Kochemea, that his father used. Palos is part of Rosalio's paternal grandmother's name, a name she acquired from her mother, Julia Palos.

---

[18] Beals, "Aboriginal Culture," p. 49.
[19] Spicer, *Pascua*, pp. 91–116.

Hurtado is the Spanish name adopted by Rosalio's mother's family instead of the Yaqui name Liowe. I always knew him as Simon Palos, a name he adopted in 1934 when my father visited Torim village and Rosalio was asked by the Torim village officials to be his interpreter. At an earlier date he had gone by the names of Miguel Venegas and José Ramos for a time. If he used the Mexican naming pattern whereby the father's last name precedes the mother's last name, he called himself Rosalio Valenzuela Hurtado, and that was his official name for legal purposes.

Such a multiplicity of names is not unique to Rosalio, but is found among many Yaquis, especially those of his or an older generation. During the period of active persecution and deportation, many, perhaps most, Yaquis took Spanish names. It is my impression that family names were not strongly formalized, nor did they have a great deal of continuity before this century. The selection of family names is much less patterned than the usual Mexican system. Many Yaquis' names that Rosalio has reported seem to be descriptive of something that happened within the last one or two generations. One example is Juhuazula (meaning "frozen"), a name reportedly attached to a man when he got so drunk he passed out on his way home on a cold night; he was said to be frozen, but thawed out and lived to a ripe old age. His immediate family became known by that name. A particularly tall family is known as Yaqui-largo, or "the tall Yaqui." The Yaqui name of Vicente Tava's family was Huila-jaa-mua, a reference to the long stirrups effected by Vicente's father, who never assumed a Spanish name like his sons did. Many women may be known by the name of the man they are living with, whether he is a legal spouse or not. On the other hand, many legally married women never use their husband's name at all. Rosalio's mother and grandmother used only their maiden names. When Rosalio referred to women by their "husband's" last name, it has often been because he did not know the woman's real name, having known her only in the context of living with this one particular man.

Normal Mexican practices of applying certain names to members of one sex are not necessarily observed. Jesús, for example, tends to be a masculine name for Mexicans, but several women known to Rosalio bore that name, and it was the name by which they were customarily addressed. In some instances, two living children in a family are given identical names. It is to be expected that younger Yaquis would conform to the dominant cultural pattern of limiting one's names. The technicalities of social security, the selective service, and other official facets of modern life encourage the selection of one name, to be adhered to for a lifetime. Rosalio's youngest daughter has only used the name Tara Valenzuela or Tara Valenzuela Castro; she confesses bewilderment about the fluidity of naming patterns older Yaquis use. Recently one of the girls in the Tucson household where Tara has lived needed a social security number. Her uncle filled out the forms, entering a last name she had never used, although it was her mother's maiden name. While the girl's reaction was not strong enough that she corrected the forms, she was nevertheless uncomfortable about the incident.

Both male and female homosexuals were known to Rosalio, who maintained that a smaller percentage of Yaquis fall in this category than Mexicans. Male homosexuals are known as *joto* and *frescos* in Spanish and *sevi* in Yaqui. Female homosexuals are *marimacha* in Spanish. Rosalio did not give a Yaqui word in this case. Sometimes the Spanish or Yaqui terms become an informal but lasting part of an individual's name. Of the several cases related by Rosalio, about half were said to "prefer" younger members of their own sex, but also maintained relations with members of the opposite sex. Others never married. One man in Tucson kept a camera, photographed all of his boy friends, and pasted their pictures all over his walls. Rosalio said that no one liked that man. I asked if the dislike arose from his being a *joto*, and Rosalio said, "Oh, no, no one cares if a person is a *joto*. But this man caused all the youths to gather at his house." This individual was a *maestro*, and Rosalio said, "All the *maestros* are like that." A *maestro* and a *sacristan* of one of the Yaqui villages lived together in a stable relationship that lasted for years. They took turnabout cooking. Rosalio knew one *marimacha* who often assumed men's clothing.

A strong tradition of folk history, largely oral, exists among older Yaquis. This is combined with a fine development of rhetoric in the Daniel Webster tradition. Many of the men who become *maestros* and political leaders have polished their talents in the field of declamation or public speaking to a bright luster. While Rosalio was not an accomplished orator, he was something of a folk chronicler. Throughout his early life, he was steeped in an oral historical tradition. His grandmother, María Daumier Valencia Palos, acted as a funnel through which a wide range of medicinal, mythological, genealogical, and historical information flowed. Rosalio's father, talkative like María, was also a liberal donor of this sort of information. When Rosalio learned to write in the Arizona public schools, his father had him sit at the kitchen table as he dictated a genealogical record of the family and an account of Yaqui military matters, which Rosalio duly inscribed in a dime store composition book. This sounds like a *Book of the Dead*, such as Spicer describes,[20] except that the historical coverage probably was fuller than in the books Spicer mentions.

The following letter, translated by Dr. Charles B. Qualia, offers an example of the sort of preoccupation with the past common to many Yaquis. It also demonstrates the sort of distortion of historical events that one finds in a verbal folk tradition about events of deep and passionate interest to the teller. This letter was written by Vicente Tava in 1939 from Vicam Switch, Sonora, to his daughter in Tucson. She was not unaware of the things written in the letter, but the occasion for sending the letter was simply that my father was returning to Tucson from the Yaqui country, and Vicente took the opportunity to have a letter hand-delivered to his daughter. Since Vicente did not write, the letter was dictated to the village secretary, who typed it on the ancient typewriter at the *guardia*. We have a lengthier and somewhat more rambling version of this obtained during a taped interview with Vicente Tava in 1953, in which many of the same phrases are repeated.

REPORT:

The Yaqui tribe has been victim for some sixteen years of some men who like to live always at the expense of the tribe. These men are interested in the Yaqui tribe only for acquiring their property. So that we are always victims of these men on account of this piece of territory of which we are natives, and which belongs to us and for which we have suffered much. We have spilt much blood, and we have lost many lives, and we have lost much wealth, and we have suffered a thousand miseries, and we are despised. Both the soldiers and the civil population look upon the Yaquis with scorn. They call us Indians. They never say Yaqui. The sons of the soldiers and the civil population are accustomed to look upon the Yaquis with scorn. We are scorned on account of our possessions. We have rights in this part of the land, and we never complain when we lack food. From the year 1880 to 1887 the General of the Yaqui tribe was chief of the Yaqui towns. His name was José María Leyva Cajeme. This man it was who weakened the eight towns in three battles. The tribe met its downfall. The eight towns lost the Battle of Pitahaya, the Battle of Anil, and the Battle of Buatachive Cautorreon in 1887. The tribe was scattered right and left. General Cajeme went to join his group at Guaymas because he is from Guaymas. There he studied, and when he was already a man he became a soldier of the government. He came to be captain in Guaymas. In a battle which he fought with the tribe he lost his two brothers. He was angered over

[20] Ibid., p. 34.

the loss of his two brothers and in order to avenge the death of his two brothers he came to the Rio Yaqui to unite himself with the tribe. The tribe made him chief of the eight towns. No sooner was he made chief of the eight towns than he began to kill off the most intelligent men. The enemies of the tribe were in accord with the Cajeme. This was quite evident when they wanted to fight because he would stop them in the battle and give the advantage to the enemy; thus, the tribe failed, and to this day we have been deceived in some manner or another. The same treachery which Cajeme inflicted on us we are still suffering. In 1910 came the Madera Revolution, and we joined the Madera cause because at first the Maderistas promised us they would leave us our property. The revolution triumphed, and they still remained the enemy of the people. That same treachery which José María Leyva Cajeme played on us continues. About the year 1915, during the last days of December, I was victim of treachery. I was going to a conference with an escort of 38 men. The conference did not take place. The plan of Cajeme was already made, and there was nothing to do for the tribe; so I was sent to the jail on the 27th of December with all the escort. I asked a North American whose name was Enriques a favor that he should go and make known how the tribe was being treated. That was the man who saved my life, and though they did not take my life, they took me to the Islas Marias. On the 5th of December, 1916, they took us out of the jail at Guaymas to a boat. On January 9, they put us on the Islas Marias, and there we remained five months. On the 20th of June they took us over to Mazatlán, and thence, to Manzanillo on the 24th of June, 1916. Still prisoners, the thirty-eight of us were made soldiers for four years. In 1920, I came here to the Rio Yaqui with my brother. Now here I am, thanks to God, in Vicam. We are natives of Vicam; we are the founders of this little town, or camp. In 1927 we returned to our house, and we found the whites, both military and civil, in our house. They had taken possession of our house. Both the civil and military wish to command in this region. They think they are the only ones who are important, and we Yaquis are good for nothing. In 1919–1936, the Yori soldiers and civil officials have more guarantees than the tribes. They are in command. By telegraph, telephone, and letters, the government has ordered that they give guarantees to the tribe as soon as we arrived in Sonora. The tribe has no eyes to see or mouth to speak. It does not know how to write, and we do not speak Spanish; we speak only Yaqui dialects. The commissioners who come to talk with us promise a great deal, but never do anything. The President does not know what is going on here. Here they take advantage of us. They have it said in the newspapers of Mexico and in foreign countries that they have given to the tribe tools with which to work. That is not true. That is merely used as an excuse to exploit the tribe. They are accustomed, both large and small, to impose upon the Yaqui Indian. Now they are trying to take legal possession of Vicam. They ask for things for the tribe, but the one who asks for the things does not get them. They exploit the tribe at the expense of the government.

If an inspector comes here, they buy him off, in order that the government may
not know that everything is in disorder here.

*Vicam, April 13, 1939.*

### About the Personal Chronicle

When my father, W. C. Holden, went to the Yaqui River on an
ethnographic expedition in 1934, the Torim village council asked Rosalio
Moisés (or Simon Palos, as he called himself then) to serve as interpreter
to the expedition because he was trilingual. Rosalio served as interpreter
and informant on each of several subsequent expeditions that my father
undertook between 1934 and 1955. Aside from these personal encounters,
the two men corresponded at some length over the years. In December of
1949, Rosalio wrote a despairing letter about the general hopelessness of
his future in the Rio Yaqui. My father arranged for him to come to Texas
for six months as a laborer. Arriving in May, 1950, he built a Yaqui
ramada for the museum at Texas Technological College and helped with
house construction, and during the summer he accompanied us on an
archeological field school as a shovel hand. This was my first personal
contact with him. Rosalio and I spent long days in the fall of that year
washing potsherds at the same table. Many days were passed in complete
silence before he began to talk, and it was many years before he talked
freely to me.

When his six-month permit expired, Rosalio returned to Sonora with
a comparatively large bankroll which he used to start a small store in
Torim. A period of relative affluence eventually gave way to renewed
hardship and despair as he lost all his money. After his wife and son died,
he again thought of working in the United States. When my family
visited the Yaqui villages at Christmas of 1953, Rosalio returned to Texas
with us. Texas was his main residence thereafter; he followed a pattern
of living on the Texas farm during the agricultural year and returning to
Tucson and the Sonoran Yaqui villages each winter.

This personal chronicle began in the spring of 1954 when he had little
to occupy him on long evenings. My father supplied him with a stack of
lined composition books and sharpened pencils, suggesting he write his
life story. He preferred to write in English, although he was considerably
less fluent in spoken English than in either Yaqui or Spanish; however, his
only formal schooling had been in English in the Arizona public schools.
Rosalio found the idea of writing his life story extremely compatible with
his own aptitudes and personal habits. He was already accustomed to
spending long hours writing, as he maintained a regular and prolific

correspondence with relatives and friends. He worked at his autobiography faithfully, and over the next four years he produced a personal document filling twelve spiral notebooks, totaling 527 pages. When I was in Lubbock, I would spend a few hours now and again reading over what he had written, asking for additional details, and making a few notes. Insofar as I can tell, my questions had no effect on what he wrote, as we always discussed what was already written, and he never rewrote or amended. This entire autobiography must be considered as a solicited but undirected document.

Over the years, my father has assembled quite a lot of ethnographic and historical data about the Yaquis and the Yaqui wars in the form of taped interviews with Rosalio and other Yaquis in the Arizona villages, in Torim, and in Vicam Switch; movies and tapes of the Torim Easter ceremony; interviews with Sonoran Mexicans about their attitudes towards the Yaquis; and so forth. Many of the stories Rosalio told my father through the years were woven into his novel about the Yaquis, *Hill of the Rooster.*

Rosalio's laboriously written autobiography remained in my father's possession for several years. A verbatim copy was typed, from which my father eventually created what was essentially a liberally edited version with certain sections amplified in the light of his personal knowledge. This was submitted to a press. It was suggested that the manuscript was too full of colloquialisms—too quaint, and that the identity of many of the characters was seldom clear; the manuscript needed revision.

The various manuscripts and raw data were filed away for future revision. In the summer of 1967, my father was deeply involved in preparing two other manuscripts for publication. He asked me if I would like to take over Rosalio's life story, and I readily agreed. Inasmuch as Rosalio's story was told in terms of unnamed aunts, uncles, and cousins, my first step was to take the original autobiography and clarify exactly what individuals were involved in each episode. As the interviews progressed, the episodes began to be associated with individuals equipped with names, histories, genealogies, and biographical details. Genealogical data were collected on well over five hundred individuals. As these data were woven into the original stories, the episodes ceased being isolated events. Known individuals began to thread in and out of the stories, and social groupings became discernible. A recurrent group of miners dominate Rosalio's early years, and countless crossties, many of them kin-based, weave through the story.

It was my original intention to revert to Rosalio's original manuscript, inserting appropriate names and adding minor clarifications in footnotes, but before my interviewing was through, I had accumulated almost as much data as were contained in the original autobiography. It became obvious that footnotes would occupy roughly half of the book. The new data could not be interspersed with the old as the style difference would be too great. Placing in footnotes half of the information, much of which formed an integral part of a particular story, would be distracting. On the other hand, it was clear that the less I acted as a screen between Rosalio's story and the reader, the more valuable the result would be.

During 1967 and 1968, Rosalio and I worked together on the auto-biography. Our conversations were in Spanish. I would take an episode from his autobiography and ask about the individuals concerned. From this starting point, he would relate who they were, give genealogical data, amplify the story at hand, and go off onto other subjects and stories. It was, in other words, a slightly directed or extremely open-ended type of interview situation. I got all of my questions answered, eventually, and collected reams of data along the way. It was not my purpose to collect generalized ethnographic data. Throughout the whole process, my basic premise was that I was a recorder of what he felt was important to his own life story. This is not, and was never intended to be, *the* story of *the* Yaquis. Rosalio was a good informant about Yaqui culture. Indeed, we have tapes and notes about many aspects of Yaqui culture, such as legal procedures, obtained from Rosalio. But in the context of relating his own life story, he was thinking at a highly personal level about actual events and personalities as they impinged upon his life. Rosalio the ethnographic informant was distinct from Rosalio telling his own story.

One final consideration was instrumental in my decision to rewrite the book. Rosalio was verbally fluent in two languages, Spanish and Yaqui. His Spanish was basically the Spanish of Sonora at the turn of the century. He had an appreciation of beautiful Spanish and was openly contemptuous of the present-day Spanish that one hears in the United States. His spoken Yaqui was that of a native speaker. The Yaqui language was a matter of tremendous importance to him, a yardstick of his and other people's degree of "Yaqui-ness." A true Yaqui speaks Yaqui. Those who choose not to speak Yaqui, and who do not teach Yaqui to their children, are not good Yaquis. The use or nonuse of the Yaqui language is a fairly accurate gauge of where a person fits on an acculturation scale. The Yaqui tongue has assumed a nativistic role in Yaqui culture.

Here was Rosalio, a fluent and conscious connoisseur of two languages, writing in a third language in which he was less than proficient. His sentence structure was not normal English usage. His vocabulary was drastically curtailed. Most of the time he wrote with a Spanish-English dictionary at hand, and his selection of terms from among the synonyms listed in the dictionary led to curious results. He also translated some words from Spanish to English on his own; thus, a hangover was described as a cruddity, from the Spanish *crudo*. His spelling was marvelously fluid in English, Yaqui, and Spanish. As we went over each story in Spanish, the new oral version was considerably expanded and, of course, fluent.

The final version used in this book is a compromise. I have stayed close to the original autobiography, filling out the stories from the information obtained in interviews, rewriting most of it, but trying to retain his style of speaking. I have attempted to introduce as little investigator bias as possible, although it is inevitable that I have shaped the whole. While it is regrettable that Rosalio cannot speak directly to the reader, his story probably could never have been published as he first wrote it. To further keep the life history as Rosalio wished it to be, he read and corrected each chapter as it was written, and we went over the final manuscript again together.

Rosalio's original handwritten autobiographical notebooks are to be placed in the archives of the Arizona State Museum, University of Arizona, Tucson, for anyone wishing to use those documents. The names of all but major historical figures have been changed throughout. A key to the real identity of the characters in the personal chronicle, on file at the University of Arizona, can be made available for serious scholars doing research on the Yaquis.

Interpersonal relationships between Rosalio and the members of my family may be of some interest for people evaluating this document. Rosalio viewed my father as an authority figure who made many important decisions affecting Rosalio's life. My father was instrumental in effecting some minor concessions for the Yaqui tribe from the Mexican government in the 1930s, and thus has been a person to whom the Yaqui officials of Torim and Vicam Switch have appealed for help on numerous occasions since that time. In Rosalio's eyes he was therefore pro-Yaqui. Also, as a historian who solicited the Yaqui view of Yaqui history, my father has had a consistently good reception among some Yaquis. At a more personal level my father aided Rosalio in many ways, and for eighteen years he and his brother were Rosalio's Texas employers. My father and Rosalio were almost the same age, establishing a generational bond that reinforced the other bonds of long association and common interests. Their relationship as investigator and informant was impaired by two factors: they spoke in English, and Rosalio would never have corrected my father.

On the other hand, he had little hesitation in correcting me. During the time we actually were working on this book, the physical setting of the interviews was the reverse of an anthropologist going to the field. Rosalio was in my house, observing my child-training and household habits, and eating food I prepared while we talked about him.

The question arises, how accurate is this information and how reliable is the informant? This is hard for me to judge objectively when so few published crosschecks are available. The historical data seem to be well within the range of Yaqui folk history, with no more discrepancies than normally occur with oral transmission. One system of crosschecking that we have been able to implement is the collection of the same story at different times. We have two base lines as it were: the original auto-biography written in 1956, and the verbal interviews of 1967 and 1968. Considering Rosalio's age, the two sets of information correspond remarkably well. On the more important and often told stories, even the phraseology is almost verbatim, time after time. For the period between 1934 and 1950, we also have the letters Rosalio wrote to my father, as well as a few letters written to other individuals in Lubbock with whom Rosalio was acquainted. Some of the individuals mentioned in the story are known to me and to my father. Other corroborating evidence is to be found in taped interviews with other persons. Some individuals are mentioned in Spicer's *Pascua*, verifying their existence and presence in Tucson. For example, the close relationship between Miguel Palos and Juan Pistola described by Rosalio is given an added dimension and verification when one realizes that the fascinating document Spicer quotes on pages 23 and 24 was signed by Rosalio's father.[21] Spicer gives the date of one individual's death as 1928, while Rosalio places his death in 1927, illustrating the approximate correctness or margin of error in Rosalio's dates.

Minute details are a crucial and important element in Rosalio's story-telling. In collecting the same stories at intervals over several years, the minor details might change from story to story, but the basic outline and the type of details remained the same. For example, he seldom used generalized time or space referents such as "early morning" or "late in the afternoon." Rather, he was quite specific and said at 7:00 A.M. or 10:00 P.M. He was equally specific about longer periods of time, such as

21 Ibid., pp. 23–24.

the number of days, weeks, or months that he stayed in a certain place. If the number of weeks or months specified from one calendar date to the next fail to add up, it is not, I think, too surprising for someone relying exclusively on memory. Most of his dates must be interpreted with a small margin for error. Certain dates seem to be correct, and they form the anchor points from which he dated other events. His birth date, the year the family left the Colorada Mine, the date of his grandfather's deportation, his marriage, and the year in which his father and grandmother died are some of the key reference points in his chronology. When describing a trip from one place to another, he was likely to specify the route, direction, and distance. His repeated listing of menus and recital of genealogical relationships are other examples of the importance of details. As mentioned above, genealogical data have been collected on over five hundred individuals, and I am convinced Rosalio could have supplied similar information on many more.

Rosalio was only an individual relying on his memory. While he could read and write, he did not crosscheck his data against, for example, histories of the revolution. He was aware of some of Spicer's publications and knew when Spicer lived in Pascua and in Potam, but he had no interest in checking his data against Spicer's, since he felt that Spicer only wrote down what he was told by other Yaquis, and Rosalio was certain he knew as much as any other Yaqui. It is inevitable that his view of past events was selective and biased. It seems probable that certain stories were slanted or changed to place him in a more favorable light. The one incident for which we have definite conflicting evidence concerns the death of Francisca (Pancha) Castro in Torim. This woman lived with Rosalio, and at her death (?) left him an infant daughter. Because of the legal complications of bringing the daughter to the United States some years later, we obtained a number of affidavits from Mexican officials to the effect that the mother was dead. Recently, Tara has received letters from a woman purporting to be her mother. The outcome of this episode is not known at this time. Whichever version is true, I think one can safely say that Pancha was "dead" to Rosalio.

Toward the end of his life, he was concerned about the reliability of his memory. His vision became progressively more impaired due to cataracts which he refused to have treated. When we found discrepancies between the autobiography written in the mid-1950s and the oral information of 1967–1968, he often wrote to friends or relatives asking for clarifications. I have been in independent correspondence with Señora Josefa Moreno of Hermosillo, Sonora, about events in the early period of

Rosalio's life. He said quite frankly that the earlier information was more reliable than recent data because his memory was not what it used to be. A few stories show such a duplication of elements that I have wondered if the same event was not being introduced in more than one guise. Two stories concerning Miguel Palos's exploits in the Sierra share (1) a battle or ambush near Gavilan, (2) with a single companion, (3) who was killed, (4) by a larger force of *torocoyoris* or Mexicans who, (5) did not realize that Miguel's companion had been killed, or (6) they would certainly have stayed to kill him. Rosalio said his father recounted these as two separate episodes, and so they have remained in the chronicle, and both could have occurred.

Rosalio had a hard life, developing his share of prejudices, resentments, and ill-feelings along the way. He never occupied high status roles within the tribe. He was never terribly successful with women. Although he lived with quite a few, none of these liaisons were long-lasting. Several times he said to me that he got along best with his relatives from a distance, that he was "too sad" and did not react well to prolonged interpersonal contact. If he did not act out his life at the center of the Yaqui stage, he nonetheless was a knowledgeable observer of the many and varied scenes that passed before his eyes. His observations about Yaqui culture were sharpened by his contacts with other cultures, giving him a wealth of comparative cultural information against which to project Yaqui culture.

It is our belief that, except for possible instances of alteration of the "facts" as in the Pancha story, Rosalio constituted a reputable informant. I would hesitate to say that any single fact could not be challenged, but the sum total probably is a close approximation of reality as interpreted by Rosalio and the people on whom he relied for information.

Dr. Spicer kindly consented to read the manuscript. His knowledge of Yaquis and Yaqui culture is unparalleled and he was in a position to evaluate Rosalio's general reliability in a way that I could not. He took the trouble to check events and persons mentioned in the narrative with Yaquis in Arizona and Sonora. It was his feeling that Rosalio's reliability was exceptionally high.

Rosalio's story points up the remarkable persistence of many core values of Yaqui culture. In spite of living in non-Yaqui environments much of his life, he maintained a deep commitment to the Yaqui way with its abiding interest in a Yaqui homeland.

# Selected Bibliography

Acosta, Roberto. *Apuntes historicos Sonorenses: La conquista temporal y espiritual del Yaqui y del Mayo.* Mexico D. F.: Imprenta Aldina, 1949.

Beals, Ralph L. "The Comparative Ethnology of Northern Mexico before 1750," *Ibero-Americana* 2 (1932), pp. 93–225.

————. "The Aboriginal Culture of the Cahita Indians," *Ibero-Americana* 19 (1943).

————. *The Contemporary Culture of the Cahita Indians,* Bureau of American Ethnology Bulletin no. 142. Washington, D.C., 1945.

Fabila, Alfonso. "Las tribus Yaquis de Sonora: Su cultura y anhelada autodeterminación." In *Primer congreso indigenista interamericano,* pp. 3–313. Mexico: Departmento de Asuntos Indígenas, 1940.

Hernández, Fortunato. *Las razas indígenas de Sonora y las guerras del Yaqui.* Mexico: J. de Elizalde, 1902.

Holden, W. C., *et al.* "Studies of the Yaqui Indians of Sonora, Mexico," *Texas Technological College Bulletin* 12 (1936).

Johnson, Jean B. *El idioma Yaqui.* Mexico: Departmento de Investigaciones Antropologicos, Instituto Nacional de Antropologia e Historia, 1962.

Mintz, Sidney W., and Eric R. Wolf. "An Analysis of Ritual Co-Parenthood (Compadrazgo)," *Southwestern Journal of Anthropology* 6 (1950), pp. 341–368.

Nicoli, José Patricio. *Yaquis y Mayos, estudio historico.* Mexico: Francisco Díaz de Leon, 1885.

Pérez de Ribas, Andrés. *My Life among the Savage Nations of New Spain.* Trans. in condensed form by Tomás Antonio Robertson. Los Angeles: Ward Ritchie Press, 1968.

Spicer, Edward H. *Pascua, a Yaqui Village in Arizona.* Chicago: University of Chicago Press, 1940.

Spicer, Edward H. "Potam, a Yaqui Village in Sonora," *American Anthropological Association Memoir* 77 (1954).

————. *Cycles of Conquest*. Tucson: University of Arizona Press, 1962.

————, ed. *Perspectives in American Indian Culture Change*. Chicago: University of Chicago Press, 1961.

Troncoso, Francisco P. *Las guerras con las tribus Yaqui y Mayo del estado de Sonora*. Mexico: Tipografia del Departmento de Estado Mayor, 1905.

Villa, Eduardo W. *Historia del estado de Sonora*. Hermosillo, Sonora: Editorial Sonora, 1951.

# A YAQUI LIFE

# CHAPTER 1

# *The Colorada Mine, 1896–1900*

I WAS BORN at dawn, September 4, 1896, at the Colorada Mine, where my father had many good years mining for gold. My father often told me the exact hour of my birth. People born in September are a little *sabio* (wise), like a *tecolote* (owl). I do not know when they first went to live at the mine, but it was before my older sister, Antonia, was born in 1892. Many friends and relatives from the Rio Yaqui worked in the Colorada and Suviete mines or at the Minas Prietas five miles away where they dug for graphite.

My father was called Miguel Valenzuela at the mine, although in our pueblo of Torim he was known as Miguel Palos. After he left Colorada, most Yaquis called him Miguel Palos again, although he still used the name Valenzuela with Mexicans and Americans. Even as a little boy in Torim, he never used his father's Yaqui name of Cochemea. People always liked my father and he had many good friends. He liked to drink mescal and played cards almost every day. He was a captain of the *coyotes*, and had been ever since he made a *manda* or *promesa* to the Virgin of Guadalupe. He was never without a medal of the Virgin. Dancing at fiestas took a lot of his time. Several times after I was born he went to the Sierra to fight the Mexicans, and by the time he died in 1918 I guess he had killed scores of them.

My father's father and mother lived with us. Abelardo Cochemea never took a Spanish name as younger Yaquis did. Cochemea is a Yaqui word meaning *mataron dormido*, or "they killed (him) asleep." The Cochemea family from Potam, including the famous General Cochemea of the Sierra army, was not kin to my grandfather. Mexicans called him Abelardo Zapatero because he was a shoemaker. There was not another shoemaker in Colorada. When he was not working, he sat perfectly still with his arms folded across his chest, never saying anything and never smiling. He was a *chatito*, which is to say that he had a flat snub nose. This nose goes from generation to generation, and two of my grandchildren are *chatitos* like Abelardo. The only thing my grandfather Abelardo ever did for me was to teach me to make shoes, and I did not like that. He learned shoemaking from his father, Manuel Cochemea, a saddle maker, shoemaker, and leather worker who died in Torim before they moved to Colorada.

Abelardo's wife was María Daumier Valencia Palos. She was my *mama grande*. She had no memory of her father, who they say was a Frenchman from Guaymas named Daumier. He is supposed to have had children by other women besides María's mother. My *mama grande* looked upon Arturo Frías as her half brother through the Frenchman Daumier, even though Arturo was twenty years younger. Both María and Arturo had light-colored skin. Since the Frenchmen came to the Sonoran coast without their own women, they left descendants in every Yaqui village. A French priest performed *mama grande*'s marriage to Abelardo at the church in Torim shortly before her mother, old Julia Palos, died.

*Mama grande* was small and never got fat. When I was a grown man, she came just below my shoulder. Her daughter Camilda and many other descendants inherited her French light-colored skin. If my grandfather Abelardo never spoke, *mama grande* was just the opposite. Everyone called her the *habladora*, or the talker, because she talked all the time. She talked about everything. When happy, she told jokes to the men and imitated the *pascola* dancers; she had to ask permission to dance as a *pascola*, but they always let her do it because she made everyone laugh. Often she talked about the saints and about the past of our people. She talked about our relatives and our friends and their relatives so much that years later, when I finally went home to my pueblo of Torim, I already knew who everyone was although I had never seen most of them. In all the years I lived with *mama grande* I never talked to her, because I was more like Abelardo and never talked much. One could not grow up around her, however, without hearing a lot.

My mother, Cecelia Hurtado, was born in Vicam. Although she did not know the year she was born, she remembered the earthquake of 1874, when she was about ten years old. She was fairly dark, perhaps five feet two, slender, with gray eyes like a rattlesnake. I have inherited her nose and her feet. She never believed in God or the saints, not until the day she died. She sang a great deal around the house and was always happy. My mother liked fine clothes, and while we lived in Colorada she had cotton dresses of many colors, silk dresses for fiestas, lots of *rebozos*, and wore nice shoes every day.

All of these people lived in our house, along with me and my older sister, Antonio, and sometimes there were more. All of us ate in our house, as did my aunt Camilda Palos (my father's sister); her husband, Pedro Omogon; and their daughter Viviana, who was a year older than I. Camilda's family slept in a small one-room house just a few feet away from our house.

My mother's mother and father also lived in Colorada in their own house on the other side of town. Francisco (Chico) Liowe belonged to the pueblo of Vicam. His wife, Esperanza Cocomorachi, was a Tarahumara who came to the Rio Yaqui with her mother and father after they had to leave their own Sierra. The Cocomorachis settled in Torim, and Esperanza stayed with her parents till they died. Then she married Chico Liowe. They had two daughters: my mother and a little girl named Juana just two years older than I. As so many Indians were doing, they changed their name, to Hurtado, to appear more Mexican. Esperanza once took my mother to see Teresa, the Saint of Cabora, when my mother was just a little girl. Esperanza believed in the saint; my mother just laughed at Teresa.

Francisco Liowe worked in the mine on the 7:00 A.M. to 3:00 P.M. shift. Nearly every day after he got off work, he took one of his rifles and went hunting. He was often lucky and brought home meat. Usually he went alone, although sometimes he took along older boys. I was too little to go. Even though Chico Liowe and Esperanza Cocomorachi were my grandparents, I never called them *papa grande* and *mama grande* because they never talked to me. My mother went to see them almost every day, taking me along. Juana would come outside and play with me while my mother visited with her mother. I never entered their house and my grandmother Esperanza never gave me anything to eat.

Abelardo's half brother lived nearby with his family. The two men had not been raised together. When Abelardo was a boy, he lived with his father, Manuel Cochemea, and his mother, Juana Sewa, in Guaymas, where Manuel was working for Rosario Moreno, the *dueño* of some boats. Rosario fathered Francisco. Manuel kept on working for the *dueño* and of course Juana remained his wife, but he never liked Francisco and Francisco, who had his father's red hair, grew up with other relatives. When he grew up, his long mustache was red, too. Early in life he took the Spanish name of Moreno. Francisco was a *pascola* dancer. His daughter Josefa was always called Chepa, as most Josefas are. Chepa carried me, played with me, and cared for me, but her sisters were older and never paid any attention to me.

These were our closest relatives who lived at the Colorada Mine. Other relatives and people my family had known in the Rio Yaqui lived close to us. There must have been over one hundred men working in the mine, many of them Yaquis.

Boys over ten went to work at the mine. Their first job was to carry the rocks out of the mine in pigskin bags. Later the company put in a cable to carry big skin bags and the rocks were taken out that way. Nearly all the women washed for gold; my aunt Camilda was always lucky and found gold nearly every day.

Accidents occurred in the mine from time to time. When I was about two years old, a terrible explosion occurred about eleven o'clock one night. Most of the people from the village went to see what had happened, and my mother carried me in her arms. I can remember the scene vividly. Fifteen men were blown to bits because someone was smoking too close to the dynamite. Pieces of flesh and bone were plastered all over the walls of the cavern. They could not separate one from another. So they picked up what they could in a sack and buried them together in a wooden box.

Men were paid eight pesos a day for an eight-hour shift. The mine ran around the clock with three shifts, 7:00 A.M.–3:00 P.M., 3:00 P.M.–11:00 P.M., and 11:00 P.M.–7:00 A.M. Eight pesos a day was good pay in Sonora in the late 1890s. On the haciendas they were only paying thirty-three centavos a day, with weekly rations of lard, flour, corn, beans, and other basic groceries issued on Sunday. The mining company did not issue rations, but with eight pesos a day the men could buy everything they needed. The miners were paid in silver. When you needed something from the company store before payday, you could go to the store and ask for a five-peso or ten-peso coupon book, and they took away that many pesos next payday. The coupons of five, ten, fifteen, twenty, twenty-five, and fifty centavos and one and five pesos could be spent only in the company store. Payday came every fifteen days. Real silver coins were brought from the bank at Guaymas. Soldiers living at Colorada would go with the American *pagador* (paymaster) to Guaymas to bring back the money.

Torres, fifteen leagues away, was the closest that the main railroad came to Colorada. A narrow-gauge train ran from Torres to Colorada. When the pay train came in, it took two or three mules just to carry the silver used to pay the miners to the company office. The pay train also brought in the mail. Every payday lots of people came up from Guaymas on the little train with things to sell. Women came with oranges, cloth, and clothes.

Some men living in Colorada did not work in the mines at all. My grandfather Abelardo was a full-time shoemaker; Leonardo Valdez made his living hauling water; and there was a man who made pottery. A photographer who lived in Colorada for a while made the big framed photographs of my father and mother that hung in our house.

Others worked in the mine and had businesses on the side. Felipe and Lucas Robles were relatives of my *mama grande*'s from Torim, but they did not look like Yaquis because they were so white. They brought a herd of cows with them from the Rio Yaqui. One Mayo and two Mexican vaqueros, hired to care for their cows, also lived in the town. Milking was done in the morning. The three vaqueros and their families worked every day making cheese, which the Robles brothers sold at their house, or which their wives peddled from house to house. Yaquis came from the other nearby mines of Suviete (or Zubiate) and Minas Prietas to buy this cheese.

The town of Colorada was built in two parts. Americans lived south of the mine in floored wooden houses with flowers in the yards. All of the American children went to the school held in the big dance hall. The miners could send their children to school, but few wanted to. I know of two Yaqui girls who learned to read and write there, Natalia Valencia, a daughter of Delores Valencia, and Ventura Baumea, the daughter of Rosalina Baumea. Both were relatives of my *mama grande*.

Miners lived about a quarter of a mile away, to the north of the mine. The thirty or so houses were made of rocks or of woven branches plastered with mud. Many kinds of branches were used, as the carrizo cane used in the Rio Yaqui did not grow in the Sierra. No flowers grew around the miners' ramadas.

The nearest real church was at San José de Pima, five miles away, and it was there that everyone went for marriages and baptisms. A priest from Guaymas came to San José de Pima every Saturday and Sunday. In Colorada an empty house was used by the *maestros* to hold mass every Sunday. The house had an altar and *santos* but no bell. A priest came occasionally to hold services in Colorada. In our family just about everyone went to Sunday mass. Even my mother, Cecelia, who never believed in God or in the saints, went to mass. Only my grandfather Abelardo would never go to church or to the fiestas.

Colorada always had Yaqui *maestros*, *cantoras*, and dancers, so the Yaqui fiestas were observed there, as indeed they have been wherever groups of Yaquis have lived together. Even in the days when thousands of Yaquis lived in the Sierra they held their religious rites whenever they could.

At Colorada the Easter fiesta was the most important, and the mine closed down from Good Friday until the Monday after Easter. During the Fiesta de Gloria, the *maestro* had to call on everyone in the village who was blind, sick, or otherwise incapacitated.

Other important fiestas in Colorada were San Ignacio on July 31 (which lasted one night), San Francisco (which lasted only one night in Colorada, although it lasts ten days in Magdalena), Santisima Trinidad, Virgin del Camino on July 1 (when everyone marries), San Juan Bautista on June 23 and 24 (characterized mainly by horse races and cockfights), and the Twelve Pastores on December 24, when everyone goes to see the baby Christ at the church.

One year Valentín Rahju, a grandson of Delores Valencia, got to be the Christ child. Valentín was five years old at the time. In order to get the part of the Christ child one had to have been an angel in the ceremony for the preceding two years. At the mass Valentín, dressed in white with large wings, carefully gave the talk that the *maestro* had spent months teaching him. This part of the Twelve Pastores ceremony has never been performed by the Arizona Yaquis so far as I know, but we did it every year in Colorada.

Yaquis at the nearby mines of Suviete and Minas Prietas took part in the Colorada ceremonies. When someone in one of the other mines made a *promesa* to have a fiesta, everyone from Colorada went over there, and that fiesta was not celebrated in Colorada. That happened once that I can remember. The fiesta was held in Suviete. My father had two burros equipped with big leather baskets on either side in which food and children were carried. Everyone else walked. I remember riding along in the big basket feeling very excited about going to a fiesta away from home and drowsing off as the basket swayed.

The company store, the company office, a dance hall, a cantina, and a *fonda* (inn) were together on a street in the American part of town. The company store must have been over 15 feet high, 150 feet long, and 100 feet wide. Groceries, cloth, ready-made clothes, and ever so many things were sold there. One corner of the store was a meat market; nearby ranchers brought in fresh meat every day, as well as salted dried beef.

Whenever anyone bought something, the clerk put the money or the coupons in a little basket that was pulled on wires into the office building next door. If a person had change coming back, it was sent back from the office, as they kept no money in the store.

Sometimes my mother took me to the store. My father never took me there, although he sometimes took my sister Antonia. Rujelio Moreno, nicknamed Loih (Crippled) because he was lame from a mining accident, used to pick me up under one arm and carry me to the store, where he would buy me an ice or maybe a banana. Loih's wife, Loreta (called Loy), referred to my *mama grande* as *sobrina* (niece), but I do not know how they were related.

Loih was the only man who ever picked me up when I was a little boy. Mostly I was carried around by *tia* Chepa, who was eight years older than I. *Tia* Chepa (Josefa Moreno Domínguez) still lives in Hermosillo, and I can say now that she has been good to me all my life. She has never done anything bad to me, and has helped me many times.

Every Saturday and Sunday nearly all the miners went to the dance hall and to the cantina. Some American men went to the dance, but of course the American women never did. The women in the cantina were Mexicans, many up from Guaymas for payday. Some local men could play guitars, harps, and other instruments, but most of the music at the dance hall and at the *fonda* was supplied by musicians from Guaymas. An organ grinder who often came up from Guaymas and played along the streets was popular with the children. My mother never went to the dances, although she liked music and dancing. My father went every week, usually meeting Augustina Preciado there.

At this time, my father spent as much time at Augustina's house as he did at home. He often went to the Preciado house when he got out of the mine at three in the afternoon and many times he ate supper there before he came home to sleep. I have a half sister, Dominga Palos, who is the daughter of Augustina and my father. She was born in 1897 when I was about a year old. Dominga was always sad, like my sister Antonia. We called her Dominga *güera*, Dominga *blanca*, and *la francésa* because she was so white; she is more like *mama grande* in appearance than anyone else in the family, except that she is taller. She is the prettiest of all.

While my father, Miguel, was going to Augustina's house, his cousin José González was coming to our house to see my mother. José got off work at three o'clock, like my father, and he often spent the afternoon with us, eating with the family before he went home. He never took my mother to the dances, although he usually went. José and my father were good friends in Colorada, and often played cards together.

Card games were an almost daily part of life. They often began when the seven to three shift got off work, usually at our place; playing was the heaviest on Saturday, Sunday, and payday. Perhaps eighteen men played together fairly regularly, and many members of this card group stayed together for many years. Three women played cards with these men; all were *borrachas* (drunkards) who supported themselves by playing cards and selling tequila. They always walked around drunk.

Among the men who never took part in the card games were Abelardo Cochemea, Delores Valencia (a relative of *mama grande*'s), and the brothers Felipe and Lucas Robles.

The luckiest of all the card players was Chico Liowe, and as a result, my grandmother Esperanza always had a sack of money in the house. My father was lucky too, always winning.

Card games were accompanied by a lot of joking and storytelling. One of the earliest songs I can remember was sung by Sacramento Somoochia, a Mayo *compadre* of *mama grande*. He was a violinist who played at Yaqui fiestas. This song began:

> Tu marido es celosa
> Echele hueso en el plato
> para que contenta. . . .
>
> [Your husband is jealous
> Throw him a bone in his plate
> So he will be content. . . .]

It is still sung sometimes in Torim.

The constant pastime of the men as they played cards or just sat around was talking. When I was present, I listened to their stores about Tajéchino, a famous joke teller of Torim who was old when Abelardo Cochemea was young. Stories about Yaqui generals and Yaqui soldiers and Yaqui traitors were told repeatedly. Everyone agreed that my father was the best storyteller in Colorada.

Abelardo Cochemea had been in the Sierra with José María Leyva, known as Cajeme, and while Abelardo never talked about anything, *mama grande* told many stories about Cajeme, whom she had known well. She said he had wives in all eight pueblos and he used to stay busy just walking from town to town to see his many women. Cajeme had once gone to California with his father to look for gold, in 1850, as many Yaquis did.

Vicente Tava told me a story about hunting for gold in California during the gold rush days. Vicente's uncle, José Luis Tava, went with one of the last groups to leave Torim for California. Fifteen Torim men went. As they were coming home, they got lost in the desert just south of the United States line. They knew that if they did not eat soon, all would die of hunger, and not a deer or a rabbit could they find to kill. Late one afternoon they decided that if they could not get some game the next day, they should eat one member of the party. Accordingly, as no game was killed, the next afternoon they again had a conference, and it was unanimous that one should die. They felt that the logical way to decide who should be killed was to choose the fattest. All stood in a line, while they pinched each other to see who was the fattest. Acusti Cungo was selected. He was killed with a knife, cut up, and roasted. With this food, the remaining fourteen men got closer to Magdalena where deer could be found. This is the only time I know of that the Yaquis ate a man. The Mexicans used to say that we were cannibals, but it is not true. During World War II, I read in a magazine that a man in Germany ate his fat sister.

Before the days of Cajeme, my great grandfather Manuel Cochemea fought by the side of General Mateo Wichamea of Torim. The name Wichamea means "with thorns" or "thorny." The card players in Colorada were very fond of hearing *mama grande* tell of General Wichamea and his one-time friend Yorilipti. This Yorilipti (translated "the blind *yori*" or "the blind traitor") was for years General Wichamea's main advisor, as Yorilipti was an exceptional administrator. Then Yorilipti became a *yori*, joining the Mexican forces against General Wichamea. After he became a *yori*, he would have his son guide him to a battle between Yaquis and Mexicans, asking his son to point his long rifle toward the Yaquis. After he pulled the trigger, he asked, "How many did I kill?" The invariable answer was "Two with one shot, my father." Yorilipti would exclaim, "That is what those crazy Indians want."

Yorilipti was married to a woman named Anna, the mother of Refugio, the half-wit son who guided him around. In spite of his affliction, Yorilipti considered himself to be the great lover of Torim. In those days, one way of declaring one's interest in a girl was to take a big wheel of cheese and steal close to the edge of the clearing where she lived, wait until the girl could see you, and then wave the big wheel of cheese, being careful, of course, to avoid detection by other members of the family. Yorilipti was enamored of a particular girl. He acquired the wheel of cheese and told Refugio to take him to a big tree on the edge of the clearing and tell him when to wave the cheese. Instead, Refugio led him into the clearing, stationed him behind the tall cross that stood in the bare yard, and told him that the girl could see him. The whole family was seated in the ramada where they had a clear view of the suitor. The father said, "What do you think the blind one is doing?" Yorilipti had to take his cheese and go home. My grandmother was very funny when she acted out this story.

Augustina Valencia was a grown woman in Torim when my grandmother María was a little girl. Those two were relatives and lived close together. They had been close in Torim, and now lived side by side in Colorada. Long before the days of Cajeme, Augustina fled to the Sierra with her husband, Chico Contreras, staying there for several months. A French priest from Torim went to the Sierra with them. The whole band was captured by Mexican soldiers at Apelahuecheme, a hill that has always made noises like rocks constantly falling, as the Yaqui name describes. I slept there once, and this noise went on day and night, but rocks were not really falling. The whole captured band, including Augustina and the French priest, were stood in a line to be shot. Three times the soldiers tried to shoot with their muzzleloaders, but the guns would not fire. The Mexicans walked the Yaqui band to Guaymas as prisoners. Augustina said that there were no houses in Guaymas then, just the wharfs where the boats came. In those days the deportations had not begun, and after a few weeks the soldiers turned the group loose and they went home to Torim. Upon their return, they found that Mexicans had stolen all their chickens, turkeys, and goats. They were especially sad about the turkeys, as these had come from the Sierra Madre of Chihuahua. Yaquis have always made special trips to get turkeys from the Tarahumaras of Chihuahua.

Augustina Valencia remembered many things that happened long before I was born, and everyone always listened when she started to tell about these things. She talked almost as much as my grandmother. In fact, they talked to each other all the time. Both remembered when the Apaches raided as far south as the Rio Yaqui, killing a great many people, including children.

Augustina had seen lots of sickness. About every year there were epidemics of yellow fever, smallpox, and cholera from China. Every time one of these sicknesses went through the Rio Yaqui, many died. Augustina remembered a big earthquake. Once when she was a little girl, the world was covered with red clouds when the sun came up. The French in Guaymas also saw this, and everyone was afraid.

Both María and Augustina told us about *argolitos* (called *suawáka* or *suaguaca* in Yaqui) and *sierpas*. *Argolitos* come from another world, traveling through the air so fast you just see a little light and hear a "whoosh."

If he comes close, you can see a long rope trailing behind. *Sierpas* are creatures that live in caves and caverns, growing bigger and bigger. They were once people who committed incest or did some other bad thing. When they get very large they leave their caves and go to the sea with a terrible roar. The earth shakes. *Sierpas* can be big snakes, giant tarantulas, or other animals. They are very dangerous. Once they go to the sea, they never return to their cave. Many still live in the sea.

Once a *chivatero* (goatherd) named Wite from Torim was spending the night close to Cenyoa-Baam where a great rattlesnake *sierpa* lived. I guess this was not so long ago, as the Yaquis already had goats and lambs from the Spaniards. Whenever people passed near the canyon, a woman dressed in white would walk out and stand. She must have been one aspect of the *sierpa* but she never hurt anyone. It is believed that this *sierpa* was once a man from Torim named Tomás, who became a *sierpa* because he married a close relative. The *chivatero* saw a bright light trailing a long rope flash down into the canyon, and he crept over to see what was happening. A terrible fight between the *sierpa* and the *argolito* went on for four hours; about daylight the *argolito* killed the *sierpa* and began to cut up the meat, which he tied with his long rope. All *argolitos* carry long ropes coiled over their shoulder. When he had tied up all the *sierpa* meat, he saw the *chivatero* and asked him if he wanted to go to his, the *argolito*'s, home. The *chivatero* agreed and they flew away to another world. For three days the *chivatero* was left alone, locked in a room. He could hear the children of the *argolito* asking when they could eat him. The *argolito* replied that the *chivatero* was the son-in-law of the rain. Finally the *argolito* took him back through the air and left him on the hill north of Torim. He told everyone about his experience. My grandmother said it was true.

One of my mother's relatives who was living at the Colorada Mine was a champion at doing tricks. He did many kinds of tricks, and often he had me swallow a bean or kernel of corn.

"Are you sure you swallowed it?" he would ask.

"Yes."

"You just thought you swallowed it; it is in your ear."

I would feel in my ear, there it would be. I asked him, "How did you learn to do tricks?"

"I never did learn it," he said, "it is magic."

He told me that when he was a boy, he went to a spring very early one morning. The water was clear and cold, and in the bottom of the spring were some beautiful little rocks. In looking at the rocks, he saw one round like a marble and crystal clear, except in the center where there were some little figures or forms. One could hold it one way and see a snake, another way and see a cat or a coyote. Since then he always carried the crystal marble, and when he had it he could do wonderful tricks. His name was Remetio, and the spring where he found the crystal marble was Pueblo Viego, twenty-seven miles east of Hermosillo.

He lived with us and worked in the mine at night. One morning he came home to breakfast, and my mother said to him, "Why do you look so sad? Has something happened to you?"

"Nothing has happened to me; I am all right."

When he finished breakfast, I asked him to do a trick for me.

"I don't want to do anything," he said, and he went to bed and to sleep.

I waited all day for him to wake up. At five in the afternoon, when he was awake, I again asked him to do a trick for me. He did not answer me, not a word. He did not seem to hear me, but ate his supper in silence and went to work.

About midnight the boss man at the mine came to our house and called, "Hello. Are you asleep?"

My mother said, "No, I am not asleep."

"Something has happened at the mine. Your cousin died half an hour ago."

My mother woke my father up and said, "Get up. There has been an accident at the mine."

The boss man said, "No, there was no accident. I saw something like a whirlwind where Remetio was working. When I went to the place, he was dead. But he was not hurt."

We were all awake and heard what the boss man said. My father got up and built a fire. Then he went to the mine to bring the body back. I wanted to go with him because the first thing I thought of was that I wanted to go and search in his pocket for the magic marble, but my father said that I was to stay with my mother.

When my father and some more men got back with the body, I said to my father, "Did you inspect his pockets?"

"Yes. I looked in the pockets for the magic marble, but it was not there. I guess that is what the whirlwind was; the Devil came and got the marble."

"What does the Devil look like?" I asked.

"He is an ugly man, with a long face and a horn, and he has long claws."

I said, "That man comes to see me every night after I go to bed. He is not a bad man. He shows me many wonderful things each night."

My father did not believe me, but it was true. Ever since I was three, the ugly man would come to see me. He told me about large cities and the wonderful things to be found there, how to learn to do tricks, and how to make money when I grew up. When other children came around, the ugly man would leave. He did not like children. Only I did not scare him. Sometimes I would get very angry with the children when they came just when the ugly man was telling me something. The night after Remetio died, I was waiting for the man with the claws. I thought he would bring me the crystal ball, but he never came again.

Our life in Colorada was comfortable and pleasant. We had plenty to eat every day. My father bought fruit jelly at the company store. My mother was a good cook, making enchiladas, chili *relleños*, *chimole*, and frijoles. No one makes *chimole* any more. It is sort of like a gravy made with wheat flour instead of corn masa, with ground red chili and maybe some meat. *Chimole* is dipped out of the *olla* with tortillas. For fiestas there was always a garbanzo stew with flour tortillas. Several bread bakers lived in Colorada. A Chinese who lived on the American side of town came to the miners' ramadas every day peddling bread. A big, flat, round loaf of *pan virote* cost only ten centavos and smaller sweet breads with a squash or sweet potato filling cost only five centavos. We usually bought our bread from Nicolasa Chora, a Yaqui woman who lived close to us and who was one of my grandmother's many relatives from Torim. Her house was always the favorite for all the children, as she sometimes gave us freshly baked bread. We wanted to stay at her house all the time. Her daughter Paola was the same age as Chepa and we were together all the time. Sometimes Nicolasa's son-in-law brought a load of salted fish from Guaymas to sell.

Our kitchen ramada was built apart from the house. My father built two high stoves out of clay for my mother, my *mama grande*, and my aunt Camilda. A wooden table, two long benches, and some short benches were in the kitchen. Big metal fry pans, wooden masa bowls, white china plates and cups, and porcelain coffee makers had been bought at the company store. *Mama grande* made *ollas* (pottery vessels) and *comales* (the flat earthenware griddles on which tortillas were cooked) for us and sometimes she sold them to other people. We never bought very much from the man who made pottery because *mama grande* was such a good potter. Neither my mother nor my aunt Camilda ever wanted to make *ollas*.

We slept on beds made of pitahaya wood covered with *petates*. We bought our *petates* (mats woven of cane splints) from peddlers. They were made in the Rio Yaqui and around Guaymas where carrizo cane grows. Warm covers were on all the beds and no one was cold at night. On the walls were large, framed, oval photographs of Miguel and Cecelia. A picture of San Francisco hung on the wall. Every time someone went to the annual fiesta of San Francisco in Magdalena, they bought a new picture of the saint for the house. A small room was used as a closet for storing our clothes.

Not only did we eat well and live in a comfortable house, but we all dressed well. My mother did not own a sewing machine, but other women in the pueblo did. My mother had some of our clothes made and others we bought in the company stores or from the peddlers who came from Guaymas. Our clothes were always well ironed. I was dressed in short pants, white shirts, socks, and shoes. My mother was especially proud of my wide-brimmed straw hat with long ribbons.

I can remember a number of things that happened when I was quite young. One of these memories is of a time when I was left outside during dynamiting at the mine. The women were afraid of dynamiting, and the miners always sent word to town when it would occur. Everyone went indoors and hid and said their rosaries and *padre nuestros* (Our Fathers). One day everyone ran to hide and only two were left outside, me and a *loco* (half-witted) boy of eight or nine. The *loco* threw himself on the ground in terror, but I loved the dynamiting noise and laughed all the time.

Another early memory is of my official baptism at San José de Pima when I was about eighteen months old. Rafaela Charavan was my baptismal *madrina* and Javier Aldamea was the *padrino*. The priest got something in my mouth and I got mad and grabbed the white scarf from around his neck. They gave me the name of Javier after my *padrino*. I had also been baptized when I was born, by the *maestro* in Colorada, at which time they gave me the name Rosalio Moisés Valenzuela. So by the time I was a year and a half old, I had lots of names, and I have used many others in my life.

At the time of my baptism in San José de Pima, I was unable to walk because I had been born with a "dry" leg. A *curandera* made my leg well by applying a warm mixture of olive oil and tobacco.

While I was a little boy in Colorada, everyone liked me and was good to me. We lived comfortably. No one was afraid. The Yaqui men at the mine were skilled laborers making good, steady wages.

Early in 1900 many people at Colorada received word from relatives in the Rio Yaqui that new trouble was brewing. A few families left Colorada to go back to the Yaqui villages. My mother's parents, Chico and Esperanza Liowe, took their little girl Juana and went to Torim. Chico Contreras (husband of Augustina Valencia) and Domingo Charavan (husband of Rafaela Charavan, my *madrina* of baptism) returned to the Rio Yaqui, leaving their families in Colorada. It turned out that their return to the Rio Yaqui was badly timed, as they soon had to flee to the Bacatete Mountains. Eusebio Bruno (husband of Nicolasa Chora, the baker) went directly to the Sierra from Colorada because he had relatives in the Sierra that he wanted to help. These six people were killed at the Massacre of Mazocoba in January, 1900. I have since met people who survived that infamous day, but these six, including my grandparents and their little girl Juana, who had been my constant companion and who was only six years old when she was killed, are the six people I knew at Colorada who were killed at Mazocoba.

Sacramento Navogoki was one who escaped the massacre when he was only six years old. He has told me how it was. All Yaquis know about it. They say thirty thousand Mexican soldiers were hunting the Yaquis in the Sierra. They rounded up over four thousand Yaqui men, women, and children. Several collecting points were being used in the Sierra, but only at Mazocoba did they kill Yaquis that year.

The Yaquis were herded into a big corral. Women and children were placed in the center by the disarmed Yaqui men. Our general, Juan María Maldonado Tetabiate, was prisoner there. Mexican soldiers started firing into the corral. Tetabiate gave the orders for everyone to escape as best they could. The Yaquis then charged the Mexican soldiers with their bare hands. A few escaped. Over one thousand Yaquis died that day at Mazocoba. Women and children were shot. Babies were killed by hitting their heads against trees. Many women and children jumped or were pushed off the cliff.

The news of Mazocoba came to Colorada and my mother learned that her parents and little sister had been shot. After that my mother cried and cried every day and was always sad. She said she could no longer stay at the Colorada Mine. Mexican soldiers came from Hermosillo to tell all Yaqui men they had to register with the government. From this time on, our lives changed.

It was decided that Abelardo, *mama grande*, and Camilda would move to Hermosillo, taking along Camilda's daughter Viviana, my sister Antonia, me, and my great grandmother Juana Sewa. I am not sure if

Camilda's husband, Pedro Omogon, went with us or not, but I think he went directly to the Sierra, where he was soon killed. We had six burros to carry our things. Nicolasa Chora and her daughter, Paola Chora, made the trip with us, as did old Augustina Valencia. Like Nicolasa Chora, Augustina was a recent widow because of the Mazocoba Massacre. She brought along her three children, Luis Contreras, Guillermo Contreras, and Tula Contreras. About fourteen of us moved together to Hermosillo, and every family had some burros.

My father, mother, and my brother Francisco, who was just a new baby, moved to the Copete Mine. José González went with them. It was not long until my father left Copete and moved on to the Sierrita Mine. My mother and Francisco stayed in Copete with José González for five years. I did not see her again until I was grown. I think she was a bad mother because she abandoned her older children.

My father moved to Sierrita after he got a letter from his old friend Eugenio Valencia saying that there were good jobs there. Eugenio, his brothers Cayetano and Ignacio, and his father, Gregorio Valencia, had gone straight to Sierrita from Colorada. Other miners who moved from Colorada to Sierrita were my uncle Francisco Moreno, Lino Sopomea, the entire Siguello family, and Carlos Rahju. Carlos Rahju was Valentín Rahju's father (Valentín being the little boy who played the Christ child on the day of the Twelve Pastores) and Delores Valencia's son-in-law (since he was married to Eufemia Valencia). Carlos was hung at Sierrita by the Porfirista soldiers because they found guns in his house. After he was killed, Eufemia, Valentín, and all of Delores Valencia's family came to Hermosillo. This was about 1901.

Juan González went to Hermosillo from Colorada to join the Mexican army. They made him a captain right away because he knew so much about the Yaquis, having been in the Sierra; in fact, he was a Yaqui general under Tetabiate, and he had a Mexican bullet in his neck. After Juan became a *yori*, he made it his business to hunt for my father, as José González, his brother, was by then living with my mother at Copete. Because soldiers were hunting him, my father left the Sierrita Mine and went to the Sierra to be a Yaqui captain with General Sibalaume.

# CHAPTER 2

# Hermosillo

MOST YAQUIS IN the vicinity of Hermosillo lived on ranches, farms, or in orchards where the men of the family worked. One large farm was called Ranchito. The *dueño* there, Arturo León (a Spaniard with a big black beard), fathered many children by Yaqui women, as he merely took any of his workers' women that caught his fancy. The main crop at Ranchito was sugar cane, and they grew both the white and red kinds. Some fields were planted in wheat and vegetables. Realito was another nearby farm where many Yaquis worked. Here they planted garbanzos, frijole beans, corn, and wheat. Quite a large group of Yaquis lived at Rincón del Burro, a little village that was not part of a ranch or a farm, located about two miles northeast of Hermosillo. A few Yaquis lived at La Iglesia Vieja, south of Hermosillo. Still another place where Yaquis lived was at La Matanza, inside the city where there was, and still is, a big slaughter-house. Most of our friends lived at Ranchito and Rincón del Burro. We seldom went to La Matanza. I think more of the *torocoyoris* lived there.

When our party reached Hermosillo from Colorada, we went to the house of José Juan Bakasewa at Rincón del Burro. We all stayed in a big ramada at the side of his house until each family got their own house. My *mama grande* knew him and his family well, and she and his wife, Prudencia Bakasewa, were *comadres*.

José Juan Bakasewa was known all over the Rio Yaqui as the best *curandero* of witch sickness. He was not a witch himself. To cure a be-witched person, he sucked the affected part of the body, removing a needle, centipede, rock, worm, or some such thing, which he put in a glass of water to which he added *chiltipiquines* (small, hot chilis). The whole thing was thrown in the fire, making the witch who had caused the sick-ness cry a lot.

My grandmother had always been able to do a little curing; she had learned a lot about curing from Victoriano Torre in Colorada, but it was from José Juan Bakasewa that she learned the most. She became very well known for treating children, *locos*, and the kind of ghost sickness that caused peoples' guts to rise. Only Yaquis came to her. Of course she never charged anyone for curing, but people she cured left us whatever money or food they could, and these "gifts" were often what kept us alive. One thing that María did for just about every sick person who came to her was to shave Brazil wood in water. The sick person drank part and left part in the glass. If the water in the glass remained red, the person could be cured, but if the water turned gray, nothing could be done and she told them she could not cure them.

One hot summer day at Rincón del Burro, my *tía* Chepa went into the dark house to get her blanket about seven o'clock in the evening. A ghost scared her; she ran to the outside fire, trembling, sweating, and crying out that a skeleton had climbed on her shoulders. No one else saw it. María was at the fire, and she immediately understood what had happened. She calmly began gathering the ingredients for the remedy. First she got holy water, making the sign of the cross on Chepa's forehead and putting three drops in some water that Chepa drank. Second, she burned a piece of palm cross left from Palm Sunday, and with the ashes she made another cross on Chepa's forehead. The last thing she did was to shave up some Brazil wood from the supply she always had on hand and make the bright red drink; Chepa drank part of it, and what was left in the glass stayed red. My grandmother's treatment was good, because the next day Chepa woke up feeling very well, without a trace of a fever.

Nicolasa Chora brought enough money with her from Colorada to pay for the construction of a house and a large bread oven in Rincón del Burro. When she moved into her house, my great grandmother, Juana Sewa, went to live with her. They baked bread for the Yaquis in that pueblito and made enough money to live on.

Many relatives and old family friends were already living in Hermo-silla when we arrived. My grandmother had not seen many of them in years. She was especially glad to see Lucrecia Sewa, who, like my grandmother and grandfather, had been born and raised at the Corasepe rancheria on Torim pueblo lands. They were about the same age and both were married in the old church at Torim. Lucrecia's husband, José María Sewa, had died of natural causes in Torim about 1898 or 1899. After one of her relatives was killed at Mazocoba, she decided that she should bring her family to Hermosillo, as too many people were being killed in the Rio Yaqui. Lucrecia Sewa, her two sons, Trinidad Sewa and Abato Sewa, and her daughter Selma Sewa More with her young children lived at an orchard called Graneo owned by Ignacio Martínez. Trinidad was the only grown man in the family who could work in the orchard. Abato was closer to my age, as was Selma's oldest daughter, Nacha.

Many Yaqui men came daily to talk to José Juan Bakasewa. One of these friends, Pedro Sosa, brought word that the Italian foreman at La Playita, where he worked, needed more workers in the orchard. José Juan Bakasewa sent my grandfather Abelardo to see Señor Antonio Terelli. Abelardo got the job. Three weeks after we arrived in Hermosillo from the Colorada Mine, we moved into one of the workers' houses at the La Playita orchard, just one-half mile south of Rincón del Burro. Augustina Valencia and her three children lived with us there. Our adobe house had four rooms, and the women cooked in a big ramada built to one side of the house. Pedro Sosa and his wife, Luisa, lived alone in a small house located in a different part of the orchard. They had no children.

One day Señor Terelli told my grandfather that he needed a night watchman to guard the oranges, so Abelardo went to Rincón del Burro and got Antonio, the son of Rafaela Charavan (my *madrina* of baptism) and Domingo Charavan (killed at Mazocoba). They had left the Colorada Mine about three months after we did, going to Rincón del Burro, where they were living in the house of Aneseto Alvarez, an old friend of my grandfather Abelardo. Both Aneseto and Abelardo were from Torim and both had served with Cajeme.

Antonio Charavan moved his family, including his mother, into the third workers' house at the orchard, which was about a quarter of a mile away from our house. Antonio's wife was named Pancha Chino because of her curly hair, which always looked as though she had a permanent. Their eldest son, Leonardo, was about twenty years old in 1900; the middle son, named Pedro, was my age. Both Pedro and Manuel, the youngest son, were born at the Colorada Mine.

Jesús Alvarez moved to La Playita with the Charavans. His job was inside the big house, acting as a houseboy and gardener. He ate with the

Terelli family instead of with Antonio's family. One day while the
Terellis were gone he took me inside their house. I walked around and
looked at everything. Jesús told me not to touch anything. A gold pin
cushion shaped like a shoe was so pretty that I took it. I knew it was real
gold because I knew all about gold since my father had been a gold miner.
After the Terellis got home, Doña Concha missed her little gold shoe and
asked Jesús about it. He replied, quite truthfully, that he knew nothing
about it. I took it to a henequen field and threw it as far as I could. I was
glad they did nothing to Jesús, but I wouldn't have admitted I took it if
they had.

Pedro Charavan and I used to go dove hunting in the brush. Once we
came upon an *olla* sitting in the fork of a mesquite tree. We knew just
what it was, although we had never seen one before. Older Yaqui women
sometimes talked about these witching *ollas*. The witch who placed the
*olla* there was Luisa Sosa, the fat wife of Pedro Sosa. She often offered
cups of pinole to boys, but we never accepted anything from her because
we knew she was a witch.

The way the witching *olla* was prepared by Luisa, or by any witch
wanting to use one, was to take a little *olla* about eight or nine inches in
diameter and put in all sorts of thorns, needles, thread, poisonous herbs,
*toloache* (jimsonweed), the milk of the *howocuta* bush, some leaves from the
Don Juan plant, and maybe some ground-up roots of a plant the Yaquis
call *ochani*. The *olla* is put out in the brush, up in the fork of a tree. In
two or three days it starts to boil, and on the sixth night it explodes with
colored lights like firecrackers. A wind blows the odors and whoever
smells them will get sick.

When Pedro Charavan and I found the *olla*, it was boiling strongly,
giving off a terrible stench. I am sure it was almost ready to explode and
that Luisa Sosa was planning to use it that night. We threw it in a nearby
creek. The next day Luisa lay face down on the floor of her house all day
long with her face covered. She cried a lot and was sick for three days.
She never did anything to us.

Pimas and Papagos make these "firecracker" witching *ollas*. Years later
when I worked around Yuma, lights could be seen in the sky almost every
night, and my Papago friends told me they were caused by witching *ollas*.
I have also seen these lights in the Rio Yaqui and in Tucson.

Señor Terelli gave Antonio a pistol for his night guard duty. Before too
long, Antonio took the pistol and went to the Sierra. He found life in the
Sierra to be uncomfortable, and returned to his night watchman's job
after only three weeks. Three days after he got back, the Mexican soldiers

came, tied his arms, and took him to jail. Three days later they took him to one of the places where they shot Yaquis. This place is called Cruz Gálvez now, and a school stands there. In 1900 there was only a little wooden house where the Mexicans kept dynamite. They shot Antonio there. Friends came to the orchard and told his family that he was dead. We had to go get him at once, as the Mexican soldiers just left dead Yaquis for the dogs to eat. I went along to get the body with Antonio's oldest son, Leonardo; his mother, Rafaela; his wife, Pancha; José Juan Bakasewa; Loreto Bakasewa; and Luis Contreras (Augustina Valencia's oldest son, who lived in the orchard with us). We made a heavy mat of *batamote* on which to carry him, covered him with a cloth, and took him home to the orchard. He was buried in the cemetery at Ranchito with his arms all swollen from being tied so tightly. The day the Mexicans killed Antonio he was the only one they shot. Usually they killed more.

After Antonio was killed, his family could not stay at La Playita any more with no men to work in the orchard, so they moved into an empty house in Rincón del Burro. Rafaela and Pancha made tortillas to sell in Hermosillo. Leonardo went to work for another Italian, Señor Marcus Krikorovich. Pedro, who was my age, worked in the fields. Pancha died of sadness six months after Antonio was killed, leaving the grandmother Rafaela Charavan to care for the three children. They lived in Rincón del Burro until 1907 when the four were deported to Yucatán. Only Pedro returned in 1911; I never heard what happened to him after that.

Our family had better luck, at least for a while. We lived at La Playita from 1900 until 1904. Abelardo worked all day in the orchards. The work was not hard. Mostly it involved cleaning around the trees and gathering oranges. He fixed shoes until late every night, as he did all day Sunday. Everyone in the house worked. *Mama grande* and Augustina Valencia washed clothes for Mexicans in Hermosillo. Augustina, by now very old, did the laundry for at least ten families, including Toni Agnelli, the owner of La Playita.

My aunt Camilda got up early every morning to make tortillas. By ten o'clock she left the orchard to walk two miles into Hermosillo to sell the tortillas from house to house. When I was not working in the fields, I went with her to the edge of town, as any unaccompanied woman might be molested. I never went in town with Camilda because Mexican boys would beat me up. Instead, I usually stayed at the Tevecare orchard, where Nicolás Arpero (Nicolás the harpist) was one of the workers. He was a relative of *mama grande*'s from Torim. His wife, Maruja, was half-witted (*medio loca*). I played with their daughter Mariana, who was half-witted like her mother, and Juan Tecu. We would take a branch of the Don Juan plant, slash it, put it on the ground, and throw mesquite thorns at it, like darts. The Don Juan plant is soft, and the thorns could stick into it. We also made mud figures (*monitos de lodo*), called them Mexicans, and shot them down with slingshots or blow guns made out of lengths of carrizo cane. Maruja usually fed me whatever they had to eat; more often than not it was just beans and corn tortillas. Sometimes she had pinole. I always enjoyed staying at the Tevecare orchard. When Camilda was through selling tortillas, she picked me up and we walked back to La Playita.

Camilda also made palm fiber hats for sale, and sometimes she helped her mother do the washing. Antonia helped with the washing, too.

From the time we moved from Colorada when I was four years old until I started work as a man when I was thirteen years old in Arizona, I was treated like a slave in the family. I had to find grass for our burros every day. Whenever there was an errand, I was sent. If I was sent to the store two miles away, *mama grande* would spit on the floor as I left, telling me that if I was not back before the spit dried, she would beat me. For several months we bought bread from a Mexican who lived south of the river. He passed a half mile from our house about four o'clock in the morning on his way into Hermosillo. I was the one who had to get up and go wait for him in the cold without a coat. I was given the oldest, thinnest blankets and was cold all winter. My *mama grande* was friendly to everyone else and she had been nice to me in Colorada, but she became my bitter enemy in Hermosillo. My aunt Camilda had never paid any attention to me in Colorada, but at La Playita I had to go to town with her all the time. She got mad at me every day, and she used to chase me through the orchard because she wanted to beat me; she could never run fast enough to catch me. When she got really mad at me, she would say I was going to turn into a witch.

About this time I started having severe nosebleeds every day. María put large coins all around my head, held in place by a big handkerchief. That cured me. She often had to cure Abelardo, who was subject to the throat ailment that has killed so many Yaquis. When he lost his voice, María would gather chollas, pound them until she had a soapy substance that she put in hot water, and give the mixture to Abelardo for three days, and his voice would be all right again.

The most pleasant job I had was when I worked at the big house in the orchard for the Terelli family. Sometimes I took care of their baby girl, María, pulling her up and down in a little wagon. Sometimes I planted flowers. When oranges fell off the trees in the orchard, Señor Terelli let me pick them up. On Sundays I would put these oranges in the big skin baskets and go to Rincón del Burro and Ranchito to trade the fruit for beans and bread.

Every Sunday my grandmother took me to town. Sometimes we went to sell eggs or some of the few chickens we had. When we got to town, Mexican boys always followed us, trying to start a fight. I could do nothing to them because I had to hold onto the chickens. My grandmother could not do anything because there were too many boys. They jeered at me, threw rocks at me, some spit on me and my grandmother, and threw dirt in our faces. Sometimes they tore my cotton dress off me. Several times I went home without any hat or dress. At that time I had never worn long pants. They would snatch my straw hat and tear it to pieces.

One time when my grandmother and I had sold our chickens at the market, we bought something to eat. We had not eaten that day and were very hungry. We sat down on the sidewalk to eat, and the Mexican boys came and spit on us and threw horse manure on the food we were eating. They never let us eat in peace, even in a restaurant. The mothers of the Mexican boys only laughed and encouraged their children in what they were doing to us. We were very sad from these things but there was nothing we could do.

When I was six, I started working in the fields. Chico Romano, a Mayo foreman at Ranchito, was in charge of work teams of boys from the ages of six to ten years old. He had a whip that was used if the boys worked too slow, and more than once he whipped a boy till he could not work at all. He was sometimes called Chico Chicotero because of his whip (*chicote*). The work with Chico Romero was not steady. We worked hard during planting, weeding, and harvesting, for a few days or weeks, then we laid off for a while. Whenever Chico needed us again, he came to our houses and got us. Pedro Charavan and Jesús Valenzuela were in my work group. The worst part of our job was planting onions. When you plant onions for a week, down on your hands and knees, you itch all over in a terrible way. We were paid twenty-five centavos a day, while grown men working in the fields made thirty-three centavos a day. Of course no one really got any money: every Sunday we drew rations instead. Each man got ten kilos of corn, five kilos of beans, one kilo of sugar, one kilo of coffee, and one kilo of lard. That was all the provisions they got each week.

The Urias family lived at La Matanza near the slaughterhouse. Ramón Urias was a Mexican married to Chavela Macochine (the name is Yaqui for the huamuchil tree), and they had six sons. Anastasio was about my age. He walked all over Hermosillo selling the *tripas* from the slaughter-house and carrying buckets of blood. Some poor Yaquis bought blood instead of meat. When you cook it a little, it looks like hamburger meat, then you put in onions and what-have-you and it is not so bad. Even today hog blood can be bought in Obregón.

Our house was a meeting place for Yaquis in Hermosillo, just as it had been in Colorada and as it was in later years in Arizona. Almost every day Yaqui men and Yaqui families came to talk. *Mama grande* served coffee to the guests and tamales when there was money enough to buy them.

Some Saturday nights a great *sabio* came to our house. He lived in Ranchito at that time, although he belonged to the pueblo of Vicam. His name was José María Nóteme, and he was very, very old. No one slept when he talked, and he would talk all night long. When he arrived, he stood as he smoked a cigarette held cupped in his right hand. First he blew smoke to the east, then to the north, west, and south. José María Nóteme told us of many things that would happen in the future; nearly all the things he said have come true and all of his predictions will come to pass in due time. He said that the men who killed the Yaquis would soon fight each other like dogs, and they did in the Mexican revolutionary wars beginning in 1910. He said the Yaquis would someday return to their rightful land, and they have. He said the Yaqui River would dry up, as it has, due to a big dam that took all the water out of our river and gave it to the Mexicans south of the river. He said there would be carriages that ran without mules, and soon we saw automobiles. He told of big things that would fly like birds, carrying people all over the world. I saw my first airplane in Tucson in 1908. Everyone was terrified of the plane, but I knew what it was because José María Nóteme had said it would come. He spoke of big iron balls that would fall from the sky and kill people, and there are bombs. He also foresaw a time when all the big nations of the world would fight each other, and only a few people would be left in the world. This is the part that has not happened yet.

Many people say that all these same things were said long ago, before there was a Yaqui tribe, by the *palo seco*. The older people said that there used to be many great *sabios* among the Yaquis; José María Nóteme was the only one I ever knew and he must have been one of the last.

It was well known among the Hermosillo Yaquis that *mama grande* knew almost everyone and talked to everyone she saw. Many people came to our house to find out about their friends and relatives. My father, Miguel, slipped in at night every few weeks, bringing news of people in the Sierra, and *mama grande* would pass along this information to their relatives in town. One of the people who often came to see *mama grande* was Juan González, the *torocoyori* brother of Jose González, who was at that time living with my mother at the Copete Mine. He would tell *mama grande* when the soldiers were going to round up Yaqui boys, and she would dress me in girls' clothes on that day, or hide me in the orchard. He told her when certain water holes in the mountains were to be poisoned, and she would send word to the Sierra Yaquis to leave that part of the mountains for a while. *Mama grande* was always nice to Juan González and he was always nice to her.

During the time we lived in Hermosillo, Mexican soldiers regularly brought in Yaqui men and Yaqui families from all parts of Sonora. The Yaquis were usually just laborers on the farms and ranches, but the soldiers always said they were *broncos*, or wild Yaquis. Every week they killed some Yaquis, and after 1902 many were deported to Yucatán or the Islas Marías. Mexicans often took the children. Those between two and twelve were given away like puppies. Girls over twelve were given to the Mexican soldiers. Babies were killed by knocking their heads against trees or rocks. Many shipped from Guaymas died at sea and were thrown overboard.

Every Sunday morning every Yaqui man in the vicinity of Hermosillo had to present himself at Cuartel Catorce (military *cuartel* number 14). If a man skipped a Sunday line-up, the Mexican officers would say, "Oh, I know, he is taking *lonche* (lunch) to the Sierra Yaquis." It was assumed that he had gone to the Sierra, and his name was automatically put on the roll of those Yaquis to be killed.

The *cuartel* covered about a square block. Along each of three sides a row of rooms opened onto a covered *portal*. The central space was a large open area like a parade ground. Enormous gates opened onto the street.

Governor Izábal was called *el segundo dios* (the second God) by the Yaquis. This was the man who began the deportations about 1902. He liked to preside at the Sunday morning sessions, sitting on the *portal*. Out in the middle of the *cuartel*, Yaqui men were sorted into three lines. Men in one line were to be killed; men in the second line were to be deported; men in the third line were released to work another week.

The soldier in charge was Luis Medinas Varón (also spelled Barón and Harrón). A captain in 1902, he was promoted to lieutenant colonel by 1904 because of his wholehearted attention to the Yaquis. Sometimes Luis Medinas Varón personally sorted the Yaqui men into the three lines. At other times he was helped by one or several *torocoyoris* who stood to one side, their faces covered by red bandanas so no one would know who they were, but of course everyone knew very well who they were. Luis Medinas Varón would call a man forward, asking the *yoris*, "Do you know this man?" A no meant that that man should be deported. A yes nod meant that the man was known to be a Sierra Yaqui and should be killed. No response from the *yoris* allowed a man to stay in Hermosillo for another week. Many friends and relatives were killed or deported during the time we lived in Hermosillo and in the years after we fled to Arizona.

On a Saturday night in 1902, Juan María Silvas made a *cumpleaño* fiesta (the one-year anniversary of the death of a near relative) at his house in Rincón del Burro. Most of the Yaquis from Rincón del Burro and Ranchito were there, and most of my family went from La Playita. Only my grandfather Abelardo stayed home, because he never went to fiestas. Among those at the fiesta were José Juan Bakasewa and his family, Nicolasa Chora and her daughter Paola, and Manuel Valenzuela and his wife, Merehilda. Juan Goih Maesto was the *cantador* for the *coyotes*. Esteban Flores was the *maestro*. Manuel Salinas was the harpist for the *pascolas*, playing with the blind violinist Juan Esuki Labeleo, a wonderful clown able to dance on one leg. He was *muy chistoso* (very funny). When he began to play, he would seesaw up and down on his chair. Some boys put a cholla thorn on his chair one night at Ranchito and he landed on it hard. As is usual for *cumpleaño* fiestas, it lasted all night. About nine o'clock Sunday morning, Mexican soldiers took every man attending the fiesta to Cuartel Catorce, saying that the fiesta was being held for the Sierra Yaquis. They held the men at the *cuartel*, telling the women and children that all the men would be shot the next day. The women and children went home to cry all day and all night. There must have been a hundred Yaqui men in the *cuartel*.

Monday was a gay holiday for the Mexicans. Stores were closed and hundreds flocked to Rincón del Burro, where the Yaquis were to be killed. All the Yaqui women and children walked to Rincón del Burro on Monday afternoon to see their men. Soldiers brought the Yaqui men under heavy guard. At the last minute they selected three and turned the others loose. Juan María Silvas, Juan Goih Maesto, and Esteban Flores were shot by six soldiers at 3:00 P.M. Juan María Silvas was from Torim, and my *mama grande* was his baptismal *madrina*. After Juan María was shot, his wife, Magdalena Muñoz, and their only son, Abrán Silvas, were shipped to Yucatán; they never returned.

In 1903, soldiers went to the Colorada Mine for Yaqui men. They brought down all the Yaqui men who were left there, including Javier

Aldamea, my baptismal *padrino*. He was hung before his family could walk to Hermosillo; friends took his body to Ranchito. His daughter, Venancia; his wife, Lupe; and Lupe's brother Cayetano and sister Pancha arrived in time for the *velación* (wake) and funeral. Lupe's mother, Marcelina, was living between Ranchito and Rincón del Burro at this time, as she had moved there after her husband, Pedro Chino, usually called Piochino, had been killed by the Sierra Yaquis in 1902 at a little hill just outside Torim. The Sierra Yaquis said Piochino was a *yori* because he never went to the Sierra. Lupe soon returned to Vicam Switch, where she lived with Luis Conemea of Bacum. Luis was killed by Sierra Yaquis in 1917. So poor Lupe's father and one husband were killed by the Sierra Yaquis and one husband was killed by the Mexicans.

At about this time in 1903, the Preciado family was taken into custody in Colorada and seven of them were deported. My half sister Dominga; her mother, Augustina; Augustina's mother, Charla; Charla's mother and father, Simón and Julia Preciado; and Simón's brother Rosario Preciado with his wife, Jesús, were all sent to Yucatán. Two of Rosario's and Jesús's three children (Espiritu and Juan) were given to Mexican families in Hermosillo as servants. The Mexicans did not send Charla's brother, Francisco (Chico) Preciado, to Yucatán because he was a Yaqui captain in the Sierra and they could not catch him.

Dominga and Augustina returned from Yucatán to Torim in 1907, only to be deported a second time in 1909. This time they were just taken to Mexico City and turned loose. Augustina and Dominga returned from their second deportation in 1917 with José María Cajeme, a colonel in the Mexican army. This man, son of the great Yaqui general of the same name, was born to Otaviana Wokoyery and General Cajeme in the pueblo of Cocorit in 1862. Otaviana Wokoyery died in Cocorit in 1890. Cajeme, Jr., had been among the first to be deported to Yucatán, and when the Yaqui slaves were freed in 1910 he joined the federal army. He, like his father, was a good soldier, and he soon got to be a colonel. Augustina lived with him until his death on October 3, 1930, when he was seventy-seven years old, in the pueblo of Cocorit, where he had been born.

In 1904, Aneseto Alvarez and his son Jesús were killed in the Sierra. Aneseto's brother, Juan Alvarez, was sent the same year to Yucatán with his entire family, which included a number of small children. Aneseto's son Pedro Alvarez married my *tia* Chepa in Hermosillo. They were deported together in 1907, along with her father, Francisco Moreno Sewa, her sister María, and María's husband, Manuel Yomaiza. Of that family, only Jesús Moreno was left in Hermosillo; her husband, Manuel Ochoa, was shot by the Mexicans at Cruz Gálvez that same year, leaving Jesús with three daughters.

*Tia* Chepa has told me many things about their deportation and slavery. They were each sold separately. Chepa was sent to Santiago del Valle. She saw her father once after that. He told her he had been dancing as a *pascola* for other Yaqui slaves. Francisco Moreno must have died there. Neither María nor Manuel Yomaiza was ever heard of again. Hacienda slaves were freed in the 1910 revolution, and there are stories about the freed slaves turning on their overseers and the hacienda owners, killing them with sticks and hand tools. Chepa came back to Sonora in 1913 with a Mexican soldier, who was killed that same year in a battle at Santa María, just outside Guaymas. She never took another man and since 1913 has lived alone in Hermosillo. Pedro Alvarez escaped from Yucatán and made his way to Arizona in 1913. Pedro and Chepa never bothered to see each other again.

One Yaqui woman in Guaymas was very important to the Yaquis being deported. Her name was Matilde Anciano. She was the wife of Pablo Matuz, who was later a general with Pancho Villa. Pablo was killed at Naco in 1911. Matilde Anciano always lived in Guaymas. She spoke very good Spanish and talked for many of the Yaquis, saying that she knew them to be good people, interested only in working hard on the ranches. She persuaded the soldiers to free a number of them. Even when she was unable to have a Yaqui freed, she could see who was being deported and send word to their friends and relatives. After she died in 1908, there was no one to talk for the Yaquis at Guaymas. They say she was a *marimacha*, preferring young girls to men, and I guess that is true.

It was also in 1904 that a man named Joaquín Perez went to a hill outside Hermosillo, collected a big pile of wood, set it on fire, and then climbed on it and burned himself up. No one knew what he was going to do. He just burned himself up. The next day his mother came to our house at La Playita and talked to my grandmother for a long time. She said Joaquín had been very quiet and thoughtful, and he had told her that he had done many bad things. I think the reason he burned himself is because the *maestros*, in every ceremony, tell everyone that if they are bad (by killing people without reason, hurting poor people, or stealing eggs) they will have to burn for salvation. I have heard of other Yaquis who burned themselves up for salvation.

Late in 1904, my father, Miguel, got word that Governor Izábal would be at Gavilán on a certain day. He and Juan Tecu, who was still a worker at the Tevecare Orchard in Hermosillo, decided to wait for the governor outside of Gavilán to see if they could kill him. They found a good place to hide near the road, and when the governor and his bodyguard of fifteen Yaquis passed by, they shot. Izábal ran away, but they killed seven of the Yaqui *yoris*. Juan Tecu was killed, but the *yoris* did not know it, or they would probably have stayed there to kill my father. My father was sad he had not killed Izábal. A short time later he decided it was wise to go to Arizona.

Augustina Valencia was supporting her family by washing, as I mentioned before. Once or twice a week I would take a burro and go with her to pick up dirty clothes and deliver clean ones. Augustina's daughter, Tula Contreras, over seventeen years old at this time, helped with the wash and went with us to the houses. One of the people whose laundry we collected every week was Ignacio Martínez. Antonia's youngest son, Guillermo Contreras, walked to work every day at an orchard owned by this same Señor Martínez. One day Señor Martínez reported to the police that a small gold shoe pin cushion and good gold rings were missing from his house, charging that Tula and Guillermo had taken these gold things. I do not believe they did, because if they had, we would have known it at La Playita. They were arrested and deported and never heard of again.

Augustina's oldest son, Luis Contreras, married Nicolasa Waibel in Ranchito. Everyone from La Playita except my grandfather Abelardo and me went to the wedding in the church in Hermosillo and on to the fiesta in Ranchito. After that Luis lived with Nicolasa's family in Ranchito, along with her mother (Amalia Valenzuela), her father (Juan Waibel), and her sister Josefa and Josefa's husband, Pedro More. Josefa and Pedro were not married in the church. He had been married to Selma Sewa at the church in Torim, but he ran off and left Selma when their daughter Nacha was only six months old, going to live with Josefa Waibel. Josefa had been married previously to Gregorio Perico of Vicam, who died of natural causes in Hermosillo. Her three sons by that marriage were living with her in Ranchito. Her oldest son always used the name Fernando Cupes, while Rosario and young Gregorio used the name Waibel.

The deportation of Tula and Guillermo Contreras was the beginning of a lot of bad luck for our household. After we had been living four years in Hermosillo, Mexican soldiers and some *torocoyoris* surrounded our house at La Playita early one morning. Lieutenant Colonel Luis Medinas Varón asked my grandfather, "Is your name Abelardo Zapatero?"

My grandfather answered him, "Yes, sir, it is."

Then the lieutenant colonel looked him up and down and said, "Where is your son, Miguel?"

My grandfather said, "I do not know anything about my son."

"Ah, yes," said the officer, "you do not know where your son is, but I know exactly about your son, Miguel. He is going up and down the mountains with a whole band of Yaquis. And I know too that he is captain of the Indians."

My grandfather did not answer, not a word. The lieutenant colonel said, "All right, sergeant, tie this man." A soldier tied both his arms tightly against his body and they took him away to Hermosillo.

After they took him away, my grandmother, Camilda, and the children began to cry. Only I did not weep. I was thinking about my grandfather, and I was very angry. How could he save himself? What could I do? I did not know the best thing to do. I was like a blind boy.

The next day we got up early and my grandmother and I went to see some rich men we knew in the city. We wanted to tell them what had happened and ask if they could save my grandfather.

We went to the home of the first rich man, Toni Agnelli, the owner of La Playita. My grandmother started to speak to him about what was happening with her husband, saying, "Please, Don Antonio, won't you do something to help us? Can you save my husband? He has no fault. He is only a worker. We have known you for a long time, and you know us very well. We have many children. What can I do with them?"

The rich man shook his head, and he answered my grandmother, "I am sorry for my old friend, the Zapatero, but I cannot help. I am afraid that if I arrange something for my old friend, the authorities will fine me a lot of money."

My grandmother then said not a word, and we went to see the next rich man, Antonio Terelli, the manager of La Playita. He said the same words as the first rich man. Then we went to Antonio Davila, with the same result.

It was in the afternoon when we got back home, and my grandmother was very angry; she was crying. My aunt and the children came running to meet us, all very happy. "What did the rich men arrange?" said my aunt.

My grandmother said, "Everything is very sad. The rich men said they cannot save him. That is all we could get from them." The children started crying again.

My grandfather was in the jail seven days. I guess the trainload of Yaquis was ready then. In the evening the train pulled out of Hermosillo for Guaymas with eight boxcars filled with Yaqui prisoners. That was the last time we saw my grandfather. He was gone forever. We never heard from him again. He was the last shoemaker in all the Yaqui tribe.

After my grandfather was shipped to Yucatán, we could no longer stay at La Playita because we no longer had a grown man in the family to work in the orchard, since Luis Contreras had just moved to Ranchito. We built a house in Ranchito, where we had many friends. Now our household was smaller. There remained *mama grande;* my Aunt Camilda, her daughters Viviana Omogon and Carmen More, and a new baby; Simón Valenzuela; my sister Antonia; and old Augustina Valencia. Nicolasa Chora and her daughter Paola gave up their house and came to live with us.

Now we did not live well. Some days we ate only once a day, and we were always hungry. At times my grandmother could not find anything at all to eat. Then I went out at night or about daybreak to a garden and got some onions, or tomatoes, or potatoes, or beans. One morning I had bad luck. The watchman saw me in a vegetable garden and shot me with a shotgun. He was two hundred feet away and the shot were small, so he did not hurt me very much, but I was scared nearly to death. I ran until I came to the railroad, and I ran so fast I got away from the watchman. Then I walked along the railroad ties so I would not leave any tracks. When I got home and told my grandmother, she was frightened, too. That was the first time I had bad luck, and I did not want to ever go back again to steal vegetables. But the family was very hungry, and my grandmother said to me, "You must pray to our God. If you do not move yourself our God cannot bring us anything, because He said, 'Help yourself and I will help you.'" I took her advice and prayed to our God before I went out. Before the Mexicans took my grandfather away I did not steal, but now my sister and all of us were hungry and it was a great necessity. So I prayed to our God and went out at night to find food. There was always danger, and I was always afraid. Sometimes I could find nothing. For twelve months we had no money to buy food and we were scared and hungry all the time. Many times we would have starved if it had not been for the gifts given my grandmother for curing.

I went to a ranch near our house that belonged to a Greek man who had a dairy. I asked him for work. "All right," he said, "you can herd my cows."

I worked for three weeks. About six o'clock one morning four dogs belonging to the Greek caught me and bit me badly. Those four big bull-dogs wanted to kill me and undoubtedly would have if some Mexican women had not heard the noise and come running to drive them off. The next morning I could not stand up, and for two weeks I could not walk. The Greek told me I could not work for him any more and paid me twenty-five centavos for each day I had worked. I still carry the scars.

During the time we lived in Hermosillo, my aunt Camilda had a number of men friends. Her real husband, Pedro Omogon, was killed by the Mexicans around 1900. For a while she knew Sergio More, who came from Potam. He never came to our house. She saw him in town somewhere. He and his wife lived in La Matanza. We never visited with his family, and I never saw his wife. Sergio worked at Hacienda Chana Baam, as the Yaquis called it. It was owned by Governor Izábal, and Sergio maintained the irrigation canals. Governor Izábal also owned the Hacienda Siaricutu (paloverde in Spanish) and the Hacienda Muucahui (Cerro de Tecolote). Sergio More was the father of Camilda's little girl, Carmen More, who was born at La Playita in 1902.

Simón Valenzuela was born to Camilda in La Playita in 1904, not long before Abelardo was deported. Simón's father was Manuel Valenzuela, the older brother of Jesús Valenzuela, who was in Chico Castro's work group with me. An older brother, Mariano Valenzuela, was deported in 1907, but at this time (1904), all the brothers lived in Ranchito. Camilda was a good friend of Manuel's wife, Merehilda, and they used to meet often in Hermosillo, where both went daily to sell tortillas. I do not think that Merehilda knew Manuel was seeing Camilda at that time, although she found out later. After we all moved to Arizona, Merehilda and Camilda remained close friends, and today Simón goes to see his two half brothers, Calistro and Carlos Valenzuela, who are the sons of Manuel and Merehilda. Just before we left Hermosillo, a Mexican soldier named Juan Guzmán started coming to see Camilda.

Crecensio Murillo used to come see us in La Playita, and after Abelardo was deported, he called on my grandmother regularly in Ranchito. Crecensio lived with friends in Ranchito; he was not married and so he did not have his own house. Whenever Crecensio came to see us, he would always bring a big sack of crackers. His only brother, Celso, lived for years at Bachomobampo in the Sierra.

Luis Lara started coming around our house at Ranchito to see Antonia, who was then about thirteen years old. He had no family in Hermosillo, and soon he sort of moved in, sleeping in the ramada. Every day he went into Hermosillo to his job as a bricklayer, often taking me along and sharing his lunch with me. Antonia was not very interested in Luis, and when he asked her to marry him she refused.

One morning my grandmother called all of us together and said, "We will have to go away from here. We will leave here Saturday for Nogales. I think we can get money to ride the train if we sell all of your grandfather's tools.'' She warned us not to tell Luis Lara or anyone else that we planned to leave. The next morning we went to town carrying the tools. We sold most of them to the second-hand store. What we were unable to sell we left behind in our little house.

On Saturday we waited until Luis Lara left for work. He said he would see us that night, but we knew better. We tied our few possessions into bundles and walked to the water station on the railroad several miles outside Hermosillo. We were afraid to go to the depot in town. Crecensio Murillo went with us. It was October 15, 1905, when my grandfather was taken away, and now one year later we were going away in the opposite direction.

# CHAPTER 3

# *Across the Border*

WE ARRIVED AT Nogales late in the evening and went at once to the border. The American inspector stopped us and asked my grandmother for some letters of recommendation.

"I am sorry, señor, but we have none. We go to my son, who lives in Tucson."

The inspector said, "What is the name of your son?"

"He is called Miguel Valenzuela."

"All right," said the inspector, and he started to write down our names. First he wrote down Miguel Valenzuela, Tucson, Arizona. Then he took down the names of my grandmother, María Daumier Valencia Palos; my aunt Camilda Palos and her three children, Viviana Omogon, Carmen More, and Simón Valenzuela; my sister Antonia Valenzuela; my grandmother's friend, Crecensio Murillo; and my own name, Rosalio Valenzuela.

A Mexican carriage driver from Nogales had heard the talk between my grandmother and the inspector. "I know her son, Miguel Valenzuela. He lives in Tucson." This was not exactly true, because my father was not in Tucson, but working at a mine. Besides, the driver had never even heard of Miguel Valenzuela. However, the inspector believed him and let us enter the United States.

The carriage driver took us to the Yaqui village about three miles east of Nogales, Arizona, to the house of Guadalupe Sinjuego. He was once married to Diana Frias, one of my grandmother's relatives who had died, and that was why we went to his house. At this time, his wife was Juliana Wiikit; their children were named Luis and Manuela.

The day after we arrived, Locaria Rodríguez, hearing that my grandmother had arrived from Hermosillo, came over to ask about her sister, Rufina Moroyoki. Locaria Rodríguez stayed all afternoon, and she and my grandmother were friends from that time on. They later became *comadres* and baptized many babies together.

Crecensio Murillo left right away to go work at Patagonia, Arizona. My grandmother had Guadalupe Sinjuego write a friend of his in Tucson to ask where my father was. In two weeks a letter came from the friend saying that my father was working at the Silver Bell Mine west of Tucson. Guadalupe then wrote to my father, and in three weeks a letter came from him saying he was glad we had come to the United States, and enclosing fifty dollars.

The following day my grandmother went to a store and bought some dresses for the women and girls and long pants for me and Simón. These were the first long pants for both of us. In Hermosillo I had worn dresses and in Colorada my mother dressed me in short pants. Everything was cheap in the store and all our clothes together did not cost much.

The next evening my grandmother sent me to the spring about a half mile from the Yaqui village to get some water. As I was coming back four Yaqui boys stopped me. Three of them held me while the other one beat me on the nose and threw the water over me. When I got home with the empty bucket I was wet and bloody. My grandmother was furious and started to go see the mothers of the boys, but I stopped her.

"Don't say a thing, *mama grande*," I said. "If you talk to the mothers, the boys will only make it worse for me. I will pay them back sometime."

Six years later, in Tucson, I was carrying some things home from a grocery store and I had the good luck to meet the boy who hit my nose. I was very angry. I took a can of corned beef out of my sack, hit him on the head, and knocked him around plenty. Then I told him, "You hit me on the nose and threw water on me six years ago." He never said a word and he went home very bloody.

A few days after we got the letter and the fifty dollars from my father, an old man offered to hire me for thirty-five cents a day and board. I talked to my grandmother, and she said, "All right, you can help him until your father comes to take us to Tucson."

I went to work with the old man. He had six burros, and we would go to a mountain six miles east of Nogales to get wood. It took us two days to get a load. When we got back he sold the wood, and we would go back for another load. I worked with him two months before my father came from Tucson in a wagon with four mules.

The day after my father got to Nogales, we started on the three-day trip to Tucson. It was raining and the river near Tucson was full. We had trouble crossing, but we made it and went to Barrio Libre, the Yaqui village on the south side of Tucson. At the time Tucson was a small city, and it was not far from one side to the other.

That evening all the Yaquis we had known in Mexico came to see us. Many of them, like us, had left Sonora to escape persecution and deportation. This was early in 1907. Among those who came were Lucrecia Sewa and her family, who had been in Barrio Libre since 1904. They had a good house. Her daughter Selma was living with Juan Buamea Valdez, who had come with them from Hermosillo. Juan was the father of Selma's youngest child, José Sewa Valdez, who was about a year old when we arrived.

Luis Moreno and his family told us that they had walked from Torim across the Sierra to Arizona in 1902, living first at Mesquital, and then moving into Barrio Libre. Luis was a singer for the deer dancers. His son Angel Moreno was a deer dancer and a *matachine*. This Moreno family was related to my grandmother from Torim.

Bonifasio Cuchubuasia (his Yaqui name means *cola de pescado*, or fish tail) of Vicam pueblo left Sonora in 1898, taking his family to California. He was the same age as my father. Both were captains in the Sierra army, and they had been friends years before. Bonifasio's wife, Bartola, was also from Vicam. Their oldest daughter, Cristina, was born in Vicam, while Lucas and Eugenio were born in Fresno, California. Neither Lucas nor Eugenio ever went to school and neither can read or write. About 1903 the family moved to Arizona, and Bonifasio and his two young sons went to work on Mr. Nash's farm at Mesquital. They had a house in Barrio Anita, another Yaqui barrio on the northwest side of Tucson. My father and Bonifasio spent a lot of time talking together.

The next day we moved to Barrio Anita. Mr. Dupree owned the land there. He sold house lots to the Yaquis for twelve dollars each. My father bought a lot near Bonifasio Cuchubuasia's house, got some lumber, and built a one-room house about ten by twenty feet with a corrugated lean-to roof. A platform about four feet off the ground was built along two walls; some of us slept up there and some slept on the floor. Luis Contreras (Augustina Valencia's son who had lived with us at La Playita until he married Nicolasa Waibel and moved to Ranchito) helped my father build our house and the cooking ramada in one day.

After the house was built, my father bought me a suit. On the next Monday he took me to Davis school and presented me to the teacher, Mrs. Goose, saying that he hoped I would learn to read and spell and speak English. Mrs. Goose was a good teacher. She did not speak either Spanish or Yaqui. Before long I could understand English, but learning to speak it was very slow. The Davis school was two stories high with about six rooms. A number of Yaqui, Mayo, and Mexican children went to school there in 1907.

In 1908, after I had learned how to read and write, my father bought a notebook. I sat at the table in our house in Barrio Anita while he dictated the names of ancestors and relatives along with their birth and death dates. He also dictated an account of the Yaquis telling of battles he had been in. Of all the people in my family, my father, Miguel, and my grandmother María were the most interested in family and Yaqui history. My mother, Cecelia, never cared about the past, nor did my aunt Camilda; none of my brothers, sisters, or cousins talked much about relatives or Yaqui history. Chepa Moreno in Hermosillo remembers a lot about things like this, and we often talk. It is sad that the book my father had me write has been lost.

For some reason I started craving sweets about this time. I wanted nothing to eat but sweets. This went on for days or weeks. Finally María made a medicine out of *batamote, saus* tree, and *yerba del indio* ground up together and dissolved in water with a little salt. She made me drink a very big glass of this horrible, bitter medicine, followed by as much water as I could hold. I laid down and she rubbed my stomach hard. In five minutes I began to throw up white balls of worms. After the worms left me, I did not crave sweets all the time. My grandmother had cured me again.

The young Mexican soldier named Juan Guzmán followed my aunt Camilda to Tucson from Hermosillo. I think he wanted to marry her. He stayed a few days with us in Barrio Anita, and then he went off to work at a ranch north of Tucson. Lots of the Tucson Yaquis knew that Juan had been active in rounding up Yaquis and killing them. He just never came back to Tucson. We found out later that some Yaquis killed him at Mesquital. Camilda said nothing when she heard he had been killed.

Not too long after we got to Arizona a man killed his daughter in Mesquital. The man was Juan Buichileme or Humo. His daughter, Laura Buichileme, was over sixteen years old. Her father caught her talking to a boy by the river. He got so mad he beat her hard. She died a week later. No one ever reported this to the American police because no one spoke

English. It is too bad she died, but girls should never talk to boys before they marry. She should already have been married at sixteen.

My father stopped working at the Silver Bell Mine because it had a bad reputation; many miners there died of lung sickness. Also he wanted to be closer to Tucson now that we were living there. His new job was at the Amole Mine, owned by Mr. Charles Carter, some twelve miles west of Tucson. Mr. Carter, who became a good friend of my father, is still living today, a very old man.

At the Amole Mine, shifts ran from seven to three, three to eleven, and eleven to seven, just as they had at Colorada. Miners lived in little wooden houses owned by the company or in long dormitories. Camilda went to live with Claudio Vacamea in one of the company houses, taking along Simón and Viviana, but leaving Carmen in the Barrio Anita with us. Camilda cooked for my father and some other Yaqui miners who lived in the dormitories, including Cayetano and Ignacio Valencia. Neither of these brothers ever married; they were always with my father. All of them liked to buy guns and ammunition. Cayetano died in 1908 and Ignacio died two months later. My father was very sad when his two old friends from Torim died. They had been miners and card players together in Colorada, Copete, Sierrita, the Silver Bell, and Amole. Just the year before, their father, Gregorio Valencia, had died in Hermosillo of tuberculosis.

Most members of Delores Valencia's family were living at the Amole Mine. Delores, his son Lazaro, his son-in-law Esteban Velásquez (married to Natalia), and another son-in-law, Juan Peña (living with Eufemia, whose first husband, Carlos Rahju, was hung at Sierrita) all worked in the mine. Another daughter, Paola, and her husband, Luis Samorano, also lived at Amole, although he worked at a nearby farm.

Marcelino or Lino Sopomea lived there with his family. Lino had married Philomena Somoochia at the Colorada Mine. She was the niece of old Salvador Somoochia, the violinist. Lino's brother, Raimundo, was at Amole too. Lino and Raimundo were great card players and they were always with my father. Other Yaqui miners at Amole that we had known in Sonora were Juan María Siguello, Lauro Taurik, Juan Buanamea Ronquillo, and Jesús Rios (the son of Lázaro Rios, a Colorada miner).

Luis Contreras and Nicolasa Waibel had moved from Ranchito with their children and two of Nicolasa's nephews, Fernando Cupes and Rosario Waibel. They had a house in Barrio Libre where Nicolasa and the children stayed while Luis worked at Amole. Rosario Waibel and I were the same age, and we once walked to Amole for supplies from the company store. Luis Contreras was killed in a fight with some Mexican miners when they were drunk.

A few weeks after Luis Contreras was killed, Juan María Chiquito Frías killed his wife, Juana. Juana was his second wife. His grown daughters from an earlier marriage started telling him that Juana was a witch. Finally he believed them. He killed her with a hatchet and buried her in a shallow grave in front of their door, sprinkling ashes over the grave to hide it. Juana's two brothers, José Luis and Locario Jiménez, came to see her. They looked for her for a long time before they went to the police. All sorts of sheriffs and policemen came and found Juana's grave. Juan María Chiquito Frías was sent to the state pen at Florence, where he died right away. Juana's little baby grew up with José Luis and Locario Jiménez.

Twice, on Saturdays, I walked out to the Amole Mine to get provisions from the company store. I stayed at Aunt Camilda's house and then walked back on Sunday carrying heavy sacks of groceries. My grandmother never went out to the mine. It was a sad place, in spite of having a big store, cantinas, rows of houses, and dances every Saturday night.

As long as my father, Camilda, Claudio Vacamea, Viviana, and Simón lived at Amole, our house in Barrio Anita was not so crowded. There was just me, my grandmother, and Carmen. It was well known that this was Miguel Palos's house, and people coming from the Sierra or the Rio Yaqui often came to stay with us.

About 1908 Ramona Robles came to live with us after her father died at Pitiquito. She had been at the Colorada Mine. A few months after she arrived, she married Anastasio Vapil in the church at Tucson. Not long after they married, Anastasio was hunting rabbits in the mountains, something he did whenever he got the chance. He shot an unusually large rabbit about six times, and it would not die. Anastasio's stomach turned over. In about two weeks he died.

Rabbits and deer can be dangerous to hunt; they are very powerful. If a rabbit shakes his ears from side to side, you should not shoot it, or it will make you sick and maybe kill you, like that one did Anastasio. A person can go blind hunting. There are lots of bad rabbits and bad deer, like witches (*brujos*). The person who knows all about such things can tell which will hurt you. Deer with red and black hooves are *brujos*. Rabbits with worms (*gusanos*) in their neck are *brujos*.

Usually the Sierra Yaquis coming to Tucson to buy *lonche* and provisions stopped and rested at Mesquital. This Yaqui settlement, only four or five miles southwest of Tucson, was on land owned by Mr. Nash. Many Yaquis worked there clearing land. When Sierra Yaquis came into Tucson, they turned their pants backwards because the front part would be so torn from walking three hundred miles through the brush. Many times I have seen men come into town with their pants on backwards, and I always knew they came from the Sierra.

The first man the Sierra Yaquis went to see was Alejandro Paamea, as he was the one who went from house to house collecting gifts and money for the Sierra Yaquis. When the Sierra Yaquis brought money with them to buy provisions, they did not stay long. Sometimes they had to stay and work in order to make some money or wait for Alejandro to raise more before they could buy what they came for.

A grown man could walk from Tucson to the Sierra in two weeks, carrying over fifty pounds. Guns and ammunition accounted for most of the weight, but the men always carried along needles, scissors, cloth, hair ribbons, hair combs, and other things as gifts for the Sierra girls, who were reported to be the prettiest of Yaqui women. The men in Tucson were always talking about the Sierra girls. That is the reason so many young men were eager to go to the Sierra. They asked me to go when I was about fifteen, but I thought of walking three hundred miles and said no.

Lola Kukut of Torim was a Yaqui soldier. Everyone called her the Señora of the Sierra. She was married to José Kukut, a Yaqui captain, also from Torim. These two always walked together in the Sierra and killed many Mexicans. They came to Tucson for supplies in 1907 and again in 1912. Both times they stayed at our house because they were old friends of my father's from the Sierra and from Torim.

Three different times, I think it was in 1907, 1908, and 1909, two Yaqui generals came from the Sierra to Tucson and stayed with us. They were General Cante Mayo and General Juan Gómez, both of Bacum. Each time they came, General Gómez brought a girl and left her with us. Emelia Vaecogoih of Bacum was the first. She stayed a few months, then married one of my father's old friends from the Sierra, Alfonso Saila, who was working for the Water Users at Guadalupe.

Luz Esperanza of Torim came with General Gómez on his second trip. She married Alfredo Perico of Torim, who had been in the Sierra with my father from 1900 to 1904. They moved to Guadalupe, where Alfredo worked for Micho Yomoto, a Japanese who went to all the Yaqui fiestas, learned to speak some Yaqui, and later married a Yaqui girl. Alfredo and Luz often came to visit us in Barrio Anita.

Micaela Catota of Bacum, the girl who came with General Gómez on his last trip, was called Bocona (*Boca Grande* in Spanish, or Big Mouth in English). She did not really have a big mouth, but they called her that just the same. She married Teodoro Muella, who was also with my father in the Sierra from 1900 to 1904. Everyone called him Papache (Apache) because he wore his hair long while in the Sierra. Both Micaela and Teodoro still live in Guadalupe and are very old. Teodoro was a grown man when I was a boy in Hermosillo.

Chico (Francisco) Preciado, a captain in the Yaqui army and the uncle of my father's old girl friend Augustina, came to Tucson to buy arms in 1908 and again in 1911. Each time he stayed with us about three weeks. He was killed in the Bacatete Mountains in 1912. Later that same year his son, Joaquín Preciado, came to Tucson to stay. Joaquín was about eighteen at the time, and already he was a good *pascola* dancer. He lived in our house in Barrio Anita for some months before he went to live with Charla Bacotmea Sánchez. They did not like each other, and he soon left her to marry (in the church) a Mayo girl named Teresa Moroyoki whose family came from Navojoa. Teresa was a cousin of Rufina Moroyoki and her sister Locaria Moroyoki Rodríguez. All of their three children were born in Tucson. They named their first son Francisco (Chico), after Joaquín's father. This younger Chico has lived at the Elliott Ranch near Eloy for several years now, and I always go see him when I go to Arizona. Joaquín's other children are Felipe, now a garbage collector in Tucson, and Dorotea, who married a Negro mechanic. Joaquín died in Tucson about 1927.

As I have already related, many members of the Preciado family were deported together in 1902 or 1903, and two of Rosario and Jesús Preciado's three children, Espiritu and Juan, were sold, or given, to rich Mexicans in Hermosillo. Their oldest daughter, María, had married my grandmother's half brother, Arturo Frías, in Torim, and their first children were born in Torim. María and Arturo Frías saved up enough money in 1904 to make the trip to Hermosillo, where they "kidnaped" the two younger Preciado children from the Mexican homes where they were servants and escaped across the border to Arizona. Arturo Frías first worked at Patagonia, where their last two children were born. Later they moved to Guadalupe, where he worked for the Water Users until he died in 1927 of the ailment caused by wearing rubber boots for irrigation work. Many Yaquis have died of this foot trouble brought on by wearing rubber boots. María Preciado Frías continued to live in Guadalupe. She must have been at least ninety years old when she died there in 1962.

Late in 1908 my father and his friends left Mr. Carter and went to work at the newly opened Sasco Smelter, forty-five miles northwest of Tucson. He took all of us with him and we built a four-room lumber house. Camilda and Claudio Vacamea built a smaller house next door. Some of our friends and relatives working at the smelter did not have wives to cook for them. They slept in our ramada and ate with us. We had to build an unusually big ramada to accommodate all of them.

Crecensio Murillo came from Patagonia to work at the smelter; it was the first time he had worked with my father, as he was not a miner. His brother, Celso Murillo, walked up from the Sierra in 1909, leaving his family behind. Chico Petrigo, Manuel Salinas, and his sons Micky and Juan all slept in the ramada with Crecensio and Celso Murillo.

Celso Murillo ate so much bologna and salami one afternoon that he got sick. My grandmother fixed him some medicine. He kept eating bologna while he took the medicine, and before long he died. We held the all-night *velación* at our house and buried him the next day in the new Sasco cemetery. Crecensio organized the *velación*, the funeral, and the *novena* (a second funeral ceremony) nine days later, but we never had a *cumpleaño* for him.

Manuel Salinas had left Torim with his father, José Juan Salinas, and his mother, Antonia Santomia Salinas, about 1888. In Torim they had known Abelardo Cochemea and María Daumier Valencia Palos; in fact, Antonia was kin to Abelardo: he called her *tia*, or aunt. They were working for Arturo León at Ranchito when we got to Hermosillo in 1900 from Colorada; Manuel was the harpist for the *pascolas* at the ill-fated *cumpleaño* given by Juan María Silvas. Manuel married his first wife, Jesús Soteo, in Hermosillo, and Micky and Juan were born there. After José Juan Salinas was deported about 1902, Manuel and his mother, wife, and sons moved to Arizona, where he worked in the rock quarry at Patagonia. Both Antonia and Jesús died at Patagonia, and about 1907, Manuel and his sons moved to Tucson, going on to Sasco with us in 1908.

Old Lucrecia Sewa and her family lived in Sasco because her son Trinidad Sewa was working in the smelter. Her other son, Abato, went to school and learned to read and write. Selma had died of pneumonia in 1907, leaving her baby boy with Lucrecia. While living at Sasco, Lucrecia *se junto* with José María Mavis, a farmer at Cerro Prieto, about one mile from Sasco. Selma's widower, Juan Buamea Valdez, also farmed at Cerro Prieto. He had a house in Sasco and was now living with Julia Serano.

Delores Valencia moved his large family to Sasco. Others who came to work at the smelter were Lino Sopomea, Juan María Siguello, Juan

Buanamea Ronquillo and his two sons, Jesús Rios, the Tapia family (Mayos), and Tomás Muina and his family. Diego Vargas, then living with Nicolasa Waibel (Luis Contreras's widow), also worked at Sasco. Much the same group played cards here as had played together at the Colorada, Silver Bell and Amole mines through the years.

Rudolfo Rivera Kuka was one of my grandmother's relatives from Torim who lived with us off and on. Like my grandmother, he was a *blanco* (had white skin). He always wore a long mustache, the longest mustache I ever remember seeing. He was sort of a criminal. He loved to steal. Just about every night he went out and stole a pig, some eggs, a turkey, or some chickens. Along about 1908, he, Tomás Bustamonte, and a Mayo named Juan Matuz (later known as Juan Pistola) were caught by federal authorities selling liquor to the Papagos, something that was strictly against the law in those days. They were sent to prison in Atlanta, Georgia, for a few years. So Rudolfo did not stay with us very long in Sasco. Tomás Bustamonte was a nephew of the Hermosillo *yori* Alejandro Bustamonte, who rode with Izábal's bodyguard and who was killed by my father near Gavilán in 1904.

My father's job at the smelter was easy, although the heat was very bad. He drove a little train up and down the dump to throw away the slag after the copper was taken from the ore. He got paid $42.50 every two weeks.

While we lived at Sasco, my grandmother sold tortillas and pinole to the Mexican workmen at the encampment. She made pinole by toasting corn in a pot; part of the corn would pop and the rest would parch. Then she ground the corn on a metate and cooked the meal with either water or milk and sugar. Wherever we lived, she cured people. More people came to her every year as her fame as a *curandera* spread among the Yaquis.

Fewer Yaquis attended school in Sasco than had gone to the Davis school. Viviana and I walked three-quarters of a mile from our house to the big wooden school in the white barrio. Most of the one hundred or so students were white. My teacher, Mrs. Kerr Carter, had a nine-year-old daughter named Ida. She said they were Irish. She was my teacher in 1908 and 1909, and she was always especially nice to me. She gave me thirty-five cents every Friday to go to the movie show; that was enough to get in and buy something. Every time I saw her in the company store she stopped and talked to me. After I quit school, she always asked when I was going to return to school and said I was a good student.

When I was thirteen I quit school and went to work at the Andreas Matos ranch nearby. After that my grandmother, father, and aunt

Camilda could not treat me like a slave any more. They could no longer send me on every disagreeable errand or threaten to whip me. I began to play baseball with the young men from the smelter as a center fielder.

My cousin Viviana was about sixteen in 1911. She had quit school, too, because she was too old to be allowed away from home. Carlos Conemea wanted to marry her, but she said she did not want to have anything to do with him because every few months he was going off to the Rio Yaqui to kill some Mexicans. Carlos was a good friend of my father's.

About dark one evening I went to a Mexican shop to buy some bread. When I started back, I saw a *bulto* (apparition or ghost) walk out of the trees ahead. It looked like a man without a hat, staggering and falling as though drunk. The *bulto* walked in front of me until I got within sight of home, and then disappeared. Then I knew I had seen a *bulto*, and not just a drunk. I was not scared at all.

We heard something about the Pitahaya Peace Conference, which took place in 1909. Years later I heard more about it from my half sister Dominga Preciado Palos. Dominga and her mother, Augustina, had been deported in 1903 from Colorada, as I have related, and they had returned to Torim in 1907. Dominga, about ten years old at the time, was taken to the peace conference at Pitahaya (Pitaya) by her mother, and this is what she told me. A priest stood at a table between two lines of armed Mexican soldiers. Next to the table stood a big wooden box. The hated Rafael Izábal was there. General Luis Bule and Captain Santiago Veteme, Yaquis, stood on either side of Izábal and Captain Francisco (Chico) Preciado stood behind him. Yaqui soldiers were told to surrender their guns, and the Yaqui General Bule told them to put them in the big box, which they did. The priest put holy water on each gun as it was put in the box. Having expected to give up their guns, they had arrived with old, worn-out rifles. All their new guns were hidden in the Sierra.

When Izábal said they had to give up their knives, General Bule and Chico Preciado picked Izábal up by his arms and said, "No. With our knives we eat and make everything. We won't turn in our knives. If you want to do harm to my people, this is your last moment." Izábal was so scared he shit in his pants and his guts came up in his throat. He agreed that the Yaquis could keep their knives. Then he asked General Bule to come with him to Hermosillo; he said he would give him money, a house, and girls. So General Bule went to Hermosillo, and Izábal gave him a big house on Chihuahua Street near the old Carmen Capia Church, and found a girl in a cantina to marry him. Her name was Lorenza Robles.

Luis Bule joined the Porfirista army, and was killed at Santa María, near Empalme, in 1911. All the other Yaquis at the Pitahaya Conference went back to the Sierra and got their new guns out of hiding.

The scare that Izábal received at Pitahaya eventually killed him. A bad scare causes the guts to rise, and medical doctors are unable to cure this, as it is not a natural sickness. Izábal got sick right away. Doctors in Hermosillo could do nothing for him. He went to Mexico City, and the famous doctors there did him no good either. He died on the return trip, somewhere around Mazatlán. His casket, returned to Hermosillo for burial, was not opened at home.

My mother, Cecilia, was working as a cook in Mexican homes in Hermosillo at this time. She later told me that some poor people dug up Izábal's casket because they heard he had been buried with gold. When they opened the casket, all there was inside was a log and a piece of iron. After that the poor people knew that Izábal's body had been thrown away in the sea.

One day in Sasco, Carlota Villegas, the wife of Tomás Muina, came to our house. She was a *cantora* and knew how to read and write. She came to ask my grandmother María if Antonia could marry her son, Ignacio Molina. Part of the family had taken the Mexican name of Molina because it was a translation of Muina. María did not say anything to Antonia, but she talked it over with Miguel. They were very happy for Antonia to marry Ignacio because he knew how to read and write in Spanish, having gone to school in Hermosillo. Still they told Antonia nothing. Two days later Carlota brought a white *rebozo*, dresses, shoes, and silk fabric to Antonia for the wedding. Antonia knew then that she was to marry Ignacio, who was forty years old at the time. Antonia never said a word.

Most of the family went to the wedding at the San Augustin Church in Tucson, but I stayed home in Sasco with Crecensio Murillo. Delores Valencia's family went to the wedding, too. The wedding party went in Fords owned by the Valencia Brothers' Stage, which ran twice a day. It cost $3.50 a person to go the forty-five miles into Tucson.

The wedding fiesta was held in Sasco. First they ate at our house, and the *pascolas* danced. Then everyone moved to the Molina (or Muina) house, where we all ate again. Antonia and Ignacio lived with the Molina family, as did several of his married brothers and sisters.

Tomás Muina and his family were already in Hermosillo when we arrived there in 1900 from Colorada. Tomás worked at Ranchito for

Arturo León. That Spaniard took any Yaqui woman that caught his eye. He fathered innumerable children by Indian women. Carlota was very attractive in those days, and as a result she had one son fathered by Arturo León whose name is Ramón León. Her other six children were fathered by Tomás Muina. Another poor woman who had a child by Arturo León was Celestia Sosoky, wife of Martín Sosoky. Her son Perfecto León is still living in Tucson.

In 1908, Tomás Muina and his family left Hermosillo on the train and came to Tucson, building a house just one hundred feet from ours in Barrio Anita. They moved to Sasco when the smelter opened. Tomás Muina was now too old to work regularly, but his sons and stepson, Ignacio, Nicolás, José, and Ramón, and his son-in-law, Pablo Avaso, all worked in the smelter. Ramón León Molina Frías married Felipa Chiquito the same year that Ignacio married Antonia. He soon left her to go with a Papago woman who had many cows. He finally left the Papago woman for another woman and went to California, where he died. The youngest Molino son, Loreto, went to school with me at the Sasco school.

The company went broke and the smelter closed down in 1910. The workmen left, most of them with only their clothes and blankets. We left what furniture we had in our house at Sasco and went back to our house at Barrio Anita. The smelter company left two white men at Sasco as caretakers. They were ordered to kill the dogs left by the workmen. It is said they killed over seven hundred.

Back in Barrio Anita, I found that three Yaquis planned to kill Carlota Muina's father, old Hector Juan Villegas, because it was well known that he had been a *yori* in Hermosillo. Everyone knew this was true. Three men abducted him, tied his arms, and started walking toward the railroad tracks. Leaving a person tied on railroad tracks was a common way of killing people, and some Yaquis committed suicide that way. I knew what those three Yaquis planned for Hector Juan because I know very well how the Yaquis think, so I picked up three bricks and quietly, quietly followed them. About two miles out of town, I crept up to within ten feet of the men and threw the bricks. The men got scared and ran off. I untied Hector Juan and we walked home. It would have been half a pity (*medio lastima*) for the grandfather of my brother-in-law to be killed, even if he was a *yori*.

Soon we learned that exciting events were taking place in Mexico. Porfirio Díaz had been run out of the country. Madero was president. The Yaquis had helped him to be president because he said he was for the

Indians, but he did not give the Yaquis back their land, so the mountain Yaquis decided that the time had come to drive the Mexicans and foreigners out of the Rio Yaqui.

More of the Sierra Yaquis came to Tucson to buy arms. Every three or four weeks some came for supplies. One storekeeper was especially sympathetic to the Yaquis, selling them everything they had money to buy. His store was on Meyer Street, and the Yaquis called him the Texas Man. So many people were making the trip between the Sierra and Arizona that we had lots of news of what was happening in Sonora.

The Yaqui *torocoyoris* who had been informing on other Yaquis to the Mexican federal officials were very sorry to hear that the Yaqui slaves were freed. Years later my mother, Cecelia, told me about what happened when the *yori* Preciliano Cuamea heard the news. He had caused many Yaquis to be deported and had ridden with Izábal for years as a personal bodyguard. He was one of the bodyguards who escaped when my father ambushed Izábal in 1904. The government paid him good money as an informer. He came to Arizona briefly with his wife, Hortencia Tapia, and his son Preciliano. The Arizona Yaquis warned him that they would kill him as a *yori*, and so he went back to Hermosillo, leaving Hortencia and young Preciliano in Tucson. He continued to send them money that he got from the government. For a time Hortencia became my father's girl friend, but he never moved in with her. In Hermosillo, Preciliano Cuamea lived in La Matanza, as did my mother at that time. He was sitting in his own house reading a newspaper when he read that the deported Yaquis were being freed. He fell off of his chair, dead of a heart attack. Preciliano Cuamea had two brothers, Alejandro and Jaime Cuamea, who were working on the ranches around Tucson by 1908, and both are still alive in Tucson today. Preciliano Cuamea (the son) is about my age and we have always been friends. I always go to see him when I go to Tucson. We never talk of his father.

Modesto Robles was another *yori* who always went from house to house in Hermosillo spying. He was paid regularly by the government. When he heard that the Yaquis were returning from Mexico, he ran away to Mexicali and so escaped being shot.

Lucas Tacruesco, belonging to the pueblo of Vicam, was one of the *yoris* who stood with a red bandana over his face at Cuartel Catorce, nodding to the questions that caused many Yaquis to be killed or deported. He was killed by returning Yaquis about 1911.

Perhaps the worst *yori* of all was Nicolás Lugo. When he saw a pregnant Yaqui woman, he cut open her belly, grabbed out the baby and killed them both. He was shot in front of his own house in La Matanza early one morning by Julian Repamea, who had watched his father shot at Realito, on Nicolás Lugo's recommendation, and he himself had been deported to Yucatán because of Nicolás Lugo. When Julian was released in Yucatán, he joined the revolutionary army and was sent to Sonora. The first thing he did in Hermosillo was to go to Nicolás Lugo's house with ten soldiers. He just called Nicolás out of the house and shot him. Julian was later killed near Hermosillo when Pancho Villa's army entered the city. Many people were killed by Villa.

Juan González, the *yori* who made it his special business to hunt my father, was killed at Naco during the revolution. From 1900 until he was killed, he lived in La Matanza, Hermosillo, with his wife, Chepa Buanamea. My mother lived in La Matanza after about 1905. José González left my mother in about 1907, taking their two sons to Torim. Cecelia then lived with a Mexican named Francisco Acosta, and their daughter Julia (my half sister) was born at La Matanza in 1908. José had left, but my mother continued to be good friends with Juan and Chepa González.

Octavio and Rafael Pare, as they called themselves although they were sons of Gregorio Valencia and brothers of Eugenio, Cayetano, and Ignacio Valencia, had become *yoris* when they left the Colorada Mine about 1900. Both Octavio and Rafael spoke fluent Spanish. They often hunted Yaquis up near the Arizona line at Altár, Cucurpe, and Pitiquito. They attended the Sunday morning presentations at Cuartel Catorce with red bandanas over their faces to "know" (*conocer*) the Yaquis. Rafael had, for a while, been in charge of the *cuartel* where young Yaqui children were kept after their parents were shot or deported and before they were given to Mexicans as servants. Octavio married one of my grandmother's relatives, Teodora Torre Bakasewa. Teodora's family had been in Colorada, where her father was a miner, and Teodora and Octavio married in Hermosillo. Octavio and Rafael were usually together, and they died in the same revolutionary battle near Empalme about 1911. The battle took place at either Santa María or Santa Rosa. Teodora is still alive in Torim.

There were many battles in Sonora during the revolution. The *Federales* (federal troops) held many towns, and the revolutionaries were outside the towns. During a long seige at Naco, Carranza forces were trying to take the town from federal troops. The Carranza forces were moved by railroad from Hermosillo to Tucson, and then shipped on the Southern Pacific to Naco, Cananea, Agua Prieta, or wherever they were told to go.

Many of the men and their families who were shipped into Tucson decided they did not want to go on to Naco. It was easy to jump train and stay in Arizona. One of the men who did this was Pedro More. His two brothers, Juan María and Juan, went on to Naco on the train and were killed by booby traps left by the *Federales*. Their families were with them, and none have ever been heard from again.

Pedro More had his family with him. He was living with Josefa Waibel, the sister of Nicolasa Waibel Contreras. He was the church husband of Selma Sewa More Valdez. The three More brothers were the Torim-born sons of José and Juliana More. They took the family name of More in the 1880s or early 1890s; before that they had a Yaqui name. Pedro and his family had never been deported because they spoke excellent Spanish and had good Mexican friends at Ranchito, where he worked; but he was never a *yori*.

While many Yaquis sought refuge in Arizona, others who were perfectly safe in Arizona went back to Sonora to join in the fighting. Mariano Otero left Tucson to fight in the revolution, taking his mother and father (Juana and Leonardo Otero) with him. They were captured by Porfirista troops in the rock house that stands at the edge of Torim and shot. Mariano Otero's brothers, Adolfo and Miguel, stayed in Tucson. Adolfo later married Angelica Tapia, who was in school with me at Davis. He left her and returned to Hermosillo in 1937. There he robbed a girl whose mother had good friends among the officials. He was captured near the coast and put in prison in Hermosillo. He died within a day or so, so soon that I think he was poisoned. Miguel Otero has lived in Cocorit since about 1936, sharecropping with a Mexican. Angelica Tapia (Otero) never took another man. She spoke English well and always had good jobs working as a maid for white people in Tucson. She kept a house in Pascua, where her brother Marques Tapia lives, but "slept in" where she worked. She died in the house of her employer in 1966.

In Tucson my father talked with Yaquis who came to buy ammunition, and he got a great desire to return to Sonora and fight the Mexicans. He had begun fighting them when he was ten years old, and was a captain in the Yaqui army when he left in 1904. His old chief, José Sibalaume, was now at Bachomobampo in the Bacatete Mountains. Each group that came to Tucson for supplies brought my father a message from General José Sibalaume to gather some Arizona Yaquis and come help drive the Mexicans out. My father bought a .30-.30 rifle, three cartridge belts, and several boxes of ammunition. He got together several friends, and they went to fight the Mexicans. He was very happy. This was in 1912.

The men who went with my father were Tomás Muina, Bonifasio Cuchubuasia, Jaime Reyes and his son Guillermo Reyes (called El Herrero, or the blacksmith), Beto Ortega (seventeen years old), and his brother Nacho Ortega. Guillermo Reyes, Beto Ortega, and Nacho Ortega were captured in an encounter with American soldiers at Tascosa, before they got out of Arizona. Nacho was shot in the neck, but not seriously. These three were first taken to Nogales, then to Tucson, and finally turned loose.

The others got across the border and to the Sierra. They stayed in Sonora several months and fought many battles with the Mexicans, both in the Sierra and in the Yaqui Valley. The four men decided that the Mexicans were not going to be pushed out of the Yaqui territory, and came back to Tucson. Several other Sierra men, including the brothers Rudolfo and Loreto Vatereo and old Alejandro Wapo, came with my father's group across the border. The Vatereo brothers probably left wives in Sonora, although I never knew. In any event, Rudolfo moved in with Regina Guzmán and Loreto *se junto* with María Cruz Teran. The brothers lived at Mesquital until they died, and they never went back to the Sierra. Old Alejandro Wapo belonged to the pueblo of Bacum. He left his wife, Teresa, in Bacum and they never saw each other again. He never took another woman, but lived with his son Martín Wapo, who was already in Arizona.

After my father returned, he worked for a few months at the Ray Mine, sixty-five miles north of Tucson, because the Sasco Smelter was still closed. I was working for a Mexican named Juan Gálvez at his little farm five miles north of Tucson, where I had worked ever since we moved back to Barrio Anita from Sasco. While my father was at the Ray Mine, Camilda's eleven- or twelve-year-old daughter, Carmen, ran off with Juan Sasueta. After marrying in a civil ceremony, they returned to live with Camilda and Claudio Vacamea.

When Rudolfo Rivera Kuka was released from prison in Atlanta, Georgia, about 1913, he came back to live with us. We were glad to see him because he was gay like my grandmother, and soon he was supplying us with eggs, chickens, and other food he stole at night. Even if we didn't need anything, he would go out and steal something just to keep his hand in.

In 1914 my father decided to go to the Sierra again. His old friends Bonifasio Cuchubuasia and Tomás Muina went with him, along with some other Yaqui men. Five of the young men were under twenty years old: Raul Siguello (younger brother of Juan María Siguello, the miner),

Esteban Goih, Eduardo Chávez, Ernesto Ronquilla, and a boy called Juan Pascola Noriega because he danced *pascola*. Armando Urrea (a distant relative of my grandfather Abelardo) and Gabriel Rivera (son of Rudolfo Rivera Kuka) completed this party. My father was in command. This time he took along combs, ribbons, scissors, needles, thread, and cloth for María Palos, a mountain woman he had lived with on his 1912 trip.

Armando Urrea had been to the Río Yaqui many times. Once he was captured near Magdalena by some cowboys; Reyes Estrella and Ricardo Sewa were with him. The cowboys tricked the three Yaquis by saying: "Come go with us to Magdalena and take the train to the Río Yaqui. There isn't any danger. Now we have peace." When they got to Magdalena, the cowboys took them to the jail, where they were disarmed. The officials in Magdalena sent word to Hermosillo that three Yaquis had been captured, and they were waiting for orders to kill them.

Armando Urrea always carried a book called *El justo juez*, which is always to be recited carefully and completely in times of danger. Armando read the book, then he repeated the *oraciones* (recitations) again. He finally finished the *oraciones* about midnight of the third day. The three Yaquis had given the guards money for some food and the food arrived about midnight, too. Only two guards were on night duty, and guns and ammunition stood in the guard room. Armando was able to open the big iron gates with the power he got from making the *El justo juez* recitations; the two guards stood like they were frozen. They didn't make a move while the three Yaquis selected guns, ammunition, and water canteens. Armando said later that he was disappointed that there were no blankets, as it was a chilly night. Not a dog barked as they walked away from the jail and out of Magdalena, because of the power of *El justo juez*.

I once had a copy of *El justo juez*, but I did not like it. You have to say the long *oraciones* all the way through without any mistakes, or else it backfires. People who are able to recite them have great protection, especially on dark nights.

*El justo juez* saved Armando Urrea's life on another occasion. He and a band of Yaquis were at a ranch near San Marcial, about seventy miles east of Hermosillo. They had eaten with the cowboys and were getting a few hours' sleep in the corral before daylight. They did not know that a troop of soldiers was on their trail, or they would not have stopped. Armando was the night guard, but he fell asleep sitting against a post. The soldiers slipped right up to the Yaquis and then opened fire. One soldier shot at Armando's head, point blank; Armando was not hurt, just powder-burned around the mouth. Not a single Yaqui was killed, because of the protection Armando had from *El justo juez*. Some of the Mexicans were killed. The Yaquis took lots of cheese when they left the ranch.

Armando Urrea's uncle was magical. My father and my grandmother frequently told of the things Juan Tecu Yoimeri did. Yoimeri means "killed by the *yori*"! He had the name because the Mexicans killed him many times, and he came back to life. My father said that once in Guaymas, during the 1880s, the Mexicans took Juan, sewed him inside a cowhide, and dropped him in the bay. In a little while he was walking around the streets of Guaymas. The Mexicans never knew that there was a Yaqui that they could not kill, but the Yaquis knew. Juan Tecu finally died of old age. The Yaquis gave him the name of Yoimeri after he died.

While my father's troop was in the Sierra in 1914, my father was out on a raiding party with Severo Valenzuela, the relative from Torim who had crossed to the United States with him in 1904. Near Gavilán they met about a dozen Mexican cowboys. Several of the Mexicans were killed and the rest ran away. Severo was killed. If the cowboys had known he was dead, they would surely have closed in on my father. After the remaining Mexicans ran away, my father gathered wood and burned Severo's body.

They stayed eight months in the Sierra. Young Gabriel Rivera was killed at Las Botellas, near the Arizona line, on the return trip. All the others got home safely. A few other Sierra Yaquis crossed the border with him as well. That was the last time my father went back to his own country (*tierra*).

Shortly before my father returned, Camilda got sick. She got progressively worse, and it was only a few days until she died. Poor Camilda. She had been pretty once, with her light-colored skin. She weighed about 175 pounds when she died, and she was not very tall. She left us four children. Viviana was nineteen and still unmarried. Carmen and her new husband, Juan Sasueta, had been living with Camilda. Simón was about ten. Mariana was a little girl of three. All of these children moved in with us. Only her husband, Claudio, did not come. He soon moved in with Luisa Valencia.

Yaquis do not like to live where someone has died. Sometimes the ghost of the dead person will come back to see the family, and most people are afraid of ghosts. Therefore as soon as my father returned from the

Sierra, we moved to a new house which we built about one-half mile to the north of the first, closer to the river. The new one was quite large, with three sleeping rooms. A long lean-to room running the length of the house served as our kitchen. We built a large ramada of cottonwood logs covered with *batamote* branches gathered along the river. The house and the ramada were built in two days by all the men in our household, my father's *coyote* soldiers, Guadalupe Sinjuego, the *pascola* Cayetano Tecu, Juan Tecu, and Salvador Montenegro and his sons Jesús and Ramón. My grandmother cooked enormous amounts of food for the men while they built our new house.

Crecensio Murillo died that same year. He got very sick and did not want to stay in our house any more. He rolled up everything he owned in a blanket and went to Hector Jaime Villegas's house near Barrio Libre, where he died two days later. He had no relative to give him a *velación* or a funeral, and so he was given a pauper's burial by the county. Hector Villegas and his wife, Jacinta, were Carlota Muina's parents. They had lived at Ranchito, Hermosillo, when Crecensio was there, and they had long been friends.

My father did not go back to the Ray Mine. Instead he went to work for Mr. Nash at Mesquital. It was the first time he had done farm work and he did not like it. I went to work with him and it seemed to help that I was by his side. We worked all year for Mr. Nash.

Our larger house was soon filled up. In addition to the nine or ten who normally lived there, more people from Hermosillo came to live with us during 1914, and they stayed in our house for several years: Marcelina Chino, her bachelor son Cayetano (who had been a baker at Colorada), her daughter Pancha, and Pancha's family. Pancha was married to a Mexican, Abrán Martínez, who said he had been Pancho Villa's secretary. They had three children, all born in Hermosillo, when they came to Tucson. Marcelina's other daughter, Lupe (whose first husband, Javier Aldamea, was hung by the Mexicans at Ranchito), was living in Vicam Switch with Luis Conemea.

In 1915 we added more people to our household. My youngest brother, Francisco Valenzuela, had always lived with my mother until now, but he left her and came to live with us. Old Augustina Valencia had stayed in Hermosillo with a relative named Cecelia Morales when we left in 1905. This Morales family was also kin to my grandmother María. Cecelia Morales had two daughters, Paola and Juana. All three Morales women were deported in 1914; Cecelia's husband had been deported in 1902. With that household gone, Augustina Valencia got on the train by herself and came to us in Tucson in 1915. She worked in Tucson as she always had, as a washerwoman.

Another person who came to live with us about this time was Pedro Alvarez. He had escaped from Yucatán, making his way to Arizona. He was my *tia* Chepa's husband before they were deported, but they never made an effort to see each other after they returned from Yucatán. With Pedro, our household numbered nineteen. Viviana, now grown, helped our grandmother María take care of our household.

In 1915 the Sasco Smelter reopened, and a lot of us went back to work there. The war in Europe had raised the price of metal. My grandmother stayed at our house in Barrio Anita and looked after all the people living there. Only the men went to Sasco. My father, Rudolfo Rivera Kuka, Pedro Alvarez, my younger brother Francisco Valenzuela, and I slept in a small company house, next door to Guadalupe Sinjuego's family, where we ate. My father was given his old job of running the dump engine, and I got a job unloading the ore cars from the mines.

Rudolfo Rivera continued his customary nighttime stealing, supplying Guadalupe Sinjuego's wife with fresh eggs and other products. He got caught when he killed a cow and was sent away to the state penitentiary in Florence. He was released in a year and came back to Sasco. Soon he started living with Josefa Matuz, who had recently arrived from Hermosillo. She already had a daughter, also named Josefa. I understand her first husband had been deported, but we did not know her family in Hermosillo. Rudolfo and Josefa built a small house nearby and he never lived with us again. When the smelter closed, he and the two Josefas moved to Guadalupe.

Prices and wages kept going up. In a few months I was making from ten dollars and twenty-five cents to thirteen dollars and fifty cents a day at the smelter. Three of us were paid two dollars and twenty-five cents each for every car of ore or coal unloaded. We could unload a car in about an hour and a half. Starting at five-thirty in the morning, we had the first car finished by seven. We would have breakfast and unload two more cars by eleven or eleven-thirty. Then we would play baseball until lunch time. Two or three more cars could be unloaded in the afternoon. When we did only two, we would play ball again before supper.

After supper I went to the pool hall to play billiards. Every evening we started to play about seven and kept on until one or two the next morning. We played for cigars and candy, but not for money. I was getting only three or four hours of sleep each night, but I never seemed to get tired. I could not stay at home. My father and Guadalupe Sinjuego became worried about me. They were always telling me I should get home earlier at night and get more sleep.

One day when I was in Tucson, my grandmother said, "Why don't you take a good rest for a few days? Your face is very pale. Week by week you look more like a sick man."

I said, "I never get tired or sleepy. I cannot stay at home because I love to play billiards."

They were sorry because they could not do anything with me. They thought, too, that I was going to see the girls. I was going to see them.

One day my father said, "My son, now we will have to look for a girl for you, so you can get married." I did not answer. Not a word.

A few days later I guess they had found the girl. When I came to supper, my father said, "My son, we are glad now because we have found a girl for you. She is only fifteen years old. Her father and her mother are pleased that you can marry her." I did not answer him, not a word.

My father added, "We must go to Tucson December 15, because you are to marry in Tucson." I did not answer, not a word.

# CHAPTER 4

# Marriage and Misfortune

THE GIRL MY grandmother found was Loreta Sánchez, whose mother, Charla Sánchez, was a *comadre* of my grandmother's; they had arranged the marriage between them. Loreta was born in 1901 on one of Rafael Izábal's haciendas, Muucahui (as the Yaquis called it), near Hermosillo. Her father was Jesús Sánchez. Jesús and Charla walked from Hermosillo to Arizona carrying Loreta when she was just a year old. There had been other babies, but Loreta was the only one who lived. Jesús began to work for the Southern Pacific Railroad. The family lived in Barrio Libre in an adobe house with a corrugated roof. They moved to Sasco the first time the smelter opened, and Jesús worked for the Fundición (Smelter) Railroad. He died of a heart attack while at work on a day that Loreta and her mother were in Barrio Libre visiting Charla's mother and father. Rafael Picacho was sent to tell them of Jesús's death. His body was laid out for two days until his family arrived and the funeral was held.

When Joaquín Preciado arrived in Tucson in 1912, he lived in our house for a few months before he went to live with the widowed Charla Sánchez. They separated soon after their baby Lola was born, and when Lola was only four or five months old, Charla went to live with Manuel Salinas, whom she had known in Sasco, when he was living in our ramada with his sons. Charla and Manuel started living together in the house Jesús Sánchez had built. Charla's parents, Alejandro and María Bacotmea, lived in another house on the same lot.

In 1916, Manuel Salinas was again working in the Sasco smelter as a weigher. Charla, Lola, and Loreta were also living in Sasco. So Loreta and I had both lived in Sasco the first time the smelter was working, we both lived around Tucson, and now we were all back in Sasco. All this time I never paid any attention to her, and I never talked to her. Not once.

On the day before the wedding, we all went to Tucson. My father and I went to our house in Barrio Anita. My sister Antonia and her husband, Ignacio, were living at the Matos ranch near Sasco, and they came to our house along with Ignacio's family. My marriage *padrino*, Guadalupe Sinjuego, was with us too. When we got home, my father and his friends took all the old brush off of our ramada and burned it, re-covering the ramada with fresh *batamote* branches. My grandmother was excited and worked very hard getting ready for the fiesta, which was to be an unusually big one, as we were having the wedding fiesta during the day and my aunt Camilda's delayed *cumpleaño* during the night. This was the first time we had enough money to hold a big fiesta. All of Loreta's family went to their old house, where María Bacotmea had everything ready for a fiesta there.

Early on the morning of the wedding, December 16, 1916, Loreta and her family came to our house in Barrio Anita. It was our first meeting face to face. The ones who accompanied us to the big Catholic church on Stone Street were my close family and my marriage *padrino*, Guadalupe Sinjuego, Loreta's family, and her marriage *madrina*, Clara Contreras. After the Catholic ceremony, we all went to Loreta's mother's house, where a *pascola* was entertaining the guests. He acted as if he were the bride, with a comb, ribbons, and flowers in his hair. We stayed at the Salinas home about two hours, then everybody walked three miles to our house in Barrio Anita. The fiesta had already started. Another *pascola* was dancing. When the *pascola* from Loreta's house got there, he kissed the other *pascola* and still pretended he was the bride. All the rest of the day the two *pascolas* showed what newly married people are supposed to do. When the wedding dinner was served, Loreta and I ate out of the same plate. The *pascolas* did the same.

In the late afternoon the *maestro* gave us a lecture. He had a great deal to say about Adam and Eve and the mistakes they made. He told us the world was full of pitfalls, and we must avoid water (the evils of drink), we must beware of iron (not engage in needless fighting), and we must avoid darkness (not stray away from the good faith). He told Loreta she must not look to the left or the right when she went out, because the

Devil was lurking there and would tempt her. Then he had us swear to heed the advice by the sign of the holy cross, made with the thumb and forefinger. That was the Yaqui wedding.

The wedding celebration ended about dark, and then we started my aunt's *cumpleaño*. Over fifty people attended the fiesta. My grandmother María had organized the whole thing and she was very happy. Every few minutes she started dancing. She asked permission of the *pascolas* to dance as a *pascola*, and they were happy to have her do it; she clowned all night. She told about all her boy friends and how when she was younger they used to stuff money down the front of her dress. When she got to imitating how men stuffed the front of her dress, I told her to stop because children were watching.

The *pascolas* dancing that night were Cante Huasula, Juan Castillo, Navor Pocheria, and Miguel Valencia. Navor played all sorts of animals. First he was a raccoon, going up to each of the other *pascolas*, touching and smelling their hands like a raccoon would. The other three *pascolas* buried seeds for the raccoon to dig up and eat. Navor was also a lion, climbing up poles set up outside the ramada. He repainted his face every time he played a new animal.

The deer dancer was Juan Sasueta, now a very old man in Tucson. He is not the Juan Sasueta who married Carmen. The *matachines* were Salvador Montenegro and his two sons, Jesús and Ramón (in from Mesquital); the three Fernández brothers; Juan Mosen; Bernaldo Ursua; Antonio Cepeda (the *jefe* of the *matachines*); Luis Medina; and Mariano Ortiz (Loreta's cousin). The *malinche* dancing with the *matachines* was Rafael Ortiz, another of Loreta's cousins. My father's *coyote* soldiers also danced. *Maestros* recited and sang all night in front of the altar that my grandmother kept in the house. She had about seven *santos* on our house altar.

My grandmother had bought some big firecrackers called *cohetes correos* (running rockets). Two tall poles, one near our ramada and the other about a half mile away, were connected by a cord, to which the *cohetes correos* were attached. When lighted they ran from pole to pole, going as fast as sixty miles per hour. Their final explosion was accompanied by a bang and lots of pretty lights. We set off three of them, which had cost my grandmother at least fifty dollars, about eight o'clock in the evening. Everyone was very happy. Everyone except me. I did not like Loreta.

An abundance of food was available. My grandmother had *atole de panoche* (a sweet gruel), garbanzo stew, flour tortillas, breads, coffee, and chocolate. Barbecue was reserved for the *maestros* and *pascolas*. Nearly every family brought more food.

At daybreak the *pascolas* said a big rainstorm was coming. One rubbed a big drum for the thunder; they flicked their tongues in and out to represent lightning and threw gourds full of water on the crowd. Everyone had to run or get wet.

After the musicians stopped playing about nine o'clock in the morning, they had the deer "play." Three of the *pascolas* acted as deer hunters, using bows and arrows without points. Navor Pocheria took the part of the hunting dog. Navor made a very good dog, walking on all fours, with a cow's tail attached to his pants. Juan Sasueta, the deer dancer, played the deer.

The crowd stood in two lines outside the ramada, on either side of the three poles stuck in the ground. Children and women ran from line to line and the hunters shot arrows at them, pretending they were deer also. A canteen of homemade wine (*tepache*) had been buried and the "dog" dug it up so the *pascolas* could drink it.

The "deer" hid around the poles for about half an hour; he went through all the motions of a deer hiding in a forest. At one point he surprised one of the hunters and knocked him down. The hunter started to cry, and the other two hunters had to whip him to get him to stop. At the third tree (or pole), the "deer" was caught and the hunters "killed" him. The "dead deer" was then carried to the ramada, where the hunters proceeded to skin, cut up, and weigh the meat. Then they started measuring the skin.

One *pascola* asked another, "Were you born in a kindergarten?"

The other replied, "Yes," beginning to count: "One kilometer, four kilos, fifty miles, thousand, a thousand eight hundred," and such nonsense.

The skin and meat were then sold to the crowd, the money being placed in a little pile. That was the end of the fiesta. All of us who had mourned for my aunt Camilda took off our black bands. Later that day we returned to Sasco.

The first evening in Sasco I went to the pool hall, as I had done before, and stayed until 2:30 A.M. I had five Mexican girl friends in Sasco, and they were all very mad with me.

One said, "You are crazy. Why did you marry that fool girl? She is like an alligator!"

The next day I saw another, and she said, "You are a fool. Why did you marry that wildcat?"

Later I met a third, and she said, "You are *loco*. You will not like what happens to you. I will pray to God every night for you to have bad luck."

I know she did, because the next day I fell thirty-five feet from the unloading chute to the ground. Workmen carried me unconscious to the hospital. When I came to, I could scarcely get my breath. My ribs were broken, my chest crushed on one side, and I was bleeding from my mouth and my nose.

The doctor came and asked, "How do you feel?"

"I feel better," I said.

The doctor said, "I do not think you are going to get well, because you are very badly hurt."

This was what I was afraid of, and I knew then that I had to go home. I told the doctor so.

He said, "No, you can't go home. You must stay here so we can look after you."

I got up and walked around the room. "See, Doctor, it is not so bad. I do not feel any pain."

The doctor let me go, and I walked home, which was about a mile. When I got there, my wife was crying. She was surprised when I walked in.

"They told us that you would die." I could not answer her. I lay down on my bed. The hurting was very bad.

That night my wife did not sleep with me. Every movement of the bed was painful and the blood kept coming from my mouth and nose. For several days it was the same, I could not eat, not a bite, and I could not sleep. My wife kept asking me how I felt, giving me medicine with a spoon. They sent for my grandmother, who came from Tucson to make me medicine.

One day I began to feel better and that night I slept a few hours. I dreamed that a beautiful woman, dressed completely in white, was standing at my feet.

"Do not worry, son," she said, "you will live. Look at this tooth." She had a tooth in her hand, and it was my tooth that she showed me. I could see that the tooth was very old. While I was looking at the tooth, she faded away.

I awoke. My grandmother was sitting by my bed, and I told her about the dream. She was very happy.

"That is good," she said. "You will get well and you will live to be an old man."

The next day I felt better, and the blood stopped coming from my mouth and nose. I ate some food for the first time, but I wanted to scream every time I moved. During the next few days I got a little stronger.

My father said, "We must send you to Tucson, where there is a Yaqui *curandero*, Butom Acuña. He can cure you."

My wife and I went on the train to Tucson, and the *curandero* said he would cure me. He made a poultice of parched cornmeal mixed with some herbs and put it on my side. Then he had me blow in an empty gallon glass bottle. In three days he cured me, and I got strong little by little. I never did play billiards again.

When I was strong enough, I started to work for the Southern Pacific. We would go out every morning on the work train to repair the tracks. Sometimes we would go toward Benson to the east, and at other times toward Casa Grande to the northwest. The work was easy. We never put in more than five or six hours after getting where we were going.

Juanito Sewa came from Torim in 1916 or 1917, moving in with us in our house in Barrio Anita. He was almost my age; I think he was born in 1898. None of us had known him before, but Yaquis without families live wherever they want when they come to Tucson. Juan stayed with us for a few years, working for Mr. Nash and the Southern Pacific Railroad.

In 1917, Lola Posoi and her husband, Chico Vica, a captain from Vicam, stayed in our house in Tucson for about a month. Chico was the brother of the famous Yaqui general Luis Matuz, and Lola Posoi was one of those Yaqui women who carried a gun and fought with the men. She said she had been in on the 1912 train robbery, as was Antonio Moreno. About thirty Yaquis stopped a train carrying a good deal of American money south of Empalme. I told Dr. Holden all about the robbery, for my father and I knew many of the Yaquis on the raid, and he put the whole story into *Hill of the Rooster*. Most of the stolen money was sent to Tucson to buy guns, but some was kept in the Sierra. Lola Posoi now lives in Hermosillo and visits Tucson every year on a passport.

One night in 1917, Pedro Alvarez and I were settling down in the ramada, talking a little before we went to sleep, when we saw a girl dressed all in white drift by. Pedro was a witch (*brujo*) and he explained that this meant that a young girl would soon die. Less than three weeks later, Desederia Tecu, the young daughter of the *pascola* Juan Tecu, died.

María and Alejandro Bacotmea died within a few weeks of each other that same year. Loreta was glad we were in Tucson when they died. After that their little house stood empty and no one lived there.

Pedro Ortiz died at Andreas Matos's ranch, two miles from Sasco, the place where I had first gone to work when I was thirteen. Pedro had worked there since Andreas came to Tucson looking for workers in 1914. He was buried in the Sasco cemetery. His oldest son, Mariano, had worked for Matos as a cowboy, and his youngest son, Rafael, was born there in 1914. After Pedro died in 1917, the family returned to Barrio Libre in Tucson, and Mariano married Merehencia Bacotmea, the youngest sister of Loreta's mother.

The war between President Wilson and the Kaiser began in 1917. The Sasco smelter shut down and my father came back to Tucson. He said to me, "Lio"—he always called me Lio—"you know about the war. I hear about one thing the newspapers say. All young men over twenty-one must go to the war."

"I guess that is right. I have signed papers three times already," I said.

He bought a .22 rifle and every day we went out from our village, and he taught me how to shoot, how to be quick, and how to wrap sacks around my feet so the enemy could not tell which direction I was walking. He showed me many tricks about how not to get shot by the enemy.

But in Europe the war was over. One night we heard noises in the city, and all the Yaquis got up. We were all asking each other about the noises, but nobody knew. The Yaqui chief, Juan Pistola, came to our house. "I come here asking you. There are many noises in the city."

My father said, "We better go ask Mr. Anderson."

Mr. Anderson lived a half mile from the village and he was a friend of all the Yaquis. Juan Pistola and my father went off to see Mr. Anderson. In half an hour they were back.

Juan Pistola said, "Boys, it is peace. The war is over."

That was November 11, 1918, and my daughter Marcelina was seventeen days old. She had been born October 25.

My father was very good friends with Juan Muñoz, known at this time as Juan Pistola. Juan, a Mayo Indian, had lived at Pitiquito on a ranch owned by José Cuervo. He worked for a while in a placer mine near Altár, but he was not a miner. When he moved from Pitiquito, he brought his wife, Manuela, and their two children, Juan and Yomumule. His wife and son died right away. He then married Antonia Matape in the church, and they had one daughter, Eulogia. Juan had been in federal prison in Atlanta, Georgia, along with Rudolfo Rivera and Tomás Bustamonte for selling liquor to Papagos, but he was a good chief, and he always tried hard to find jobs for poor Yaquis. My father and Juan Pistola had good friends in the border patrol. The two of them, along with some other friends, went to the courthouse three times a week to talk with their friends there. This made some Yaquis hate my father and Juan Pistola.

Two months later bad luck came to us. My grandmother died in the evening of December 23 and my father died the next afternoon.

On Saturday morning, December 21, my father was well and feeling fine. He went to a fiesta at Barrio Libre with his old friend and *compadre* Juan Buanamea Ronquillo. They both liked to play cards and they always won money because both had *buena suerte* (good luck). This time they played cards until about two o'clock in the morning. They lost all their money. That was bad luck. They went outside to stand around the big fire. Someone came up to my father and hit him on the nape of the neck with a cigarette. My father got home about six o'clock in the morning. My grandmother María had already cooked breakfast.

He said to my grandmother, "We had bad luck this time. We lost all our money. I feel very sick."

My grandmother said, "I told you not to go to the fiesta."

He went to bed. Soon he said, "I feel like something hit me in the back of my neck." He knew then that the Papago witch had used a magic cigarette when he hit him on the neck.

María made some medicine. She took a cup with some water, put in some medicine, and put the cup on the hot coals. In a few minutes the cup fell to one side, spilling all the medicine. My grandmother filled the cup again with water and medicine, and put it on the hot coals. In a little while it boiled over and little was left in the cup.

My grandmother became very sad (*se puso muy triste*) and began to cry. "Oh, my heaven, something is going to happen to us. I will not put it on again," she said.

She became very sick and went to bed. My wife cooked some food for my grandmother and my father. My grandmother could not eat a thing and my father ate very little. Hour by hour my grandmother said she felt worse, and my father said the same. He wanted to get up, but he could not raise his head because of the pain in his neck at the base of his skull.

On Monday morning my grandmother could not talk any more. She would open her mouth, but no sound came out. Juan Sasueta and I went off to find a *curandero*. We walked up and down, but could not find one. They had all gone away to work. Someone told us about a Papago Indian in Barrio Libre who was very wise and a good medicine man. We went to his home but he was not there. His wife said he had gone to his ranch about thirty miles southwest of Tucson. His name was Calistro Carretero.

"He will be back tonight or tomorrow," she said.

"Please tell him to come to Miguel Palos's house as soon as he gets back, as Miguel and his mother are very sick."

We went back home very sad because we could find no one to help my grandmother and my father. Both of them were worse.

We went to see all our friends and relatives to tell them that Miguel and María were dying, and everyone came to see them. We sent a telegram to Antonia in Chandler, Arizona, but they never got the telegram. Day and night our relatives came to see them.

About six in the evening my grandmother made signs that she wanted to talk to all of us. She could not speak a word, but made signs, and we could tell what she meant. She wanted me to take care of all the family. In a little while she died very quietly.

My father told Juan Sasueta, Carmen's husband, to go to the houses of the other Yaquis and select the *padrinos* and *madrinas* to prepare my grandmother's body for the funeral. Juan came back with three *padrinos* and three *madrinas*. The next morning my father gave us money to buy lumber, which the men made into a box. The funeral ceremonies were planned for Tuesday night and the burial for Wednesday morning. Yaquis always have burials in the morning.

About three o'clock on Tuesday afternoon my father called me. "Lio, you had better bring all my guns to me."

I brought his Mauser and two .30-.30 Winchesters. He gave me the Mauser and two cartridge belts. He gave one of the .30-.30 Winchesters to my brother Francisco and the other to Carmen's husband, Juan. They were all the possessions he had, except a hammer and a watch which I kept for many years.

He said, "Lio, you can take care of your brother and your cousins. Only God can help you. Do not be thinking of me, because I go to take a little rest."

Then to all of us he said, "My children, this is all I tell you. I am very tired. Lay me down, Lio." I laid him down, and he did something like a hiccup, then three times more he uttered hiccups, and he died.

Juan went out to get the *padrinos* and *madrinas* for my father. The *padrinos* sent me to town for more lumber for another box, and the *padrinos* and *madrinas* prepared my father's body for the funeral. All our relatives in Tucson got to see my grandmother and my father when they were dying. The only relative who did not get home was Antonia, because she never received the telegram.

That night the two bodies dressed in white were placed side by side on benches in front of my grandmother's altar. Each one's clothes were made into a bundle and placed under their head. Rosaries and breechclout strings were placed on the bodies. Members of the family, one at a time, knelt by each body and said good-by. Then the relatives, the *padrinos*, and *madrinas* met at the cross in front of the house, and I thanked them for what they had done. The *padrinos* and *madrinas* passed by the relatives and touched hands. They then circled around and touched hands two more times. The rest of the night the *maestro* read the litany and the *cantoras* chanted.

On Wednesday morning the *padrinos* put the bodies in the boxes, and the boxes in a delivery wagon pulled by one horse. We all followed, walking, to the cemetery. When we got there, the family went some distance from the graves, because it is bad luck for a relative to see a body put in a grave. The *padrinos* lowered the boxes, and the *maestro* sprinkled holy water on them. The *padrinos* and *madrinas* filled the graves. When they were finished, the family came and prayed over the mounds. Then the family and the *padrinos* and *madrinas* touched hands three times as they had done the night before. That ended the funeral, and we went home.

When we got back to our house, the Papago wise man was there. He said he had come as quickly as he could. We asked him what had happened to my grandmother and my father.

"I had a dream last night, and I saw it all. They were killed by a Papago witch," he said.

"Why would the witch man kill them?"

"Because your father had enemies among the Yaquis."

This was true, because the *torocoyoris* had been trying to get my father ever since he left the Colorada Mine.

"Do you know who the enemies are?" I asked.

"Yes. Several Tucson Yaquis made contributions to a Papago witch so that he would kill your father. Their names are Tomás Cosío, Alejandro Paamea, José Lorito Moreno, Lino Sopomea, Andreas Velasco, Hilario Villa, Delores Ruíz, Juan Torreon, Sacramento Navogoki, Valentín Teran, Anselmo Castillo Cuñes, the brothers Rudolfo and Loreta Vatereo, and Alejandro Wapo (the father of Martín Wapo). If I had been here I might have saved them. My medicine is stronger than the other Papagos'. I am sorry I came too late."

Not one of the men named by the Papago *curandero* was a *torocoyori*. Many had been my father's best friends. Tomás Cosío was married to one of my grandfather Abelardo's nieces from the Buetemea family. He is the only one of the men who harmed my father and grandmother who is still alive. He is old and so crippled that he can hardly walk. Hilario Villa was married to Luz Frías, the daughter of my grandmother's half brother, Arturo Frías. Juan Torreon was married to another of my grand-mother's relatives, Micaela Naponohi. Some of these men had been in the Sierra with my father. Lino Sopomea had worked with my father on just about every job from the Colorada Mine to the Sasco smelter. So it was not the *torocoyoris* who killed my father and grandmother, but some crazy Yaquis who were afraid that my father and Juan Pistola were going to sell the Rio Yaqui to the Americans. Juan Pistola was not very inter-ested in the Yaqui wars. After all, he was a Mayo. But my father still wanted to fight the Mexicans, and he was talking to his American friends about getting some help the next time he went back to try to free the Rio Yaqui. A few years later Juan Pistola died while I was in California. When I returned home, I was told that he had been killed like my father.

So that is what happened to my grandmother and father. This was our great misfortune of 1918.

We had the *novena* nine days later. It was held at our home, and we did everything we did before, only the bodies were not there. The *padrinos* provided the food and the coffee for both ceremonies.

Three nights later, my father came back about ten o'clock. I had gone to bed, but I was not asleep. He came into the room and stood close to me. He sat down beside me and touched my face, nose, and lips.

He said, "Lio, do not worry about me. I am all right." I did not answer him. He stood up, walked to the door, and went away.

As I have said, my father always called me Lio, as did people we knew in Hermosillo. Miss Ida, my teacher, called me Little One. Every morning when she came to school she would say, "Good morning, Little One." The children at school started to call me the Little One. Some of the ones I went to school with now live in Guadalupe Village near Phoenix, and their families and their friends still call me the Little One. On the Rio Yaqui in all the eight villages they call me Rosa Lingo or Rosa Lino. How I came to have so many names I do not know.

The next morning I told everyone in the house about my father's visit. "My father came back last night. He was here in this room. He touched my face, my nose, and my lips and he talked to me, but I did not answer him."

Simón said, "We had better move away from this place at once."
"Yes, we must hurry," said my brother Francisco.

That same morning we started to tear down the house. In three days we had hauled it on a wagon about a half mile north to what was to become Barrio Pascua. There was enough lumber in our four-room house to build two new houses side by side. Viviana became the head of one household with Carmen, Juan Sasueta, and their two babies, Simón and Anita. Augustina Valencia and her grandson Rufino Contreras also moved in with Viviana. Loreta and I lived in the other house with Juanito Sewa and Pedro Alvarez. Marcilina Chino and her family, who had been living with us for four years, moved to the Ajo smelter and then on to California. My father did not know where we moved, because he never came back again.

I went to work in Tucson for the gas company at $2.50 a day. Wages were already going down, although the war had been over only two months.

Soon we had another misfortune. Carmen died on January 11, 1919, leaving us two children, Simón, a boy of four, and Anita, a girl of eighteen months. Carmen was short and pretty, with white skin like our grandmother María. In fact she was very much like María in that she was gay and happy, singing and dancing around the house. She would have looked almost exactly like María except she inherited our grandfather Abelardo's flat nose. She died because she thought so much of my grandmother.

After my grandmother died, Carmen got to thinking that my grandmother and my father needed her in Glory more than her children needed her here. When my grandmother died, Carmen became sad and was not aware of what was going on around her. She wanted to sleep nearly all the time and would eat only once a day. After a few days she looked very sick. We wanted to bring a *curandero* but she said, "No. I do not need the medicine. I only want to go to my grandmother and my uncle. Please do not do anything for me. Leave me alone."

We were all very sad, but there was nothing we could do because she wanted so much to go to Glory to my grandmother. She began sleeping all the time and never taking any food. Eighteen days after my grandmother died, my cousin went to be with her in Glory.

A few weeks later Carmen's little girl died. Juan took his little boy and went to live with one of his relatives, Nacho Soto. Nacho and Juan both came from Altár, Sonora. Little Simón died a few months later. Juan was the only one left of his family and he was very sad.

Our home was not the same any more. My grandmother had always held the family together. She fed us when we were hungry, encouraged us when we were sad, scolded us when we were lazy, and doctored us when we were sick. Everyone depended on her and wanted to be near her. That is why our family and our household was always large. Sometimes there were ten or fifteen of us, all living in our one-room house, and we were happy. Now it was all changed, and we were not happy. In the spring of 1919, our family began to scatter.

# CHAPTER 5

# *Around the West*

MY BROTHER FRANCISCO VALENZUELA and several of his friends went to California in 1919. My wife and I went to Goodyear, five miles south of Chandler, where we both worked in the fields. We stayed there for nine months and saved some money. On November 20 we quit. The time was drawing near for the *cumpleaños* for my grandmother and my father.

I said to my wife, "What shall we do now? Shall we go on the train to Tucson, or shall we buy a wagon and one horse?"

"I guess we had better buy the wagon and horse," she said.

We went to Mesa and found an express wagon and horse for seventy-five dollars. It was 120 miles from Mesa to Tucson, and it took five days for us to go in the wagon. When we got to Tucson, Francisco had already arrived from California.

The next day we arranged for the *cumpleaños* of my father and my grandmother. We went to the river for fresh green boughs to enclose three sides of the ramada in front of our house. Nights are cool in Tucson in December, so we gathered quite a lot of firewood. We arranged for all the dancers: the *matachines*, the *coyotes*, the *pascolas*, and the deer dancer. Also we had to get the *maestros* and *cantoras*. They were widely scattered and it took much time to find them. Many provisions were needed, because all the Yaquis in the country were invited. It was the Christmas season, and many would be back from the cotton fields.

The *cumpleaños* lasted forty-eight hours, from Friday morning to

69

Sunday morning. The first twenty-four hours were devoted to mourning services. A *maestro* put black cords about the necks of the relatives. The *maestros* and *cantoras* read and sang. They changed off, first one and then another, all day and night. No food was eaten the first day and night.

On Saturday the *maestro* took the black cords off of the relatives and burned them before the cross in front of the house. This ended the year of mourning for my father and my grandmother. Then the fiesta began. Three *pascolas* and the deer dancer, with their musicians, took their places under the ramada and danced all day and all night, one after the other. The *matachines* danced from time to time in front of the ramada. Hundreds of homemade firecrackers were shot off.

More than a hundred Yaquis were there. The women kept making tortillas without stopping, to eat with the tamales, beans, pinole, and stew. Coffee was made in a washtub.

When the fiesta was over on Sunday morning, much food still remained. I asked my mother-in-law (Charla Bacotmea Sánchez Salinas) what we should do with it.

"You should give it to the people. Let each one have a portion," she said.

I did as she said, keeping back only enough for the family to eat that day. I had some money, too, and I gave each person sixty-five cents. When I finished not a cent was left.

That day the family ate the last of the food. On Monday morning we got up and made the fire, but there was nothing to cook. Our little Marcelina began to cry for something to eat. My wife took Marcelina to her mother's home in Barrio Libre, four miles away. In the late afternoon she came back, bringing me some tortillas, the first food I had eaten since the afternoon before, and I was very hungry.

That night it rained and on Tuesday it rained, and still we had no food. I had to go out and find something to eat. I went to the city dump to pick up scraps which people had thrown away from their Christmas dinner. I found bread, turkey bones with some meat on them, bits of cake, and a hog hide. We made cracklings of the hog hide and soup from the turkey bones.

For a few weeks we had a very bad time. After that I never wanted to make fiesta any more. It only brought misfortune and suffering. The earnings of a whole year were gone, and my little girl was hungry. I wondered if my grandmother would have thought that a good thing.

The Yaquis always like to make *cumpleaño* fiestas because the *maestros* tell them they should. When someone dies, the priests say the fiesta causes him to go straight to Glory. The Yaquis believe the priests, and so most of the money they make is spent making fiestas so that some dead relative can go to Glory. The first thing they do when they get some money is to make fiesta. The first priests to the Yaquis long ago tricked the Yaquis into making fiestas and believing in God. The trick was this. The priests knew when an eclipse would occur. They told the Yaquis that unless they repented and believed in God and made a fiesta, the moon would get black and die, and when the moon died, so would they. At first the Yaquis did not believe them, but when about a third of the moon was black, the Yaquis said they believed in God and made a big fiesta. The priests said they were saved and that the moon would come back to life. Ever since, the Yaquis have made these big fiestas, and the people are always poor.

After several weeks I got a regular job in Tucson working for the city pouring concrete curbs, and then we lived better. My brother Francisco came back from his second trip to California with money. They said that California was a much better place to work than Arizona.

In April, 1920, we all went to California on the train. My wife, my little girl, and I; my brother; my cousin Viviana and her new husband, Tomás Torre; and Juanito Sewa made the trip together. Ricky Alvarez made arrangements for us to go on the Southern Pacific. We went first to San Luis Obispo, where we worked for several weeks. We did not like the place, so we quit and went to Fresno.

When we got to Fresno we had good luck. We met a Mexican we knew in the railroad station. He took us to where he was working, and there we found a number of Mexicans and Yaquis we had known in Tucson. The owner of the orchard said that we had come just in time. An Italian friend of his needed some workers.

The next morning he took us to the Italian's place. Francisco and Juanito were out in the street when the Italian came, so they got left behind as we had to leave in a hurry. The Italian was very friendly, providing us with a lumber house with a stove and a twenty-five-gallon barrel of wine. He gave us some kind of food every day, and Marcelina played with the Italian children. Pretty soon she was speaking Italian.

The Italian had a big orchard of oranges, grapefruit, figs, pears, and grapes. We made good money. When picking was over we went back to Fresno, staying in a hotel run by a Mexican married to an Italian.

Tomás Torre and I got jobs with a section crew of the Santa Fe Railroad. We were sent to Slaton section. The railroad had a long house of about twelve rooms where the workers lived. Viviana and Tomás had one room, and Loreta, Marcelina, and I had another. Every room had a wood-burning cook stove. The big supply house for that part of the Santa Fe was Bakersfield. Every week we made a list of food and clothes we needed and gave it to our *mayordomo*, or section foreman. The next day the express dropped off our supplies, which were deducted from our wages. We made good money—four dollars a day.

Juanito Sewa, working at the Añola section, heard we were at Slaton, and the next Sunday he came looking for us. Later he transferred to the Slaton section. They gave him a room, and he ate with us until he got sick and returned to Tucson. He soon married Candelária Seamo, who already had two children, José and Lola. Her first husband was dead. Juan and Candelária lived in Guadalupe, where he worked for the Scottsdale Water Users until they both died in 1925.

After a few months I had bad luck. The boss man of the section crew was an Austrian. He was a very bad boss. He was always standing behind the workmen, watching them like a hawk. He did not want them to talk to each other or even look up from their work. If he heard someone talking, he would say, "This is no time to talk, you can do that at night."

One day we started to change some track, and the boss man was very nervous. The passenger train was soon due, and it goes by there very fast because the railroad from Bakersfield to Fresno is nearly straight for a hundred miles and the trains pick up speed. The boss man roared at me, "What do you mean always looking up?"

"What are you talking about?" I said.

Then the boss man wanted to fight with me. "I will knock your block off," he said, and ran at me.

I drew my shovel back to hit him, and he stopped. Then I threw the shovel at him, but he dodged it. I grabbed a crowbar and got ready for him again, but he walked off, muttering to himself. When we got back to the section house he gave me my time.

Loreta, Marcelina, and I took the train to Phoenix, and the next day to Tucson. Viviana and Tomás Torre stayed at the Slaton section for two more months.

When we got back to Barrio Pascua, we found the village abandoned. Nearly all the Yaquis had gone back to the Rio Yaqui. A hundred and seventeen of them left July 16, 1921.

José Molino Valencia brought a letter from Sonoran Yaquis to all the Tucson Yaquis which said:

You had better come to the Rio Yaqui and have a good time with us. Peace has come. Our friend, Señor Obregón, is the president. He has promised to take our lands away from the Mexicans and the foreigners and give them back to us. We do not have to wake up early in the morning and go to work, or go looking for work. The Señor General Obregón helps the Yaquis very nice. He gives us food, and we ride free in the passenger train anywhere we want to go.

Tomás Muina was very happy with the letter his son brought, and he and his wife, Carlota, took their granddaughter Francisca (the oldest daughter of my sister Antonia) and returned to Torim. I never saw Tomás and Carlota again, because they both died two years later in Torim of pneumonia or tuberculosis. After that Francisca married a Chinese, Chico Chifu, and moved to Cocorit, where they ran a little store.

When Tomás Muina and his son asked us to go, I answered them, "It sounds very nice, but I cannot go to the Rio Yaqui at this time. Maybe I can get there in the next eight or ten years."

Lucrecia Sewa and the remaining members of her family left Tucson in a two-horse wagon for Torim. They wanted Viviana, Simón, Loreta, and I to go with them, but we refused again. Lucrecia had lost her daughter, Selma (who died in 1907 of pneumonia), and her son, Trinidad (who died later of the same ailment), since she moved to Arizona in 1904. She was returning to the Yaqui River with only her youngest son, Abato, and her two grandchildren, Nacha and José, and her man, José María Mavis.

In a few weeks Loreta, Marcelina, and I went to the Yaqui village at Scottsdale, east of Phoenix, where I went to work for the Water Users Association irrigating fields from the canals. After thirteen months I quit because many of the Yaquis were dying from a disease of the feet which was caused by wearing the rubber boots.

The rubber boots are very dangerous when they are worn a long time. The Yaquis who stayed there all the time never lasted over three or four years. They all died, or became crippled or paralyzed. About thirty Yaquis died at Scottsdale of this disease.

I became afraid to wear the rubber boots, and I told the boss man I would not wear them if he paid me ten dollars a day. For a while he had me cut Johnson grass with a scythe. Then I helped the Water Users' carpenter for a few months.

I quit in December and went back to Tucson, where I began doing odd jobs. I knew some plumbers, bricklayers, carpenters, and truck drivers, and from time to time one of them would use me as a helper for a few days. But the prospects were uncertain, and we were never sure of having food to eat.

One day a Yaqui friend named Jimmy said, "I had a letter from my brother in Los Angeles. He said there are lots of good jobs there. Let's catch a freight train tomorrow morning for California."

I said, "I would like to go, but I have no money."

He said, "Do not worry about that. I have twenty-five dollars, and that is enough for both of us."

The next morning we caught the fast freight. We had bad luck. When the train stopped for water at Red Rock, thirty-five miles from Tucson, the brakemen put us off, and they watched us so close we were not able to get back on. We stayed there until late afternoon, when another freight stopped for water. We got on it, and at midnight we got off the train in Yuma and walked across the Colorado River on the railroad bridge. In about an hour the same train came along. It ran slow over the bridge, and we were able to get on. At Indio, California, the next morning, we got off two miles from the town. We had heard that there was a bad policeman in the railroad yards who beat up hobos and kicked them out of the yards. We walked into town down the highway.

Jimmy said, "Let's eat some breakfast in that restaurant."

Two boys were eating in the restaurant. They asked us, "Which way are you fellows going?"

"To Los Angeles," Jimmy said.

"That is where we are going. You can ride with us. The highway police have stopped us because we are carrying an overload on the truck. We are waiting for a telegram from the company. If you want to wait a while, you can ride with us."

They were from the Imperial Valley, and were hauling a big load of alfalfa hay. A few hours later the telegram came and we started. There is a long grade between Indio and Belmont, and the day was hot. The engine boiled and about every two miles we had to fill the radiator. We began to understand why they had invited us to ride with them. It took eleven hours to go from Indio to Belmont, which was only about fifty miles. We got there at two o'clock in the morning and slept for two hours on the ground beside the road. Then we started on. We passed through many towns, but the truck driver did not stop to eat. We rode on that truck all day, very hungry.

In the late afternoon we got to Del Monte and met a German girl in a car. She had been waiting for us a long time. That was the reason the truck driver would not stop to eat. She told us to follow her, and she led us to a dairy owned by her father. We started to unload the hay, and one of the boys asked the German if we could have some supper.

He said, "I am sorry, but we have not cooked supper yet. We will make some sandwiches for you."

In a few minutes he brought us a big pile of sandwiches. Then we unloaded the truck in half an hour. The truck driver gave Jimmy and me a dollar and a half each. This was all the money I had.

We went on to Los Angeles. The truck driver told us that if we did not have any place to sleep we could go home with him and sleep in the yard, but we got off at the Southern Pacific station and went to the rest room and changed our clothes. We took a streetcar into the town and went to a hotel and rented two beds for twenty-five cents apiece. Then we went to a restaurant and ate a big meal for twenty-five cents.

The next morning Jimmy went to see his brother and I left for Stockton, near Sacramento. I rode freight trains for three days to get there. I had fifteen cents when I arrived.

Plenty of jobs were available in Stockton, but a worker had to register at the employment office. It took $2.50 to buy a chance. I was tired and sad because I could not buy a chance. I went into a pool hall and sat down on a chair to rest. A Chinese came in the room and looked at all the men sitting in the chairs. Then he came up to me and said, "Do you want to work in the onion fields for three dollars a day and board?"

"Yes," I said.

"Then meet me at the boat dock at two o'clock," he said.

I decided to spend my fifteen cents for food. I went to a bakery and asked for day-old bread, because that is cheaper than fresh bread.

"How much?" the man said.

"All I can buy for fifteen cents," I said.

He gave me a big package of bread, and I ate it all. At two o'clock we started out from the dock in a boat to the island where the Chinese man lived. We had a good supper, and the next morning at seven we started to work with the onions. We worked ten hours. The work was not hard, but dusty, and the dirt contained an acid which made a man's body itch all over. Without a bath at night, a person could not sleep; he would be scratching and rubbing all the time. Even though we scrubbed hard, our skin got raw and itched. For this reason the Chinese man could never keep hands very long.

After nine days I quit and went back to Stockton with twenty-seven dollars. I sent fifteen dollars to my wife in Tucson and got on a freight train that night for Sacramento. The next day I went to the employment office and paid for my chance. I got a job in a sawmill 150 miles to the northeast. I did not like the sawmill, and after eight days I went back to

Sacramento. I spent two days there and bought another chance at the employment office.

This time the job was in a lumber mill in Modoc Point, Oregon. Nine of us made the trip in a special Cadillac and got there the next day. I had good luck. The boss man gave me easy work on the measuring machine. But in a few days I had bad luck. I was walking through the mill and passed a danger zone where big timbers were thrown out of a machine. A log struck me in the stomach and knocked me out for a while. It did not hurt me very much, and I kept on working. The next morning the boss man gave me another job. I helped the engineer who ran the locomotive for the log train. I was the fireman, and I liked it very much.

After three months with the log train I got a telegram from my wife saying that she was very sick and wanted me to come home at once. I went to the timekeeper to get my time.

He said, "It is too late today. I will fix it up for you tomorrow."

I told him about the telegram and that I had to catch the train at seven the next morning from Klamath Falls.

"Come back at eight tonight and I will have your check ready."

When I got my check, I started walking to Klamath Falls. It was dark and I was scared because there were bears in the woods. The path went along the railroad track, but it was so dark I could not see the track. I got a stick so I could feel the track. It took an hour to go two miles. In Klamath Falls I got a room in the hotel. Then next morning I could not buy a ticket to Los Angeles because I had not cashed the check, but I had enough money to get a ticket to Redding. When I got to Redding late in the evening, I went to a hotel run by an Italian I knew.

When he saw me he said, "Hello, *compaño*. I have not seen you for a long time. Where did you come from?" I told him from Klamath Falls, but I did not tell him about the check. The next morning I went to a store to cash my check, but no one would take it.

The man said, "I am sorry, but many of the lumber companies are broke, and do not have any money in the bank."

I went to three stores, and they all said the same thing. I thought I would have to go back to Klamath Falls to get the money. I must have looked very sad, because when I got back to the hotel, the daughter of the Italian said, "Something must have happened to you."

Then I told her about the check and I showed it to her. She said, "Don't worry. We know about the Modoc Lumber Company. We can get it cashed."

She took me to a big store and explained to the manager. He said, "I can cash the check, but he will have to buy something in the store."

I spent twenty dollars in the store, and he cashed the check, which was for $217. I tried to give the girl five dollars for what she had done, but she would not take it.

I went to Los Angeles on the passenger train. There I sent my valise by express and caught a freight. I got to Indio the next morning, and I did not pay a cent for the long ride because the brakemen did not find me. When they found you, they made you pay a dollar.

I jumped off the train just as it entered the yards at Indio, and ran into town so I could get some breakfast. I ate in a little restaurant by the railroad, and a mean policeman watched me very close. When I finished, I walked out the highway toward Yuma. The policeman followed me a little way and then he stopped. When I was at the edge of town, the same freight came by. It was still moving slow enough for me to catch it. A few minutes later a brakeman came along.

He said, "Where are you going?"

"To Yuma," I said.

"All right. One dollar, or I will push you off."

I gave him a dollar. I was very sleepy because I had not slept any the night before. I got in a boxcar and went to sleep. When we were within five miles of Yuma, the brakeman came and woke me up.

He said, "All right, wake up. We are close to Yuma. The train will slow down at the bridge. You can drop off on this side."

It was midafternoon and I walked into Yuma and got something to eat. About sundown the same freight started out of the yards. I rode it all night, and the next morning I was in Tucson.

When I got home, my wife was well and looked healthy.

"I thought you were very bad sick," I said.

"I was sick, and I felt very bad in my body, and I thought I might die," she said.

"This is bad luck, because I left the best job I have ever had," I said.

Our son Salvador had been born four months before, but she had not had any trouble with that. She just wanted me to come home.

I rested two weeks and got a job in Tucson. It lasted a few days and I was out of work again. One day my wife said to me, "Tomorrow you better go in the wagon and get some wood."

The next morning I filled a bottle with water and went after wood. I went about six miles west of Tucson to a place called Cerro del Gato, or

Cat Mountain. In Yaqui we called it Missi Kawe. When I finished loading
the wagon with wood, I looked at the mountain. Then I remembered I
had heard about the treasure that was supposed to be hidden there.

Looking toward the side of a cliff at the top of the mountain, I saw a
small opening about twenty feet from the top which was partly closed
with a large rock. I went up as near as I could to the opening, which was
about two feet in diameter. Rock filled part of the hole, leaving three or
four inches at the bottom of the hole. It was dark under there, as if it led
to a cave. I was about fifteen feet to one side of the place, but I could not
go closer. The cliff was almost straight from the top to a hundred feet
below the opening. On the other side of the hole it was about six feet to
where the mountain sloped. I took off my shoes and went up over the
top of the cliff and came down on the other side, but I could only get
within about six feet of the opening.

I went down the mountain and back to my wagon. When I got home
I told Manuel Salinas about what I had seen. He was very excited.

He said, "I guess you have found the treasure people have always said
was on Cerro del Gato. How wide is the opening?"

"About two feet."

"I would like to go with you and see this thing tomorrow, but I cannot
get off. I will get my *padrino* to go with you." The *padrino* was his brother-
in-law Joaquín Inigo, who was married to Venancia Bacotmea, the oldest
sister of Loreta's mother.

We got some ropes, a steel bar, some food, and blankets, and went to
the mountain that afternoon. It was late when we got there, and we slept
at the foot of the cliff. At daybreak we took the ropes and steel bar and
climbed to the top of the cliff, going up the sloping side. I tied a rope
securely to a tree at the top and threw the other end over the face of the
sloping side. We pulled off our shoes and went down until we were even
with the opening. I tied the rope around my waist, then I fastened a
short rope to me so that Joaquín could pull me back. He stayed at the
side and held the short rope, and I took the steel bar and swung over the
face of the cliff to the opening. The flat rock which closed the opening was
standing on edge. I put my hand in the open space at the bottom as far
as my arm would reach. All I could feel was dust. A bad smell came out.
I guess it was from bat guano. I could see nothing but darkness through
the narrow opening.

I started to work trying to move the flat rock with the steel bar. In a
few minutes my partner said, "There is someone up there looking at us.
He is on a black horse."

I listened a few seconds, but could hear nothing. I said, "Is he still there?"

"Yes, he is there, looking at us."

I could tell Joaquín was badly scared, and I was too. In a little while I felt the rope shake above me. My heart nearly stopped. I knew the ghost on the black horse was up there and thought that he had cut the rope or broken it, but he only wiggled it very hard.

I looked at my partner. He was shaking from top to toe, and was very pale.

I said, "You had better pull me back."

He did. I looked up, but did not see anything. I climbed up and untied the rope, and we went down to the wagon as fast as we could move. We did not look back. When we got home we were both sick. My partner was still shaking like he had a hard chill.

When we got to his home he said to Venancia, "Fix us some medicine. We are both very sick."

She said, "What is the matter with you?"

"We saw a ghost on a black horse at the top of the cliff. The ghost was wearing a deerskin jacket."

Venancia said, "What did the ghost look like?"

"He was a tall man, with long whiskers."

"What did he do?"

"He did not do anything. He just looked at us." I guess he had not seen the ghost wiggle the rope.

For four days I was sick and could not eat anything. I could not even drink water. My mother-in-law gave me all kinds of medicine. She went to the church in town and got some holy water from the basin near the door and made me drink it. She rubbed me with holy candles she found burning near the altar of the church. She gave me medicine she got from the *curandero*. After a few days I was well again.

Joaquín Inigo never got well again. After a month he could walk around, but he was not well. He went back to the Rio Yaqui with his family, but in a month we got a letter from his wife saying he had died at Vicam.

I thought about the lady in white and the tooth she showed me when my chest was broken. I guess she saved me. I do not know whether there was any treasure there. I could not see behind the rock and all I felt when I ran my hand into the cave was the dust.

I never went back, and I never told anybody except Manuel Salinas that I had been there. He never did go to look for the treasure, but it would be very easy to find. There is no other cliff on Cerro del Gato, which is located six miles west of Tucson.

As soon as I was well from the ghost sickness, I found a job in Tucson working for the gas company digging ditches; I worked steady for six months. In March, 1923, my job ended. Three days later several of us caught a freight train for California, and we had good luck all the way. Micky and Juan Salinas, sons of Manuel Salinas, and several other friends went along. At Indio we got on a train of empty refrigerator cars going west. We found one with the little doors open at the top where they put in the ice. We got down in the ice compartment and went to sleep. There was no ice in it, and the little open door let air in. We slept good. I woke up and the train was stopped. I thought we were stopped at a water tank or that we were waiting on a siding for another train to pass, and I went back to sleep. After several hours I woke up again. We were still stopped. I woke Micky up.

"Do you know where we are?" I asked him.

He said, "No, but we must be getting close to Colton."

I said, "But we have been on a switch a very long time."

He said, "We had better look and see where we are." We looked out and saw that we were sidetracked in the Colton yard.

Micky said, "We must get out of here in a hurry. There is a very bad policeman here."

We climbed down and ran to the gate, about a hundred yards away. We had good luck, because the policeman did not see us. It was still not daylight, but we went to the bus station and found a bus ready to leave for Los Angeles. The fare was $1.75, and that was all it cost us to make the trip from Tucson. We did not meet a brakeman all the way.

In Los Angeles we went to the Southern Pacific employment office. They said the only jobs they had were in Oregon. We signed up and left that night on a passenger train for the north. When we got to Sacramento the next day we deserted and ran away. We had decided we did not want to go to Oregon. We told the *mayordomo* that we were going to the bathroom and just did not go back. Of course, we lost our suitcases, but mine only had an old blanket in it so I did not care.

By this time I knew Sacramento well, since I had been there so often before. We went to the employment office and bought job chances. They gave us jobs with the San Francisco Water Supply Company, and our work was in the mountains north of Stockton. The company was making tunnels through the mountains to bring water to San Francisco. We went to Hatchy Hatchy and found they were working three shifts a day. That night I went to work on the graveyard shift, from eleven to seven. Micky got on the day shift, from seven to three.

People from many nations worked there, Greeks, Italians, Germans, Russians, Poles, Scandinavians, Irishmen, Mexicans, and many others. Work in the tunnels was dangerous. Men were hurt every day, and some were killed. Micky and I had good luck. We worked six months and did not get a scratch. The pay was $4.25 a day and board, and every three months we got a $25 bonus. We saved nearly all of it.

We quit in September and went down to Stockton, where we spent one night in a hotel. The next morning we expressed our valises to Los Angeles. We caught a freight and rode all night. When we got to Los Angeles we were very sleepy, and we went to a hotel. We slept all day and all night.

The next morning we went to a tailor and ordered suits. Mine cost sixty dollars and Micky's cost forty-five dollars. They were ready the next day. We went to an auction and bought watches. For forty-five dollars I got one with twenty-one jewels and Micky got one with seventeen jewels for twenty-five dollars. We went to a Chinese tailor and ordered silk shirts. We got different colors, and they cost twenty-five dollars each. I bought a twelve-dollar hat. My cousin spent a hundred dollars for clothes and I spent more. This was the first time I ever had clothes like that.

We stayed three days in Los Angeles, then we put our new clothes in our valises and sent them by express to Tucson. We walked five miles east of Los Angeles in our old clothes to catch a freight to Indio. Many policemen in Lost Angeles watch the railroad yards. We got to Indio without seeing a brakeman, but east of there we had to pay the dollar. When we left Yuma it was dark and we were very sleepy. We went to sleep on top of a boxcar. About three in the morning, the brakeman came and woke us.

He said, "Boys, we are close to Maricopa. There is a bad Texas policeman in the yards. You had better get off and walk across town and catch the train on the other side. We will be here until the crew eats at the railroad restaurant."

When the train started out, about forty minutes later, we were on the other side of town waiting for it. We had good luck; the Texas policeman did not see us.

When we got to Tucson, everybody was glad to see us because we had brought home money from California. We found that many more Yaquis had gone home to the Rio Yaqui. People remaining in Arizona kept getting letters telling them to come home to the Rio Yaqui. Two of the men who paid the Papago witch to kill my father, Delores Ruiz and

Valentín Teran, were among those who returned with their families. Nestor Fregoso Moreno moved to Torim. Nestor and I were always good friends, and he had been in the Sierra with my father. His father, José Loreto Moreno, was one of the Yaquis who helped kill my father. The father was usually called José Loreto Lampareo because his job on the Southern Pacific Railroad for many years was to fill and light the lanterns. José Loreto stayed in Tucson when Nestor went back to Torim, and they never saw each other again, as José Loreto died the next year. The two Vatereo brothers died in Mesquital about this time. One by one the men who killed my father were having bad luck and dying.

In a few days my wife said, "Now we have lots of money, we will go to the fiesta at Magdalena."

I did not want to go to the fiesta of San Francisco, but my wife said she would not go without me.

I said, "All right, we will go."

Magdalena is in Sonora about fifty miles south of Nogales. The church of San Francisco there is especially sacred to the Yaquis. A lot of miracles have happened there. Every Yaqui tries to go there at least once. We always had a picture of Saint Francis in our house at the Colorada Mine, and my grandmother had kept a *santo* of Saint Francis in our house at Barrio Anita.

I gave my wife a hundred dollars to buy what she and the children needed for the trip. She went to town with Micky's wife and bought more than she ever had before in her life. Manuel Salinas went to the courthouse to arrange permission for us to go across the border at Nogales. He had no trouble because he was the chief of the Yaqui village of Pascua. When Juan Pistola died, September 18, 1922, Manuel Salinas was made chief, and he called himself chief until he died in 1927. Manuel Salinas was not a good chief. I think he was *loco*. In fact I think that at least five percent of the Yaquis are crazy.

My wife and I had been in the United States for many years. We were considered permanent residents, and both our children were natural-born citizens. There was no problem about getting permission to cross the border.

On October 1, 1923, we took the stage to Nogales, getting there too late to catch the morning train to Magdalena, so we spent the night in Nogales, Sonora, and got on the train in the next morning. We arrived at Magdalena about ten o'clock and found the town full of Yaquis. More than six hundred were there; all of the men and some of the women carried guns.

My mother was there. I had not seen her for nineteen years. My half sister, Julia Acosta, whom I had never seen, was with her. My mother was very glad to see me and our two children, who were her grandchildren. She looked my wife up and down and did not like her.

We had a good time at the fiesta. There were many Yaquis I had known in Colorada and Hermosillo. Many had lived in the mountains, and some had moved back to Sonora from Arizona.

I never did go to the church. The reason was, I did not believe in the church at that time. I believed only in magic and tricks.

The last night we were in Magdalena, I had a dream. I thought I was at the church. Saint Francis was there, and he kissed all the people who came to church. But he did not kiss me. He just kept his eye on me, and did not say a word to me. The next morning I told my wife about the dream.

I said, "I dreamed I saw Saint Francis last night. He was kissing all the people who came to see him at the church, but he did not kiss me."

"He did not kiss you because you do not believe in him, and you do not have faith," she said.

When we returned to Tucson to live with Loreta's mother and Manuel Salinas I was always thinking about Saint Francis and why he did not kiss me. Every day I thought about it more and more, and I would wake up in the night and think about it.

Augustina Valencia died in this year, at the age of 113, so it was said. She had lived with Viviana since my father and grandmother died. All her life she worked as a washerwoman, and she was still taking in washing until the week she died. As old as she was, her hair never turned gray. I will always remember Augustina because she was a lifelong friend of my grandmother's, and she was very wise, teaching me much of what I know.

Augustina Valencia's grandson Rufino Contreras received a letter in 1923 saying that his mother and little brother had been executed by the Yaqui authorities at Vicam pueblo. Rufino was living with us at the time. His mother was Nicolasa Waibel, who married Luis Contreras at Ranchito, as I have already related in another chapter. After Luis was killed at the Amole Mine in 1907, Nicolasa went with Diego Vargas for a few years, leaving him for Domingo Lorenzo, another Yaqui. Nicolasa and Domingo lived in Sasco and in Guadalupe, where he worked for the Water Users. For many years Nicolasa drank so much mescal that she walked around drunk all the time.

Early in 1923, Nicolasa and two of her young children left Domingo

and went to Vicam, where her sister Josefa Waibel lived with Pedro
More. Nicolasa and her children moved in with Antonio Tupea, who
was living in his mother's house. One night about midnight Nicolasa
and Antonio got drunk and had a terrible fight. Nicolasa cut off his head
with an ax. Her son Luis got up and saw what his mother had done; he
agreed to help her carry Antonio's body out into the brush and bury it.

The next morning Antonio's mother started looking everywhere for her
son, but she could not find him. After three days she went to the Yaqui
*guardia* and put up a notice saying that Antonio Tupea had disappeared
after a terrible fight with Nicolasa Contreras. The Yaqui soldiers arrested
Nicolasa and started questioning her. Finally she took the soldiers to
where Antonio was buried. Three Yaqui generals gave orders that she
and her son were to be executed: General Luis Matuz, General Juan
María Morre, and General Luis Huicha.

Yaqui law says that condemned prisoners are to remain in the *guardia*
three days with their arms tied, without food or water. Three *madrinas*
and three *padrinos* made a brown burial robe for Nicolasa; three *madrinas*
and three *padrinos* made a brown burial robe for Luis. Each *madrina* and
*padrino* put a Yaqui rosary around the prisoners' necks. For the three days
that the prisoners stayed at the *guardia*, *maestros* chanted the funeral liturgy.
Just about everyone in Vicam gathered at the *guardia*, as though it was a
fiesta. Everyone ate well, except Nicolasa and Luis, who got neither food
nor water.

The generals would not let anyone intercede on behalf of Nicolasa or
Luis, because they had committed a terrible crime. The generals would
not even let anyone talk to the prisoners, saying they would shoot anyone
who tried. Nicolasa's sister, Josefa More, and daughter, Clara Contreras,
cried and cried, but there was nothing they could do.

Early on the third day, Nicolasa and Luis were shot by six Yaqui
soldiers. I think it is too bad that Luis was killed, because he was just a
boy helping his mother. But Yaqui law is very hard. Nicolasa's daughter,
Clara, went to live with Josefa More.

# CHAPTER 6

# *A Candle in Heaven*

ONE DAY I WAS visiting friends in Barrio Pascua. First I stopped at my cousin Viviana's house. Then I started to walk along to Claudio Vacamea's house. Claudio had lived with Luisa Valencia since my aunt Camilda died; Luisa's first husband had died in Sasco. Mariana, Camilda's youngest daughter, now lived with Claudio and Luisa. I felt a pain in my neck as I walked along. When I got to Claudio's house I was much worse.

At the door Claudio said, "You look sick. Come and sit down." He brought a chair for me, but I could not sit still. I kept moving one way and another.

He said, "How do you feel now?"

"Much worse."

"You had better lie down on the bed."

I lay on his bed, and hour by hour I kept feeling worse. Different kinds of devils came, and they began to torment me. They pulled my hair and my nose, and they spit on me. They prodded me and pinched me.

In the evening Claudio said, "Can you eat something?"

"No," I said.

"How do you feel now?"

"Much worse."

"How can you get to your home?" he asked.

"I don't know."

"I will see if I can find a car to take you," he said. In a little while he returned with one of his friends who had a Ford car.

"My friend has a car, and he will take you home," he said.

I got in the car, and the man drove me to Barrio Libre, where my wife was living with her mother. When we got there, my wife came out and looked at me.

She said to the driver, "What is the matter with him? He must be drunk."

"No. He is sick," the driver said.

When I got out of the car I could not walk straight, but reeled one way and another like a drunk man. I went to my bed, and when I lay down I felt worse and worse. I could see all kinds of devils. Some of them threw something like a gas at me and it smelled like burning wool. That night my breath began to smell like burning wool, and it was awfully bad. My mouth and my nose smelled too.

I did not sleep any that night or the next day. The next night the devils built fires under me. Everywhere I would get, they would come and build a new fire under me. Still I could not sleep or eat. The next day I told my wife that I had to go to town.

She said, "How can you go to town looking like that? Your eyes are red and your teeth are dirty."

I took a mirror and looked at my teeth. They looked as if I had been eating dirt. I took a razor blade and scraped the dirt off and cleaned them very good. Later I looked in the mirror again, and they were as bad as ever. Then my wife said I became like a crazy person.

I was awfully tired, but I could not rest. I could not sit, or stand, or lie down, because whatever I did the devils came and built fires under me. I tried walking round and round, but they would never give me a minute's peace. But I was not thinking yet. I had not remembered Jesus Christ. The only thing I wanted was to take a rest, but I could not. Every moment I saw many different things. Some women came to see me and brought ribbons of many colors, which they put across my chest and over my heart, but I did not like the ribbons and I threw them off.

They said, "He does not like what we do for him. We came to help him with these blessed ribbons, but he will not let us. We had better leave him alone." They went away, and when they did I knew that it was the Virgin Mary and the other Marys.

When they were gone, the candle began to drip in my face. It dripped on my nose and in my mouth, and it never stopped. It was the fifth night

I had not slept, and the candle kept dripping, drop by drop by drop, and I thought I could not stand it for another minute.

Three old devils came in, and one of them put a table in front of me and sat down on the other side. "I am your king," he said.

I looked him up and down, and then I looked at the other two. One of the two said, "When do we take him?"

"Tomorrow," said the old devil across the table. "This is the last day for him." All the devils laughed.

Then a man came to help me. He wore a red dress that came to his knees and he carried a long sword. When the devils saw him they ran away. They were afraid of the man with the sword. But in a little while he left, and the devils came back to taunt me again.

Another thing happened. My spirit went away from my body. My spirit went to a place under the ground where the people were all very old and ugly.

The old people told me, "You have no hope for getting back to your relatives. Look at your body over there."

I turned around and looked. There was my body. It was red hot, like a stove. I tried to get back in my body, but I could not. Then I saw my body in a long white burial sheet.

I said to the ugly people, "What has happened to me?"

They said, "Now you have to go all over, from place to place, everywhere you have been before, and pick up all of your spit and all of your sweat."

I started away, going everywhere I had worked before, everywhere I had walked, and everywhere I had ridden. In my winding sheet I went everywhere in California, in Arizona, in Sonora, on trains, on buses, in railroad stations.

It was early in the morning of the sixth day. My wife told me later I was like a crazy person. Medicine men and medicine women came and rubbed medicine on my eyes to make me sleep. But nothing would make me sleep.

I said to my wife, "I am very tired. How can I take a little rest? The candle drip is still falling on my face. Do you see the drip on my face?"

She said, "There is nothing on your face."

Two devils came to me. "We have come to throw you down the cliff," they said. I threw my shoes at the devils, and they ran away.

My wife said, "What is the matter with you? Why do you throw your shoes away?"

I said, "Two devils came after me to throw me down that cliff. See that cliff over there?"

She said, "There is nothing. There are no devils and no cliff."

Through the sixth day and into the sixth night I was in torment. I was awfully tired, but the devils would not let me rest. Every way I turned, there they were. They would spit in my face, and I would spit on them too.

Toward morning of the sixth night I began thinking. Everything that had happened in my whole life became clear. I remembered how my grandmother María and the *fariseos* always talked about Jesus Christ. I never believed what they said. They said that Jesus Christ was our father and that he loved all people, young and old.

Then I remembered all the things I had done against Jesus Christ. Every year during Lent, the *fariseos* carried Jesus Christ from house to house taking up the collection for the Fiesta de Gloria and I would not give them a cent. When I saw the masked men coming I would lock my door or my gate and go away. That I did all the time. I never gave anything.

Now I remembered that my grandmother said that Jesus Christ could cure any person who was awfully sick or who had been hurt. Any person who would promise to be a masked man, or a *fariseo*, Jesus Christ would cure. Why? Each one of us has a candle when he is born in the world. Any person who has a short candle has not long to live. Anyone with a tall candle will live a long time. I remembered all that my grandmother María said about the candles and Jesus Christ.

I said to Jesus Christ, "Forgive me for what I have done. I did not know what I was doing. If you will give me rest and peace, and a little more time to live, I will be a *fariseo*, and I will wear the mask for you to the last day I live."

When I had finished my words to Jesus Christ, I saw a little white fence around me, and there were two children, one on either side of me. Each had a staff about four feet long in their right hand. My hands were clasped across my chest like a dead person. I moved my head from side to side, looking for the devils, but I did not see any. They were all gone, and the candle drip had stopped falling on my face.

Two old men with long white whiskers and dressed in white robes came and stood at my feet. They looked at me, and one said, "Is this the man who is going to wear the mask for Jesus Christ?"

The other said, "Yes, he is the one."

The first said, "You had better take him up."

The bed on which I lay and the little white fence started to go up with me and the two children. As we passed along, some women came to me with food on a plate. But I did not take the food, and they were angry with me and threw away the plate. As we went along we met many people, and they stopped and followed us, looking at me over the little white fence.

We kept going up very fast, to Glory, and we went through a great pine forest. We went faster and faster, and I was very scared, and I began to sweat. We came out of the pine forest and there were rows and rows of lighted candles, and I could hear people singing, like in church. We came near the gates of Glory, and I could hear the big bells ringing.

The little children on either side of me were like statues, holding their sticks. They never moved. I still had my hands clasped when I arrived at the gates of Glory. An old man with white whiskers and a white robe was standing in front of the gate with a big key in his hand. Thousands of people were waiting outside the gates.

I heard someone say, "These are the people who died in accidents. Their candles have not burned out yet, and they are waiting for their time to go through the gates."

When we went through they wanted to go with us, but the old man pushed them back. As we passed the gates, I saw two devils, one standing on either side. I kept my eyes on them, but they did not want to look at me.

Soon we arrived at a beautiful church, big and white, and glorious, with two tall white towers. The little white fence stopped in front of the church, and Jesus Christ came out of the door and stood in front of the church between the two towers. A multitude of people were around him.

He said, "This is the man who is going to wear the mask for me."

Everybody looked at me. Jesus Christ blessed me with his hand where I lay on the bed.

"Come and follow me," he said.

I got up and looked down at the ground. I wanted to see what it was like. I walked to where Jesus Christ was standing, and the two children followed me. Jesus Christ looked at them and said, "Now, my little angels, you had better take a rest," and he blessed them. The little angels then went in the church, and I never saw them again.

"Now I will show you what it is like if you truly follow me," he said.

He started around the church, to the left, and I walked behind him. Suddenly the elements seemed to break loose. We were in a great storm, lightning, thunder, wind, black threatening clouds. The wind was blowing sand, rocks, timbers, and scraps of metal. The air was filled with them, but nothing hit us.

"We will now see the war," he said.

We walked into the war. A great battle was on, explosions, smoke, smells like gas. Bullets and pieces of steel were whining and whistling. Shots and shells were coming right at me, but not a thing touched me. I was scared, but I kept my hands folded and followed right behind Jesus Christ.

The war was calm, and Jesus Christ said, "Now we will go this way."

We came to thousands and thousands of candles. As we passed along he stopped and said, "This is your candle. It is very tall, and it is burning still." There were many candles which had burned down to the ground. "Do you see those?" he asked. "They are for persons living on earth. Their time is up."

Then he took me to a wonderful place of clear streams and flowers and clouds. There were people there, millions of them, dressed in white, all of them very clean. They were happy, and they talked to me, but I could not understand what they were saying. I did not see a single house where they were living. Jesus Christ said to me, "These are the good people."

Next he took me to another place which was hot and sultry. It was a plain, from which the heat waves rose like mirages, and it was covered with cactus and thorns. The plants were parched and crisp. It looked as if they had not had a good rain there in many years. There were many millions of people there, and they were ugly and distorted. Some had long tails, some had heads like roosters, some had horns like a bull, and some had feet like birds. Some were walking round and round, some were hopping like frogs, and some were crawling on the ground. Most of them were dirty and sweaty. Some were bleary-eyed, and some smelled like a pulque vat.

Jesus Christ said, "These are the condemned people. They are here of their own choice. They are here just what they made of themselves on the earth."

We went back to the church, and he said, "Remember that no bad luck can come to anyone who has faith in me. I will give you a sign. When thunder and lightning come dangerously close, make this sign and they will go away."

The sign he gave me was to cross the index finger and thumb of each hand. I have used the sign many times since then. When a storm would catch me out in the open and the thunder and lightning were very bad, I would make the sign, and the storm would go away.

We went into the church, and it was as beautiful inside as it was outside. There were many people there. I saw my father. He went to the priest and said, "You had better baptize my son again." He did not come to me or speak to me. Instead, he went away.

Next a man had me sit at a table. He took all the bones out of my body and laid them on the table. Then he took out all my teeth and laid them on the table. I was there in my dead, red-hot body. He took out my heart and told a bird to fly with my heart three times across a lake. The bird returned and gave the man my heart. After this the man put all my bones, my teeth, and my heart back in my body.

Jesus Christ called two angels to him and said, "Now you had better take him down to the earth."

The angels were young and tall and very clean. They took me to my bed in the little white fence. I lay down on my bed, and we started down through the pine forest, the clouds, and the blue sky. We did not go fast, but slow like an elevator. The little white fence touched the ground, and the angels went away.

I wondered how I was going to get back inside my body that was lying there like dead, still red hot. It was hard to do, but I managed to do it. I opened my eyes, but I could not see very well. It seemed as if the room was full of smoke. Jesus Christ appeared to me again and told me to get up and walk. I took one step and fell on my hands and knees, and Jesus Christ said, "This is the way you will come to me." It was another promise of long life. I looked around, and there were many people in the room. Some were sitting up, and some were sleeping on the floor. My wife was sleeping on the bed by me, and I woke her up.

"How long have I been on this bed?" I thought months had gone by.

"About two hours," she said.

"What time is it?" I asked.

"About three o'clock in the morning," she said.

I was still not sure where I was. I saw a pile of valises against the wall and decided to see if they were real. I got out of bed and started toward them, but my vision was blurred and my head swam, and I fell on the floor. Everyone awoke and looked at me as if they had seen a dead person come to life.

Charla, my mother-in-law, said, "He must be worse."

Another woman said, "I do not think he will last until morning."

"She does not know about the candle," I thought. I said to my wife, "I would like some water."

She brought me a cup of water and I drank it. Then I went to sleep, the first sleep I had had in a hundred and thirty hours. It was almost noon when I woke up.

My wife said, "How do you feel?"

"Much better, and I am hungry," I said.

My wife ran to her mother and told her that I felt better and that I
was hungry. Pretty soon she brought me some breakfast, and I ate it all.
Then I walked to the door and looked out. It looked like a new world, but
I still could not see very good. I closed the door and went back to my bed.
Soon I was asleep, and I did not wake up until about sundown, and I
was hungry again. They brought me food, and when I had eaten it I
felt very good. I could see clearly, and my head did not swim.

After supper I explained to the people what had happened to me when
I went to Glory. I told them everything I have related here, and many
other things which I saw in Glory and have since forgotten. When I had
finished, I said, "Now I have to be a *fariseo* and wear the mask for Jesus
Christ every year during Lent."

Manuel Salinas said, "That is good. We will all be glad to see you
wear the mask."

Everyone believed that I went to Glory and that I saw Jesus Christ.
They asked me many questions, and we talked about it until midnight.

I went to sleep at once when I went to bed. Soon I was having a
beautiful dream. Angels were around me instead of devils, and all was
calm and serene. I slept late the next morning and when I got up I told
Charla about my dream and the angels.

She said, "That is a sign of good luck. You will live a long time."

After that I did not dream any more, and I was happy because I had
found peace of mind. Now I knew that the chastisement of God is worse
than any physical pain or sickness. I knew that I could perform no more
tricks, or play cards for money, or drink mescal, or act with the consideration of an animal.

In February, 1924, I made my first *fariseo* mask. I bought a fresh goat
hide from a Mexican, and when I had fleshed, stretched, and dried it in
the sun, I made it into a sacklike shape, with the hair out. It fitted over
my head and came down to my shoulders. With scraps of the hide I cut
and sewed on a big, long nose and a pair of large, floppy ears. I cut little
holes for the eyes and a hole for the nose to breathe. I made a wide mouth,
and outlined the big teeth with black paint. The ears I painted white on
the inside and put red flowers in the centers. The red painted lips made
the mask look happy. I shaved the hair from the skin on the face, but left
the long hairs on the chin to look like whiskers and beside the eyes to look
like long sideburns.

A new *fariseo* must have one *padrino* who is a *fariseo* and one *madrina* who
is a *cantora*. Javier Cardenas was my *fariseo padrino* and Vincela Fernández

was my *cantora madrina*. These two put rosaries around my neck but did not have to run around the church with me when the *maestro* said "Gloria Patria HALLELUJAH" on the Saturday of Glory. My other *padrinos* had to do that. My first *padrino* who ran with me in 1924 was Martín Riesgo; Chepa Armenta was my *madrina*.

The first time I wore the mask I had a bad time. I could hardly see at all. I kept the Yaqui rosary in my mouth and prayed inside the mask. My teeth hurt every time I wore the mask for three years; after that it was not so bad. I wore the mask whenever I was in a Yaqui village at Easter from 1924 to 1948. Then I had so much trouble breathing inside the mask that the captain made me a *cabo* (corporal) in the Soldiers of Rome, and I danced without a mask for two more years, 1949 and 1950. Every Easter from 1951 to the present I've been in Texas and so I have not been able to dance as a *fariseo*. I will dance as a *fariseo* again. Every December when I am in Tucson, I buy three big candles and leave them with my granddaughter Manuela (my son Salvador's oldest daughter). She takes the candles to the church on Good Friday and lights them for me.

# CHAPTER 7

# *Loreta Leaves*

WHEN THE EASTER FIESTA was finished, my wife and I went to Scottsdale to work for the Water Users Company. We left little Salvador with his grandmother Charla because he wanted his grandmother so much. We only took our six-year-old Marcelina with us. Sometimes I walked from Guadalupe to Tucson and back.

As I was walking alone from Tucson to Guadalupe one night, I laid down on my stomach at a canal to get a drink; a wooden bridge was nearby. A noise like someone stomping on the bridge sounded close to my head. Then some dirt was thrown on the bridge. I drank from my hand, and the noise came again. By then I knew it was a ghost, so I left in a hurry.

That same year, 1924, Pedro Alvarez was living with us in Guadalupe. Hearing there were jobs with the railroad crew at Maricopa, we decided to walk all night and get to Maricopa in time to go to work. In the evening we started walking along the tracks. The moonlight was bright. We heard a terrible crying near some tall bushes about eleven o'clock. Pedro said the cries belonged to a woman who had been killed near this place. We walked on, and got to Maricopa about daylight. The *mayordomo* said we could work, and so we stayed a few weeks.

Late one night in the ramada when Pedro Alvarez and I were talking, he offered to show me how to use the magic cigarette. Pedro was a witch; his father, Aneseto Alvarez, had been a witch. Only a witch can use magic cigarettes. They are made from a strong native tobacco called *hiacbibam* or *macucho*. The tobacco is wrapped in a cornhusk; the cigarette is about as big around as a little finger, and some are six inches long. The witch makes a speech to God, the *Justo juez*, and a saint, tells the cigarette where to go, and then sucks on the lighted cigarette three times. It sort of explodes and goes off to wherever it is supposed to go. Pedro sent it a few miles away. In about a half hour we saw a faint light far away, then another light closer, finally a third light nearby, and the cigarette came back. It whispered in Pedro's ear, about as loud as a mosquito buzzing. That night all it said was that the place to which it had been sent was dark and there was nothing to be seen.

Whenever someone uses the magical cigarettes, they have to be sure to stay awake, for if the cigarette finds its "driver" asleep, it will hit him on the side of the head and he might die. Some witches can kill people by having the magic cigarette hit the person on the nape of the neck. This was the way my father was bewitched. It is also the way Lino Sopomea was killed in 1923, or so I was told. They say Lino played cards all night with a lot of Papagos, winning all their money, leaving them cleaned out. One of those Papagos was a witch and hit Lino with his magic cigarette. The next morning Lino was dead. I decided that I did not want to learn how to control magic cigarettes, but I watched Pedro send off the magical cigarettes many nights.

Pedro told me about the way tobacco came to be. Long ago there was an ugly woman. She was the ugliest woman in the world. No one loved her. Finally she went to a wise man (there were lots of wise men in the old days) and asked what she could do to make someone like her. He told her that he could turn her into tobacco and then everyone would like her, and every time a man smoked a tobacco cigarette, he would caress her. So she said she wanted to be made into tobacco, and she was.

Pedro Alvarez knew all sorts of magic. He kept a *chone*, which is a scalp or a doll to which the scalp is attached. *Chones* can go through the air wherever they are sent; troops of Yaqui soldiers in the Sierra liked to have someone along with a *chone* because the *chone* would go ahead and tell when they were in danger. It could paralyze Mexican troops. *Chones* can be used by witches for bad reasons, or they can be used by people for good reasons. Some people use *chones* as guides on dark nights.

When the person using the *chone* is bad, they can make the *chone* kill a person by wrapping the scalp hair around their neck and strangling them. Everyone was afraid of *chones* sent out by a witch. Whenever people hear a whispering noise in a house or a ramada, everyone starts looking for a *chone*. They grab it, throw ashes and ground chili on it, and throw it out. This scares the *chone* and it goes home to the witch who sent it. It will not return again.

While I was working in Guadalupe for the Water Users, I ordered a book for $2.98 called *El oculto talisman* (The Secret or Hidden Talisman) from San Antonio, Texas. At this time I did not believe in God or the saints, but I did believe in *El oculto talisman*. This little blue book had a pleasant odor. It told how to be a good robber, how to win at cards, how to steal money, how *not* to get caught, and many useful things. The *oraciones* were much shorter and easier to say than those in *El justo juez*. Most of the recitations were no longer than an Our Father.

I would lay on my cot and read the *oraciones* for flying. My body stayed on the cot, but I could fly or flit from place to place, scaring people. When they chased me, I would disappear and then reappear behind them.

The *mayordomo* at the Water Users was a Cuban named Blacky. Several of the men went to him and said that a *bulto* was appearing every night. Blacky organized a search that night. All the men carried rifles and looked all night for the *bulto*. I helped. It was very funny that I was helping look for myself. The next night I started scaring people again. I never did hurt anyone. I just had fun, throwing rocks on tin roofs, flying like a bird, and scaring people. I was like the wind or a shadow.

The little book told how to become a good thief, or rather, how to find out if you would be a good one. Take a black cat, cook it whole and alive in a large *olla*. When the flesh has cooked off the bones, stand in front of a mirror and bite each bone. If you can see yourself, you will not be a good thief. If you are invisible, you can enter banks and houses and steal whatever you want.

To be a good cowboy, catch a hummingbird at a flower, bite its head off, and put the feathers in a little bag which you always wear under your clothing. Once in Phoenix, Jaime Cernas won the rodeo. He was wearing a bag containing bright-colored feathers, so I guess he knew about *El oculto talisman* too. One day I caught a hummingbird, but I could not bring myself to bite its head off, so I just turned it loose. I did not really want to be a good cowboy anyway.

A way to see in the dark is to take a bat, bite its head off, and put the bat's blood on your eyelids. *El oculto talisman* told me many things, and I believed in its power. I never did any harm with it. I just had some fun.

After I had been working around Guadalupe for a few months, I got a letter from my sister Antonia at Tucson. Her husband, Nacho Molino Valencia, had died and she could not make a living for the children. She wanted me to come and take them to Scottsdale.

I said to my wife, "Where can I find the money to bring them?"

"That will be easy because you have so many relatives here. Anyone can lend fifteen dollars."

I started out to borrow the money, but the answer was "We are sorry, but we have no money." I went to four families, and it was always the same.

The next Saturday I told my boss about my sister, and I said, "I need fifteen dollars; can you loan the money to me?" The next morning he came to our house and brought the money. We rented a car and got to Tucson by noon. Within an hour we had started back, with my sister, her four children, and their few belongings.

We had a hard time for several months. My wages were two dollars a day, and at that season of the year there was no work for the rest of the family. Our food all that summer was beans, tortillas, and coffee without sugar.

When cotton picking started, I quit the Water Users, and we moved to Guadalupe Village and began picking cotton nearby. I could pick only 85 pounds a day, but my wife could pick 110; our little Marcelina was good for 50. My sister and her children could pick 400 pounds between them. With all of us working we began to live better and save a little money. Each Saturday, Loreta and Antonia went to Phoenix for provisions. My sister had not bought anything for almost a year and her children needed clothes.

Her husband had been sick for six months before he died. One night when he was drunk, he had a fight with three Yaquis at Barrio Pascua. The Yaquis whipped him with a bicycle chain all over the body, and put out one of his eyes. He was badly hurt. My sister wanted to call the sheriff, but he would not let her.

He said, "When I get well I will pay each one back."

But he never got well. Day by day he got worse. He had a big wagon, four mules, and a cow, but he had to sell everything. The medicine man tried to cure him, but did no good. Every day he talked about getting well so he could pay back the three Yaquis. He wanted so much to live for that purpose. When he died, all the money was gone.

I always liked my brother-in-law. When he married my sister, he taught me how to read and write Spanish. Until then I spoke Spanish, but could not read and write it. At school in Tucson and Sasco I had learned to read and write English, but could speak it very little. Yaqui was the language I learned first because we had always spoken Yaqui at home, but I learned Spanish almost as soon as Yaqui. My mother and father both spoke Spanish, although my grandfather Abelardo and my grandmother María learned to speak very little. My brother-in-law knew how to read and write Spanish very well. He was a good teacher, because he taught me how to write in three months.

We picked cotton near Phoenix until Christmas, 1924, when we went to Tucson. We had a happy Christmas in our little house in Pascua Village.

During 1924 a sad thing happened in Pascua Village. Three sisters committed suicide. The first was Linda Valencia, only fourteen years old at the time. She boiled several coins in a cup of water, and when it cooled she drank it. When anyone drinks "money water" it causes them to stop eating and they get thin and turn a darker color, dying within two months. My grandmother often told me how dangerous "money water" was. After Linda died, Yolanda and Consuela committed suicide the same way. I do not know why they did it; probably just because they were sad. These girls were daughters of Tirbusio Valencia, the chief of the *matachines* in Pascua that year.

Men don't commit suicide with "money water." They hang themselves in the middle of the night in front of their house, throw themselves in the river or under a train, shoot themselves, or, like Joaquín Perez in Hermosillo, burn themselves up. Many Yaquis commit suicide.

After New Year's, I found a job in the wood yard in Tucson, and my sister and her oldest daughter got jobs doing housework. I worked three months and quit, because Lent of 1925 had already started and I had to make a new *fariseo* mask for Holy Week. Wearing the mask and keeping the rosary between my teeth made me very sick with my eyes and my mouth again.

The Yaquis say that if a *fariseo*'s *madrina* or *padrino* falls down in front of or inside the church while running with their *'hijado* (ceremonial godchild) they will not live to see another Easter. I know this is true. It has happened to five of my *fariseo* godparents. They fell down and died before the following Easter. The first time it happened was in 1925, when Chepa Armenta fell down as we ran in the church, and she died a few months later. I have seen many Yaquis who fell down while running in the Fiesta de Gloria die before the year was over. White people cannot believe this is so, but it is a sign from God.

After the Easter dances, I rode a freight train to California and got a job with the extra gang of the Southern Pacific. I was sent to Mount Shasta, where I stayed a month. Then I went to San Francisco, where I worked until the grape picking began. I could make more money picking grapes, although I was not nearly as fast as the other workers. I could pick two hundred planks or boxes a day. Others could pick three or four hundred planks.

When the grapes were gone, I and fourteen other Mexicans and Yaquis took a contract to gather 160 acres of sweet corn. One of the men cooked and the others worked in the field. When we finished, we divided up the leftover provisions. I got one box of matches, as that was all I needed. Some of the other men got food because they had their families nearby.

In September I started back to Tucson. At Bakersfield, I got in an empty boxcar at midnight and found about fifteen hoboes in there. I was afraid to go to sleep, because I had nearly four hundred dollars with me. But they were all good people. They only asked me for smoking tobacco.

My wife and children were very glad to see me because I brought home money. I gave it to them and went to sleep, as I had slept very little for three days and nights. They went off to town to buy some things.

When I got home, everyone was talking about poor Micaela Naponohi, the widow of Juan Torreon, who helped pay the Papago to kill my father. Juan had died of pneumonia. Afterwards a Mayo asked Micaela to go live with him. When she refused, he got a witch to give her the stomach of a horse and she ate herself to death. She stayed so hungry that she had to carry a sack of food with her everywhere she went. Soon she died.

I started working for the gas company, and would get home about five-thirty in the afternoon. After a few days I began to notice that only Marcelina, who was seven years old, was there. Salvador spent most of the time with his grandmother in Barrio Libre. My wife would not get home until late in the evening.

One day I said to Marcelina, "Does your mother always stay away until late?"

"Yes. Always."

"When does she leave?"

"Early in the morning, right after you leave."

"How long has she been staying away?" I said.

"A long time."

"Do you get scared staying here by yourself?" I asked.

"I did at first, but I got used to it."

I got to thinking about what my wife did every day. The next Saturday night I said to her, "Where have you been all day?"

She said, "To see my mother. She is not well, and I go to help her with the work."

The next morning, which was Sunday, I went to see Charla. After we talked a while, I said, "Was my wife here with you yesterday all day long?"

"Oh, no. I did not see her yesterday. She did not come here at all."

"That is funny. She was gone all day, and when she got home she said she had been here helping you all day."

"She was just trying to make a joke with you, I think."

When my wife got home Sunday night I said, "I went to your mother today and I asked her if she had seen you on Saturday, and she said you had not been there at all." I did not know who to believe, my wife or my mother-in-law.

A few nights later I was passing a neighbor's house after dark, and I heard my name mentioned by people talking in the house. I stopped to listen. I heard a woman say, "That Rosalio really has a fast wife. Every day she goes out and Rosalio never says a word. I guess it is all right with him."

My blood boiled and it was hard for me to breathe. For a little while I wanted to kill my wife. Then I got to thinking about the children, and by the time she got home I was not so mad. I said to her not a word, but that night I did not sleep, and I slept little for many nights.

A few days later Pedro Alvarez came to me and said, "Something has happened to you."

"No. Nothing has happened to me. Why do you say that?"

"Because I saw you in my dream. I know about your wife, and that you worry very much. For sixty dollars I will make an end of your fool wife." As a witch, Pedro could do things like that.

I said, "No. I cannot do that. Go away and leave me alone."

I realized that everybody knew about my wife. Still I could not decide what to do. If we broke up our home I did not know what to do about Marcelina. Salvador had already been taken over by Charla, but there was no place for Marcelina.

Several months went by, and the time came to make my mask for the Easter dances. I was very unhappy during the Fiesta de Gloria, and that was the last mask I ever made and wore in Pascua Village. My first *madrina* had died, and my *padrino*, Martín Riesgo, got me another *madrina* to put rosaries on me and run with me on Holy Saturday. Her name is Regina Suárez, and both Martín and Regina still live in Tucson.

After Easter I told my wife I was going to California. She seemed pleased, and said that she and the children would get along fine.

I left home in the spring of 1926 with five dollars; when I got to Sacramento, enough was left to buy a chance at the employment office. I got a job on the section of the Western Pacific Railroad. For two months I felt miserable. I slept from two to three hours at night, ate very little, was always tired, restless, and never wanted to be still. I gave up that job and went to Los Angeles. I could not get interested in the many wonderful things to see. I would go into a moving picture show and leave before it was over.

I moved on to San Juan Capistrano and took a job with Mr. Matson, who had a big orchard and a large family of seven children. The next morning we had a breakfast of hot cakes, eggs, bacon, and fruit. I was not hungry and ate very little. Mr. Matson noticed it and thought it was because I did not like American food.

"I guess you do not like our kind of food. If you would rather have Mexican cooking, we have a family of Mexicans here with whom you can take your meals. They are very fine people."

I said, "I like American food, but I will be glad to eat with the Mexican family."

He took me to the home of José Rivera. Señor Rivera's wife was named Juana; and his daughter, named Javiela, was twenty-two years old. They were glad to see me.

Señor Rivera said. "Where are you from?"

"From Tucson," I said.

Señora Rivera said, "Do you have a family?"

"I have two children. I lost my wife several months ago," I said.

"That is too bad. We are very sorry," Señora Rivera said.

I worked two months for Mr. Matson. He and his family and the Rivera family were good to me, and I liked them all. When I told them I was going to quit, Señor Rivera said, "Has something happened to you?"

I said, "No. Nothing has happened to me, but I am worried about my children and I must go back to Tucson to see how they are. I hope I can come back in two or three weeks."

Señora Rivera said, "Don't forget us, and write to us when you get to Tucson."

This was in 1926, the last year of open fighting between the Yaquis and the Mexicans. It was the last year in which Yaquis died in military action. One of those killed was Rosario Waibel, son of Josefa Waibel and the stepson of Pedro More. In 1921 the More family had returned to Vicam from Tucson, where they had been since Pedro, Josefa, and their family jumped the troop train in 1911. When the fighting broke out in 1926, the whole family went to the mountains; Pedro decided to come on to Arizona, leaving his family in the Sierra. While he was gone, Rosario was ambushed and killed by Mexicans.

Gilberto Cocomorachi was killed the same year, but not by Mexicans. The Sierra Yaquis mistakenly thought he was a *torocoyori* because he did not go to the Sierra. The man who killed Gilberto was my old friend Anastasio Urias, often referred to as Anastasio Loco. Anastasio belonged to the Urias family I had known in Hermosillo, when Anastasio used to peddle *tripas* and buckets of blood. By 1926 he was a captain of the Sierra Yaquis. He came down to the valley to steal provisions; he was stealing corn from Gilberto's field when Gilberto saw what he was doing. Anastasio shot him and escaped back to the Sierra, where he stayed for several years. He was made a colonel in the Mexican army, and eventually became one of the military paymasters for the Yaqui Zone. His mother, Chavela Macochine, died in Hermosillo about 1905. She belonged to Bacum pueblo; his father, Ramón Urias, was a Mexican from Hermosillo who rode with Pancho Villa, along with Valentín and Eusavio, his oldest sons.

All three of the Uriases who had been with Villa came to Tucson in 1917, and Ramón and Valentín soon died there of influenza. Eusavio went back to Vicam in 1923, and was in the Sierra with Anastasio in 1926, as was the youngest Urias brother, Gregorio. José and José María Urias came to Tucson in 1917 with their father. They stayed on. José is still living in Barrio Pascua with Isidora Valenzuela and José María still lives in Barrio Libre. After Anastasio came down from the Sierra, he started farming a lot of land in Bacum. He had many women. He married Maruja Kutam, and they had a son, Manuel. Both Anastasio and his son are said to be killers. Manuel is said to have killed many Mexican peddlers, bootleggers, and even bread men, just to get their money to buy mescal. My father always said that the Yaquis of Bacum pueblo were the worst assassins, and I believe it.

Nacha Sewa was in the Sierra with José María Mavis, the man her grandmother had lived with since Sasco, when a small unarmed group of Yaquis were captured at Misa, northwest of Vicam. From the time they were captured, the men were not allowed so much as a drink of water. Nacha fixed a cup of pinole for old José María and a soldier knocked it from her hand. The soldiers gave the captured men picks and shovels and had them dig a long trench. When it was finished, the sixteen men and boys were machine-gunned into their newly dug grave. The women and children were shipped to central Mexico and turned loose. The soldier who ordered this terrible act was the very ugly General Manso, who they say was an Indian from elsewhere in Mexico. Poor old José María Mavis was not a soldier, and was unable to use a gun. He was nothing but a farmer.

Nacha Sewa's brother Abato Sewa was killed that same year. He was at that time the secretary of Torim pueblo. He was trying to get to the Sierra when a detachment of soldiers cornered him in the big cave that you can see from Vicam (Matuecame cave) and shot him. Nacha's grandmother, old Lucrecia Sewa, was in the Sierra, but she was never captured.

Another place the Yaquis were slaughtered in 1926 was at the Cerro del Gallo, or Hill of the Rooster. Delores Ruiz, one of the men who paid the Papago witch to kill my father, and his wife, Juliana, were killed there, as was Pascuala Wivis. This Pascuala was about my age and I had known her in Hermosillo. Her parents were deported early and she grew up in a Mexican home till she was old enough to run away to Tucson in 1915. In 1917 she went with Eugenio Castillo. They returned to the Rio Yaqui in 1923 and died together at the Cerro del Gallo. Six children of Juan and Juana Valencia of Torim perished there also. Carlos Conemea, who once wanted to marry Viviana in Sasco, was killed at the Hill of the Rooster and his two brothers deported to Yucatán. Both Lola Kukut and her husband, José Kukut, died in this battle. Lola Kukut, the Señora of the Sierra, was as good a soldier as the men. She always carried a rifle and wore cartridge belts just like the men, and she had killed as many Mexicans as most Yaqui soldiers. As mentioned before, she and José came to Tucson in 1907 and again in 1912 for supplies, staying about three weeks in our house each time. My father thought she was a fine soldier. Many believe José Kukut is not dead but still walks in the Sierra because he made a pact with the Devil. I told Dr. Holden about Lola Kukut and she served as the model for Chepa in Dr. Holden's book *Hill of the Rooster*.

Because of these new Yaqui troubles in Sonora, hundreds of Yaquis fled to Tucson. They got jobs picking cotton or working on the railroad.

I arrived in Tucson in the late afternoon, going directly to our home in Pascua Village. Only Marcelina was there, and she was glad to see me. "Where is your mother?"

"She went to town this morning, and I don't know when she will get back."

About dark my wife came in. She was surprised to see me. "Oh, hello, when did you come?" she said.

"About an hour ago," I said. I saw that she was wearing a black dress. Yaqui women wear black only for mourning. "Why do you wear mourning? Has one of your relatives died?" I said to her.

"Oh, no. No one has died. Times have changed. Women can wear black at any time now." I did not answer. Not a word.

The next morning she said, "I am going to see my mother, and will get back before sundown." She went away.

After she had gone, my cousin Viviana came to see me and explained what my wife had been doing. She said, "You had better leave her alone. She is no good for you. She leaves little Marcelina alone all the time. She takes the money you send her and spends it with her friends. Do you know why she wears that mourning dress? Well, I'll tell you. She started wearing it when a friend's aunt died. You let her go. You are still young, and you can find another wife."

That night when my wife came home I was sitting at the table, and I had the cards in my hand. I laid the cards on the table and said, "The cards tell me everything." My wife kept her eye on the cards. She did not know anything about cards. Neither did I.

I said, "See here. The cards never tell a lie. This is the truth what the cards say. From now on you can wear the mourning dress all you like."

I was very angry with her. She did not answer, not a word. That night I did not sleep.

The next morning I had a pain in my left chest and my left arm. When I tried to walk I could hardly breathe. For two months I could scarcely walk across the room. Then I sent for Pedro Alvarez. He rubbed my chest over my heart.

"You have been thinking too much. That's what the matter is with your heart."

I gave him five dollars, but he did not do me any good. Then I sent for the Mexican doctor. He looked me over and said, "The heart is very bad. I am afraid you have tuberculosis, too. Eat only rice, without salt, and coffee."

He gave me a few dozen pills and charged me ten dollars. I took the pills every two hours, but nothing helped. The money I brought from California was gone. Antonia and Viviana brought me rice and coffee. My wife was never home in the daytime, and she never fixed me anything.

After three months I was a little stronger, and the pain was not so bad. One day I wrote to the Rivera family and told them I had not come back to California because I was sick. In a few days I received a letter from Javiela. She said, "We are all very sad that you have been sick. We are sending you ten dollars. In a few more days we will send some more."

The Rivera family started sending me fifteen dollars every two weeks. All this time my wife had money, but she never offered to help me or bring food to me. I never asked her where she got the money. She began staying away on Saturday night. She would leave Saturday morning and not come back until Sunday night. Sometimes Marcelina stayed with me, and sometimes with her grandmother.

Pretty soon my cousin Simón told me where my wife went on Saturday nights. She went to Manuel Salinas's house in Barrio Libre. My father-in-law, Manuel Salinas, was chief of the Arizona Yaquis, and his house was the week end headquarters for many of the Sierra Yaquis who were in Arizona during 1926. The Sierra Yaquis had money, and they bought ample supplies of mescal and whiskey. They would get drunk and dance and fight all Saturday afternoon, Saturday night, and Sunday. My wife liked very much to be there. Simón went there several times on Saturday night and he saw what was happening.

Early one morning one of my wife's friends came to see my wife. She said, "Good morning, Liowe." All the Yaquis called my wife Liowe, which means "wild hog" in English. "I came to invite you to my daughter's wedding next Sunday at our home. We all will have a good time."

My wife said, "I will be glad to come to your daughter's wedding."

On Saturday my wife stayed at home, but she left early Sunday morning and was gone all day. In the late afternoon she came back with three Yaqui girls. One of the girls said, "Let's go back to the fiesta tonight."

My wife said, "Good. Let us go back."

The girl said, "All right, we will come back for you later."

When the girls went away I said to my wife, "You spend all day making fiesta over there; why do you want to go back?"

She said, "Never mind. No one can stop me. I do what I want to do."

I said, "I do not want you to go back."

She said, "Why not? I am going back anyway."

I said, "We will see what you do."

I was very angry, and I became like a crazy man. I got up from the bed and locked the door, and went to a box where I kept my knife. I caught her hair and threw her down on the floor. Holding her down by the hair, I put the knife to her throat.

I said, "Now you tell me the truth, every fool thing you have been doing. If you do not tell the truth, this will be your last night."

"Please. Don't. You are crazy."

"Tell me!"

"Please leave me alone."

"Tell me the truth or I use this knife."

"I will tell you the truth right now. I am just having a little fun. You were gone so long in California that I got tired just staying at home."

Then I threw away the knife, and I caught her throat. "You make a fool of yourself, and you cause me to be sick many months."

I held tight onto her throat until she was limp like a rag, then I let go. In a little while she opened her eyes. Blood came out through her mouth. I brought her a cup of water. She threw the water on me and then threw the cup at me.

"Why don't you go ahead and kill me?" she screamed. I answered her not a word, and she did not speak to me again. Marcelina was asleep and did not know what happened.

I guess someone passed by and heard the big noise we made and told the neighbors. They came and tried to get in the door, but it was locked. They heard my wife say, "Why don't you go ahead and kill me?" They beat on the door and called to me, but I did not answer them. When things got quiet, they went away.

The next morning my wife left early, taking Marcelina with her. She went to a neighbor's house and watched our home all day. I did not cook any rice, because I did not want to eat that day. In the afternoon I went to the river and was gone about an hour.

When I got back everything had been moved out of our house except my clothes, one old blanket, and some rice thrown on the floor. My wife must have had a lot of people to help her, or she could not have carried everything away so quickly. My watch and my father's watch were gone. Everything.

The next day no one came to see me, not even my sister and my cousin. For several days no one came. The next Saturday night one of my wife's friends, Julian Tacruesco, and two of his cousins came to Pascua Village and got drunk. They walked up and down in front of my house and shouted insults at me. I was standing inside the door, and I was so angry I shook all over. I had my .38 revolver and five cartridges. I kept holding it in my hand and praying to Jesus Christ. "Help me so I will not kill this devil," I said.

The three drunks would go away, and then come back with new insults. I kept thinking, "If I kill him I will not be able to run away. I am too weak. I have been sick eight months, and weigh only 122 pounds, and I do not have any breath when I walk fast. If I kill him, I won't have a chance to get away. They will catch me and put me in prison." Finally I knew I had better not kill him.

About three o'clock in the morning, one of the cousins got so drunk he fell down in front of my house. The other cousin said, "We had better take him home." They got him up on his feet, and they all staggered off. I knew they would take him along the path by the irrigation ditch, and that Julian and the other cousin would probably come back the same way.

I put the .38 away, and got two rocks and a stick. Then I went to the irrigation ditch to wait for them. Pretty soon I heard them coming back. When they were about twenty feet away from me, they saw me and stopped.

"There is Rosalio," said the other cousin.

I ran at him and tried to hit him with the stick, but I missed and he ran away. Then I turned and threw a rock at Julian, but I missed with that too. I threw my last rock in a hurry; it hit him on the wrist and broke the bone. He kept on running, shouting, "I am coming back to get you, you son of a bitch."

He got some of his Mexican friends from elsewhere in Barrio Libre. Soon they were back throwing rocks at my door and shouting more insults. They beat on my door, but I had locked it. They tried to break it down. I got my .38 gun again and pointed it at the door, ready to shoot if anyone came in. Again I prayed to Jesus Christ. "Please help me so I do not kill anyone."

Simón Valenzuela heard the noise and came to my house. "Hey, what are you doing to this sick man?" Simón said to his brother-in-law.

Julian said, "Your cousin hurt me very bad. He broke a bone in my wrist."

My cousin said, "All right, what did you expect? Now get away from here, every one of you, before I knock your blocks off." Nobody wanted to fight with my cousin. He was big and strong. They all went away.

After that, very bad luck came to Julian. He lived with my wife for three years, then she quit him when he lost his job. The bone in his wrist never healed, and after my wife left him he died. After that, Loreta went with Lucio Reyes, after his first wife, Aurelia, died. Loreta and Lucio are still together. This Lucio Reyes is the son of old Jaime Reyes and a brother of Guillermo Reyes, both of whom went to the Sierra with my father in 1912.

The night of the big noise I did not sleep any. The next morning, which was Sunday, I decided to go see my mother-in-law, Charla. When I got there, they were all under the ramada.

"Good morning."

Nobody answered me. They were all very angry. No one would talk to me. My mother-in-law went in the house and lay down on her bed. I went inside to speak a few words with her.

"I have come here for my wife. I will take her back to help the children. I want to raise my children."

My mother-in-law said, "Leave her alone. She is better off without you, and don't worry about your children."

I repeated again what I had said.

She said, "You have nothing to arrange with me. You hear me. Now go. I don't want to hear another word, and I never want to see you again. I never want to hear your dirty words again. Leave and don't ever come back."

I said, "You hate me. All of you hate me. But I tell you that you are not going to be happy. You are going to regret what you do to me. Do you think there is no God to see what you do? Every word you say to me is going to bring you bad luck, every one of you. You will not forget what I say."

Manuel Salinas said, "If you wanted to keep your wife, why did you go away and leave her? Why didn't you take her to California with you? She had a right to look around when you stayed away so long." Then he quickly got his harp and started playing. The *pascolas* began dancing. I left. As I left they all laughed at me.

All the way home I prayed to Jesus Christ. When I got there, I was very tired because of the long walk. When I had rested, I cooked all the rice I had left. I did not have a cent left either. No one came to see me that day, not even my sister or my cousin. That night at midnight I went outside my house and prayed that Jesus Christ would take away all the bad people from the earth. I made this prayer every night for three nights.

The next morning I decided to see if any of the neighbors would invite me to eat. I went to the first neighbor, Juana León, and I said, "Good morning."

They said not a word, and did not look at me. Then I went to the next neighbor, Cenovio Bruno, and said, "Good morning." They said not a word, and pretended that I was not there. I stood in the door a few minutes and went to the third neighbor, Luisa and Claudio Vacamea, and said to them, "Good morning." They said "Good morning" very softly. They were sitting around the table, eating. I stood there a while but they did not ask me to eat with them. Then I went to the fourth house, where my *compadre*, Marcelina's godfather, Hilario Rodríguez, lived. "Good morning, *compadre*. Good morning, *comadre*." My brother Francisco Valenzuela was living with them, as he had since our father died.

"Good morning," they both said, and Locaria brought a chair for me. "Sit down, and how are you?" she said.

"About the same," I said.

"We are sorry your wife left, but do not worry about her," she said.

"I do not worry about her, but about the children."

"Well, I tell you one thing. You stay with us until you get well. I want to make some medicine that will help you. Tomorrow you will take a bath in the big tin tub, and I will put the medicine in the tub."

The next morning I took a bath with the medicine, and I took these baths each morning for three days. I began to feel better day by day. After a week I was strong enough to look for work.

I had good luck. I found a job in the plumber's shop. That day I did not go back to my *comadre*'s house to eat at noon, because it was too far to walk. When I went back in the evening, she was glad that I had a job. The next morning she prepared a lunch for me.

A few days later, my *comadre* said to me, "I saw someone from Barrio Libre today. They said your mother-in-law is very sick."

"Oh, is that so?"

"Yes. They are very worried about her."

I did not say another word.

Each day my *comadre* had news that Charla was worse. Then one evening my mother-in-law's brother, Eufemio Bacotmea, was waiting at Hilario Rodríguez's house when I got back from work. He said, "Oh, hello. How are you?"

"I am all right. What brings you here?"

"My sister sent me to see you. She is very sick. She wants you to come see her. She wants to arrange a few words with you."

"Is that so? She told me she never wants to speak to me again, or to see me. She said for me to never come back. Go and tell her I have not forgot what she told me. I will never go back."

He went away, but two days later he was back. "My sister is calling for you again. She is very sick, and she will not live very long if you do not come and talk with her. Will you come?"

"No. I have not changed my mind. I cannot see her again, not even at her funeral." He went away very sad.

When he was gone my *comadre* said, "Please, why do you not go see your mother-in-law? She has sent for you two times already. I do not know what she wants to arrange with you, but I think you better go."

I said, "I cannot go."

She did not say any more.

My mother-in-law died on Saturday morning, and the next morning they brought her to the Yaqui church at Pascua for the funeral ceremony. They all made a big noise in the church. I did not go to the funeral, but I watched from my *comadre*'s house, which was near the church, and I said to myself, "Jesus Christ is answering my prayers."

The next Sunday morning I was at my house when my wife came in.

She had a whole bunch of children with her because her mother left two young daughters, Lola Preciado and little Loreta Salinas; she had our two, Marcelina and Salvador, and all of them were with her.

She said, "Good morning. How are you?"

I said, "I am all right."

She started to cry.

I said, "Well, what brings you here?"

"Now I believe what you told me some weeks ago. You said I would have the chance to wear mourning all I wanted to."

"That is right, but it has only started. Now who do you think is to blame for this, you or me?"

She said, "I blame you. You tried to kill me, and you helped to kill my mother. You put the curse upon her, and you would not come when she sent for you. You did not even go to her funeral. I cannot forget that."

"So that is the way it is. And that is the way it will always be. Everybody knows what you are. Everybody knows that you didn't want to take care of your children. I do not want to hear another word from you. Now get out." I spit in her face.

"You dirty, yellow devil!" she said, and she ran from the house. The children all followed her.

That was the last time we had a great big noise together in our house. Every time I saw her in my dreams after that I did the same thing. I spit in her face.

CHAPTER **8**

# *Javiela and After*

I KEPT WORKING in the plumber's shop and buying the food for my *compadre* and *comadre*. One day I wrote to the Rivera family at San Juan Capistrano, telling them I was well again and working, but that I was making only two dollars a day and could not save any money. I told them as soon as I could I would pay them back.

In a few days a letter came from Javiela. She sent fifty dollars, which they hoped I would use for bus fare back to San Juan Capistrano. There was plenty of work there, she said.

I guess I made a big mistake. I told some of my friends about the fifty dollars, and said I intended to leave for California pretty soon. The next Saturday afternoon I bought provisions for my *comadre*. Then I went to my house, and soon two of my friends came by, Miguel Valencia (a Mayo) and Lucio Muñoz. They were riding up and down in a Ford car, drinking as they went.

"Hello, Rosa. We have come to see you, and we want to have a funny time with you because we know you have been very sad. Now you are not to worry about a thing. Here, take a drink. This will make you very happy."

"I should say so," I said, and I took a big gulp of the wine. Then we all kept drinking, and soon the gallon jug was empty.

"Let us go buy more wine," I said.

We got in the car and drove to find a bootlegger. From him we bought

111

two more gallons. I paid for it. Then we started riding up and down. We met Juan Sasueta and picked him up. This was the Juan who had been married to my cousin Carmen. Later we passed the pool hall and saw Pablo Ronquillo, son of my father's old friend Juan Buanamea Ronquillo. He got in the car. We kept riding until the gasoline ran out. We pushed the Ford to a station, and I paid to have the tank filled. Then we met my brother Francisco Valenzuela and he joined us. The six of us rode up and down all night and all day Sunday. The wine and the gas would run out about the same time, and we would go buy more wine and more gas. I paid for everything because I was feeling very rich.

Sunday night I went home without a cent. The next morning I woke up very sick in my head. I was sad, too, when I discovered I had spent all my money. I had not even bought a pair of socks. The only good thought was that I had already bought the food for my *comadre*.

I got to thinking. Now I could not go to California until I made some more money. I could not even go to work that day at the plumber's shop because of my head. My condition was caused by the wine. Whiskey and wine have always been poison for me, making me lose my reason. I thought and thought, and then I made a vow to Jesus Christ that I would never drink again. Ever since I have never liked the taste of whiskey or wine or anything of that kind, and I have never had another drink.

On Tuesday morning my head was clear and I was hungry again. After I had eaten at my *comadre*'s, I went home and wrote a letter to my wife: "Tomorrow morning I go away from this village where we have been unhappy and where you spit on me and I spit on you. I hope I never see you again. You are free now. You can do anything you like from now on."

I took the letter and walked to Manuel Salinas's in Barrio Libre. When I arrived only one person was there, Jesús Lopez Salinas, the wife of Micky Salinas. She had always been good to me and had never talked against me.

I said, "Good morning."

"Good morning, how are you?"

"I am very well."

"What brings you here?"

I said, "I only came by to see you for the last time."

"Do not say that. Has something happened to you?"

"Nothing has happened to me. I came to say I am going away to-morrow to California."

She was really sad. Then Marcelina came home from school to eat her lunch, and she was glad to see me. I said to her, "I have come to tell you I am going away to California for a long time. I am sorry to leave you here, and I hope you will not forget me. If you ever need me, or need some money, write to me. My sister in Pascua will know where I am and will have my address. I have a letter for your mother. You can give it to her."

She took the letter and put it in her valise. I told her and Jesús good-by. Marcelina kept her eyes on me and looked very sad. I did not see Salvador, and it was just as well, because he did not like me. I did not see Marcelina again for nineteen years. Then she came to the Rio Yaqui. By then she was married and had three little girls. I never saw Jesús again, as she died the next year.

I left Pascua Village August 6, 1926, with a dollar and a half in my pocket, going to live with Simón Hernández in Scottsdale in order to work for the Water Users Association.

One day my boss man said to me, "Did you know the Yaqui chief in Tucson? His name was Manuel Salinas."

"Yes, I know him."

He said, "I read in the newspaper that he was killed yesterday. He was crossing Meyer Street in Tucson and a car hit him."

I did not tell the boss man that Manuel Salinas was my father-in-law.

My prayer was still being answered. One by one the bad people died. I found out later the people in Pascua thought I was a good witch because my enemies in Tucson died, but I was not a witch. I only believed in Jesus Christ, who answered my prayers.

At Easter I decided to dance in Guadalupe because I could not bring myself to return to Tucson, where I had been so unhappy. Whereas fourteen masked *fariseos* had been dancing in Tucson, there were seventeen of us in Guadalupe. My *padrino*'s name was Adolfo Bernal and my *madrina* was Micaela Feliz. On Holy Saturday we were running very fast. One fell down on one side and one on the other side, inside the church. I could not stop, but kept running to the altar. A few seconds later they came and knelt by me to make the sign of the cross on my front. They were very pale, like ghosts, because they knew what it meant. He died in June and she died in September.

It was about this time that my sister Antonia remarried. Perfecto Valencia Wahuechia had wanted to marry her, but she did not like him very much. He bought a little Chevrolet car, and then she liked him better. They were married in 1927. Wahuechia is a nickname given to this Valencia family meaning "he who plants by the side of the river," a reference to a lazy man's way of farming without clearing land. Perfecto was a relative of Juana Tacruesco Valencia Wahuechia, the first wife of my cousin Simón Valenzuela. I was glad that Antonia had someone to support her. Now she would not go hungry.

After Easter, 1927, I wrote to the Rivera family in San Juan Capistrano that I could not come to California until I earned some more money. In a few days I received a letter from Javiela enclosing twenty dollars and a note saying, "This is for your fare on the train or bus."

I left the Water Users company the next day and went to Phoenix. I found out the fare would be twelve dollars, and I decided to ride the freight train. I got to Los Angeles without spending a cent, and went to San Juan Capistrano by bus.

Everybody was glad to see me. They asked me many questions, and I answered them the best I could. They wanted to know about the children, but they never mentioned my wife. I started working in Mr. Matson's orchard. Javiela and I worked together.

I said to her on the first day, "I will have to save all my money for a long time."

She said, "Why will you have to save?"

"So I can pay back all the money you have loaned me."

"We did not loan you the money. We sent it because you needed it and we wanted to help you. We never expected you to pay it back."

I said, "I thank you and your family, but I must pay the money back."

Three months later Javiela and I were married by a judge, in his office. Only two other people were there, and they were the witnesses. Señor Rivera said it would be best not to invite all the neighbors to the wedding, because we would have to spend a lot of money.

The first night of our marriage I had a dream early in the morning. I thought that Javiela, dressed in white, got on a ship and sailed away toward the west, leaving me on the shore. I woke up very frightened, because this meant bad luck for me and my wife. It was a bad sign, and I was worried. Every time I have had this dream about someone, they died. I did not tell my wife about the dream.

I dreamed about her every two or three weeks, and every time she was leaving me. I was always worried and sad, because my dreams never lie. My wife noticed that I was worried. She said, "Why are you sad? Are we not very happy?"

"Yes, we are very happy. I have never before been so happy. I guess I keep thinking about the children." I did not tell her it was the dream that kept me worried always.

I worked in the orchard for a long time and Mr. Matson paid me four dollars a day. One day I said to Javiela, "I think I have to do one thing. I know a man in Oakland. I want to write him for a job. We can't save any money here."

"That is a good idea. You better write him right now."

I wrote to Nicolay Palayut, a Greek foreman in the Sherwin Williams paint factory. In a few days I received a letter from him. He said he had all the help he could use, but if I would come he would lay off a man and hire me. I wrote that I would be there the next Sunday morning, and would meet him at the electric railroad station in Sacramento at ten o'clock. He had said he would meet me there and take me to his place.

We traveled to Sacramento by bus, and went to the electric railroad station to wait. I saw him getting off the car, and in a little while he came in. He saw me and came to me.

"Hello, Valenzuela, you are here already."

"Yes, sir. I brought my wife. Her name is Javiela."

He said, "Oh, is that so? Why didn't you tell me before? I did not know that you are married."

He was glad to see us and asked about our trip. He said he would leave for Oakland at one-thirty, and he would meet us at the station at that time.

Mr. Palayut took us to his house in Oakland. He did not have a wife, only a cook. He put us in a little house near his home. The company had many little houses for the workers.

The next morning I started to work in the shipping department pushing hand trucks and loading boxcars with boxes of paint. The pay was $4.06 a day for eight hours, and extra pay for overtime and Sundays. I put in two to four hours of overtime every day and worked nearly every Sunday. So my wages were much more than I made at San Juan Capistrano.

The first Sunday I did not work; we went across the bay to San Francisco. My wife liked the city very much, everything except the smell of fish, which made her head ache.

Javiela never felt well in Oakland. After we had been there a year, she got terribly thin and her face became very pale. She could hardly eat. Day by day she got a little worse. Finally she had to lie down most of the day and she was always coughing. I was very worried about her and kept having the bad dreams.

One day she said, "I would like so much to go home, back to San Juan Capistrano."

"All right, we will go. I will ask for my time next Saturday."

That made her happy, and a little color came back in her face. I went to see Mr. Palayut and told him about my wife. He said, "Yes, I think you should take her back home. Maybe the change of climate will be good for her."

We went by bus to San Juan Capistrano. When we got home, only Señora Rivera was there. She was so excited and glad to see us that she did not notice how pale and thin Javiela was. When we were in the house, my wife sat down, tired and exhausted. Señora Rivera noticed how thin she was.

She said, "What has happened to you?"

"I am very sick, mother."

Señora Rivera fixed a bed and laid her down.

Then she said to me, "Tell me what has happened. How long has she been sick?"

I told her all that we knew. When Señor Rivera came home he was very sad when he saw Javiela and heard about her sickness. The next day we all took her to see the doctor. He examined her and asked many questions. Then he shook his head and said, "This is very bad. I will give you some medicine for her, but the main thing is that she must stay in bed all the time and eat as much food as she can." He gave us a list of what she should eat: milk, eggs, meat, and other things.

We put Javiela to bed and did everything the doctor said, but nothing seemed to do any good. She got thinner and could not eat, and the cough never stopped. She could not sleep for coughing, day and night. Then we bought every kind of medicine that people told us about, in bottles and in boxes, but nothing did any good.

One day she said, "Do not buy any more medicine. It does me no good. You spend too much money. The doctors and the medicines cannot help me." This made us very sad. We did not know what to do. I prayed to Jesus Christ, but I knew that her candle was about burned out, and that soon she would join the good people. That would be wonderful for her, but I did not see how I could do without her. She had given me the only happiness I had ever known.

She died October 18, 1930, and we buried all that was left of her frail body the next day. My bad dreams had come true. All the time I had known something like this was going to happen.

I stayed a week with Señor and Señora Rivera. Javiela was their only child, and their sorrow was so great they could not eat or sleep. It was a bad time for all of us.

I began to get restless, and I could not stay still for more than a few minutes. I decided I could not help the father and the mother. I said to them, "I must go back to Sacramento."

My mother-in-law started crying. She said, "Why don't you stay with us for several months?"

I said, "I hope I will not be gone long. I will come back to see you when I can."

She said, "You must write to us and let us know how it is with you."

I took one suitcase and my jacket. All our other things I left. I never wrote and never saw them again.

I went to Sacramento and rented a room in the Japanese hotel for two months. I still had $140. We had $690 when we returned to San Juan Capistrano from Oakland, but the doctor, medicine, and funeral had cost a lot of money.

In Sacramento I felt like I could not work for a while, because I was restless and was always thinking about Javiela. Nothing would interest me or hold my attention. After a month I got a job and worked for three weeks, but I could not keep my mind on what I was doing. I forgot about my relatives in Tucson. All the time we were in Oakland I sent them fifteen dollars a month. Now I even forgot to write them. They did not know where I was. I did nothing for another month, and then got a job with a Japanese farmer, but I stayed with him only a week. I still was restless and could not concentrate. I went back to the Japanese hotel for another month. After working for another farmer for three weeks, I had to quit again.

One day I passed the Salvation Army house and saw a lot of people eating inside. I stopped to look at them. Each one looked like he had been having bad luck. One of the Salvation Army men saw me standing there, and he came straight to me.

He said, "Why don't you come inside? There is room at the table."

I went in and sat at the table, and they brought me a lot of food. I ate it all. Then the man had me sign my name; for some reason I cannot explain I did not sign my real name, but José Ramos.

The man said, "Where are you from, José?"

"From Tucson."

"What is your address in Tucson?"

"The only address we have is what we call Barrio Pascua, or Pascua Village."

"Well, then, you are not a Mexican."

"No, sir, I am an Indian."

"That is all right. We would like for you to come to our meeting from seven to nine this evening."

I said, "I will come."

That was the first Salvation Army service I ever attended. They played horns, beat a drum, and sang songs about God. One of the Salvation Army people would talk sometimes, but I could not understand him very well. I liked the singing much better.

The next day I went back for breakfast and lunch. They did not have supper, just breakfast and lunch, and singing and preaching for the poor people who did not have a home. For several days I only had to buy my supper, and it cost about twenty-five cents.

One day in May I saw a crowd of Mexicans looking at a sign in front of a pool hall. The sign said, "I need sixty laborers to work in the beet fields in Montana. Inquire inside." I thought this was my chance to get out of Sacramento, so I went inside and signed up, but like a crazy person I did not sign my name, but Miguel Venegas.

It took two nights and a day to get to Montana on the passenger train. When we got to the beet field, the boss man said, "Boys, we will divide you into three teams. The fastest workers will be in the first team and will get six dollars a day and board. The next team will get four dollars a day and board. The slowest will be in the third team and get three dollars and a half and board. I got in the third team because I could not work fast. I did not like working with the beets, and after two weeks I quit. I had made forty-two dollars.

I took a bus to Walla Walla, then a freight train back to Jamestown, North Dakota, another freight to Pierre, South Dakota, and still another across Nebraska to Kansas City. Here I found a Salvation Army. I stayed a month, eating and sleeping with them; it did not cost me anything. Next I went to Chicago, where I put up with the Salvation Army people for another month. Then I went to Cleveland, Pittsburgh, and Philadelphia, always riding the freights and spending several days in each place with the Salvation Army.

I caught a freight for New York City and arrived there September 23, 1931. First I found the Salvation Army; they let me have a free bed, and I found that they served three free meals a day. My clothes were dirty and ragged. The Salvation Army people gave me a suit, shirt, socks, shoes, and hat. I stayed there a month, going to their services. I spent the rest of the time seeing the city.

The thing I liked to do most was to watch the ships come in and go out, load and unload. I spent days going up and down the waterfront. When a Spanish, Italian, Chinese, or Japanese ship came in, I would talk to the sailors and learn where they had come from and what it was like.

Every day I saw some kind of free shows on the street. A strong man lifted weights of five hundred pounds and held them over his head. Another man sold medicine and told how the medicine was made of herbs discovered by the Indians long ago. The strong man, an Indian, had taken the medicine all his life, and that was how he got to be strong. The strong man said he was a Yaqui; but I talked with him, and he could not speak either Yaqui or Spanish.

Another street merchant did many sleight-of-hand tricks. He would do the tricks until he got a crowd around him and then sell clothing, jewelry, and kitchen utensils. I went many times to see him do his tricks.

I read in the newspaper about an airplane with nine motors. It was at the airport, getting ready to fly to South America with a load of freight. I went to the airport and saw it being loaded with many boxes, some of them containing pianos.

The tall buildings did not seem as high as the City Hall in Los Angeles, which stood up so much higher than all the other buildings around it.

I did not see any Mexicans in New York, and never heard Spanish spoken except when a Spanish ship came in. There were some Mexicans in Chicago, but not many.

I stayed four weeks in New York, then went to Boston on a freight train. There I went to see the Witch House at Salem and the places where they burned the white witches. I stayed a week in the Salvation Army house, and went back to New York, where I stayed two more weeks with the Salvation Army people.

I liked the Salvation Army very much. No one ever asked me where I was from, or what tribe I belonged to, or what I did, or where I was going. I was just there. The Salvation Army seemed better to me than the Church, because I had seen many Catholic families fight, brothers against brothers, children against parents, parents against each other. The Salvation Army people were like brothers, singing all the time about God and never fighting. I lived with the Salvation Army several months and I never did have to work. There was always plenty of food, and table waiters and cooks.

It was the middle of November, and the weather was getting cooler day by day. I knew I would have to get back to Arizona before it got too cold. It took nine days to get to Salt Lake City. Sometimes I rode day and night, but every second or third day I would have to stop to sleep and rest. The weather was very cold all the way. I soon found I should have started a month earlier. I stayed in Salt Lake City only two days. There was no Salvation Army there, and I had to pay for my meals and bed. I still had about thirty dollars.

I rode a Union Pacific freight from Salt Lake City to Colton, California, and took a bus to Los Angeles. The bus fare was $1.76, and this was the only fare I paid from the time I left Sacramento, three months before.

In Los Angeles, I found the Salvation Army, but they charged ten cents for the meals and did not have any beds. I had to pay twenty-five cents a night for a cot in a flop house. I stayed in Los Angeles two days, and went to Phoenix. I had ridden the freights over this country so many times I knew every water tank and every stop. I got to Phoenix on November 30, with a bad cold.

I bought some groceries and took the bus to the Yaqui Water Users camp at Cactus, nine miles east of Phoenix. I went to the house of Luciano Hernández and his wife, Philomena. Both Luciano and Philomena were nearly one hundred years old. He had been with Cajeme in the 1880s. Both were born in Torim, they married in Torim, and their first child, María, was born in Torim. They moved to Guaymas for a short time, and then came to Arizona in 1889. They must have been among the first Yaquis to move across the border. Their son Simón, about my age, was born in the United States. They lived in Sasco in 1908, and Simón was in my room at school. They were relatives of my grandmother María, and all the families knew each other in Torim long ago.

When I got to their house, I said, "Good evening."

They answered me the same way. Philomena said, "Where are you from?"

"Oh, I have come a long way."

She said, "You are sick with that cold."

"Yes, I caught a cold on the freight trains from New York. The weather was very bad."

She fixed supper for me, and I asked about a job with the Water Users' Association.

Luciano said, "It is very hard to get a job. The cotton is nearly all picked and there is not much irrigation just now. The Water Users laid off many workers last week. The ones still working are repairing the canals."

This made me very sad, because my money was nearly gone. I wondered what I would do. I had found out that many people were without work everywhere because of the Depression.

After four days I felt very well again and I started looking for work.

One Sunday the Yaqui laborers in the camp got some whiskey, became very drunk, and made a lot of noise most of the night. I thought, "Some of them will not go to work tomorrow, and maybe I can get a job."

I got up early and went to the bridge on the irrigation canal, where the trucks came to get the workers every morning. The ones who did not drink came out, and some of the drunk ones staggered out. But many did not come. The truck drivers blew their horns, but still they did not come.

The boss man saw me standing on the bridge and came to me. I had known him a long time, and he recognized me. He said, "Hello, Valenzuela. When did you get back? I read your letter from New York City a few weeks ago. Do you want to work?"

"I am ready," I said.

"Get on that truck."

I had not had breakfast, but at noon some of the other workers gave me some beans and coffee, and I got through the eleven-hour day. The next day Philomena fixed me some lunch: beans, tortillas, and a bottle of coffee.

I worked for the Water Users from December, 1931, to October, 1932. The pay was $1.80 a day. Every two weeks I received $21.60. After I bought food for Philomena and went to Phoenix on Sundays, I had nothing left, not a cent.

After I had been working for the Water Users for nine months, I got to thinking about the Rio Yaqui in Sonora and all the stories I had heard about the place. The valley lands were rich, and there was gold in the mountains. The lands needed a little water; all kinds of seeds would grow very fast. A man could raise two crops a year because there was never any frost in the winter, and there was wild meat, deer, javelina, and quail. A man did not need money there because he could raise his food; and few clothes were needed, as the weather was always warm.

I got to thinking and thinking, "What is the best thing to do, to go to the Rio Yaqui or back to California?" I had never been to the Rio Yaqui but according to what people said, a man could live there without working for wages. Everybody said jobs were very hard to get in California, and people were living in shacks.

I decided to go to the Rio Yaqui. It was September 1, 1932, and I had no money. If I did not go to Phoenix any more on Sundays, and saved all my money not needed for food, I would have enough to get to the Rio Yaqui. This I did, and on October 1, I had sixteen dollars. Then I had an idea. It was payday for all the Yaqui workers at the Cactus camp, and I knew how they loved to buy whiskey.

I learned where there was a bootlegger in a Mexican village called

Cuatro Milpas, south of Phoenix. I went to his house and knocked on the door. A man opened it and said, "Hello. Come in."

I went in and he brought a chair for me.

He said, "What brings you here?"

"I wonder if you could tell me where I can buy a gallon of whiskey?"

The man looked me up and down, and said, "I have never seen you before."

"No, but some of my friends know you very well, and they told me about you."

"Who are some of your friends?"

I thought quickly of all the Yaquis and Mexicans I knew who bought whiskey from the bootleggers. I named three or four, and then I mentioned Severo Rodríguez, who worked for the Water Users and bootlegged on the side.

He said, "Oh you know Severo?"

"Yes. He is my one good friend."

"That is good. Maybe I can find you one gallon of whiskey."

"How much will it cost?" I asked.

"Not much. Just ten dollars."

"All right," I said.

He brought the whiskey in two half-gallon fruit jars. I wrapped them in a newspaper and took the bus to Cactus. I sold all the whiskey, and Sunday morning I counted my money. Instead of sixteen dollars I now had thirty-three dollars. It did not come to my mind that if I stayed on at Cactus and sold whiskey to the workers I could make lots of money. All I thought was, "Now I can go to the Rio Yaqui."

The next day I put all my clothes in a suitcase and expressed them to Nogales, and that night I caught the freight for Tucson, and got there early the next morning. I did not want to see any of the Yaquis in Tucson, not even my sister and cousins. My memories of Barrio Pascua and Barrio Libre were still very bad.

I jumped off the train when it slowed down at the edge of the city. I walked the old railroad track to the west of the city until I came to Congress Avenue. Then I walked east to the Armory Park, where I spent the day sleeping on the grass. In the late afternoon I took a bus to Nogales.

I got to Nogales about sundown. When I went to the express office to get my suitcase, the office was closed and a sign on the door said it would be open at nine the next morning. I found a hotel for the night, and was waiting at the express office when it opened the next morning.

I went back to the hotel and changed my clothes before I went to a bank and changed all my money into pesos except two ten-dollar bills.

At the port of entry a Mexican officer asked me for my passport.

I said, "I do not have one."

He said, "Why not? Are you lost?"

I said, "No, señor. I really do not know what you mean by a passport."

He said, "Where were you born?"

"In the Colorada Mine in Sonora."

"Where is the Colorada Mine?"

"In the mountains, east of Torres."

"When did you go into the United States the first time?"

"In 1906."

"What day of the month?"

"That I do not know, because my grandmother could not read or write."

He said, "Then you went across with your grandmother."

"Yes, señor."

He asked me a lot of other questions, and at last he said, "All right, go on."

I went on to a little park just beyond the Mexican customs house, and pretty soon I was surrounded by Mexican beggars of all ages. Little boys wanted to shine my shoes, men wanted to be my guide, an old wrinkled woman with a dirty, ragged dress wanted money to buy food.

One of the men said, "What part of the United States do you come from?"

I said, "Los Angeles."

He said, "What kind of work do you do?"

I said, "All kinds, carpenter, mechanic, electrician, many kinds of work."

He said, "Maybe you earn good money?"

I said, "Yes, I made good money."

He said, "We do not have any work. Maybe you can buy us some coffee and some tortillas."

I said, "Yes, I would like to help you, but I sent nearly all my money to Hermosillo. I can help you just a little."

I gave one peso each to the old woman and the men, and some centavos to the boys. They went away, but I noticed they kept watching me. I watched them, too.

I asked a Mexican when the next train left for Magdalena. He said at seven o'clock in the morning. I asked if there would be a bus during the day, and he said that all the buses left early in the morning, too. Then it turned out that he was a beggar, too, and I did not know whether to believe him. In a little while a bus passed the little park; it had a sign, HERMOSILLO, on it. Magdalena is on the road to Hermosillo, so I knew the beggar had not told me the truth. The bus was full, and I did not try to stop it.

I was sitting on a bench, and pretty soon I noticed a Mexican girl sitting on the other end of the bench. She kept moving up, closer and closer. She looked me up and down, and said, "Have you come from the United States?"

I said, "Yes."

She said, "Do you know anybody in this town?"

I said, "No. I do not know anyone."

She said, "Maybe you are lonesome and would like to spend the night in my house. I live on the south side."

I looked at her and did not answer. I wondered which one of the beggars had sent her.

She said, "I will be back, so don't go away."

A Ford truck stopped by the little park. On the door it had the sign of a Magdalena company.

I asked the driver, "Are you going to Magdalena?"

He said, "Yes."

"When do you leave?"

"Right now."

"Can I ride with you?"

"Yes. Come on."

On the road to Magdalena the truck driver asked me all about what I had been doing in the United States. We talked all the way and became very friendly. When we got to Magdalena, he asked me if I had any relatives there. I told him I did not have anyone living there. He said, "The fiesta of San Francisco is going on, and the town is crowded. If you would like to spend the night in my aunt's house I will take you there."

I said, "That will be very good."

The truck driver drove me to his aunt's house and explained to her that I was his good friend and did not have any relatives in town. He asked if I could stay in her house.

She said, "Yes. I will fix a bed for him."

I said, "Thank you, señora, and with your permission I will go back to the fiesta for a while."

She said, "That is good. Come back whenever you wish."

We went back to the fiesta, and I bought some supper for the truck driver and myself. Then he said, "Would you like some tequila or beer?"

I said, "No, thank you. I never drink anything like that, but I will take a bottle of soda water."

He drank two bottles of beer and said, "Now we will go watch the dancing."

I said, "No. I had better go back to your aunt's house."

He took me back to his aunt's house. She was waiting for me. She said, "I have your bed ready. Now you had better give me your money and other valuables, and I will put them in the trunk in my room."

I gave her my pocketbook and watch. The next morning when I woke up, she was already up. She said, "I have some hot water, and you can wash."

I washed my hands and face, and she brought my pocketbook and watch to me. I did not count my money, but later I found it was all there, every cent.

She said, "I will soon have some breakfast ready."

"Thank you very much, but I want to go on to the fiesta to see if I can find any of my relatives from Hermosillo or the Rio Yaqui. I will come back later for my suitcase."

I went to the church of San Francisco, but I did not go in. People were everywhere. Some were still sleeping on the ground, some were going to or coming from the church, and some were cooking on little charcoal burners. I walked around for some time, but I did not hear anyone speaking Yaqui, only Spanish.

After a while, I heard a woman say to a little girl, "Basotch nen buise nana," or "Give me that cup, young lady."

I asked the woman, in Yaqui, "Is there anyone here from Hermosillo?"

"Oh, yes, we live in Hermosillo."

"Which barrio?"

"Barrio de la Matanza."

"That is the place where my mother lives."

"What is her name?" she asked.

"Cecilia Hurtado."

"I know your mother very well, but she did not come to the fiesta this year. She is very well."

I said, "Do you know Josefa (Chepa) Moreno Domínguez?"

"I know her too. She is here now, camping on the west side of the church. I will take you to her. But first, let me give you some coffee." She gave me a pottery cup of very strong, thick coffee which made me sick. It was the first strong coffee I drank in Mexico.

When she finished breakfast for her family, she took me to Josefa Moreno. She said, "Good morning, Josefa. I bring you this young man. He comes from Tucson, and he is looking for you."

Chepa said, "Who are you?"

"I am Rosalio."

"My cousin Rosalio Javier?"

"Yes."

Then she asked me about my sister and cousin in Tucson.

"I am sorry, but I have not seen them for several years. I came here from Phoenix and I did not see anyone in Tucson when I came through, but I think they are all well."

*Tia* Chepa was glad to see me, and she thought I had brought a lot of money from the United States. Because she expected me to be rich, I began to feel as though I were. I bought soda pop, cactus candy and sweet bread (*pan dulce*) for Chepa, her family, and her friends. After three or four hours I suddenly realized that I had not bought my railroad ticket to the Rio Yaqui, and had not paid the truck driver's aunt for my bed. I counted my money and found I had ten pesos left. I went to the railroad station and saw a sign giving the prices of the fare. It said, "Ten and a half pesos to Vicam Station."

"Ave María, la Purisima," I said to myself.

I went back to the church and walked around the fiesta again, but I did not feel rich any more. Then I went back to the station and looked at the sign. It still said ten and a half pesos. I walked back to the church feeling very sad.

I remembered hearing my grandmother say that the Saint Francis in the church at Magdalena worked miracles for those who had faith in him. This Saint Francis is a very good friend of the Yaquis. He has helped lots of Yaqui prisoners. Many people make promises to give him candles or walk a mile on their knees if he grants their prayers. Many people try to raise the saint. You can pick him up if your faith is strong. Some people who try cannot do it, and that shows their faith is weak. When that happens, the women cry. Usually there are some crying women in the church.

I went into the church and prayed to Saint Francis. Then I went up to him and told him everything that had happened to me. I said, "If you can help me in my necessity, I will give you a candle worth twenty-five centavos. If you really do something good for me, I will bring you another candle worth one peso.

Then I kissed his foot, his knee, and his face. This was the same Saint Francis I had seen in my dream the time he kissed all the other people and did not kiss me. I guess he had forgiven me, because as I left the church he caused me to think about my two ten-dollar bills I had completely forgotten about.

I went to the bank to exchange my dollars for pesos. The cashier kept his eyes on the bills, ran his fingers over them lightly, and put them in the drawer. Then he counted out the pesos and gave them to me. I went straight to a store and bought a candle for a peso and took it to the Saint Francis. I said to him, "Here you are, my good Saint Francis. I know now that you are really a miracle saint."

I prayed in the church to Jesus Christ, and went to the railroad station and bought a ticket to Vicam Station. I was very hungry because I had not eaten all day. I bought three pesos worth of bread and took it to Chepa. Two of her sister's daughters were with her.

She said, "Where have you been all day? I have been waiting for you."

"No place. I have just been walking around the fiesta."

"Sit down, and I will give you something to eat."

"No, thank you. I am not hungry."

I was very hungry, but I was ashamed to eat their food. There were so many in Chepa's family, and they never seemed to have enough to eat. I was feeling very sorry for them. In a moment I was like a crazy person. I started giving them my money: twenty-five pesos to my cousin and a peso to each of the children and the relatives from Hermosillo. I gave away about fifty pesos. In order to make it seem I was very rich, I went to a restaurant to eat. The meal cost me five pesos, because prices are always high during the fiesta in Magdalena.

When I came out of the restaurant, Chepa was waiting for me. She said, "It is time to go to the railroad station." We were all going to ride together to Hermosillo.

I remembered about my suitcase. "All right. All of you go ahead. I will go get my suitcase and meet you at the station."

The truck driver's aunt would not accept any money for the bed. Although she was very poor she had great dignity and was above letting rooms for money.

The train left about sundown. Soon I was buying soda pop for the children. At midnight the train got to Carbo Station. Mexican women were selling food along the platform. I was still feeling rich, so I purchased something for each person in my cousin's group.

Before the train got to Hermosillo, Chepa said, "You should stop at Hermosillo and not go to the Rio Yaqui. It is no good. Everyone there is poor. There are no jobs for money. Only the people paid by the government have enough to eat. There is constant trouble there. Someone is always getting killed. It is a bad place to go."

I said, "Anyway, I would like to see what it is like. My father, my grandfather, and my grandmother were born at Torim. I have always wanted to see the place."

Just before the train stopped at Hermosillo, I took my clothes out of my new suitcase and gave the suitcase to Chepa. She had admired it, and I was still feeling rich.

After the group got off at Hermosillo and the train started on to Empalme, I got to thinking about my money. I took it out and counted it. I had two pesos left. No longer did I feel rich. I began to wonder if I would have enough to get some breakfast.

Empalme is a division point on the Sud Pacifico Railroad, just across the bay from Guaymas; a lot of loading and unloading goes on there, so the train stops for some time. I went to the restaurant where the passengers ate and looked at the prices on the sign. A breakfast cost three pesos, so I went and found a place where the laborers ate, and got some food and coffee for one peso. I bought cigarettes and matches and had five centavos left. I did not feel rich any more. This is the amount I had when I got to Vicam Station in the Rio Yaqui at noon that day, five centavos.

# CHAPTER 9

# Hard Times in the Rio Yaqui

I GOT TO THE Rio Yaqui on October 5, 1932. When I got off the train at Vicam Switch a lot of Yaqui men were standing around. I asked if they could tell me where to find Pedro More. It turned out that he was standing there.

I went up to him and said, "Good morning."

"Well, well, how did you get here? I am very glad to see you. Let's go to my home."

Josefa More was very happy to see me, too, as was the whole family. Josefa gave me a cup of coffee and a piece of bread; in a couple of hours she cooked a big dinner. Old friends and relatives came to see me to get news of people in Arizona. The reason everyone was so happy to see me was because they thought I had brought lots of money, but I only had five centavos in my pocket. Sad because I had no money, I thought, "Oh my God, why did I fool myself into coming to this sad place?"

Pedro started advising me about how to invest my money in the Rio Yaqui. "Let me tell you one thing. You came here just in time. Do you know the best thing to do? If you have money, you can buy some cows, because cows are very cheap here in Vicam and every week Mexican ranchers come here to sell cows and calves. Cows cost only twenty-five to thirty pesos a head. This is the chance for you. As soon as your cows increase, you can make a good living in the Rio Yaqui."

Thinking about my five centavos, I answered, "Well, Pedro, this is a very fine place. But I never liked working with cows; the only thing I like is working hard all the time."

"If you like hard work, I've got some in my fields," he said.

The next morning he took me to his field between Vicam Station and the river where he had some wheat, corn, and some beans. Giving me a machete, he showed me how to cut weeds. I guess he was very lazy, because such big weeds flourished between the bean plants. I worked hard in the bean patch, without any lunch; by midafternoon I was so hungry I could hardly work, but I kept on until nearly sundown, and then walked the three miles to Vicam Station.

My uncle said, "How many furrows did you take out?"

"Thirty-four."

"You did nice work over there."

My aunt gave me supper, with very strong coffee. I drank the coffee, but it kept me awake most of the night; as a result I was sleepy the next day. I worked three days for my uncle.

So many Yaquis knew me that I guess some told my half brother about me. He came to look for me at Pedro's house. He said, "Good morning," to Pedro and Josefa, and they said to me: "This is your half brother, Mariano González, from Torim." We shook hands and I was very pleased to meet him. We talked for a while. I think my poor brother thought I had lots of money, because he kept looking at my fine hat and watch.

Mariano was born to my mother in 1907. Both Mariano and his brother Manuel were born in Hermosillo. As I have already related, my mother left my father about 1901 to go with José González. José only lived with her a few years; in 1909 he returned to Torim, taking Mariano and Manuel with him. Mariano was two and Manuel was one when they left our mother. In Torim, José lived with Rita Salvador for a while. Then he left her (she was still alive in Vicam Switch in 1967) and went to live with a blonde woman, Ramona Villegas, of Torim. By this time José was old and white-headed.

Mariano asked me to walk to Torim with him. I said that I would very much like to see Torim, because it is the pueblo to which I belong. Actually I have rights in Vicam because Francisco Liowe, my mother's father, belonged to that pueblo. All of my father's people were from Torim. Both my father and my grandmother had talked so much about Torim pueblo that I felt like that was where I belonged.

We walked to Torim in about one hour and twenty minutes. Many people came to see me at Mariano's home. Nacha More Sewa, Lucrecia Sewa's granddaughter, lived close to Mariano. I was glad to see her; we were about the same age and had been together as children in Hermosillo, Tucson, and Sasco. I met María Palos for the first time. She was the Sierra woman that my father went to see in 1914. In 1932 María Palos was a strong woman. She is still alive today, but now she is very bent and old. Teodora Torre lived close to Mariano. I remembered her from Hermosillo. She was one of my grandmother's relatives, the widow of the *yori* Octavio Pare (Valencia).

At midday they made coffee. There was nothing else to cook. At supper we had beans boiled with corn and more coffee. Mariano's wife, Anastasia Hupaumea, said, "We are waiting for payday so we can buy some food." Mariano had signed up with the government in 1927. He got paid every fifteen days for not fighting the Mexicans.

After supper Anastasia brought me a *petate* and an old dirty blanket. She did not bring me a pillow because there were none. They built a big fire under a tree, and Anastasia told me, "If you put your *petate* near the fire, you will sleep well." I lay down near the fire, using a brick for a pillow.

Something started walking on me. I could feel things all over my body, stinging my feet and neck, everywhere. I got up and put more wood on the fire so I could look for what was stinging me. I did not know what the insect was. The rest of the night I sat against the tree. When Anastasia got up around five-thirty, she made coffee and gave me a cup. She asked if I had slept well and how was I feeling.

"Oh, I didn't sleep all night, because so many little animals pricked me hard all night."

"Those are our fleas. We have many fleas in this country." She started making tortillas. Our only breakfast that day was coffee and tortillas with a little salt.

An hour later I was back at Pedro's house at Vicam Switch. I was glad that Josefa cooked a big meal. When I told her that I had fleas in my clothes, she had me change into clean clothes while she boiled mine in a five-gallon can. The next morning I put on my clean clothes and went back to work in Pedro's bean patch. I was very happy working, even without lunch. I was glad to be working with my machete.

A Yaqui boy came to the field and said, "Ketchealea" (How are you?). I answered, "Ket tuih" (I am all right). He sat down, gave me a cigarette, and talked about many things.

"How much does this man pay you a day?"

"I don't know. I didn't ask him."

"Well, I will tell you something. No one likes to work for this man because he never pays his laborers."

"I don't know if he will pay me or not, but I am here to help him."

Later the boy said it was time to eat. "Come on, we can both ride home on my horse."

"No, thank you. I will work until five o'clock."

I got home about five-thirty. After supper I went to the pool hall to pick up cigarette butts because I had no money to buy cigarettes. I kept my five centavos in my pocket.

One day I was hunting deer in the brush near Vicam, when I suffered from what we call *chictura*. It is a sort of sickness; even though a person knows a place very well, all of a sudden you get lost and do not know where you are. My grandmother said this was a common sickness among the Yaquis; many Yaquis in the Sierra got this disorientation sickness and wandered until they died of thirst. When this happens, my grandmother said that the way to cure yourself is to spit on the ground repeatedly until you have made a cross of spit. Then you sit on the cross with your head hanging down, and in a few minutes you will be all right. I forgot my grandmother's advice and wandered around the brush for about two hours, until I heard dogs barking and went toward the noise. I arrived at a rancheria belonging to Gregorio Juárez, a captain of Vicam pueblo (and one of my grandmother's relatives), and he told me how to get back to Vicam.

Luis Molino, a Mayo living in Torim, and I decided to explore the big cave called Matuecame in the Cautorreon Mountains. The cave is visible from Vicam. Luis told me that a handprint in a boulder was the hand of God. Inside the cave was abundant evidence of coyotes and mountain lions. When we saw a big ball of rattlesnakes, we left. I doubt that there is any gold in that cave.

Luis was sometimes called Rosario Molino too. I think he was a relative of the Luis Molino in Tucson. The one in Torim had grown up in Mexico City because he had been deported as a child. I suppose he learned to carve saints while he was in Mexico, and he was the saint maker in Torim. The Luis Molino in Tucson is a saint maker, too. Well, Luis and I used to talk about the gold in the mountains and many times we went hunting for it. We knew where there was a little placer gold about five miles from Agua Caliente, but we never got a chance to pan the gold because we were scared of the bad Yaquis that watch everyone who enters the Sierra. Sometimes I worked for Luis as a tally keeper out in the wood forest. He was good to me. Now he lives at Wata Baam, Rio Mayo, with his daughter, Antonia Tepasuca.

Pedro still thought that I was keeping money in my pockets. One day he asked "Are those your only work clothes?"

"Yes, these are my only clothes."

"Well, you can buy some more in the store. Work clothes don't cost much. A shirt is three pesos and pants cost three and a half pesos."

I said, "I don't have any money. I lost all my money at the fiesta in Magdalena. I came here with just five centavos."

"Oh, that's too bad. I thought you had lots of money."

I finished cutting the weeds in the bean field on October 18, 1932. On Sunday, Pedro went to the store and bought me one shirt and a pair of pants. But he did not give me a peso for cigarettes.

On Monday I started pulling beans. It took three days. Then I piled the beans where we were going to clean them. Pedro helped haul them in his wagon, so that only took a half day. We cleaned the beans, filling twenty-two and a half sacks. Each sack weighed 80 kilos, or about 176 pounds. We could not haul the beans to Vicam Station in one load, so I had to sleep in the field to keep Yaqui thieves from stealing what was left. The next morning Pedro brought me some breakfast, and we loaded the rest of the beans.

A few days later my uncle sold fifteen sacks to the Mexican storekeeper for 8 pesos apiece. The storekeeper gave him 120 pesos. I unloaded the beans and waited for him to pay me. He did not give me a single centavo. "Maybe he will pay me when we get home," I thought.

When we got to his house, I sat down near the table and said, "I want to write one letter to Tucson, but I've got no paper."

"I will give you twenty-five centavos to buy paper and a stamp," he said.

That was all I ever got, besides the shirt and the pants, for working with the beans. Instead of writing a letter, I went to the store and bought cigarettes and matches. The next day he asked if I wrote the letter to Tucson. "Oh yes," I said, "I've already mailed it." He believed me.

A few days later Josefa said, "Pedro, when will you begin to gather the corn?"

"I guess we'll start tomorrow."

"You had better hurry, while you have good help," she said.

"He will never pay me for pulling the corn," I said to myself. To them I said, "I think I will go to Torim today."

"That is all right," he said, "but come back tonight, because tomorrow we start picking corn."

They went away to visit some friends. I packed my few things and started to Torim. I went to see my other half brother, Manuel González, and his wife, Rosa, who were eating dinner when I arrived. They had roast meat, which I thought was pork. Rosa fixed a plate for me.

"This is lion meat," she said. "We think it is very good."

I tried to eat, but could not. It smelled like jack rabbit, and the taste was bitter.

"What is the matter with you?" Rosa said. "You don't like to eat fat meat?"

"No. I don't like fat meat." I did not tell them that I did not relish the lion meat. I drank some coffee and ate two tortillas with salt.

At supper Rosa made lion meat soup with rice and onions. I wanted to eat it, but it smelled like jack rabbit. I ate tortillas and salt with coffee. The rest of them liked the lion soup. The next morning they ate what was left of the lion meat. I had coffee and tortillas again.

After breakfast I went to look for a piece of land where I could plant some watermelons. I found a place on the south side of the river, about a mile west of Torim. I started to cut away the brush and weeds with the machete. I worked all day without food. In the evening I went to Mariano's house, carrying a big load of grass to sleep on, because there were so many fleas on the ground.

Anastasia asked, "Did you find a good place to plant the watermelons?"

"Yes," and I told her about the place.

"I am glad," she said. "My son, Salome, and your brother Mariano can never raise watermelons."

She gave me coffee, beans, and some bitter greens called *chichi kelite*. I ate five tortillas at a time because I was so hungry. That night the fleas did not bite me so much. It takes them a while to work their way up through the fresh grass.

The next morning everyone had a cup of coffee. All the Yaquis like coffee when they first get up. Later they eat breakfast. I went back to my little field and worked until noon.

Then I went to see Locaria Sewa, who lived near Corasepe Hill, north of Torim village. A number of families lived at Corasepe, including the Vega brothers, Valentín Teran Cohuetero and his family (they made fireworks; Valentín was one of the men who paid the Papago witch to kill my father in Tucson), and Juan Jacom. But it was old Lucrecia I was going to see.

"Sit down," she said, "What brings you here?"

"Not a thing. I just came to see you."

She fixed some dinner for me, and it was the most food I had seen since

I got to the Rio Yaqui. She gave me real meat (beef), beans, flour tortillas, cheese, and decent coffee that was not so strong.

We walked around Corasepe and she showed me where my grandmother and grandfather had been born and which fields had belonged to my great grandfather, Manuel Cochemea. She was now using the land that the Cochemeas had farmed. *Tia* Lucrecia knew all about my family. She even remembered my grandmother's mother, Julia Palos. She told me how Torim looked in the 1880s and 1890s. No Mexicans lived in Torim then. Where the pueblo center is now, there was just the old Spanish church. The Yaquis lived scattered around at small rancherias like Corasepe.

After we had walked around, my aunt asked, "What are you going to do in Torim?"

"Yesterday I started clearing a piece of ground on the other side of the river."

"That is very nice. What are you going to plant?"

"Some watermelons, chili peppers, and pumpkins."

"Do you have the seeds?"

"Not a single seed."

"Then I will give you some. I have many kinds of seeds." She gave me watermelon and pumpkin seeds.

"Do you have any tools?" she asked.

"Only a machete that belongs to my brother."

She gave me a grubbing hoe and a knifelike hoe, as well as three pounds of corn pinole. I took all she gave me and went back to my little field and worked until night. I returned to my sister-in-law's house, where we ate tortillas and *chichi kelite;* again I took a big bundle of grass to sleep on.

When I got to my field next morning, a man was waiting for me. He looked like a Mexican, with long whiskers. His name was Juan Luis Salazar. He said, "I came to see you to let you know this is my land. I came here in 1928 and claimed it. I have never had time to clean it up. I want you to leave it as it was and not come back."

"I am sorry for what you say. If you will pay me two pesos a day for the three days I have worked cleaning this spot of land, I will go find another one."

"I cannot pay you."

"Then I stay here."

The man went away very angry. The next day he came back with his son. The son told me the same thing his father had said the day before, and that he was with his father when he marked the land in 1928.

I said, "I don't care who marked the land, you have not worked it. It is only when you work land that you can claim it." They went away very angry, without another word. The land was only two hundred feet square.

The following Sunday I went to see Locaria Sewa. She offered me some breakfast, but I had already eaten.

"Do you know one Juan Luis Salazar?" I asked.

"I know him very well."

"He came to my little field and claimed that the land was his."

"That man does not even belong to Torim village. He belongs to Rahum. Besides, he is not really a Yaqui. He is half Yaqui and half Mexican. Keep on working the land, and don't pay any attention to him. If he comes back, tell him to come and see me."

I went on to Vicam Station to see Pedro More.

"What are you doing in Torim?" he asked.

"I am cleaning up a piece of land to plant watermelons."

"That is good."

"But a man came to stop me. He said he marked the land in 1928."

"Who is this man?"

"Juan Luis Salazar."

"I know him. He belongs to Rahum village. He is half Mexican, so don't you believe what he says. The next time he tries to stop you, tell him I want to see him."

I felt better about the land, but as I walked back to Torim I was sad because I did not have a centavo and I longed for a cigarette. As I went along, I looked for cigarette stubs. I found several, all very short. I picked them up, every one. When I got home I took out what tobacco was left in them and rolled it in corn husks. In that way I made three or four cigarettes. It was well that I had the cigarettes, because there was no food in Mariano's house. In the evening Anastasia made us corn tortillas and coffee.

The next morning we had the same thing. I went to my little field and started digging holes for the watermelons. Each hole was about a foot and a half deep and a foot wide. In three days I made eighty holes for watermelons and twenty holes for pumpkins. Then I dug a well in the bed of the river, about four feet square and four feet deep. Water would stand in it nearly two feet deep.

I spent a whole day looking for two five-gallon oil cans to carry the water from the well to the field. Not a single extra can could I find in Torim. The next day I went to see Lucrecia Sewa at Corasepe Hill.

"Are you going to Vicam?" she asked.

"No. I am looking for two oil cans to carry water for my watermelons."

"We have some old ones. I think we can find two which will hold the water."

I made a trail up the steep river bank and began carrying the water to my field. I poured a canful in each hole. When I finished, I went over the field a second time. This made ten gallons of water for each hole. When, at the end of three days, I got through carrying all this water, my shoulders were sore and my legs were tired. That was November 25. Next I spent a week building a carrizo cane fence around the plot.

For a few weeks I had nothing to do except walk back and forth from Torim to Vicam, trying to find something to eat and cigarette butts to pick up. My sister-in-law, Anastasia, could not get enough food for her family, and I did not have a centavo to help her or myself. I would go to the house of a kinsman or a friend about mealtime. Sometimes they would offer me food, and at other times they would pretend that they thought I had already eaten. Occasionally they would ignore me completely, acting as if I were not there. The only person who was glad to see me was Armando Urrea, the man who went to the Sierra with my father in 1914. He was rich, with many fields; he planted over eighty acres of wheat in all. I did not like to stay with him, because he liked to drink too much tequila. I got thinner and thinner until I had to take up my belt two notches.

One night I was visiting Nacha Sewa More Buanamea at her house near the school. As we sat, we saw a lady dressed all in black leaning against one of the school windows. In a little while she stopped looking in the window and drifted off, about twelve inches off the ground. She had no feet. She went to the old stone house and disappeared. We were able to see her face very well. It was a teacher named Loreta Aceves who had recently moved to Obregón. Her apparition was yellow and sick, and we knew she would soon die. Less than a month later we heard she had died in Obregón.

One day my half sister Dominga came to Torim looking for me. I had not seen her since she was a baby at the Colorada Mine. She was sitting on a chair when I got in from the fields. I did not speak to her because she looked like a Mexican lady, with her light skin and the clothes she was wearing. Then she got up and came to me and touched my hand, saying, "I am your sister, Dominga Palos. I brought you this basket of fruit." She held a large basket of oranges, guayabas, and figs. She asked me to go see her mother. I got dressed up in my best clothes, which still looked pretty good, and we walked to Cocorit. Augustina began to cry as soon as she saw me.

"I wanted to see what Miguel's son had become. I have never been able to forget your father. I am so glad you have come to the Rio Yaqui."

She talked and cried all afternoon. I guess she really liked my father a lot. Now she was living with the son of the famous Yaqui chief, Cajeme, Jr. They had a fine adobe house in Cocorit. Everyone thought I was rich because of my fancy California clothes.

On December 15 I began planting my melons and pumpkins. Insects began to eat the little plants. Twenty-three holes of watermelons and eight holes of pumpkins were left. Every two days I carried water to them.

Christmas and New Year's were very sad for me. I would eat once a day, and some days not at all. I kept thinking how it had been in the United States, about how much money I had made, and about the food. I said to myself, "Why did I come to this dirty place?" There was no hope. How could I ever go to the United States again? The saddest of all was when I heard little Yaqui children crying in the night for something to eat, and the poor Yaqui mothers answered, "Well, my dear child, where can I find some food for you?"

On New Year's morning Anastasia could give me only a cup of coffee. I went to Lucrecia Sewa's house at Corasepe, and she gave me breakfast. Then I walked to Vicam Station, where Yaqui and Mexican cowboys were ready for the New Year's Day horse races. I never liked horse races, but I said to myself, "This is a good place to pick up cigarette stubs." I walked around and around picking up the stubs, and filled one of my pockets. In the afternoon I went to the ball game. I like baseball much better than horse races, but I did not watch the game this day because I was still walking around and around looking for cigarette stubs. I filled all my pockets.

When I got back to Torim in the late afternoon, Anastasia asked me, "Where have you been all day?"

"To Vicam Station, to the horse race and the ball game."

"Sit down," she said, "I have some *pozole*." *Pozole* is made with beans, hominy corn, and meat. She gave me a bowl. The meat looked like chicken.

"What kind of meat is this?" I asked.

"That is a big rat. It is good, like chicken."

I tried to eat it, but I could not. It smelled like a burning feather. I picked out all the meat and put it back in the cooking bowl, then I ate the beans and corn. My sister-in-law's family was glad I did not like the rat. They ate it all.

The next day I went to my field. The melons were growing fast. After I looked at each vine, I went to where I had hidden my tools. They were gone. Someone had stolen them. I spent the day pulling the weeds from my field with my hands. I looked every place for my hoe and grubbing hoe but I never found them.

The following day I went to visit one of my grandmother's relatives named Gregorio Juárez at a place called Cincuenta, three miles west of Vicam Station and eleven miles from Torim. He was the captain at Vicam pueblo. I started early and got there when the family was eating breakfast.

"Good morning."

"Good morning," they said softly.

"Sit down over there," said one old woman, motioning to an oil can. There were several empty chairs, but she meant the oil can. They kept their eyes on me and did not say anything while they finished breakfast, not even offering me a cup of coffee.

Captain Gregorio said to his son, "Let us go look at the wheat. We have much work to do." They went away, saying nothing to me. Not a word.

The old woman said to her daughter, Valeria, "You sweep around the house." She started in front of the kitchen, where I was sitting on the oil can. She stirred up a cloud of dust all around me, but I did not move.

I sat there until noon, and the women did not speak to me. Captain Gregorio and his son came back, and the women put roast beef, cheese, milk, coffee, beans, and flour tortillas on the table. All of them began eating, and the old woman brought me some beans and one tortilla in a dirty plate which she did not bother to wipe out. No beef, no cheese, no milk, no coffee.

I could not understand these people. They had much more than most Yaquis. They had eaten with my family in Tucson in 1920. And he was a relative. As I walked back to Torim in the afternoon, I prayed to my God, "These people hate me. Do not give them good luck."

My prayer was answered. Several weeks later I saw Captain Gregorio in Vicam Station. He was pale and very thin. Soon after that he died. His wife became very poor. I once saw her walking back and forth by the train, when it stopped in Vicam Station, trying to sell pinole.

When I got back to Torim after the twenty-two-mile walk, I had some good luck. Anastasia had roast beef, beans, and piles of corn tortillas for supper.

A few days later Chico Comela, a Mayo Indian living in Bacum, came to Torim to ask permission to cut crossties on Torim land. He said, "This would be a good chance for the Yaqui villages. I will willingly pay one thousand pesos a month to the governor."

Not one Yaqui wanted to give permission. "We are sorry, Señor Comela, but we do not want wood cut on our lands," said Luis Tepasuca, our first governor. "No one can take a single railroad tie from our lands."

Chico Comela said not a word. He just walked away. He had already arranged for the permission with General José María Huerta Noguera (commander of the Yaqui Zone), Colonel Antonio Zaragoza (commander of the Mexican garrison at Torim), and the *torocoyori* chief, Pluma Blanca.

Four days later I heard a lot of Yaquis talking. Comela was cutting crossties a few miles east of Torim. The governors were very mad but nothing could be done, because General Huerta had sent Mexican soldiers to protect Comela's woodcutters. Some of the men of Torim, those who were very hungry, went to cut ties for Comela. He paid them seventy-five centavos for number one ties, fifty centavos for number two ties, and thirty-five centavos for number three ties. I wanted to cut ties but had no ax and not a centavo to buy one.

José Loreto and Esteban Patón Vasquez made the arrangements for Comela's men to cut on Torim lands. José Loreto Patón Vasquez was the *commandante* of Torim and Esteban Patón Vasquez had been a captain of the mountain Yaquis. From 1907 to 1911 they lived in the Sierra and were very brave. Their father, also named Esteban Patón Vasquez, had been a baker in Torim before he was deported. After he was deported, their mother, Lola Patón Vasquez, went with General Luis Matuz. A third brother, Guillermo Patón Vasquez, never went to the Sierra, nor did he ever become a *yori* like his brothers. He was a lieutenant in the *fariseos*, and I first met him in Tucson in 1926 when he fled from Sonora with Lino Vega. José Loreto and Esteban kept all the money that the Comela brothers paid to the pueblo of Torim. While they did not get rich, like Chico and Gonzalo Comela, they got enough money to stay drunk on mescal all the time without working.

I kept my melon vines watered and spent the rest of the time walking from house to house and from village to village to get something to eat. My half sister, Dominga, lived in Potam, fifteen miles west of Torim. My friend Tiojilo Yoisanacame also lived in Potam. Every few days I walked to Potam and returned that night, thirty miles for one meal. Often I visited León Tava and Vicente Tava, who were usually generous with their food. Augustina lived in Cocorit and willingly gave me food. In fact Augustina was better to me than my own mother in many ways.

It was at Augustina's house that I met Rosa Kuka. I was visiting Augustina one day when Rosa and her aunt Bernalda Kuka Valenzuela came to visit. Bernalda said in Yaqui, "What is he doing here? I thought he was a *yori*."

I answered her in Yaqui, saying, "Oh, no, I am not a *yori*. I have always remembered the Yaqui language and now I have come home to live in the Rio Yaqui."

Bernalda said she was glad I was a good Yaqui, and asked me to visit them. At this time Bernalda lived about one mile east of Cocorit with her mother, Bartola Kuka, and her father, Juan María Valenzuela. They were nice to me, probably because they thought I was rich. Rosa lived with her mother, Lola Kuka, in Bacum. Her father, who had died in 1928, was Lorenzo Kuka, the brother of Rodolfo Rivera Kuka, who had lived with us in Arizona when he was out of prison. I told Rosa that we were distant relatives because the Kuka family was kin to my grandmother María. Rosa could not have cared less. She said, "I don't want to be a relative of yours. That is all too far away to matter."

I had good luck with Rosa in 1933. I still looked young and had nice clothes. They all thought I had money, but I usually only had a few centavos that Anastasia gave me. Rosa gave me a good watch with twenty-one jewels. She never told me where she got it. Before too long I had to hock it for a little money.

Rosa's mother and Bernalda's mother and father all died in 1933. Rosa and Bernalda moved together to Esperanza, where Rosa got a good job in a restaurant. She wanted to come live with me, but of course she could not leave her job. Sometimes I visited Rosa in Esperanza and some-times she met me in Potam at Dominga's house or in Cocorit at Augustina's house.

Sacramento Navagoki Ochoa left Arizona in 1932 for the Rio Yaqui. He was known by many names. Ramón or Kino Basko or Vasco (because he was from Bacum) was what most Yaqui called him. Ochoa was his Arizona name. He had been at the Mazocoba Massacre, in the Sierra with my father, and was one of the Yaquis who felt my father was trying to sell the Yaqui Valley to the Americans and who helped pay the Papago witch to kill him. He was the drummer for my father's *coyote* society. His Arizona wife, Blanca Jiménez, had died about 1927, and he left his three sons by that marriage in Tucson. In fact, Rosario, Davíd, and Ruben Ochoa are still living there. In the Rio Yaqui he began farming on both Torim and Bacum lands. He really belonged to Bacum, but he had friends in Torim. He built a house in Bataconsica and *se junto* with Blanca Gutiérrez. He did well in the Rio Yaqui. I often visited him in Bataconsica, and he gave me food. We were always friends.

My clothes were wearing out. I had one shirt, one pair of pants, a straw hat, and one pair of huaraches. Each week I washed the shirt and pants in the water hole in the river. When they were dry, I put them on again.

All the time I was thinking what I could do. Day and night I thought about it. I never wrote to my sister or my cousin who lived in Tucson, and I never asked them for money. One day I went to see Luis Molina, the saint maker in Torim.

"How are you?" he asked.

"Not so good," I said, "because I have no way to make a living here. I stay hungry most of the time."

"What would you like to do?"

"I would like to cut wood on the other side of the river, but I have no ax."

"I have two axes," the saint maker said; "I will loan you one." This made me very happy. He brought the ax to me and I started at once to the south side of the river to chop wood.

In the United States, wood was sold by the cord. In the Rio Yaqui, it was sold by the *carga*, or load. Sixty pairs of sticks (120 sticks) about three feet long make a *carga*. Mexican truckers who came into the woods to pick up the *cargas* paid one peso a *carga*. The first day I made two pesos, the first money I had made in the Rio Yaqui. The next week I cut fourteen *cargas*, but could not find a trucker to buy it.

My shirt was torn across the back, and I needed a new one. I went to see my half brother's father, José González. He had recently left Ramona Villegas and was living with Carmen Cosío, a Mexican who had been captured by the Sierra Yaquis near San Marcial when she was about ten years old. She was given to an old Yaqui soldier after the raid on which she was captured, along with her brother, Jorge. The old Yaqui was Benito Vico, and he was still alive when I first got to Torim in 1932. He must have been over eighty when he died in 1933. It had been several years since he had been able to work. He just walked from place to place carrying a saint, asking for alms. Carmen once told me she had never seen a twenty-peso bill. I used to buy presents for her children. She was about twenty-eight years old when I got to the Rio Yaqui in 1932 and very pretty. Everyone thought José had very good luck to have such a blonde young woman when he was so old. José and Carmen had two babies, José and Paola; neither was healthy and both died young. Carmen was José's last woman.

Carmen brought me a cup of coffee and a piece of bread. José said that he had seen my watermelon patch, and that it was looking very fine.

"I came to see if you will buy me a work shirt. This torn shirt on my back is all I have to wear. I have fourteen *cargas* of wood. When I sell it I will pay for the shirt," I said.

"I am sorry, but I cannot help you," he said. "I owe many pesos at the store."

"I can pay for the shirt in two or three days, as soon as I can find a trucker to buy my wood. It would not be a gift."

"No, I cannot do it."

"Well, good-by," I said, feeling very sad. "I must go to Vicam Station."

I looked for an old sack so I could take out a string to sew up my old shirt. Finally I found one and mended the tear across the back.

I walked to the house of my *tio* Vicente Tava at Vicam Station. The family was eating dinner. "Sit down and have some dinner," said Vicente.

After I had eaten, I began to talk with him. He was very happy and able to live very well at that time. He had a good wagon, four mules, eight milk cows, and every ten days he was paid the wages of a lieutenant by the Mexican government. He was one of the Yaquis who signed the treaty with the government in 1926. I told him about the fourteen *cargas* of wood and asked him if he would buy me a shirt at the store where he had credit.

"I have helped many of my relatives and friends," he said, "but no one can ever pay me back. Never. Never."

I said, "Thank you very much. I guess I better go back to Torim."

As I walked out of Vicam, Captain Martín Maehto of Torim crossed the street to talk with me. "How are you, Rosalio?" he asked.

"Not so good."

"Did you walk from Torim?"

"Yes."

"Any news?"

"No."

"Do you have any money?"

"No."

"Here are fifty centavos. You can buy some cigarettes."

He handed me the coin and walked away. I bought two packages of cigarettes and one of matches for fifteen centavos; I spent the other thirty-five centavos for bread.

As I walked along the trail back to Torim I thought about *tio* Vicente and was very sad. "I will never ask anyone else for anything. I know

very well that only my God can help me, and all these people who deny
me the things I ask from my deep necessity, they must have bad luck."

My God heard me, because soon Vicente's daughter died. Then his
wife ran away with a Mexican. One by one he lost his mules. He sold his
cows in the hopes of getting another wife, but he never found one. In
1952 the government took him off the payroll. He became poor and had
only what his children gave him. In 1954 his son killed a policeman and
the government put the boy in jail, but I always thought about the shirt
and did not send him a centavo. He served his term and was released not
long ago. Vicente died very poor in 1956.

Bad luck also came to José Gonzáles, who died in 1936, a few months
before his pretty young wife, Carmen, died, very poor. After José died,
she went away with Juan Rios, or Juan Vaquero, as he was called, to his
ranch north of Bacum. He came in a wagon to see her, saying he would
take good care of her because he had many cows. She asked me if this
were true, and I said, "Yes, he does have many cows." I never saw her
again. They said she was buried without even a *novena* because she had no
relatives.

When I got to my sister-in-law's house in Torim, I put the bread on
the table.

"What did you find in Vicam Station?" she asked.

"Not a thing," I said.

"Do not worry," she said; "tomorrow I will tear up one of my petti-
coats and make a shirt for you." Sunday my sister-in-law made a shirt for
me. It was not so good, but I wore it anyhow.

We ate up all the bread. That night we smoked all the cigarettes, one
after another.

The next week I cut six more *cargas* of wood. Now I had twenty loads.
On January 21, I got up early, drank a cup of coffee, and went across the
river to the road used by the truckers. It was cold, so I built a big fire
by the side of the road while I waited for a truck. At nine o'clock one came
by and I stopped the driver.

"Oh, hello, are you looking for wood?"

"Yes. How many *cargas* do you have?"

"Twenty."

"That's good. Let's go load it."

When the wood was loaded, the man paid me twenty pesos and said
he hoped I would cut another load for him. That was the first twenty pesos
I had received in the Rio Yaqui, and I was very happy. When I got home,
I took off my homemade shirt and put on my old one. I was ashamed to

wear the homemade shirt where people would see it. Then I started to Vicam Station. As soon as I was out of Torim I started to run, and I ran all the way. I went to a store and bought a work shirt and a pair of pants for seven pesos. I got a package of razor blades and some food. As I went back to Torim I walked slow, because the sack of groceries was heavy. Nothing cost very much in Vicam in 1933, and I had bought a lot of food. That night we had a good supper and I gave thanks to God. My first good dinner in my brother's house was January 22, 1933.

I never cut twenty *cargas* again for one sale. Sometimes I cut 240 pairs (four *cargas*) and sometimes I cut 480 pairs (eight *cargas*). Usually I cut wood three or four days a week. I still had to care for my melon patch, and on the days when there was not any food in my brother's house, I would walk to relative's houses to see if I could get a meal.

Just before Lent began, I went to the chief of the *fariseo* society and told him I was a *fariseo*, ready to wear the mask, but that I did not have a goat skin to make the mask. They were very glad to know I was a *fariseo*.

"Do not worry," said the head chief. "We will find a skin for you." The next day the *fariseo* chief gave me a goat skin. In two days I made the mask.

Nacha Sewa Buanamea, Lucrecia Sewa's granddaughter, was my *fariseo madrina* in Torim, and Felipe Vega, who lived at Corasepe, was my *padrino*.

On Sunday morning the *fariseo* chief called us together and said, "Well, my *fariseos*, I want each of you to get ready with your mask. Why? Because we are going to make a procession to every house in Torim; we have to make a fiesta wherever we sleep. We have to collect a little money in every home."

Sunday afternoon we started out to visit every house. We spent the first night at Compuerta, where we made a fiesta. Monday night we made another fiesta at Tierra Blanca, two miles west of Compuerta. Tuesday night we made a fiesta at Baghoi, about a mile and a half west of Tierra Blanca. Wednesday we were at Labór, northwest of Baghoi. Thursday we moved to Vicam Switch to make the last fiesta.

Oh my God, this was the first time I was a *fariseo* in the Rio Yaqui; it was a hard life, but I wasn't hungry. We had plenty to eat every day. But no sleep from Sunday until Friday. Friday we went back to Torim to make our procession there. We finished late in the afternoon; I went straight home, went to sleep, and slept heavily till the next morning. My eyes were hurting from wearing the mask. They were painful for days.

All during Lent we had very little to eat. On Good Friday, I fared

better because I ate with the *fariseos* and there was lots of food. When the
Fiesta de Gloria was over, I thought, "Next year I'll eat well at Easter."

After Easter I was able to support myself a little. I got enough money
from selling wood to buy some coffee, sugar, beans, and lard. But still we
were hungry and I could not buy any clothes.

One day I found a small, sharp nail and made a fishhook. I started
fishing in the water holes in the river. The first day I caught fourteen fish
that weighed about two pounds each: twenty-eight pounds of meat. My
sister-in-law was very happy. She said, "This is the first time we are going
to eat good fish steaks." That night we had a big supper.

Other Yaquis saw my fish, and the next morning several men and boys,
with various kinds of homemade hooks, were trying to fish. Boys kept
coming to me all day, asking what they should do. That was the first time
I ever taught the Yaqui boys anything. After that I often fished in the
river, getting three or four fish a day. Sometimes I would sell a fish or two
to the Mexican soldiers at the garrison for fifteen centavos a fish, so I
could buy cigarettes.

Then, oh God, we started to eat the tender pumpkins from my field.
We had some every day. The first week in May, the watermelons began to
get ripe. Salome Hupaumea Kuka and I stayed in the field all the time,
sleeping there at night, because there were so many coyotes and so many
little animals we call *batepi* (raccoons) that eat watermelons with their
hands, like monkeys. Yaquis and Mexicans tried to steal, too. One of us
stayed awake and on guard day and night. I never ate watermelons before,
but now I did. We were not able to sell any watermelons because there
were so many watermelons that year in Torim.

The big fiesta at Vicam is the Día de San Juan, beginning June 24. I
had always been told what a pretty fiesta this was, and I was glad to be
in Vicam to see it. The fiesta began about ten o'clock in the morning
with all the Yaqui cowboys galloping by a live chicken buried in the
sand, trying to pull it up by the head. Whoever gets the chicken wins
twenty-five pesos. Two cowboys tore the live chicken in two by running
away from each other on horseback. Then a chicken leg is thrown to the
women. All women who like to fight enter the event, and they fight two
at a time for a chicken leg. They run this event until all the women who
want to fight have had a chance. The winning woman in each fight is
given a big basket of bread and three pesos.

In the afternoon the *Morom* game begins. The players are called the
*Moros*, or Moors. Six men play on each team, and the chief of the *Morom*

players is called *Moyaut*. Two ramadas are built somewhat over three hundred feet apart; lines are drawn on the ground in front of each ramada. The players of each team attempt to push and haul their opponents up to the line and then throw them over. Basically this is a wrestling match. One of the most famous wrestlers of Torim in the 1880s was Alejandro Bacotmea, my ex-wife's grandfather.

The *Moros* play about fifteen minutes, and then they rest; so it goes all afternoon and all night. Sometimes during the game the teams try to steal the big drum from the musicians on the other side. While the *Morom* game is going on, two groups of dancers are also performing, four *pascolas* and a deer dancer in each group.

All during the fiesta the kitchen keeps lots of food and anyone can eat. In 1933 the kitchen was run by one-eyed Juan María Simpatico. I was told to see if I could help him, and all night long I had to carry water. Several times an hour he sent me to the well, about a quarter of a mile away, with two five-gallon cans that I carried on a shoulder yoke. Four of us did the water carrying for the whole fiesta. After that I didn't think this was such a pretty fiesta, but I did get all I wanted to eat for the two days and the food was good.

Early in the afternoon of June 25, a mass is held in the church, and after the mass the remaining food is divided up among those who will furnish food for the fiesta the following year. If a person takes one kilo of sugar it means he will donate fifty kilos of sugar the next year; a leg of beef is to be replaced with a whole cow, one firecracker with fifty. Sometimes a pueblo spends three thousand pesos for the fireworks for a Día de San Juan fiesta.

One way a person could make a few pesos was by bootlegging mescal from Bacum. Beer was sold openly in all the Yaqui villages north of the river, but mescal was prohibited. Since Bacum was on the south bank of the river, mescal was legal there. Many Yaquis from every pueblo kept up a steady traffic to Bacum.

I never had enough money to buy mescal for resale, because it cost twenty-five pesos a gallon. Once or twice a week, from 1933 to 1938, I walked to Bacum to buy mescal for the people who sold it in their houses. They gave me the money for the mescal and a few pesos besides. I never got more than six pesos for making the trip, and sometimes it was less. If I went from Torim, it was eight miles each way. If I went from Vicam, it was thirteen miles each way. The river at Bacum was never dry, and I always had to find a log or tie up a bundle of carrizo cane to paddle across the river.

I had a good Mayo friend in Bacum, Pancho Paderes, who lived in a house belonging to Francisca (Pancha) Valenzuela Castro and her mother; like Pancho, they were Mayos. I always went to see Pancho when I went to Bacum, and that is how I met Pancha. Pancha was called Wailika as a nickname. She worked in Mexican houses as a cook and washerwoman. She was young and pretty in 1933 and had never been married. I was always glad to see her.

One day in 1933, Nestor Fregoso Sanava, his son Eduardo, and I were waiting at Chumaiumpaaku along the trail to Bacum for Anastasia González (my sister-in-law) and Nestor's wife, to help them carry their load of mescal back to Torim. All of a sudden we suffered from *chictura*, the sickness that causes you to become lost even though you know perfectly well the place where you are. For about three hours we wandered in circles; we did not remember the cure my grandmother taught me for *chictura*. We finally heard the women coming, and we became oriented again.

For a while in 1933 I worked for Luis Molino, tallying the amount of wood that each of the woodcutters cut for him each day. I would go to where they were cutting, write down the names of the men working that day, and how many *cargas* they made. One day, about 9:00 A.M., I was walking through the brush just east of Corasepe, when I saw a long *bulto* walking along slowly. It looked somewhat like a coyote with an extraordinarily long tail and big, stand-up ears. We call it a *coludo*. He stopped, then slowly walked out of sight. I went over to where he had walked to look at his tracks; as I expected, each track had seven claws. This *coludo* is often seen near that place, so probably there is buried treasure, as *coludos* are said to be a sign of treasure.

Salome Hupaumea, about fourteen years old at this time, was Anastasia's son by a man she lived with before she lived with my half brother. Salome and I have always been good friends and worked together a lot. One day I said to him, "Why don't we try making some crossties? They say a man can make four to six ties a day."

"But I don't have an ax."

"You know lots of people. Maybe you can borrow one."

"I will try," he said.

No one in Torim would let him have an ax. Then he went to another village where he had relatives. In two days he came back with a good, sharp ax. The next day we started making crossties at a place about two miles east of Torim. Mexican, Mayo, and Yaqui men were working there.

I asked one man, "Where do we find the boss man?"

"We have no boss. Every man cuts for himself. We sell to the contractor." He showed us the measurements used to grade the ties. Number one ties are eight inches square; number two ties are six to seven inches square; and number three ties are five to six inches square. All are eight feet long. We started cutting mesquite trees into crossties.

I made one crosstie in about four hours and started another one, but could not finish it. I was too weak. Romulo finished his second one. In four days each of us had made eight ties, which we sold at Chico Comela's store in the labor camp for six pesos worth of groceries and two new axes. He never paid for the ties with money.

We kept working, making about six pesos a week. After two months Chico Comela and his brother Gonzalo started paying one peso for number one crossties; then we made eight pesos a week and all the men were very happy. Comela was selling them to the Southern Pacific Railroad for twelve pesos each. He became very rich. Nobody could stop him, because General José María Huerta Noquera had Mexican soldiers in every camp. The Comela brothers built fine houses in Cajeme (now known as Obregón) and bought several irrigated farms. In February, 1934, the crosstie cutting stopped. Salome and I had bought a shirt, a pair of pants, and one new ax, and that was all we had.

Salome and I decided to leave Torim to look for work because there was nothing to do in Torim. Oh, my God, it was hot. We carried a lunch with us. We walked toward Cajeme. Finding a Yaqui, we asked him if he was working. He was working at night; he said farm laborers were getting from two to three pesos a day. We spent the night there, and early the next morning we went to see the boss man, who said he could use us pulling weeds out of the rice fields for three pesos a day.

We worked from sunrise to sunset, fourteen-hour days. All day we stood barefooted in water, stooped over, pulling weeds. It was hot. At night we could hardly sleep because of fleas on the ground and mosquitos in the air. We stayed eight days, and it was the hardest work I ever did. Groceries were very expensive. We drew our wages on February 14, 1934; each of us took ten pesos back to Torim. When we left, we said we would never again work in the rice fields of the Yaqui Valley. How could a poor man live in the Rio Yaqui? Many families had little children. How could they eat on three pesos a day? I never want to go back to work in the Yaqui Valley. Not even if it's the last job in the world.

The day we got back to Torim, we spent all of our money for food. I woke sad the next morning because I did not have a centavo in my pocket and Lent had started.

CHAPTER **10**

# *Torim, 1934–1937*

ONE NIGHT, early in Lent, I had a dream, a very good dream. I dreamed that some white men were coming to the Rio Yaqui from the north, and that they were going to help the Yaquis. I did not know when, but they were coming.

The next day I was thinking and thinking about the American friends, because I remembered the things José María Nóteme told the Yaquis long ago in Hermosillo. Many Yaquis came to hear this *sabio* as he talked about the future and what was going to happen to the Yaqui tribe. He said the Yaquis were going to have the hard life for a long time, and some of the Yaquis would go to the United States to save themselves. Some Yaquis would be very happy with the Americans. The Mexican government, he said, would try to clear the Yaqui people out of the Rio Yaqui, and the government could do nearly everything. But it would never finish off the Yaquis. He said that a big revolution against Porfirio Díaz would come, and the people would be like crazy for a few years. They would fight like dogs and kill each other. "It will be the chastisement of our God," said José María Nóteme.

He said the Yaquis of the Rio Yaqui would have a little rest and make a happy living for a few years, then the Mexican government would start to fight with them again; that would be the last fight of the Yaquis. Then some white men would come from the north to help the Yaquis. The white men would ask the Yaquis about all that had happened to them and little by little help them to make a happy living. Well, that was what the old men said when I was a little boy.

Lent of 1934 had started, and I made my mask. While we were making the fourth procession in Torim village, we heard about the white men. They were in Vicam Station, and they wanted to find some old Yaquis to tell them everything that had happened to the Yaqui tribe. When I heard this I thought, "These are the white men I saw in my dream, and my dreams never lie to me."

A few days later a white man and a Yaqui lieutenant, José Juan Torre, came to Torim. I guess the chiefs at the *guardia* could not understand what the white men wanted. Luis Overa, the governor, sent a Yaqui soldier to where the *fariseos* were at the church, and the soldier said to the chief of the *fariseos*, "Can you let Rosalio come to the *guardia*, because there is one white man there and we cannot understand what he is looking for. Maybe Rosalio Javier can understand him."

The *fariseo* chief said to me, "You had better take off your *fariseo* mask and all your *fariseo* clothes and go see this white man. Find out what news he brings us."

I said to the chief, "I do not think I can understand him, but I will go."

When I got to the *guardia*, I shook hands with the man named Dr. Holden, and told him my name was Simón Palos. Dr. Holden started to explain to the governor, Luis Overa, and to the other chiefs why he and the other white men had come to the Rio Yaqui. The chiefs were scared of the Americans.

One chief said to the governor and all the Yaqui soldiers, "This will mean trouble for all the Yaquis, because we do not know these people. Are they good, or are they *políticos* like the ones who always come to the Yaquis and explain to them with a lovely voice? The *políticos* always make trouble for us, and I guess this will be the same."

I told Dr. Holden what the chief said. He told me to tell the chief, "We are not *políticos*. We are honest people who come to help the Yaquis."

Then he showed some papers to the chiefs. I explained in Yaqui what the papers said. They told where the white men were from and what they wanted to do in the Rio Yaqui. The Americans wanted to learn what had happened to the Yaquis in their own land, and they wanted to put everything in a book for people to read. This they said, would help the Yaquis make a better life in the Rio Yaqui. Dr. Holden finally made the chiefs understand, and then the chiefs were glad, because this was the first American friend they had met in Torim village.

Dr. Holden said he wished to visit Pluma Blanca, the chief of the Yaquis, at Bataconsica, which is about eight miles east of Torim. Luis Overa said that would be all right. Then the other chiefs said, "Yes. They can go see Pluma Blanca." Teodoro Reales, the second governor of Torim, and I went with Dr. Holden and José Juan Torre to Bataconsica. It was fifteen miles by the road, and it took an hour to go. When we got there we stopped at the Yaqui *guardia* and shook hands with Pluma Blanca and all the chiefs of Bataconsica village.

Pluma Blanca was sick with a headache because he had been drunk for two or three weeks. Dr. Holden started to explain why the white men had come to the Rio Yaqui. Pluma Blanca and the other chiefs took the words the wrong way. Pluma Blanca said, "What do they want? Are we not like other human beings? We have five fingers on each hand and five toes on each foot."

The chiefs were very scared and very mad too. Lieutenant José Juan Torre and the second governor from Torim tried to help Dr. Holden, but Pluma Blanca and the chiefs of Bataconsica would not believe them, and Dr. Holden did not arrange anything. We got back to Torim about 1:30 P.M. and the second governor and I got out of the car, and Lieutenant José Juan Torre went back to Vicam Station with Dr. Holden.

The next day I did not have to do anything for the *fariseos*, so I went to Vicam Station to see the Americans. I asked Pedro More where the Texas friends were. He told me that they were camped near the depot and the railroad. Many Yaquis were standing around the camp, looking at the Americans. I stood there some time before Dr. Holden saw me. He came to me and shook hands, then he took me in the camp and had me shake hands with all his friends. They were all very glad to meet me. They gave me some magazines.

Dr. Holden showed me a letter from "General" Lucho Ramíriz, who was living in Tucson. It was written in Yaqui and was addressed to all the governors of all the eight villages. It said that he sent good regards to the governors and all the chiefs of Torim and all the eight Yaqui villages. He said, "I let you know, every one of you, that this Dr. Holden and a few of his friends come to visit the Yaqui villages, to find out what happened among the Yaquis, in the Rio Yaqui. They say Dr. Holden and his friends are honest men and you can meet them with confidence. They are real good friends of the Yaqui Indians."

Every word in "General" Lucho Ramíriz's letter was written very well. But the Yaquis in the Rio Yaqui have no relations with "General" Lucho Ramíriz. They hate him, and say, "What kind of a general is he? We didn't elect him." The Arizona Yaquis said the same things.

When I finished reading, I told Dr. Holden, "This is a very good letter, but it will not do any good. The Yaquis in the Rio Yaqui do not like Lucho Ramíriz. They hate him. They did not elect him to be general; he just took the title when he got to the United States. I would not show this letter to anybody else. I would burn it." I guess he burned it, because I never heard of it again.

Dinner was ready, and Dr. Holden asked me to eat with them. It was the first American food I had seen, or tasted, in over two years, and there were many lovely things to eat. I was sad, thinking about the U.S.A. While I was sitting at the table with the Americans, I heard some fool Yaqui boys in the crowd saying, "Hey, don't let that Yaqui eat at the table with you, because he will eat everything on the table." The Americans could not understand them, but I could. When I finished eating, I went back to Torim very happy because of the nice food and my American friends.

In the morning the *fariseo* chief ordered all the *fariseos* to work, saying, "Well, boys, we have to fix everything in the church." We worked all that day in the church, and the next day we finished getting the church ready for the Fiesta de Gloria.

The Americans wanted to move to Torim for the Fiesta de Gloria. They asked Luis Overa if they could camp near the Yaqui soldiers' *guardia*, because they said they had come to see the Yaquis and not the Mexicans. Luis Overa said, "You can camp anywhere you want," so they started unloading their truck.

The Mexican garrison, on a hill near the river about two hundred yards from the Yaqui *guardia*, was commanded by the Lieutenant Colonel Orozco. In a little while a Mexican soldier came down the hill to the Yaqui *guardia* to tell Dr. Holden, "You cannot camp near the Yaqui *guardia*. You must come up the hill and place your tent near the Mexican *guardia*."

Dr. Holden took me and one of the white boys as interpreters up to the Mexican headquarters. The colonel was very angry. He wanted to know what the white men meant by making a camp at the Yaqui garrison. "Don't you know they will cut your throats while you sleep?" he asked.

The Americans explained what they were doing and showed the colonel a letter from the president of Mexico. The letter directed the army and the navy to help the Americans in every way. The colonel did not know what to do. "I must telephone General José María Huerta at Esperanza about this," he said.

He called the general and read the letter to him. When he had finished,

he said to us, "The general says that the letter places you under the protection of the Mexican army. The army must see that no harm happens
to any of you. You must camp here on the *portal* of the Mexican garrison:
none of your party can go anywhere in the Yaqui Zone without some
Mexican soldiers to go with you. The general says you must either do this
or leave the Yaqui Zone without delay." The Americans moved to the
Mexican *guardia*.

Colonel Orozco started watching the Americans very closely. He was a
bad Mexican. He always hated white men and he hated the Yaquis too.
A few days later he called me to headquarters to ask me what the white
men were telling the Yaquis. I told him that I did not speak Spanish,
and, oh my, he sure was mad at me.

He sent for Governor Luis Overa and asked, "What is that Rosalio
doing with the white men and what do the Americans want, always talking
to the Yaqui Indians?"

Luis Overa said, "Well, these are our good friends. They come to see
our religion because many Americans don't know about our religion."

Colonel Orozco was mad at the Americans, at me, and at the governor.
Everywhere the Americans went he sent along a Mexican soldier.

One day the Americans went to Potam, and I went along as interpreter.
First we stopped at General Mendez's headquarters and asked a Mexican
soldier if we could go to the Yaqui *guardia* to see Captain Trinidad
Aldama. He showed us the way. Dr. Holden shook hands with Captain
Aldama, and then asked him what was happening in the Yaqui tribe.

Trinidad Aldama answered with foolish words, saying, "Well, I don't
know anything about what the American wants to know. Our General
Morre left me here to take care of our Virgin Mary church. I've never
asked anyone for help. I don't need help. No nation can help me. I was
in the service of the Mexican government for more than thirty years. I've
only got one bullet in me." The American medical doctor, Dr. Wagner,
told Trinidad that he would be happy to take the bullet out of his leg.

"Oh no, no. I feel very well with my bullet." Trinidad Aldama was
a brave man, but he was afraid of an operation.

Dr. Holden did not find out anything from Trinidad Aldama, because
Aldama was very stupid and he would not cooperate with the Americans.
The only thing he believes in is his religion. He tells his people that Jesus
Christ was born in Belem village. León Tava tells young Yaquis that same
thing. Most Yaquis think Trinidad Aldama and León Tava are crazy men.

The next day Dr. Holden wanted to go see the governors and chiefs of
Cocorit. We had to go see them at Vicam Station because they were under

arrest at the Mexican *guardia* there. All the Cocorit chiefs and governors shook hands with the Americans, but they were afraid and said they could not understand the Americans.

Dr. Holden wanted to meet the Vicam pueblo officials. The governor, Guillermo Acuña, was living about three and a half miles from town. We finally found his house. Dr. Holden could not make him understand what he wanted. Guillermo Acuña told the Americans that he did not know anything. He acted like an innocent little boy.

The Americans quit trying to see the governors and chiefs. They never went to Rahum, Huirivis, or Belem. They just stayed in Torim, taking notes about everything they saw. I was very happy. I had a good time, eating well every day. I had some money in my pockets, too.

The *fariseos* started working hard on Good Friday, and we worked day and night. The Americans worked hard too. They watched everything we did and wrote it all down. They stayed with us night and day, writing down every move we made, what we did in the church, and how we ran up and down every ten minutes close to the door where two little angels stand on either side of a white curtain that the Yaqui priests call the Gloria. The last time we ran, all the *fariseos* took off their masks and threw them by the big cross in front of the church that we call the *Cruz Mayor*. The *fariseo* society end their activities about 11:30 A.M. on Saturday; then the *pascolas* and *matachines* started dancing.

Oh, my Lord, I was awfully tired and sleepy, because we had been working, walking, and running since Thursday. The chief of the *fariseos*, the lieutenant, sergeant, Pilate and his assistant, the flag man and the drummer—all these have an easy time during Lent. They just sit on chairs and give orders to the poor *fariseos*. They eat very well, all day long, and at night they sleep for two or three hours. But *fariseos* never get to sleep. It is hard to wear the mask and hold the Yaqui rosary in your teeth all the time. Your eyes always hurt because the eye holes in the masks are made with a needle.

Every year the *fariseo* masks are burned when the *fariseos'* dance is over. Two masks are saved, in case any *fariseo* member dies during the coming year, so that he can be buried with a mask.

Dr. Holden wanted to buy a mask, but the *fariseos* would never sell them. Not for a thousand pesos, because we pray to God in our masks and we sweat in our masks. Dr. Holden asked me to make two masks for the museum. I did so secretly, going out in the brush to make them where no one could see what I was doing. I took the two masks to him very early on the morning he left the Rio Yaqui. No one knew.

After the Americans left, I was very sad for a few days. A few weeks later Dr. Wagner sent me a package of medicine for a sick woman at Compuerta. But the medicine was too late, because Micaela Jiménez was already dead.

Dr. Holden sent me a letter saying that he was sending many photographs for me to give to people. When they came to the Vicam post office, Lieutenant Colonel Orozco got the package out of the post office and tried to sell the photos for seventy-five centavos apiece. No one ever paid him any money, and no one ever got any pictures.

Later that year Dr. Holden and Dr. Wagner came back to Torim, bringing with them a fine interpreter, Dr. Charles B. Qualia. They started talking to Governor Luis Overa; he was very drunk, and pretty soon he started talking about the history of the Filipinos of Manila. I do not think he knew what he was talking about. I wrote Dr. Holden a note saying that the governor was very drunk. So all the Americans went back up to the Mexican headquarters.

That evening Dr. Holden and Dr. Wagner came for me. We sat on the sidewalk at the corner of the Yaqui school while they told me what they had done. The Americans wrote down a few more notes, and then they went back to the United States, taking a lot of carrizo cane to their museum.

Dr. Holden wrote again, saying he was going to Mexico City to tell some Mexican officials how things were in the Yaqui country. I guess he explained things very well, because soon some Mexican officials came to the Yaqui villages. León Tava called the Yaqui governors and chiefs from the eight pueblos to Vicam Switch. The Mexican officials listened to León Tava and the governors while they told him how the railroad ties had been cut from village lands without the permission of the pueblo officials.

General Huerta was called to Mexico City to explain all the things he did to the Yaqui people. General Jesús Alvarez Ramos was sent to Vicam as the new commander of the Yaqui Zone. He was very friendly with the Yaqui governors. Right away he stopped all the crosstie cutting on Yaqui lands, and he kicked all the Mexican thieves out of the Yaqui country.

A boxcar arrived at Vicam Switch, February, 1935, loaded with work pants and jackets, more than two thousand blankets, huaraches, and agricultural tools. The boxcar was not opened in Vicam Switch. Rather, Chief Pluma Blanca ordered that it be opened at Jori, three and a half miles from Bataconsica. Everyone walked to Jori Switch to get some blankets or something. I went too. When we got there the boxcar was already opened and empty. Pluma Blanca had fifty blankets, and his captain, Anastasio Urias, had fifty blankets. The governors of Bataconsica and Pluma Blanca's soldiers all got two or three pairs of blankets. The Vicam officials were equally well supplied.

My uncle Vicente Tava got all he could carry, but he did not say a word to me. All day I stood there watching. I did not get a single blanket. Mariano, my half brother, got one blanket, one pair of pants, and one pair of huaraches. No one from Torim got very much. Many of the things that the Mexican government sent to help the poor Yaquis were taken by *torocoyori* Yaquis and Mexican soldiers; and a lot of the things were sold in the shops of Vicam.

A few weeks later the government sent four tractors to the Yaqui tribe. León Tava and some officials at Vicam took them, because by this time they were friendly with General Jesús Alvarez Ramos. The tractors never did anyone any good because these lazy Yaquis would start working at midmorning and they quit at midafternoon. No one knew anything about tractors and they soon burned up the motors.

Dr. Holden had got the government officials in Mexico City to listen about the plight of the poor Yaquis. But the *torocoyoris* and Mexican soldiers stole everything, and nothing was changed for the poor Yaquis.

The land in our valley is good land, rich enough to grow two crops a year. All Yaquis could live comfortably and never be hungry—if there was enough water. When the river does not flow, the ground is too hard to plant; the poor Yaquis go hungry. The river was dry from 1933 to 1937, and few crops were grown. It was hard to live in the Rio Yaqui during those years. Once or twice a week I walked to Bacum, receiving a few pesos from the people who sent me after bootleg mescal. More often than not, I walked all night on the mescal hauls. Sometimes I worked for other men who were trying to farm; they could not pay me, but they usually gave me a meal. Frequently I walked to the other Yaqui pueblos to see if I could get a meal from a friend or relative. Several women wanted to live with me, but how could I feed a family when I stayed hungry all the time?

I blame the Yaqui chiefs and governors and generals for most of the misery the Yaquis suffer. They do not know how to make arrangements with the Mexican government that will stop the suffering of the Yaqui tribe. If someone even tries to talk to the Mexican officials, all the other Yaquis start to say, "Oh, I guess he is going to sell Yaqui lands to the Mexicans," as though anyone could sell land without a document. Most

Yaquis distrust anyone who speaks fluent Spanish, because they can not understand everything that is said and they are afraid he will make some sort of a deal with the Mexicans. The Mexican government might help the Yaqui people if the chiefs and governors knew how to talk to the officials for the good of the whole tribe. But every time the government has given something to the Yaqui tribe, the chiefs and governors take everything, and the Yaqui people are as hungry as before. Worst of all is when the Yaqui babies die from hunger, or when they get sick and their mothers and fathers cannot buy medicine. I was always sad when babies and little children died in Torim. About half the babies born in Torim died before they were two years old.

Dr. Holden gave me fifty pesos when he left the first time. With it I bought some shirts and work pants. The second time he came he left many shirts and pants, so for a while I dressed well. As time went on and I could not find work, I began taking a pair of pants or a shirt over to Vicam to sell for a peso or two in order to buy a little food so we would not starve. Sometimes I gave a shirt to someone for a meal. Soon the clothes were all gone.

Through all these hard years, when there was no money to buy food, we went out into the brush (*monte*) and collected things to eat. From the *hue-e* plant, we ate the leaves of the young plants, and when the plants matured we gathered the seeds. In the leafy stage, we called it *ajo* (not to be confused with the Spanish *ajo*, garlic). The tiny brown seeds can be parched and made into a sort of pinole, or boiled, ground, and made into *masa* for tortillas and tamales. Tortillas made of *hue-e* seeds look and taste like dirt. The first time I ate them, at the house of Panocha and Juana Valencia, I asked, "Where did you get this dirt? I want to make tortillas too." They thought it very funny that I believed I was eating dirt.

During June, July, and August everyone goes out to gather pitahaya. With a long, sharpened carrizo cane you spear the fruit, which may grow fifteen or twenty feet above the ground. At home the fruit is peeled, put in an *olla* without water, and cooked. The women decide when it has reached the jelly stage by dropping a little in a cup of water. The sweet pitahaya jelly, which we call *sitoim*, can be kept a long time. This sort of jelly can be made from other cacti, but that made from pitahaya is the best. When the *sitoim* is made from the nopal tuna (prickly pear), we call it *navo sitoim*.

Some cactus fruits can be eaten fresh. The *ahuesoim* does not grow in the Yaqui Valley, but there are lots of plants scattered between the low hills near the sea at Guaymas. The red *ahuesoim* fruit is thought to be very good when ripe. The *museom* cactus fruit is also eaten fresh.

It is very bad to eat the red tuna from the nopal, unless you know just what to do, because you can get a fever called *ta-he-hue-chi-a na-bom*. If you know how to yell at the nopal to scare it, you can eat the tunas without getting the fever. The tiny red fruit from the jito tree (called *San Juanico* in Spanish) can be cooked like beans.

In these three years I spent most of my time looking for food, one way or another. Either I was walking miles and miles in the hopes of getting a meal from a relative or friend, or I was working very hard for a meal or a peso or two to buy a little food, or I was out in the brush finding things to eat.

One day in 1934 I was out in the brush cutting wood, when I saw a lot of buzzards. Going over to investigate, I saw that they were clustered around a body stuffed down into a hole. From the clothes, I realized that it was Alberto Duval; the face and body had been so hacked up with an ax as to be unrecognizable. I left the body there and went back to chopping wood. Alberto was never buried. The buzzards ate him. If I had gone to the *guardia* to tell the officials, they would have said I killed him.

Alberto Duval was a Mexican soldier stationed at the Torim garrison. Some time before, he had gone to Reyes Castillo at Cenobampo to buy green corn, and Reyes had said, "Why don't you come live here with us and plant on my land." Alberto left his guns at the garrison and deserted. Mexican soldiers hunted for him, but he was well hidden at Cenobampo, a rancheria on Torim lands.

Alberto planted and raised a crop. After the corn was harvested, Reyes refused to give Alberto anything at all. Alberto was a good friend of mine, and he came to see me, telling all about what Reyes had done. Three days later I found him dead, and I am sure Reyes killed him rather than share his crop or pay him any money.

Reyes Castillo was a Sierra Yaqui for many years. He and his wife, Victoria, returned to Torim in 1927 and began farming at Cenobampo. After his sister, Mariano Castillo, married Roberto Huerta, a Mexican from elsewhere in Mexico, they lived at Cenobampo and farmed with Reyes. As far as I know, Reyes never murdered anyone else in Torim. He was a good Yaqui, never becoming a *yori*. His brother-in-law probably helped him kill Alberto.

In the following year, 1935, another murder occurred in Torim. A young man, Luis Santana, was a regular mescal runner. Every two or three days he went to Bacum to get a load. I had known Luis briefly in Tucson in 1926, when he was only in his early teens. He had returned to Torim in 1927, as did so many others.

One day, Luis left Torim on a mule about four o'clock in the afternoon, carrying about 150 pesos for buying mescal. He was killed about a mile from Torim with a knife, and his body was burned a little ways off the Bacum-Torim trail. The mule coming back by itself to Luis's house in Torim caused people to go look for the body, which was finally found by some vaqueros. The burned remains were left there and never buried.

The next day after the murder, Guadalupe Chávez of Cocorit was well dressed in brand-new clothes; he had been seen in the Torim area on the day of the murder. Everyone knew he had killed Luis, but nothing ever happened to Guadalupe.

Sacramento Navogoki, Juan More, and I went to the Sierra in 1934, looking for gold. There are supposed to be some old Spanish gold mines in the Bacatete Mountains, and we had heard many stories of buried treasure. We never found any gold, but we saw where a *sierpa* lived. We found a big hole in the ground; the ground around the hole looked like it had been swept clean. Strong winds rushed down into the hole, winds strong enough to suck a person into the cave. If you sat to one side, you were safe. We watched birds get sucked into the hole. Sacramento said that it must be a *sierpa*.

*Sierpas* are always very large. They can eat a whole cow or a deer at one time. Almost any sort of animal can be a *sierpa*—giant rattlesnakes, giant scorpions, giant centipedes, or giant fish. Some, with a white cross on their foreheads, are harmless. Ones without the cross are dangerous. All *sierpas* were once people who did something wrong like marrying a close relative. As a rule, they do not hurt people. They live in a hole, eating and growing bigger, until one day they go to the sea (*salen al mar*) with a terrible uproar, tearing up trees and knocking down anything in their way. Thereafter they stay in the ocean, never returning to the place they grew for so long.

At another place in the Sierra, Sacramento, Juan, and I saw a giant scorpion about two feet tall moving in a big wind. That was probably a *sierpa* too. We left.

I remember a story that Miguel Compoy, a *pascola* drummer, told me in Tucson. Years before he had been a cowboy on Sonoran ranches. When he worked at a ranch east of Hermosillo, he was with another cowboy at a place called Cerro del Tigres. He was sucked off his horse by a strong wind and drawn closer and closer to a cave. He hung onto branches with all his might, wet with sweat from the effort. Just when he was about to be sucked into the cave, his companion reached him and made the sign of the cross three times with his hat in his hand. The wind stopped and

Miguel fell over to one side of the opening. Miguel had not known about *sierpas* before this happened, but his companion did.

When I first arrived in Torim, an old man named Juan de Dios Meowa was very good to me. He would say, "Come Rosalio, let's go to the fiesta," and we often attended fiestas together in the different pueblos. Whenever I visited him in Compuerta, he gave me a meal. He must have been as old as my grandfather Abelardo and told me many stories about my relatives in Torim and his long years in the Sierra. In spite of his age, he had a young daughter, Anita Flores. His sister, Jesús Esuki (or Jesús Ant), kept house for old Juan and Anita. Her husband had been deported and she never took another man. Her daughters were all married. Juan and Jesús lived fairly well on his government pay. After his death in 1934, Jesús and Anita nearly starved. One day in 1935 Jesús brought the sixteen-year-old Anita to my house and gave her to me. They wanted us to marry in the church some day. Poor Anita was so hungry. She asked me to buy her some canned fruit. She ate it so fast it made her sick. About a month later she got sick and asked to go home to her aunt Jesús at Compuerta. I was not there when she died. Since old Juan de Dios had been a *fariseo*, all of the Torim *fariseos* attended her *velación* and funeral.

It was in 1935 that the Yaquis burned a witch. I attended the Día de San Juan fiesta in Cocorit that year and liked it no better than I had liked the Día de San Juan fiesta in Vicam. After the fiesta, many men went over to the nearby Corrál railroad station to drink mescal. A *maestro*, Juan Maesto of Cocorit, died; another *maestro*, Juan Corál of Vicam, was said to be the witch who had caused his death. The other men immediately bound Corál's arms and took him to the Yaqui *guardia* in Cocorit, where he remained three days and nights without food or water. He was never untied. The chiefs of Cocorit sentenced him to a witch's death by burning and sent six men out to chop wood. The fire was laid at a place about one-half mile northeast of Corrál. After Corál walked to the wood pile, they tied his feet, threw him on, and lit the fire. He never cried out or said anything. Whenever a Yaqui knows he is to be killed he never cries out. Of all the Yaquis killed by the Mexicans, none ever cried out. I went to the trial in Cocorit and witnessed the burning.

Juan Corál's family in Vicam knew nothing of what was happening until it was all over. Then they went to the place he had been burned. No *velación*, funeral, or *novena* was held for him because he was a *demonio* (devil). Everyone, including his family, knew he was a witch. For years I had been told that he was a well-known witch. Witches are the only ones condemned to die by burning, according to Yaqui law.

Lucrecia Sewa went blind in 1936 and died a few weeks later at her house in Corasepe. I attended her funeral because she was my grandmother's kinswoman. Before she died, she told me that Juan Jacom Pata de Hule (rubber-foot), also of Corasepe, had bewitched her. I am not sure he was really a witch. In any event, Juan was a nice person (*buena gente*), always sharing food with his friends. His son, also named Juan, lived very close to Mariano González's house, where I was living.

Nicho Valenzeula, who returned to Vicam from Arizona in 1932 (the same year I came to the Rio Yaqui), died in 1936. He was known as *Ju-hua-zu-la*, which means "frozen," because once, when he was a young man in Arizona, he got so drunk on mescal that he passed out as he was going home. It snowed that night. When they found him the next day, he was "frozen," but he thawed out and lived a long time after that. I had known him well in Arizona, and I often saw him in Vicam after we returned to the Rio Yaqui.

Adelina Alvarez was a pretty girl of seventeen or eighteen in 1936. Her father, Valentino Alvarez, was my old friend Pedro Alvarez's brother. Pedro was living in Cocorit at this time, and Valentino and I often walked over to see him when I first lived in Torim. Pedro was now crippled and unable to go visit anyone else. Valentino died about 1934, leaving his family without a source of income, as his government pay was cut off. Since I had been in their house so often, I had known Adelina for several years. She told me she wanted to marry me. Both her mother, Luisa, and her brother José Luis Alvarez were very happy that Adelina wanted to marry me. José Luis was a *fariseo* like I was, and we were good friends.

One day I said, "I am going to Tucson."

Adelina said, "When are you coming back?"

"Never." I meant it for a joke, but she believed it. I left and went to Esperanza to see Rosa Kuka before I left for Arizona.

At the border it was easy to get across. I just said I was a citizen of the United States. For a month I went to visit everyone I knew. I had a fine time seeing friends and relatives in Tucson and Guadalupe. I stayed with my cousin Simón Valenzuela in Tucson, and he told me all the news. He always was a talker. He told me that Juan Sasueta (the one who was married to Carmen, Simón's sister who died) had been killed. I know who killed him, but he is still alive so I will not write his name. These two had been drinking together and got into a fight. After Juan was killed, the other man put his body in his car and drove up to Casa Grande, where he threw it out of the car. Juan had lived with Rufina Valenzuela since

1917. After his death, Rufina went to live with Eufemio Bacotmea, who is now the *maestro* of Pascua. Eufemio is the youngest brother of Charla, my first wife's mother.

One day at 9:45 A.M. the immigration officials came for me at Simón's house. "Are you Rosalio Valenzuela?"

"Yes."

"How did you enter the United States? We know you are not a citizen as you claimed."

"It was easy. I just lied to the man at the border." How was I to know they had tightened the border regulations? Before when Yaquis crossed the border, everyone said whatever the border people wanted to hear.

They gave me the alternative of jail or leaving the country in twenty-four hours. I said I would leave. I had only come for a visit and to pick up some of my California clothes, anyway.

We found out that the man who turned me in was Tomás Vidal. He had bad luck after he reported me. On December 6, 1936, someone put him on the railroad track and the train ran over him and killed him.

I caught the train from Nogales to Esperanza, spending the night at Bernalda's house with Rosa. The next day I got to Torim. The first person I talked to was Anastasia Hupaumea González. She told me Adelina Alvarez died not long after I left. She refused to eat another bite after I told her I was not coming back and died of *tristeza*. It was only a joke. Her brother José Luis died shortly thereafter of a throat ailment. He had been ill for some time, and for the last few months of his life he was unable to talk.

Along about this time, Lázaro Cárdenas, president of the Republic, sent eight new trucks to the Yaqui tribe, one to each pueblo. The captain of one of the pueblos sold that pueblo's truck to Santos Suárez for fifteen hundred pesos—a gift. Santos lived then and still lives in Obregón; he is a half Yaqui–half Mexican who makes his living as a trucker and peddler, going to all the Yaqui villages, Guaymas, Hermosillo, into the Sierra, and down to Agua Calienta, selling food: flour, beans, sugar, sweets, coffee, bananas, oranges, lard; clothing, hats, blankets, thread, needles, sewing machines, and just about anything anyone would want. He traded for cheese, *petates*, or whatever people had. He also handled contraband goods, such as guns and ammunition. Santos himself went to Nogales to get the guns. The shells were mostly supplied by his half brother, Bonifasio Díaz, a Torim Yaqui who worked on the railroad out of Empalme. He went to Nogales regularly as part of his railroad job; he always brought back .30-.30 and .30-.40 shells. Bonifasio still works for the railroad, but it is not necessary to run contraband guns any more. Bonifasio's sister, Juana Díaz, ran a small store in Torim, and his older brother, Juan, now in his eighties, was the chief of the Torim *fariseos* until 1948, when he could not run anymore. Juan was called Juan Tequila for many years.

After the truck was sold to Santos, the captain was removed from office and a new captain was selected. Even though the captain was stripped of his office, he has lived comfortably, acquiring a herd of cows; his family make and sell cheese.

Once at Chumaiumpaaku, an old man named Tevelito Lipti (because he had one eye) killed a *coludo*. He lived by himself in a house built out in his field, where he kept several large dogs. Hearing a terrible racket one night, he came out to see what the dogs were fighting. He saw that it was a *coludo*. The dogs finally killed it; the next morning he skinned the animal and took the hide to the *guardia* at Bacum. Even though he was living on Torim lands and the Torim *guardia* was a lot closer, he went to Bacum because that was his pueblo. I walked over to Bacum to see it. It was rather like a coyote, but with a tail four feet long, and each foot had seven toes. In 1933 I saw a *coludo* near Corasepe, as I related earlier.

A few months later, after Tevelito killed the *coludo*, he saw a flame (*lumbre*) under a large *maco-chine* (huamuchil) tree. Digging there the next day, he found a large *olla*, covered with a heavy *comal* and a metate, containing 800,000 pesos. Tevelito showed me two of the coins, big silver pesos bearing 1874 dates. Tevelito had an old wife and no children. He never spent a penny of that money. Instead he went to the Sierra and hid it; I suppose it is still there.

These *lumbres* are said to burn now and again where treasure is buried, but I have never believed that was true. Although I have often seen *lumbres* that burned for a few minutes and disappeared, I never bothered to dig for treasure. I believe in *coludos* because I have seen them. What else has seven toes?

The two Conemea brothers returned to the Rio Yaqui in 1936 from their deportation in 1927. The third brother had been killed at the Cerro de Gallo, as mentioned earlier. Luis Conemea died in Huirivis about 1938 and Eulogio Conemea has become a school teacher at Pitahaya. Eulogio learned to read and write at Mesquital, Arizona. Recently he has been writing down old Yaqui stories on the typewriter. He knows the old stories all right, so I think he is a good teacher. It is very interesting for the modern children to know the old stories.

The Fiesta de Gloria in Torim, 1934. The man acting the part of Christ (second from left) reportedly made a *manda* at the age of seventy-five. He served in the role for three years before his death.

Envion : _____ : ___ : __ Good Friday, Taxim, 1994

The Fiesta de Gloria procession on Easter Day, Torim, 1934.

A raised hearth for cooking, Torim, 1934. A metate stands at the right.

A house compound of carrizo cane, Torim, 1934.

Dr. Charles Wagner visiting with Torim villagers, 1934.

Dr. Wagner examining a patient with severe tuberculosis.

Deer dancer (left) and *pascolas*, Torim, about 1938.

*Matachine* dancers, Torim, 1953.

A man from Hollywood, California, came to Torim one morning in May of 1936 to ask the governor and chiefs of our pueblo if he could buy one million carrizo canes, each at least nine feet long. He asked the governor to go with him to the bank in Obregón, where he would immediately open an account for Torim pueblo, after which he would pay fifty pesos per thousand carrizo delivered. He said, "This will be good business for the Yaqui people. They can begin to help themselves."

The Yaqui commander told the governors and chiefs that they could not allow this man to cut carrizo on Torim lands, because if they did they would have trouble with the officials from the other Yaqui pueblos. The first governor told the white man that Torim could not accept his offer. The man from Hollywood said, "Well, that is fine. I will go to the other pueblos."

He went back to Vicam Switch to talk to the Mexican judge, Lauro Gallardo; they made all the arrangements, because Lauro's brother, Luis Gallardo, was a good friend of General Jesús Alvarez Ramos, who was in charge of the whole Yaqui Zone. Luis Gallardo signed the contract and right away he had people cutting carrizo all up and down the river. Pretty soon all the poor Yaqui men started cutting carrizo for Luis Gallardo; he only paid thirty pesos a thousand, instead of the fifty pesos the white man had first offered. Luis Gallardo pocketed twenty pesos per thousand carrizo.

Fine carrizo grew all along the river. For twelve days I cut carrizo, making a bundle of four thousand canes. Then I had bad luck and got sick, and it cost all the money from the carrizo to buy medicine for my chills. When I got well, I had just started cutting carrizo again, when some fool Yaqui burned the carrizo cane breaks all the way up and down the river, so I lost my four hundred cut carrizo. Many other Yaquis lost theirs, and there was no more carrizo business. Luis Gallardo made over three thousand pesos in one month, even though he could not finish the contract. With his money he bought some cows and a new wagon with mules. Now he is a rich man with a big ranch at Bemela Ba-am (which means "the new water"), just east of Torim.

The Yaqui chiefs and governors did everything wrong, just as they have every time they have had a chance to make an honest business that would help the poor Yaqui people. Instead of everyone making money, only a few *yoris* made out.

Water came down the river in December of 1936, and the Yaquis were able to plant in January of 1937. I looked around for a place where I could plant watermelon and I found a good place about a mile southwest of Torim pueblo. I began clearing on January 5, 1937. The brush was not heavy and the clearing was easy. I finished in five days. Then I made eight hundred holes in the wet ground. On January 15 I planted watermelons and a few cantaloupes. My luck was good. Not a single watermelon plant did I lose. It was hard, working on my watermelon plot all day when I had so little to eat; once a day my sister-in-law fed us a little. I was so tired all the time, I could not walk to relatives' houses in the other pueblos to get a meal.

When Lent started, it was time to make my *fariseo* mask. Wearing the mask was hard, because I could not see well. Whenever I wore my mask, I got sick in my eyes and teeth. But I had to wear it because I had made a *promesa* to Jesus Christ to wear the mask. This was the last time I wore my mask.

As soon as Lent was over, I went back to my watermelon plot. Day by day the watermelons grew nicely. On May 20 I began selling the melons. Many people came to buy, and sometimes Mexicans came in wagons to buy a hundred melons for thirty pesos. As soon as I got some money, I started buying all sorts of food for Mariano, Anastasia and Salome, and Micaela. Anastasia was so happy to have food that she walked out to my watermelon plot with a lunch for me three times a day; I had to stay out there all the time to guard my melons. All that year we had food to eat; we did not gather cactus apples in June and July, nor did we have to eat other wild foods. Yaquis who could not pay money for the melons gave me sugar, coffee, or dried meat. When they gave me dried horse-meat, I used it to feed the two big dogs that helped me guard my field. Anastasia could make a good stew out of dried venison which people gave me in trade for melons.

I picked melons until the last of August. The last melons were left in the field for anyone in Torim pueblo who wanted to get them. It is the Yaqui custom to leave the last of a crop for the pueblo.

A new state governor was being installed in Hermosillo in August. They ran a special train from the Rio Yaqui and any Yaqui who wanted to go to see the governor could get a free ride. His name was Roman Yucopicio and he was a Mayo. I went along to see my mother in Hermosillo, because my crop was finished. She was very glad to see me, as was my half sister, Julia. Over and over they asked, "Why don't you come live in Hermosillo? You can live here with us. Why do you want to live in the Rio Yaqui where everyone goes hungry all the time and people are always getting killed?"

I told them, "What you say is all right, but I have to go back to the Rio Yaqui."

I also visited Chepa Moreno. She told me that Juana Cochemea had just died. I was sorry I had not seen old Juana, who was a close relative of my grandfather Abelardo. Juana had for many years lived in a little house dug into a hillside in the barrio of La Matanza. She left a son, called El Guero, but Chepa told me not to go see him, as he did not like Yaquis. Consequently I have never spoken to this kinsman. He and his family have become Mexicans and no longer speak Yaqui.

It was either 1936 or 1937 when Clara Contreras committed suicide. She was the daughter of Nicolasa Waibel Contreras (condemned and shot for murder in Vicam) and Luis Contreras (killed at the Amole Mine in 1907). Clara had lived with Josefa More after her mother was shot, until she married Rosario More (no relative of Pedro's). They had never gotten along, and after he left her, she moved back with Josefa More. One night about midnight she went out in the brush alone, drenched herself with gasoline, and burned up. She must have died of *tristeza* because of her unhappy life. Josefa was sad that another of her relatives had died.

# CHAPTER 11

# Vicam 1938–1939

AFTER SEVERAL DAYS I went back to the Rio Yaqui on the train. They were glad to see me at Pedro More's house; Josefa gave me some breakfast, and we talked about my fine watermelon crop and my visit to my mother. After breakfast I went to the Mexican store owned by the brothers Eusebio and Domingo Aleman Encinas and sat down in front. Rafael Pomala came and sat down beside me.

Rafael said, "Oh, how are you?"

"I am very well, thank you."

"Oh, say, a new doctor has come from Mexico City and he needs two Yaqui helpers. He has found one already."

"Who is the Yaqui he has found?"

"You know him very well. The Champion." We called Rujelio Cantu of Vicam Switch the Champion.

Rafael said, "If you want to work for the doctor, it would be a good job for you. If you wish, I will take you over there now."

"Well, I guess that will be all right."

We went to the doctor's office.

"Good morning, doctor," said Rafael.

"What news do you have today?"

"Well, doctor, I have found another Yaqui to work for you. This is my good friend, and he understands Spanish very well."

"That's fine," said the doctor, "that is just what I need." Then the doctor began to explain what he was doing. "The government in Mexico City sent me here to the Yaqui region so that I can vaccinate all the Yaqui children. As soon as we get ready, we can begin vaccinating the children here in Vicam. You have to wear white pants and a white shirt. I believe the government will pay you seventy-two pesos a month."

I signed my name, Rosalio Valenzuela.

"I cannot start to work right away. I have to arrange some things at Torim."

"That is fine. You can start work six days from now, on September 1."

I went directly to the store and bought white pants and a white shirt. I left Vicam in the evening and walked to Torim. I carried a lot of food and they were all very glad to see me. I told Mariano and Anastasia about my new job with the doctor. "I guess I'm going to be a vaccinator."

The next day I got a ride to Obregón and bought some more white pants and shirts. It was awfully hot, so hot that for the next few days I simply rested at Torim.

On August 31, 1937, I moved over to Vicam to stay with Pedro More. Early the next morning I dressed in my white clothes and went to see Dr. Moisés Ortiz Hernández. I had to go without breakfast because Yaqui families never cook breakfast early in the morning. They drink coffee when they first get up, and have breakfast at eight-thirty or nine o'clock in the morning. I got to Dr. Hernández's office at seven. He opened the door at nine o'clock, saying, "Oh, good morning. What time did you get here?"

"Seven o'clock."

"Come in and let me show you the office."

He showed me everything and explained what I should do every morning when I got to the office. He told me to come about six o'clock, sweep, clean the office, and boil all the tools.

Every day I had everything clean by eight o'clock and then I could go eat breakfast at Pedro's house. My partner, the champion, brought the doctor's breakfast from the restaurant every morning. We started vaccinating Mexican and Yaqui children. Many Yaquis refused to let us vaccinate their children because they did not trust Dr. Moisés.

He told them, "This is good for your children. If they are vaccinated, they will never have smallpox." All the same, many Yaquis would not let him vaccinate their children.

On September 4 we went to Bataconsica. We did not vaccinate many children there because they ran away. Many of the Yaqui families were mad at us. The boys and men of Bataconsica smoke marijuana all the time. Many die, but they do not care. They go on smoking marijuana.

Many turn crazy. It was lucky that a Mexican lieutenant from the Bataconsica garrison went with us to every house.

The next day we tried again to vaccinate children in Vicam, and the day after that we went to Potam. The people of Potam are very good; they liked what Dr. Moisés was doing, and we got to vaccinate many children. There were so many people in Potam that we had to go back. When we started for Potam the next Monday, we could not find a car or truck going that way. Dr. Moisés and the Champion rode horseback while I walked. I have never liked horses, and I could walk about as fast as the horses.

After we visited all the pueblos, the doctor stayed in Vicam most of the time; all I had to do was clean up his office by eight o'clock in the morning. The rest of the time I sat in front of the office, or sometimes I sat in front of the Mexican store. Every two weeks I got paid thirty-six pesos, out of which I had to pay Josefa More twenty-two and a half pesos for board and six pesos to the woman who washed my white clothes. That left me seven and a half pesos on payday. Every little while Anastasia asked me for money, and soon my money was gone.

My work was too easy. Just an hour and a half a day. But I did not like sitting around all day; I could never save a peso. Josefa gave me beans, tortillas, and bitter coffee three times a day, while they ate meat and had sugar in their coffee. When January came it was too dry to plant, so I kept working for the doctor. Life was very hard with just beans, tortillas, and coffee to eat.

Many times while I lived in Vicam a group of us went to the Sierra hunting for deer, javelinas, and gold. Anastasio Urias (by now a lieutenant colonel and one of the paymasters for the Yaqui Zone), Camilo Tava (one of Vicente's brothers), Pascual Murillo (captain of Vicam), Manuel Urias (Anastasio's son), Francisco Marín (a lieutenant of Vicam), and Jesús Mesa (the sacristan of Vicam) made up the group that liked to go out in an old pickup. Anastasio and I once found an old mine at Bachomobampo with the entrance covered with poles and dirt. We later learned that this was an old Spanish copper mine, and they say that the big bell in Torim was cast with copper from that mine.

One day we were out in the pickup. We left it to go hunting on foot. Anastasio and Pascual always had good luck hunting. Deer would stand still for them with their whole head in sight. When we got about three-quarters of a mile from the pickup, we could see a female fox circling the pickup with her tail straight up in the air, crying and crying. Anastasio said, "I know something bad is going to happen to us."

Within three weeks Francisco Marín had been killed. He was in bed with Victoriano Vasquez's wife, Ana. Victoriano was a Mayo from Navo-joa who lived in Vicam because he did a fine business running mescal from Bacum. He knew Francisco was seeing his wife. In the dark he slipped into his own house, lit a match to see by, and stabbed Francisco through the heart with a butcher knife. Victoriano was arrested and taken to Guaymas. He was free in less than a month, because he was a good friend of General Ramon Rivera, also a Mayo.

A few days after Francisco was killed, Jesús Mesa borrowed a forty-five from Fernando Cupes (Josefa More's son) and shot himself three times in the breast. He was sad because Francisco had been killed. They used to always be together.

Augustina Preciado Cajeme died in Potam in 1938. She and Dominga had lived in a nice adobe house in Cocorit owned by Jesús María Leyva Cajeme, Jr., when I arrived in 1932, and I often went to see them there. Dominga married Anselmo Romero Matos of Potam; in 1936, Augustina moved to Potam to be with Dominga. When Augustina died, Dominga was awfully sad, because she had always been with her mother.

When Lent began, one of the *fariseo* lieutenants came from Torim to see me at the doctor's office. "The *fariseo* chief wants to know if you have made your mask."

"I can't go over to Torim for all of Lent; besides, I don't think I can wear my mask this year because I always get sick when I wear it."

"That is all right. This year you can be a *fariseo cabo*." A *fariseo cabo* is like a boss man who does not have to wear the mask.

"That is all right. I will be happy to be a *cabo*, and I will be in Torim for the Fiesta de Gloria. I will be there before Good Friday."

"That is all right," said the *fariseo* lieutenant, "I will tell the chief what you said."

A few days later, Dr. Holden wrote from Texas that he and some friends would come to Torim for our Easter ceremony. The Texans arrived in Vicam Switch on Tuesday before Good Friday; they came to Dr. Hernández's office looking for me. I was very glad to see Dr. Holden and his friends, and I shook hands with every one of them. They went on to Torim that same day. I walked over on Wednesday, because all the *fariseos* must gather in the church at nine-thirty Wednesday night, when everyone comes to the church to watch the *cabos* whip the *fariseos*. Children have to be whipped too. We call this the *tinieblas*, or "the darkness." I was glad that I did not have to wear a mask.

Thursday morning all the members of the *fariseo* society started running

up and down. We ran all day Thursday, all Thursday night, and on Good
Friday we did the same thing. We could not sleep Friday night. By
Saturday morning I was awfully weary and sleepy. The last thing the
*fariseos* did in the Fiesta de Gloria was to lead the burro and the Judas
around, early on Saturday morning. The Judas had many kinds of music,
deer dancers, *matachines*, *coyote* dancers, and a priest too. We finished the
Judas celebration about midmorning; a few moments later the *fariseos*
started marching in front of the church to get into Glory. The curtain
was up. When the curtain opened, the *pascolas* began hallooing the
*fariseos*, calling out "Gloria, Gloria." Then the *fariseos* ran away, running around the big cross; then they stopped and started marching again.
The *fariseos* ran around a second time. On the third run every member
of the *fariseo* society must get inside the church with their *madrinas* and
*padrinos*. The *madrina* and *padrino* of every *fariseo* made the sign of the
cross on their front, and then they put rosaries on the *fariseo*, calling him
'*hijado*.

All the *fariseos* went outside with their godparents, and a *fariseo* lieutenant gave a talk, advising each *fariseo* to respect his *madrina* and *padrino*.
All this advice does little good, as I have often seen *fariseos* fighting with
their godparents, especially when they were drunk. The *fariseo* lieutenant
talked a long time, and then the *fariseo* ceremony was ended.

*Pascolas* and deer dancers began dancing at the "priests" house, which
is what we call the place where the *santos* are housed. They danced there
several hours, and then they came down to the other ramadas. The
*matachines* must dance at the church all night while the deer dancers and
*pascolas* and the *coyotes* dance all night in the ramadas.

Sunday morning four girls ran down from the church with Saint
Magdalene, looking for the Christ. They then ran back to the church to
tell Saint John that Mary Magdalene had found Jesus Christ in the fiesta.
Saint John did not believe this. The four girls, carrying Mary Magdalene,
again ran down from the church, and back. This time Saint John believed
that Mary Magdalene found Christ. So he said that he would go along
with Mary Magdalene to see Jesus Christ. Four boys carried Saint John
and four girls carried Saint Mary Magdalene, and they all ran down to
the fiesta.

Saint John said, "Oh, what you said is true. We will go back and tell
his mother."

The four girls and four boys ran with Saint Mary Magdalene and Saint
John back to the church, where Saint John said to the Virgin Mary, "It
is true. Your son, Jesus Christ, is down there in the fiesta."

The Virgin Mary said to all the saints in the church, "Let's go see my loving son and we will meet him in the middle of the road."

The Yaqui *maestro* and the *cantoras* began singing "Alleluia" in the church and the other singers sang "Alleluia" in response.

The group carrying the Virgin Mary and the saints started walking slowly toward the other group where Jesus Christ was. When the two groups met, the Virgin Mary said that she was very glad to meet her loving son again. People threw flowers and they all started up to the church again.

All the *madrinas* and *padrinos* of the *fariseos* had to make the sign of the cross on their *'hijado* again. Then all the *fariseos* and their godparents went outside the church and sat down. The *fariseo* lieutenant finished his advice to the *fariseo* society. Each *fariseo* then had to shake hands with his *madrina* and his *padrino*.

Many of the *fariseos* cooked chili con carne, garbanzos with chili, bread, and strong coffee for their godparents. The *madrinas* and *padrinos* brought along a few bottles of soda pop, and sometimes a gallon of mescal or tequila.

When everything was over in the church, around noon, everyone went to the big cooking ramada, where all the little children who had played the angels had a big dinner with their godparents. The food included fish, oysters, eggs, chili con carne, chocolate, and strong coffee. Everyone brought bottles of soda pop. After the feast was over, everyone began drinking soda or mescal. The *fariseos* started drinking mescal in the cooking ramada about two o'clock on Sunday afternoon, and they kept drinking till they ran out of it or passed out. They would drink a whole week if the mescal held out. That is the end of the Easter ceremony. This is what happens every year in every village.

During the Easter ceremony in 1938, I saw little of Dr. Holden and his friends because of my duties as a *fariseo cabo*. Dr. Anderson was an eye doctor; he brought many pairs of glasses. A number of old Yaquis were glad, because they like to use glasses. The Americans left Torim just as soon as the Easter ceremony was over. I was awfully sad when I went back to work for Dr. Hernández.

A few days later some Yaqui men came to see me. They said, "The chief of the Sierra Yaquis, Calistro Huasula, wants to see you. He wants to find out what the white men said. You can come to the Sierra any day now."

"I will willingly go to visit the chief. I do not yet know exactly what day I can go to the Sierra, but you can tell him I will be there right away."

I sent along a small present that Dr. Holden had left for Chief Huasula, a little red book he had written about the Yaquis.

A few days later the same three men came down from the Sierra. "Our chief sent us again. He wants you to come to the Sierra so you can read the red book for him, to tell him what it says about the Yaqui tribe."

"I will come next Sunday." They returned to the Sierra.

About six-thirty Friday evening, the same three men came to Pedro More's house. "Well, we came back again so you can go with us tomorrow morning to the Sierra."

One of the Yaqui captains at Vicam Switch, Juan Camasehua, took us the four and one-half miles to Wapari in his Ford pickup, about nine o'clock Saturday morning. From there we walked up into the Sierra to where the chief lived, reaching the mountain village called Ceberia Mesa about eleven o'clock. We stopped at the Yaqui guard, and then went on to see Calistro Huasula and his soldiers. I touched hands with the chief. He presented me to all his people, saying, "This is the son of Captain Miguel Palos. Miguel Palos was my best friend here in the mountains." All the Yaquis kept their eyes on me. Some were scared of me.

That was the first time I ever saw Chief Calistro Huasula. He was a tall man.

"How old are you?" I asked the chief.

"I was born in 1874 in the Bacatete Mountains," he said.

He was about sixty-five years old then and looked like he was thirty-five. He had never left the Sierra since he was born. Even after all the other Yaquis left the Sierra, he and his band remained there, scared that the Mexicans would kill them if they left the Sierra. His real name was Calistro Anwamea, or Calistro Hard to Kill in English.

Pretty soon a few of the Yaqui families brought me food of the sort they eat in the mountains, deer meat with wild potatoes and corn tortillas. "We are sorry, but we have no coffee here in our poor village. Sometimes we have coffee and sometimes we don't drink it for a month at a time."

"I don't drink very much coffee," I said.

After dinner Chief Huasula said, "Tell me what the Americans have been telling the Yaquis in Torim and in the other villages."

"Dr. Holden came to visit the Yaqui tribe here in the Rio Yaqui with all his good friends from Texas and one friend from Boston, on the east side of New York City. Every one of these gentlemen are good friends of the Yaquis. You have nothing to be scared about. Dr. Holden and Dr. Wagner came to help the Yaquis in every village. Dr. Wagner is a good doctor. He relieved many sick people in Torim pueblo. The chiefs and governor of Torim liked what Dr. Holden said and they allowed him to do what he wanted during the Easter ceremony. Now Dr. Holden and his friends have published a little book, which he said must be of some help to the Yaquis. He left a copy for you."

Chief Huasula said, "Well, I think what the North Americans did was a good thing, and I sure thank them for telling about the Yaquis in a book. Now, you read this book to me."

I started reading the book about two o'clock in the afternoon, translating from English to Yaqui. I read until it was too dark to see. The next morning I read again until I had to leave to return to Vicam. I did not get to finish the whole book.

The chief said, "Well, I like every word in the red book. This will be a little help for the Yaqui tribe."

One of the bad Yaquis named Captain Alfonso Yolimea said, "Now that we understand what the white people were doing in the Rio Yaqui, the only thing left to do is give this man a good rest." Whenever the Yaquis say they are going to give someone a rest, it means they are going to kill him.

The chief said, "No, please don't do that. He is the only person who can understand the white people." Then the chief said to me, "Don't believe what my captain says. He is just joking."

After Yaqui women brought us food again, the chief said he would call me back in two weeks. I shook hands with everyone in the village, and we left. I already knew at that moment that I would never come back there again, because I know the Yaqui people very well. They never fool me.

We left Ceberia Mesa about two o'clock in the afternoon, reaching Vicam Switch about seven-thirty that evening. Monday I went back to work for Dr. Hernández. All week long I thought about the mountain chief, because I knew what the bad Sierra Yaquis were going to do to him. The next weekend I thought, "I sure would like to go back and see the chief in the Sierra." But every night I had the same dream, and I knew I would never see him alive. I told no one about the bad luck that was coming. I just waited.

The following Monday the same three Yaquis came to see me. "Are you going to be ready to go to the Sierra on Saturday?" they asked.

"I hope so. I am sure I will be able to come on Saturday."

My dream came to me that night. A great train ran very fast from the east toward the sundown; it almost ran over me, but I quickly jumped to one side of the track, saving myself. I could see the chief standing at a curve about a quarter of a mile ahead. When the train reached the curve, it left the track and exploded. Then I saw Chief Calistro Huasula, and he was hurt.

I had this dream just three days before I was supposed to go back to the Sierra. Something bad is going to happen, I told myself, because my dreams never lie. I better not go see the chief any more because something bad is going to happen in the mountains.

Friday afternoon about three o'clock, two Sierra Yaquis brought the bad news to Captain Juan Camasehua in Vicam that Calistro Huasula had been shot about nine o'clock that morning as he went to get water from the spring. These two men said they heard four shots and ran to the spring. Four Yaquis in blue jeans were escaping down the trail. They could not chase the murderers because they had to go to their chief, who was dying with four bullets in his breast. They signaled all the Sierra village Yaquis to come, and soon they gathered at the spring and carried the chief back to the village. He died right away. Calistro Huasula's son-in-law, Loreto Vatereo, and another Yaqui soldier came down from the mountains to inform Captain Camasehua. That is what happened to Chief Calistro Huasula in the mountains.

Much the same thing happened to José María Soto in the mountains. José María was a Mexican captured near San Marcial when he was a young boy. He grew up with the Yaquis and became a Yaqui soldier. He finally got to be a captain of the Sierra army and was a member of the *coyote* society. During the 1926–1927 war he fled to Arizona, where he talked a lot to the border patrol and other Americans about the Yaqui problems. Some dumb Yaquis thought he was going to sell Yaqui gold mines to the Americans. I often talked to him, and he was a good friend of Lucho Ramíriz and Hilario Rodríguez. When José María Soto went back to Sonora, he joined Calistro Huasula in the Sierra rather than going to live in the valley.

One time Lucho Ramíriz, Marques California (the secretary of Guadalupe Village), and an American pilot named Albert flew a plane from Tucson over the Bacatete Mountains, where they dropped several bundles of cloth assay sacks (like miners put gold in) for José María Soto. The plane turned around and went back to Tucson. After that, Sierra Yaquis were sure that José María Soto was going to give away the Yaqui mines, and they killed him. People said that he shot himself but this is a lie. I know the name of the bad Yaqui who killed him; it was Selmo Perez, who hated all whites and all Mexicans.

After Chief Calistro Huasula was killed, Selmo Perez wanted to kill me, but he never could because I had so many friends and relatives. Every time Selmo Perez planned to kill me, some friend or relative would tell me, "Do not walk on such and such trail." Every Sunday when I walked to Torim I went by a different trail, there being five roads to Torim. The bad Yaquis never found me on the trail to Torim, and one by one they all died.

Why did the stupid Yaquis murder Chief Calistro Huasula? Just because the chief was glad to hear from a white man, because he liked what Dr. Holden wrote in the little red book, and because he liked what Dr. Holden told the Yaquis in the pueblos. These ignorant Indians thought that the chief was going to tell Dr. Holden about gold mines in the Sierra. There are supposed to be four old gold mines that the Spaniards worked. The stupid Indians said, "We don't have to give him any more chance to tell the white people where the mines are. We must kill him any day."

I did not hear personally what the stupid Indians said, but a few days after the chief was killed, Kino Yoisanacame, one of my relatives who lived with the bad Yaquis, came to see me in Vicam; he told me all about what those mountain Yaquis did to the chief. The soldiers who had served under General Huasula tracked the men who shot him. Their tracks led to Potam, which, as everyone knows, is full of *yoris*. The governors of Torim, Belem, Huirivis, and Rahum got together and had me write to Dr. Holden, telling him about this terrible thing and asking him to inform government officials in Mexico City about the Potam *yoris*. Poor chief— he died with a great hope for the Yaqui tribe.

CHAPTER **12**

# *Torim, 1939–1945*

AFTER THE CHIEF was killed, I worked for Dr. Hernández a few more weeks before I quit and moved back to Torim. After working for the doctor for so many months, I left with four pesos. It was a nuisance to stay clean all the time, and I did not like just sitting around. It is much better to work hard all day. In spite of having regular paychecks I stayed hungry all the time because the food Josefa More fed me got worse from week to week. It was July, 1938, when I moved back to Torim.

Not long after that, Pedro More died in Vicam of either TB or pneumonia at the age of sixty-four. That left his wife, Josefa, and their three living sons in Vicam Switch. The sons, Fernando, who is my age, Cipriano, and Bernal, are still farming at Vicam Switch. They are good Yaquis, still speaking the Yaqui language.

Bernal once married a girl named Charla More in the church; even though they were not relatives, everyone said they were because they had the same last name. After about a year they separated. They did not like each other much anyway. He then lived with Rufina Moroyoki until she died. She was fifty-six years old and had lost all her teeth when she died in 1953. Rufina was old enough to be Bernal's mother. Rufina was the sister of Locaria Rodríguez, who lived in Arizona when I did.

In 1939, Rosa Kuka had my child, a little girl named Juana. Rosa died about two weeks later; her aunt Bernalda Valenzuela took my little girl and raised her. I was very sad when Rosa died. Whenever I see Juana now, she reminds me of her mother because they look so much alike. Rosa was a kind person. She never had another husband.

Soon after I got back to Torim my mother came to visit, and she stayed five years. First we lived with Mariano. Then a friend named Guadalupe Sandoval moved out of a nice adobe house that he had built (where he had run a little store) and gave it to me. My mother and I moved into this house. That was the first time I lived in my own house in Torim.

My mother was there to take a rest from working so hard as a cook in the Mexican houses in Hermosillo, but she did not mind cooking for the two of us. She was always happy and singing, and when she heard music, she danced around the house. She still did not believe in God or the saints, any more than she had when we lived at the Colorada Mine; now she never went to church or to fiestas.

Her cousins, the Cocomorachi family, lived close to our house and we visited back and forth every day. Both my mother and I especially liked Teresa Cocomorachi, who was always good to us. Teresa was the only one of the Cocomorachi family who was always glad to see us; she always gave me a big *abrazo*.

Like my half sister Dominga, Teresa Cocomorachi had been deported twice. She and her sister, Esperanza Cocomorachi Tahacaih, were the daughters of Gilberto Cocomorachi (killed by the Sierra Yaquis in 1926) and his wife, Lola. Gilberto was the son of Lazaro Cocomorachi, brother of my grandmother Esperanza Cocomorachi, the wife of Chico Liowe Hurtado. Esperanza and Lázaro Cocomorachi are said to have been Tarahumaras who fled their Sierra with their parents, settling down in Torim.

Life was hard in Torim. The river was dry, so I could not grow any food. I started chopping dry mesquite wood. Sixty pairs of dry wood (one *carga*) sold to the Mexican truckers for one peso. Some days I could only chop sixty pairs because I was so weak. We were eating once a day, so I had to chop all day without breakfast or lunch. When Mariano got his Mexican government pay of twenty-one pesos every two weeks, we ate better for two or three days. Sometimes Mariano spent his whole check on mescal, and then we did not eat so well for perhaps a month at a time. Anastasia never got disgusted with him when he wasted all the money. My poor sister-in-law was a good and patient woman. She just went looking for rats and cactus when there was nothing else to eat.

Big rats built nests up high in mesquite trees. She had to walk three or four miles to find any rats because they were all gone around Torim village, since the poor Yaqui families hunted out every rat nest near the pueblo.

When the Yaquis have plenty of corn and beans and meat to eat, rats move back closer to the village. You can tell how hungry the people of Torim are by how close to the village rats can be found. The name of our village, Torim, means rats; maybe people here have always had to eat rats.

Anastasia could get two or three dozen rats on a good day, cooking them in an *olla* with corn or wheat. Her family ate them very well. I was sad, because neither my mother nor I could eat the rats. They smelled so bad when they were cooking. Cecelia did not like iguana, either.

I still had some clothes that Dr. Holden gave me at Easter, 1938. When my mother and I got very hungry, I would walk to Vicam with a shirt or a pair of pants, after chopping wood all day. Sometimes I was lucky and got a peso. Sometimes I just gave them away for a meal. My mother and I were always hungry. I chewed mesquite beans all day while I was chopping wood. The hunger was worse for my mother because she was used to eating good food in rich Mexican homes in Hermosillo where she was the cook.

This is the way things were during 1939. On New Year's, 1940, I was awfully sad because I did not have a cent in my pocket, and all the clothes Dr. Holden gave me were gone. Still, I did not want to bootleg mescal, and now I made the trip to Bacum only once in a while.

In January, 1940, I started cutting carrizo. Truckers were paying five pesos a thousand for cane stacked by the highway. I could cut one thousand carrizo in two and a half days; then I had to carry them across the river and stack them by the highway. I was able to save two or three pesos a week, and by March, I had bought a new shirt for twelve pesos, new blue jeans for sixteen pesos, and a new straw hat for two and a half pesos at Vicam Station.

Lent started in Torim village. I thought and thought. "Only my God can help me. How can I get through the Fiesta de Gloria, when I don't have a cent and my poor mother is hungry? I cannot cut dry mesquite wood or carrizo while I am dancing as a *fariseo*."

A few days later I saw Dr. Holden and Dr. Wagner in my dream. I woke up very early in the morning and said to myself, "I guess I have a letter in the Vicam post office; I have to go see." As soon as I had a cup of coffee, I started walking to Vicam; by sunrise I was at Vicente Tava's house. They asked me to have breakfast with them.

"Why are you here so early in the morning?" asked my uncle Vicente.

"I came here for my mail at the post office. I guess I have a letter from Dr. Holden."

When the post office opened, I was there, asking for my mail. I was very glad to get a letter from Dr. Holden, and I quickly went back to Vicente's house. "Well, I got a letter from Dr. Holden."

"Oh, I am so glad."

I opened the letter. Dr. Holden said that he and Dr. Wagner would come to Torim for Easter, probably arriving on Good Friday. Dr. Holden did not tell me about Miss Frances.

Vicente was very happy to hear that our American friends were coming. Vicente is just like my father. They both liked Americans very much. They never liked working with Mexicans. In fact, my father really hated the Mexican race. But he always liked Americans. My father started working with Americans in 1887 at the Colorada Mine.

When Dr. Holden and Dr. Wagner arrived, they had their wives with them. Dr. Holden had married Miss Frances. Vicente and I were happy to see them, as was Lucho Ramíriz. They gave us lots of clothes.

They started down the road to go back to Nogales Sunday afternoon. I was awfully sad, thinking and thinking. I said to myself, "Well, I guess there is no hope. I will never have a good time again. The only thing left to me is to work again, very hard." So I worked hard cutting carrizo and mesquite wood all year, from Easter to December.

During 1940, Lucho Ramíriz and I went to the Sierra looking for gold. Lucho Ramíriz is the same General Lucho Ramíriz who earlier lived in Tucson and who gave Dr. Holden the letter in 1934. I had known Lucho well in Arizona. Now he too had come to Torim. He, like my father, had always liked Americans, and some of his California friends wanted him to find the Yaqui gold.

We had always heard there was gold in Bejori Ba-am Mountain, but neither of us knew which was the mountain of that name. My father said he had seen gold there. Old Sacramento Navogoki Ochoa, with whom I had gone to the Sierra in earlier years, knew which was Bejori Ba-am, but he would never take us there. He would point to a hill from a great distance, but we never found it. Sacramento told us that the Yaquis always watch that place, and no one can touch it.

The Yaquis were very mad at Lucho Ramíriz because he was looking for gold, and they were mad at me because I went all over the Sierra with him. I was not scared of the Yaquis; I knew they could not hurt me because I always carried a cross and my God looked after me.

One day, after we had come home from the Sierra, Lucho went to a little village called Ba-ah Gohoih, because some friends were going to give him some *elote* (fresh green corn). When Lucho got home in the afternoon, he gave several dozen ears of green corn to his wife and said, "I am feeling very bad." That was October 25, 1940.

Every day I went to see him. On November 1, he took his Mauser and ran away from his wife while she was asleep. His wife was waiting for me when I got home from chopping wood to tell me that he had run off. We did not look for him till the next morning, when four Torim boys and I started tracking him through the brush. We followed his tracks all day through heavy cholla and cactus. In late afternoon I told the boys that we had better rest a little, and we sat under a big mesquite tree. Within a few minutes we heard a bird cry out. It was the deer guard bird, a big brown bird that looks like an eagle; this bird always cries when he sees a hunter, to warn the deer. This deer guard bird thought Lucho was deer hunting because he was carrying a Mauser.

The boys said, "Do you know what that bird saw?"

"Well, I guess he saw Lucho."

We walked toward the bird's cries. Then we heard Lucho cough close by. We went on very quietly until we could see him.

"Oh, there he is," I said softly.

There he sat, under a tree, holding one arm in his other hand, looking very sad. The boys were scared of Lucho; they said, "You know him very well; you go talk to him."

I went over to Lucho and said, "How do you feel today?"

"Awful. I am very, very thirsty."

I handed him a water canteen and he drank. The boys took his gun, and we stood him on his feet and started walking the four miles back to Torim. All the way home he kept talking and talking to us telling us that two Yaquis at Torim wanted to kill him because he had been looking for gold. They were Crecensio Buetemea, the Yaqui commandant at Torim, and Esteban Amarillas, a lieutenant at Torim.

I said that I did not think they would do that. He said, "Oh yes. I know very well what is the matter with me. Those people at Ba-ah Gohoih gave me something in the food. They have done me a great injury." When we reached his home, his wife, Micaela, was very sad; she started weeping when she saw him. His arm was swollen.

Day by day he got worse, and on December 15 he ran away again. Micaela came to me, saying, "He ran away early this morning. I did not see which way he went." For four days I looked for him in the brush, but I could not find his tracks. Finally I heard that he was at Guamochil village, west of Cocorit. I went to tell his wife where he was.

"Will you do me a favor?" she asked.

"Well, sure."

"I guess I'd better sell our phonograph. Will you go to the Mexicans and ask if they will buy it?"

"Of course."

I went over to the Mexican garrison and told them, "A lady wants to sell a phonograph."

They wanted to know for how much.

"I don't know. She didn't tell me the price. But if you want to buy it, you can go see it."

One of the soldiers walked back to Lucho's house with me. "How much do you want for the phonograph?"

"Twenty-five pesos."

"I have only fifteen pesos with me, and that is all I can pay."

"Give me the fifteen pesos, because I need the money right now."

Poor Micaela. She had to sell her nice phonograph for just fifteen pesos because she needed the money for her husband, and she gave the soldier eighteen records.

The next day Micaela asked a truck driver at the Mexican store in Torim if he would go get her husband at Guamochil. Lucho was very sick. His clothes were terribly dirty. The Mexican soldiers had taken his Mauser. They told us they found him wandering in the brush about seven miles east of Torim.

Micaela asked Lucho, "Well, how do you feel?"

"Very much worse." His arm was a mess up to the armpit.

The Yaquis around Guamochil helped us put him on the truck, and we arrived back in Torim about five o'clock in the late afternoon. His arm was split open and you could see worms in it.

Micaela had nothing to do except wash his arm and give him water from a spoon. She sold everything they brought from Tucson very cheaply —a bedspring and mattress, all their blankets, and a big black trunk. None of the medicine she bought helped him.

On December 28 Lucho sent for me. He said, "I guess I've only got a few days left before I die. I'm feeling worse all the time, and I'm awfully tired. I just wanted to tell you from now on that you better take good care of yourself, because sometime the bad Yaquis will try to hurt you."

"Don't worry about me. They have never been able to harm me and I'm not afraid of them."

That was the last time I talked to him. He stopped eating. His throat got so sore that he could take only water from a spoon. He died on January 1, 1941, in the evening. The next day his wife and a few other

Yaquis buried him in front of the church. Very few people went to see him when he was sick, and fewer went to see him when he died. Almost all the Yaquis in Torim hated him because he was friendly with Americans.

One of his American friends was Dan Cantrell, a border patrolman. Charles Dixon, a millionaire in Los Angeles, was the one who sent Lucho to the Rio Yaqui to look for gold. Mr. Dixon helped Lucho a lot in Arizona, and for a while after he came to Torim, Mr. Dixon sent him money. Albert, the pilot who once flew Lucho over the mountains to drop assay sacks to José María Sosa, came to see Lucho in Torim several times, giving him a little money, and telling him to keep looking for gold. After while all that help stopped when the Americans decided he was not going to get any gold, and Lucho was a very poor man.

I felt very bad when Lucho died. He had been my best friend in Torim. When he had food he helped me, and when I had food, I helped him. Lucho was a good person, but all the Yaquis in all the eight pueblos hated him because he looked for Yaqui gold.

Lucho was born in Hermosillo. His parents were deported in 1905 when he was about ten years old. Governor Rafael Izábal sold him to a rich man, Antonio Dávila. As a result, Lucho grew up in a Mexican home, speaking beautiful Spanish. He often told me that all through the long years that he lived among the Mexicans, he never forgot that he was a Yaqui. After Lucho died, I found out that the commandant and the lieutenant of Torim had hired Lucas Mateo to kill him.

Micaela soon went crazy. She walked around without any clothes on, never knowing what she was doing or whether or not she had eaten. Within a year she died too.

The year 1941 was another hard year. I was sick for a long time with kidney trouble and could work very little. I thought about ways that the Yaquis could be happy, making a good living. With a little money and water, the rich Yaqui lands could feed us all. Many times I walked up to the church and sat alone in the shade, thinking about the Yaquis. Why are they so poor when God gave them such rich land? I did not have a single centavo, and most days I felt so bad that I could not cut much wood. My mother would tell me that the Rio Yaqui was a hard place to live.

December 17, 1941, the river began to rise. Even though I did not have a cent, I felt much happier. Maybe I could do something. As soon as the water ran down, I began to make holes for a melon crop. I made seven hundred hills of watermelons and also sowed a few pumpkins. Every hill had good plants. Christmas night was sad, but my plants grew nicely.

When Lent began I went to see the *fariseo* chief to tell him that I could not leave my field for the whole of Lent, but that I would dance in the Fiesta de Gloria.

Three or four hours a day I chopped wood, then I went back to my watermelons. All this time I was chewing mesquite beans, like a cow or a horse. We cooked bitter weeds from our field, which could be choked down with a little salt. Even after I had a good load of wood ready, there was trouble selling it unless you were friends with the Mexican truckers, and I had no good friends in the wood forest.

On Good Friday I began dancing with the *fariseos;* I had a good time because there was so much food. After Easter I chopped wood a few hours a day and spent the rest of the time with my melons. In May I quit chopping wood and built a ramada in the field, where my mother and I lived to take care of the melons and guard them from the Yaqui boys at night. We cared for our melons like you would a baby.

Soon I was selling melons and getting money. We bought food for Anastasia, Mariano, Salome, and Micaela. Anastasia was so happy that she cooked nice meals three times a day and walked out to the field with food for Cecelia and me. I put the money in a five-gallon can, and when the melon crop was finished, the can was full of money.

Delores Hupaumea, a trucker from Cocorit, took me to Obregón, where I bought provisions for the little store my mother and I ran in our adobe house. Four Mexican stores in Torim had gone broke during 1942. It looked like Torim needed a store. So many people needed food and so few had money that our provisions were soon gone and all we had left was a stack of credit slips. Many people in Torim still owe me money for things they bought in my store in 1942. I went back to chopping wood.

My half sister Julia came from Hermosillo to see our mother. She told Cecelia that she was crazy to live in the Rio Yaqui when she had a nice house in Hermosillo where there was food every day and the stupid Yaquis were not always killing each other. This was the first time that Rosa had ever lived away from Cecelia, and she missed her. So my mother went back to Hermosillo.

In October I decided that I wanted to go to the big fiesta in Magdalena, although I had only sixty pesos. I paid a truck driver twenty-five pesos for the round trip and went from Vicam Switch on a truck loaded with Yaquis. When we got to Hermosillo, about three-thirty the next morning, the truck stopped at the river and everyone laid down on the sand to sleep. I did not feel a bit sleepy. Everyone awoke early, and we went on into the market for breakfast. We reached Magdalena in the afternoon.

I went directly to the church to salute Saint Francis. His statue is lying down. Everyone tries to lift the saint's head, and if they do, it means they will have good luck. If they cannot, all the women cry. I have always been able to raise the *santo*. After I kissed him, I bought him two long candles.

Then I went to the fiesta. Oh, my Lord. Such wonderful things to see in the fiesta. Music everywhere. I was so happy, walking up and down. Many friends and relatives from Tucson were there, and every time I met one of them, they gave me some money—in dollars. Some took me into restaurants and bought me beautiful meals.

The next day I found my niece, my brother's daughter, who was three months old when I last saw her in Tucson in 1929. I was standing with a relative when she walked up. "Here comes your niece," he said to me.

She said, "You are my uncle Rosalio."

"Yes."

"I am very glad to know you."

"How did you know I was here?" I asked her.

"Your wife, Loreta, told me about you, and that you were here in the fiesta."

"How are your parents?" I asked her.

"They are fine; they are always talking about you and how you left Tucson when I was just a baby."

She opened her purse and gave me ten dollars. She was a wonderful-looking girl, a lot like my grandmother María—like a French girl.

The next day I looked for my niece at the place where they camped. My ex-wife, Loreta, was there. I did not say anything to her. I took my niece to the bus station, and she left for Tucson. At noon we took the truck back to the Rio Yaqui. I did not waste my money in the fiesta, and I got home with 111 pesos.

In Torim I rested a few days before going back to chopping wood. With my mother gone, I had to eat with Mariano's family or with my god-mother, Nacha Buanamea. I moved back to Mariano's house, leaving my own adobe empty. I tried my hand at making railroad ties, but that was awfully hard for me to do. I could make two ties a day; I only got one peso for a first-class tie, although the man who bought them sold them for fourteen pesos apiece. I decided I could make as much money chopping wood.

In December of 1942, the river came down; I started clearing my garden on December 15, saying to myself, "This time I'm going to plant my watermelons very early so I can make a lot of money." By December 20 I was ready to plant the seeds in the one thousand holes I had prepared.

Christmas that year was one of the happiest occasions I can remember. Anastasia made a lot of tamales and we ate them all through *Noche Buena* (Christmas Eve). No one slept at all. Everyone had all the tamales and coffee they could eat. We took oranges to the church as gifts for the baby Christ.

When next I went to see my watermelons, they were doing very badly. I don't know why, because I never learned about watermelons. I carried water to every hole. When New Year's Day came, I was sad, thinking about my watermelons.

I had a dream the night of January 1, 1943, in which I saw my watermelons—nice plump melons all over the field. I woke up very sad because I knew what was going to happen to my watermelons. Anyway I kept working in my melons. I decided not to believe my dream. But the dream kept coming back. I would wake up very mad because my dream would not leave me alone.

When Lent started, I did not go see the *fariseo* chief, and he did not come to see me. I just kept working in my garden. On Holy Wednesday I went to the *fariseo* chief with my stick to dance in the Fiesta de Gloria. When Easter was over, I began watering my melons again. Day after day I carried five-gallon tins of water from the river up to my garden, but the melons grew awfully slow. I went to ask a Yaqui what was the matter with my melons. He walked out to my garden with me. "Don't you know what is the matter with your melons?"

"No, I don't know."

"Well, this land is too dry. You can't do anything about it."

I was sad and mad; this was the first time the watermelons fooled me. I had spent so many days working in my garden. I never liked to plant melons on dry land again. I went back to making crossties.

All summer I worked cutting ties. Some days I could only work for a few hours because I had a fever that came every day. My clothes wore out and I was down to two old torn shirts.

About this time, the governor of Torim, Federico Salas, was walking to his home at Babu-u one night. The bad ghost of Babu-u climbed on his shoulders, giving him a bad scare. That night he came down with a high fever. Rather than calling a *curandero*, he took medicine of his own. Within three days he died, and shortly others in his family died too. The ones who were left moved away. For a while Babu-u was abandoned.

People still see ghosts there, but the ghosts have not killed anyone since. This ghost of Babu-u is *not* the ghost of the Mexican named Enrique

Chávez who is said to have buried a large treasure there. Many bad Mexicans lived at Babu-u during Porfirio Díaz's time and are buried there. Enrique Chávez was a Mexican who knew the Yaqui people and the Yaqui lands very well, as he was raised in the Rio Yaqui. Yaquis killed him during the 1910 revolution when the Mexicans were driven from Babu-u. People are still digging holes five and six feet deep around Babu-u looking for that money.

Ghosts are people who were killed. The Apaches killed many Sonorans. As a result, ghosts have been seen everywhere. Only a few ghosts will harm people. The ghost of Babu-u is one of the bad ones.

There are also *lloronas* around, both in Mexico and Arizona. This is a bad woman, crying for children that she has killed. She is not attached to any particular locality, but moves around. I believe that there is only one *llorona* who moves from place to place, but many people think that there are various ones.

A *yoeta*, at Corasepe, is rather like a *llorona*, except it is a cowboy who cries out three times in a row. No one ever sees him. Just the three yips, or *gritos*, each one farther away. The Mexicans call the Corasepe *yoeta* by the name Santeagueño.

Christmas of 1943 was sad because we were poor and hungry; worst of all, my sister-in-law, her daughter Micaela, and Micaela's husband were sick. All three were bewitched by Clara Morales because she was infatuated with Jaime, while he, being newly married to Micaela, paid no attention to her.

On New Year's Day, Anastasia got up before sunrise, saying, "I would like to see myself in the sunrise."

"You will just scare your shadow," said Mariano.

Several boys and girls came to watch my sister-in-law look at her shadow. She stood close to the adobe wall as the sun came up. One of the little girls said, "Oh, look, her shadow has no head."

Anastasia started laughing. "Well, I guess I never will get well. Soon I will die."

She told Mariano, "Go to Vicam Switch and find a Mexican to buy my sewing machine."

"How much do you want me to ask for it?"

"I can sell this machine for at least four hundred pesos."

Mariano saddled his horse and rode to Vicam. In the afternoon he was home again.

"Did you find someone to buy my sewing machine?"

"Señor Cárdenas will come over to see the machine tomorrow."

The next day the Mexican came. He did not say a word, just gave Anastasia four hundred pesos and left with the machine. He knew he had a good price because the machine cost over eight hundred pesos.

Day by day Anastasia and Micaela got worse, and Jaime was sick too. Mariano wanted to take Anastasia to the doctor in Vicam Switch, but she sent for her uncle, a *curandero* from Bacum named Gabriel Lozas. He came and said right away that they had witch sickness. He sucked on their bodies and out came little snakes, centipedes, and lots of other things, which he put in an *olla* and burned. He was very sad that he could not cure them. First Micaela died, then Anastasia, and last of all, Jaime.

Jaime was a *fariseo*. I was with him when he died and the *fariseo* society stayed with his body all night. His body sweated after he was dead. He was still sweating when we buried him with the *fariseo* mask in front of the church the next day.

It was January 14, 1944, when Anastasia died. We took her to Bataconsica for burial the next day, as she belonged to Bacum pueblo. Her uncle, the *curandero*, was so sad because she died that he hung himself out in the brush.

After Anastasia died, her house was awfully sad. She had been so nice to Mariano and to me. Now Mariano just stayed drunk all the time. He spent every penny of the money Anastasia left him on mescal. He said he could not stay home any more, so he rode from pueblo to pueblo on his horse.

Clara Morales and her sister, Anita, are well-known witches in the Yaqui Valley. They have never practiced witchcraft for money, but they have caused the death of many people they did not like.

Clara and Anita are the youngest children of Carlos Morales and María Cocomorachi. Carlos was a Mexican who was killed by Sierra Yaquis in 1914 at a place across the river. María was one of my mother's part Tarahumara relatives. María and Carlos, who never married in the church, had six children: Luciano (the oldest), Cristina (a *chatita*, flatnosed), Marcos (who came to Tucson in 1926; he now lives in Eloy), Guillermo (who also came to Tucson in 1926; he was killed by falling off a truck in Arizona in 1927), and Anita and Clara.

Anita, Clara, and Cristina were deported together in 1926. As was the case with so many people deported that year, they were shipped to central Mexico and turned loose, rather than being sold as slaves. In Mexico the two younger sisters learned witchcraft. Cristina did not become a witch. They returned to the Rio Yaqui in 1927 on the train. The three of them moved into a house near their Cocomorachi relatives and started selling mescal in their house. The mescal, of course, came from Bacum. They always had lots of boy friends. Because of the mescal, plenty of fighting took place around their house.

Anita married Beto Valencia in the church soon after I arrived in Torim in 1932 or 1933. They built a house of their own, close to Clara and Cristina, and eventually had three children: Luz, Tomasa, and Chato (who died at four years of age). Beto's family lived close to them. Cristina had been married to someone I never met because he died before I got to the Rio Yaqui. About 1934 she started living with Felipe Díaz, a brother of Juan Díaz, the *fariseo* captain, and they stayed together until Felipe died.

I could often hear the fights and the noise from their houses. Many nights we heard gunshots. Every time Beto got drunk, he walked around shooting his rifle in the air. No one was ever shot, however.

Just about the first person that Anita and Clara killed was their oldest brother, Luciano, in 1937. He had whipped all three sisters for saying his wife was going around with a Mexican singer, although everyone but Luciano knew it was true. They put a needle in his heart and he died.

They also killed Pablo Peralez, a man they called *tio*. Pablo had been deported to Yucatán as a boy in 1907, finally returning to the Rio Yaqui about 1927. He became a baker in Torim; later he owned a lot of goats. He was a great talker (*hablador*); he did not care who he talked to and he would talk about anything. He started telling people, including me, that Anita and Clara made little cloth dolls that they called by the name of a person they did not like; they then stuck pins in them. Sometimes Anita and Clara took these dolls to the cemetery southeast of the pueblo and buried them. They did not need anything that had belonged to the person they wanted to harm. Soon the person died.

After Pablo Peralez had told everyone that Anita and Clara were witches, they made a doll of him and buried it in the cemetery. Soon he began to get very thin. Knowing he was bewitched, he went to see Andreas Tayechea, a *curandero* at Compuerta who has had a lot of luck curing witch sickness. Andreas told Pablo that he could not help him. Pablo sold all his goats, giving the money to his kinswoman, Teresa Cocomorachi, to save until he died, so that she could arrange a nice *velación* for him. Within two months of the time he got sick, he died. Teresa arranged a nice *velación* with lots of candles; she used every penny, just as Pablo had wanted. The *novena* was arranged by other relatives.

Anita caused her husband, Beto Valencia, to die in 1942. They say that she ground up some bones of a dead person from the cemetery, added cemetery dirt, and put the mixture in Beto's food. He got very thin and died within two months.

Beto had always beat Anita a lot because she had plenty of boy friends. One who came to see her every two weeks was Luis Perico, called Luis Cornicero (the bugler), a Torim Yaqui who was deported at a young age. As a result he grew up among the Mexicans. At this time he was a lieutenant colonel in the Mexican army and one of the paymasters for the Yaqui Zone stationed at Vicam Switch. He had first known Anita in Mexico. He had a lot of women, one in every pueblo; he went to see them as he went from pueblo to pueblo on payday.

Another of Anita's many boy friends was Remetio Cruz; she went to live with him after Beto died and still lives with him today at Compuerta, where he has relatives. Remetio Cruz was the first governor of Torim in 1967. Remetio and Anita never had any children; her two daughters live with them; both Luz and Tomasa are still unmarried.

After Beto died in 1942, Anita started bothering his parents. She picked up some dirt from where Juan Valencia (Beto's father) had stepped, mixed it with dirt from the cemetery, and wrapped the dirt and lots of thorns in a cloth, which she buried in the cemetery. Not long afterwards, Juan fell and hurt his foot as he was coming home from chopping wood out in the brush. He just fell down, walking along on perfectly clear, flat ground. His foot became swollen, breaking open like a tomato. Juan knew that Anita had bewitched him. He never beat her, but he never liked her either. He said she was a bad woman.

Juan Valencia was a *matachine* chief. A long time before I got to Torim, people said he lived with his two daughters like they were his wives. For this reason he did not want them to see other men, and he got furious one morning when he found a man sleeping with Macaria, the daughter who was a *cantora*. Juan started to beat the boy with a strong stick, hurting him pretty badly before he could run away. The boy friend was a *maestro* named Luis Chavez Romero, a brother of Pancha China. He had been sleeping with Macaria for a long time, but Juan did not know about it. Several months later Macaria had a baby boy.

Three days after the baby was born, Juan burned him up and threw the dead baby in the river. Juan is not the only Yaqui who killed a baby when the parents were not married in the church. I have known of babies killed in Tucson, Guadalupe Village, and Hermosillo, as well as in the Rio Yaqui. I guess there is no law for babies. Poor Macaria was sad her baby was killed. She caught pneumonia a few months later and died.

Juan and his wife, Juana, lived in the Colorada Mine when they were young. They were close cousins and were not supposed to marry; however, they liked each other so much that they ran away together in 1899, returning to Torim so they could live together. They had ten children, six of whom died together at the Cerro del Gallo in 1926. The remaining four children lived in Torim.

Anita then bewitched Beto's mother, Juana Valencia, by making a doll, sticking needles in it, and rubbing ashes in the eyes. The ashes were of the *huvacvena*, a very poisonous bush with a bad odor that grows all around the Rio Yaqui. Used in small amounts, it is good for toothache (put a tiny piece from the fresh plant in a cracked tooth, and in a few days all the pieces will come out). Juana's eyes dried out and "exploded"; she went blind.

As I have already related, Clara Morales became infatuated with Jaime Lugo from Vicam, who was many years her junior. Jaime and his wife, Micaela Hupaumea, were living with Anastasia and Mariano Gonzalez. Clara got mad at all of them and bewitched them. Micaela died first, then Anastasia, and last of all Jaime. Everyone knew Clara Morales had caused the three to die. It is said that she killed them by making an *olla* of the explosive witch medicine, such as Luisa Sosa made in Hermosillo. She left town for a while because everyone was so mad that she had done this awful thing. Soon she came back.

Clara Morales started living with Nicolás Valencia, the younger brother of Anita's deceased husband. Nicolás probably knew that Clara had helped kill his brother and make his mother and father sick, but he liked her. Clara was about fifty years old at that time, and Nicolás about thirty-five.

The last person bewitched by the Morales sisters, at least that I know of, was Luis Perico, Anita's long-time boy friend. I was living in Texas when Luis got sick and when Nicolás moved in with Clara, but Mariano González wrote me about both things, and after I returned to Torim I was told the stories several times. They say that Anita got mad at Luis, so she stuck pins and thorns in the feet of a doll named Luis Perico, and before long he got sick and could not walk. Two soldiers had to carry him on his payday rounds every two weeks. Soon he died.

Today the Morales sisters are well off. All three sisters are still alive. Clara still has black hair, though Anita and Cristina have white hair. They are still in the mescal business. Now they have a horse and wagon that they use to haul it from Bacum. Anita and Charla own about forty cows. They make cheese daily and peddle it in their wagon.

Lucas Mateo, the witch hired by certain Torim officials to kill my friend Lucho Ramíriz, was run out of Torim about 1948 because of what he did to Mona Velásquez. Lucas had a son, Locario Mateo, usually called Locario Loco, who talked and sang and stayed drunk most of the time. Both Lucas and Locario were on the government payroll. Locario wanted to live with Mona, but she refused because he was a crazy man. To pay her back for refusing his son, Lucas caused her to get worms in her nose. She went to Andreas Tayechea, who told her that Lucas Mateo had caused this witch sickness; Andreas was able to cure her.

Both Andreas and Lucas lived at Compuerta, and they were good friends. After people knew what Lucas had done to Mona, they told him he had better leave town, so he moved back to his home pueblo of Bacum. Lucas is now an old man over seventy years old, so poor that he does not even own a horse.

Juan Jacom Pata de Hule (old "rubber foot") was the witch who caused Lucrecia Sewa to die in 1936. In 1948 he caused Pedro Valdes, also of Corasepe, to get sick; Pedro's feet dried up until only the bones were left, and then he died. These were the only people that I know that Juan Jacom harmed. As I have mentioned before, he was a good sort except for being a witch. Although poor, he shared his food. He died in 1951. Salome Hupaumea's son, Cruz, now lives with old Juan's granddaughter Isidora in the house with Juan's widow, Chepa, in Corasepe.

Four days after Anastasia died I went to see my other half brother, Manuel. "Well, how are you getting along all alone?" they asked me.

"Not very well. I don't like staying over there any more because Mariano gets drunk every night and makes a lot of noise in the kitchen."

"Why don't you move over here?" Rosa asked. "We are very poor, but we can eat anything we can find." There were three houses in their compound. Manuel and Rosa lived in one, and the other two were empty. One was where José González had lived with Carmen. I moved into the other one and ate with Rosa. I caught iguanas and rats for them, but seldom ate any. We all enjoyed catfish from the river.

Six months after Anastasia died, Mariano had good luck. He found a seventeen-year-old girl name Olga Velásquez Escalante at the Fiesta del Virgin del Camino in Bataconsica, July 2, 1944. He didn't get drunk so much after that. The Día del Virgin del Camino is the time when everyone gets married, even people who have lived together for thirty years. Olga is the younger sister of Mona Velásquez, who had trouble with the witch Lucas Mateo.

Early in June I decided to write to Dr. Holden; it had been a long time since I had heard from him. I asked him if I could borrow twenty dollars to start a little store in Torim. He must have mailed the money as soon as he received my letter, because a letter containing two ten-dollar bills came right away. I did not want to go to Obregón to change the dollars, because I had no shoes and my clothes were all patches. Instead I went to see Vicente Tava in Vicam and asked him to change the money for me. He gladly went to the store.

When he returned, I asked, "Did you change my money?"

"Oh yes, but I wasted twenty pesos. But don't worry. I'll pay you back." He gave me seventy-six pesos and never paid me back.

I walked back to Torim and did not spend a single peso. I started cleaning out my adobe house, getting everything ready to set up my store. I needed a wagon to haul provisions for my store from Vicam Switch. I went to every Yaqui in Torim who owned a wagon. No one wanted to loan me one. One said, "Well, yes, I have a wagon, but I turned my horses loose." Another said, "My wagon cost me a lot of money," and so on.

Finally I went to see my *fariseo padrino*, who was perhaps the richest man in Torim: Felipe Vega, who lived at Corasepe. He and his two brothers, Octavio and Marcelino, planted 30 hectares and ran more than 150 cows, 8 horses, a burro, and mules. They are the biggest cheese makers in Torim. Their burro is the one used to carry the Judas with the *fariseos* at Easter. Marcelino is a *fariseo;* he went to Tucson in 1926, returning to Torim in 1927. He never married.

When I got to Felipe's house, he said, "How are you getting along?"

"A little better, thank you."

His wife, Isabella, brought us very strong coffee and gave me a plate of *frijole* beans. I was not hungry, but I ate it all up.

"Well, *padrino*, I came to see you because I want to borrow your wagon to go buy provisions in Vicam Switch."

"We turned all the mules loose last night, but the boys can go get them." Two cowboys went off, brought back the mules, hitched them to the wagon, and off I went to Vicam Switch.

At the Mexican store I bought one sack of sugar, one sack of flour, a five-gallon can of lard, ten kilos of coffee, a box of washing soap, and a small box of candy, for seventy-six and a half pesos. I paid Felipe twenty-five pesos of money I had saved for the hire of the wagon. I decided to move back to my house to guard my provisions.

That very same day Yaquis came to buy things at my store. Whenever I got ten or fifteen pesos ahead, I walked to Vicam to get some more provisions for my store. Small things like cigarettes were no trouble to carry, except that it was awfully hot.

A month later I had two hundred pesos, so I rented Felipe's wagon again and restocked my store with heavy things. My store was doing very well; I made three hundred pesos in a couple of weeks and then five hundred pesos. Some of the poor Yaquis started asking for credit. I let them have twenty to fifty pesos worth of groceries on credit. On government payday every one of the people who owed me money would come to the store to pay. But no one ever paid all of their bill. Those who owed me twenty pesos paid me ten or fifteen; those who owed me fifty pesos would pay twenty-five or thirty and ask for another twenty pesos of credit. What kind of business is that?

We were eating a little better, but my clothes were wearing out. I had to quit running my store in February because I was broke. Only a few provisions were left in my adobe house.

When Lent started, I presented myself to Juan Díaz, the *fariseo* chief. I stayed with the *fariseos* for the whole of Lent, since I had not danced as a *fariseo* at all in 1944 because I had been so sad about Anastasia's death. I made all the processions to the rancherias and small pueblos. We walked to Compuerta, Tierra Blanca, Baghoi, and Vicam Switch. I was awfully sleepy after we made all those fiestas.

We were living on the few provisions left in my store. All through Lent and Easter I was unhappy because I did not have a penny. From February to April I did not work a day. I just went around with the *fariseos*, thinking, "How can I pay Dr. Holden back?"

After Easter I went back to the wood forest, cutting out seven-foot mesquite posts. I was paid fifty centavos a post, of which Miguel Toledo took thirty centavos because he had the contract for the posts. The ax was in pretty bad shape, so I could only make twenty-five posts a day. All the other Yaquis working with me were making forty to fifty. We had to walk seven miles out to the place where we cut the posts and seven miles back every night, even though there was good mesquite much closer. The governor of Torim and Miguel Toledo told us, "If you folks want to cut some posts, you better go over past *Paros Hackia* (Rabbit Creek).

I was making about five pesos a day and walking fourteen miles through terrible heat. Miguel Toledo was very happy because he did not have to work at all. He just sat around the *guardia* all day and got rich off of our hard work. Such easy money for him. We cut enough posts (seven thousand) to fulfil Miguel's contract in two months, finishing on July 18, 1945. On the nineteenth, I started making ties, and four days later I went back to the wood forest.

In July, 1945, I moved in with my *fariseo madrina*, Nacha Sewa. Her husband, Nacho Buanamea, was a woodcutter too; we walked to work together every day. Nacha fixed lunches for us of two corn tortillas, beans, and a bottle of coffee to take to the wood forest. Nacha and Nacho had two little girls, Epifania, about five years old, and Aurelia, about three.

Just a week later I came down with fever sickness. Day after day I had chills and high fevers. Whenever the spells came, I would shake all over. From two or three o'clock every afternoon until about ten o'clock at night I would shake and shake. Nacha made some medicine, but nothing helped.

One day she said, "Why don't you ask Viviana or Antonia in Tucson to send you a little money."

I wrote to Antonia, and Nacha sent Nacho to Vicam to mail it. In seven days Mariano González came by. "There is a letter for you in Vicam," he said.

On August 12 I went to Vicam so weak from the fever that I had to rest several times along the road. It took a long time to get there. I went directly to Vicente Tava's house.

"What has happened to you? You look so pale."

"I've been sick with a fever for more than two weeks."

"Sit down and let me get you something to eat."

"No, thank you. I can't eat anything. I just came down to get my mail."

A money order from Antonia was waiting at the post office. I took it to the Mexican store to get it countersigned and then I went back to the postmaster, who gave me fifty-seven and a half pesos. The order had been for twelve dollars.

I went to the doctor. "What can you give me for fever-sickness?"

"How long have you been sick?" he asked.

"About two weeks."

He gave me some capsules to take three times a day, two after every meal.

"How much do I owe you, Doctor?"

"Seven pesos."

I bought some groceries for Nacha and caught a free ride on a wagon with a man who lived near Torim. When Nacha saw the groceries, she said, "What did you find at Vicam?"

"I received fifty-seven and a half pesos from my sister Antonia."

The capsules the doctor gave me were good. My fever stopped that day, and soon I was strong enough to go to the wood forest again.

On August 28 the river began to rise. All the poor Yaquis were happy because now they could grow some food. When the water ran down, everyone started clearing and planting. I planted about fifteen pounds of beans and some pumpkins early in September.

# CHAPTER 13

# *Torim, 1946—1950*

PANCHA (FRANCISCA) VALENZUELA CASTRO WAILIKA just arrived at my house one day in 1946. For a long time she had wanted to come live with me in Torim, but I always told her I was too poor. If I could not feed myself, how could I feed a family? Pancha had lived with her mother and aunt in Bacum, where she worked in Mexican houses as a maid. She and her mother often fought; once her mother cut her breast badly with a knife. It was after one of their fights that she came to me.

I was living in Nacha's house when she came. I said to all of them, "Look. How can I support a wife?"

Nacha said, "Well, Rosalio, I think you need a wife. You know very well that our God never forgets us, and I don't think you will die of hunger with a wife."

I let her stay. This was my birthday, September 4, 1946. Nacha gave us a lot of advice about married life; she wanted us to get married at the Virgin del Camino fiesta, but we never did.

The day after Pancha arrived, we walked over to Vicam to buy some things for my adobe house, because I did not own a single cup or spoon. We bought a few pottery cups for twenty-five centavos apiece and a few groceries and walked back to Torim. Two days later we had cleaned out my adobe house and moved in. Nacha gave us a few things for cooking.

Pancha's mother was Chela Castro, a Mayo; her father was Enrique Valenzuela, a Mexican soldier who was transferred to Mexicali in 1928;

they never saw him again. After Pancha moved to Torim, Chela never came to see us; in fact, she did not even come when Pancha died, and Pancha was her only child. Pancha's aunt was named Bartola Sanova.

Being a Mayo, Pancha spoke practically no Yaqui, even after living in Bacum all those years. She began teaching me Mayo, and soon I was pretty good at talking Mayo, which is a lot like Yaqui. Usually however, Pancha and I spoke Spanish.

People in Torim liked Pancha; she was so happy, always laughing, singing, and talking to everyone. She wanted me to dance and laugh like she did. "Why are you so sad?" she would ask.

"Así soy" (That's the way I am).

She loved going to the baseball games in Torim, and she yelled plenty at the players.

I built a big oven for her so she could bake bread for us and for sale. She would walk around the pueblo with her bread in a basket, selling it from house to house and talking to everyone along the way.

We made a happy living for a while. I had a garden from which we ate green beans and pumpkin every day. Pancha made bread. I cut some wood for sale and carrizo for Pancha, who made *petates*.

Valentina Castillo of Compuerta, was very fond of Pancha, and Pancha liked her very much. Pancha called her *tia* because old Valentina was like an aunt to her. Valentina was, in fact, much nicer to Pancha than any of her real family. Valentina was the mother of Reyes Castillo, the one who killed the young soldier in 1934 at Cenobampo, and the aunt of Marcelo Castillo, whom Pancha had known in Bacum. Like Pancha, the Castillo family were Mayos. The old lady came to see us almost every day. Pancha would take her to the garden and give her some beans and pumpkins.

We walked out in the brush looking for wild food. We did everything we could think of to find food, and indeed we were not often hungry. *Chiltipiquín* grew wild all through the brush, and we would pick a sackful and sell it to the Mexican storekeeper in Vicam; he paid five pesos a kilo. We could pick two or three kilos of *chiltipiquíns* a week.

On November 20, I began pulling the bean plants to get the field ready for a new crop. We had eaten so many green beans that I just saved three five-gallon tins and threw the rest away. As soon as the field was clean, I began making mounds for watermelon. With Pancha helping, we made eight hundred holes for watermelons, fifteen holes for squash, and twelve for pumpkins. I planted the watermelons by November 27, but it was still too early to plant pumpkins and squash.

Pancha and I walked over to Vicam to pick up papers so we could cover our watermelon holes to protect the plants in case of frost. We were able to find enough papers to make heavy loads for each of us. The trip home was very tiring. The next day we covered every hole, and on December 7 baby plants were born in every hole.

Every night I waited for my dream to tell me how my crop would turn out that year; all my dreams that tell me what is going to happen come about three o'clock in the morning. Well, my dream came, and I could see my garden, but not a single watermelon. At first I felt awfully sad. But then I was happy because I knew I would have luck. As soon as I drank my cup of coffee, I went to see my garden and looked at every melon plant. While the plants were growing, there was not much to do in the garden, so I went back to the wood forest.

About the second week of December, 1946, buzzards over the Valencia house started crying "Manuel, Manuel" every night. The Valencia family lived near our adobe house; I knew that soon something would happen. Buzzards roost in the cottonwood trees around Torim every night, and ordinarily they do no harm. Whenever they call a name night after night, that person will die.

Manuel Valencia was the son of Eusebio and Cornelia Valencia; they were Mayos who had lived in Torim for some years. Manuel was a good friend of mine. For years he had been one of Juana Chávez's boy friends. Her other boy friend was Victor Palma, the Yaqui captain of the pueblo.

On Christmas Eve, Juana Chávez got mad at Manuel and, going to Victor Palma, she accused Manuel of stealing a suitcase containing clothes, which of course he had not done. Victor Palma immediately sent Yaqui soldiers and a sergeant to get Manuel, and by 11:00 P.M. Manuel was tightly bound in the *guardia*. Victor quickly summoned all of the Torim officials, including Celso Flores, the governor. By midnight the Torim officials had sentenced Manuel to death. They sent a soldier to Compuerta to wake up the executioner. I walked by the *guardia* about 3:00 A.M., and Manuel was sitting silently, his arms bound tightly against his body.

At 4:00 A.M., the executioner arrived. His name was Ramón Robles, the son of Luis Robles Carretero, a Sierra Yaqui. Ramón was not a *yori*, but he was a born killer. He carried out the official executions for Torim pueblo. He had only one foot and had to go from place to place on horseback.

When he arrived at the *guardia*, the other men put Manuel up behind Ramón on the horse, and the two rode off alone. About a mile north of the pueblo, Ramón knocked Manuel off the horse and slashed his head with a machete.

Eusebio and Cornelia knew nothing about what had happened to Manuel until the next morning, when old Joaquín Babosa, who lived close to where Manuel was killed, found the body and notified them and everyone else in Torim. They left the body there and immediately walked to Vicam to get the authorities. Mexican soldiers arrived. It was clear who had done the killing. I went along to where Manuel's body was found. We could tell that he had run about fifteen feet from where he was hit before he fell and died. Blood was everywhere.

The whole pueblo felt that the Torim officials had acted unjustly. The officials admitted that they had told Ramón to execute Manuel. Everyone wanted to send the governors to Vicam to request an investigation, but the officials were afraid to go. All Christmas Day they sat in the *guardia* with their hats over their faces, very much afraid.

General Ramón Rivera, a Mayo who was the highest-ranking Mexican officer in Vicam, summoned the governors of the other pueblos; and all of them, as well as Colonel Oscar Salcedo, a Mayo stationed at Potam, Lieutenant Colonel Anastasio Urias, the crazy Yaqui who had killed Gilberto Cocomorachi in 1926, Abrán Villa, a Yaqui captain at Cocorit, and Chico Bule, son of old Luis Bule and paymaster of the Yaqui Zone, came to Torim in a big truck on December 28. They picked up the Torim officials, who had nothing to say, and the whole party returned to Vicam. Ramón Robles was not taken, and no one was mad at him, because he had simply followed orders.

The Torim officials were freed within two hours, but their government pay was suspended. They all became very poor because none of them knew how to work, as they were accustomed to drawing pay for doing nothing.

Cornelia Valencia was a very fine woman, a good *curandera*, but not a witch. She had cured my mother of a fever sickness when Cecelia lived with me. Cornelia went to see a Mayo witch living in Cocorit, Román Arpero, to ask him to harm all the ones who had anything to do with killing her son. One by one they all died except Victor Palma, who became very ill.

The first to die was Juana Chávez. She was dead by the end of January, 1947. The governor, Celso Flores, died soon thereafter. Later Sergeant Jorge Savas, who had been at the sentencing, Jesús Aldamea, the second governor and an assistant to Jorge Flores, Lieutenant Lauro Mendoza, Lieutenant Tomás Robles, and his brother, Sergeant Gonzalo Robles, all died.

The last to die were the members of the Buetemea family. Captain

Rosario Buetemea and Commandant Crecensio Buetemea had both been present when Manuel was sentenced. These two brothers, Rosario's wife (María Buetemea), Rosario's two sons (Gilberto and Juan María), and Crecensio's seventeen-year-old son (Joaquín) all died within a week in 1952. I had already gone to Texas when they died, but Mariano González wrote me all about it.

The reason that Victor Palma was only crippled instead of being killed is that Ramón Arpero died, and the great *curandero* of Torim, Andreas Tayechea, was able to save him when the witchcraft stopped. Dr. Holden sent medicine for Victor, but since his illness was caused by witchcraft instead of natural causes, the pills did not help.

They say the way Ramón Arpero bewitched Victor was by taking dirt from where Victor had stepped, mixing it with cactus thorns, wrapping it in a cloth, and burying it in the graveyard. I often saw Ramón in the graveyard, as many people visit the graveyards on Sunday in order to leave candles at graves, but I never saw him digging around.

Ramón Arpero was a *sabio* as well as a witch, and was able to find lost articles or tell who had stolen something. To identify a thief, he would take a glass of water, break an egg in it, recite the rosary, and the image of the thief appeared in the glass.

Cornelia and Eusebio Valencia both died that same year, and my brother wrote me about that too. Their other children were Ana, Aurelia, Lola, Amelia, and Delores. Eusebio Valencia was the brother of Panocha Valencia, who was once the governor of Torim, the only Mayo governor of Torim that I can remember. Panocha and his wife, Juana Quesubari (Fresh-cheese, because her family were cheese makers), were always good friends of mine. I baptized Panocha's son and named him Rosalio, in 1932 or 1933. This made me a *compadre* to Panocha. Martín Valencia was the name of Panocha's and Eusebio's father; I do not remember their mother's name.

At Christmas we were very happy. My wife did not make tamales; instead she made *buñuelos*, a kind of fried bread that the Yaquis like to eat with syrup or honey. At midnight of December 24, Pancha and I went to see the dance for the Christ child in the church. The dance lasted about an hour, and then all the Yaquis went home and ate all night. Every family that had any food at all made tamales or *buñuelos* and everyone stayed up, very happily. Some drank mescal. Musicians were playing. On Christmas Day the Yaquis all went back to the church to see the Christ child.

The Yaquis do not do anything in the church for New Year's. Those who can make tamales and *buñuelos;* many poor Yaquis are hungry on New Year's. Of course, people drink mescal whenever they have it.

Many Yaquis like marijuana better than mescal or tequila. Nearly all of the Yaquis who returned from Central Mexico used marijuana. In Torim twelve boys between the ages of ten and eighteen died of marijuana, and eight others went crazy. Many times the Mexican government has sent orders to the general in Vicam Switch to destroy all the marijuana. Every time such orders came, Mexican soldiers had to search all over the Yaqui territory for marijuana; they never found any because the Yaquis plant it out in the heavy brush or among the carrizo. The Mexican soldiers did not really want to find marijuana plants, because a lot of them like to use it too. Mexicans often came to Vicam Switch with marijuana cigarettes to sell for one and a half pesos each. A lot of marijuana is grown around Hermosillo and at San Ignacio, north of Magdalena.

My two Torim brothers, Mariano and Manuel González, both grew and used marijuana. That was one of the reasons that Mariano was always so hard to live with.

In February of 1947, Pancha and I uncovered all the watermelon plants because frost danger was past. The squash and pumpkins could be planted. Pancha said, "Aren't you going to plant some beans?"

"If someone will loan me a mule and plow."

No one in Torim wanted to loan their mule, so I walked over to Vicam to see Vicente Tava, who had four mules. When I got there, the house was empty. One of Vicente's sons came along.

"Where is your father?"

"At the billiard hall. He will be here any minute."

In about fifteen minutes Vicente came home.

"Well, *tio* Vicente, I sure want to plant some beans. I've got two five-gallon cans of beans. I need a mule and a plow. Can I borrow yours?"

"That would be all right, but now I am working with the mules."

"I could plant in just one day."

"I have to load some wood down by the river tomorrow."

There was nothing more to say. When I got home, Pancha asked, "Did you find anything?"

"No."

I did not plant any beans that year because no one would loan me a mule for plowing. Instead, I went back to the wood forest. When Lent began, Pancha asked, "Are you going with the *fariseo* society on their first procession?"

"No, I don't think I should, because we are so far behind. We have no money and very little food. I believe I had better chop wood until Holy Wednesday. Then I will dance for the *fariseos*."

"That is all right."

Everything stops in Torim on Holy Wednesday. No man can work in the wood forest and no family can wash their clothes. The *fariseos* walk around watching everyone to make sure no one is doing some work. If they catch a man or a woman working, they take them to the *fariseo guardia*, where the *fariseo* chief makes them pay a fine. If they have money, they pay three pesos right then. If they have no money, the chief makes them drag a heavy cross made of green mesquite wood around the crosses where the procession occurs on Good Friday. The *fariseo* chief in every other Yaqui village metes out the same punishment to people who are working or drinking between Wednesday and Sunday of Holy week.

Only a few families in Torim do not believe in God and never go to any of the fiestas. Locario Lopez Mejia is married to Esperanza Cocomorachi, the older sister of my aunt Teresa Cocomorachi. They do not like the Yaqui religion; they say it is a lot of foolishness. Maybe that is because they are part Tarahumara. My mother, also a Cocomorachi, never believed in anything either. Veva Valencia, the daughter of Juan and Juana Valencia, is married to a half-Mexican named Carlos Huerto Guzmán, and they do not believe in anything. Well, there are all kinds of people on this earth. I know there are people in the United States who do not believe in God or in ghosts.

When Holy Wednesday came, I did not know what to do because I had no money or food. Pancha said, "Why don't you go to the Mexican store in Vicam Switch and ask for credit. Tell them you will pay them back as soon as you sell all that wood you've chopped."

She and I walked over to Vicam Switch together and went to the Mexican store. I had known the man who ran the store for many years.

"Well, I've come to ask if I can have twenty pesos worth of groceries on credit. After Easter I will pay you back," I said.

"Are you working?"

"Oh yes. I work all the time in Torim, and I've got about thirty loads of wood out in the wood forest. After Easter the truckers will come again to buy wood."

"That is fine. I'll let you have ten pesos worth of groceries."

We took our groceries and walked back to Torim, getting home around noon. That evening of Holy Wednesday I presented myself to the *fariseo* chief. Once you have gone to join the *fariseos* you cannot go home again until the Easter dance is over on Sunday. When the dance was over and I went home again, I found Pancha sitting in a corner of the house on the floor, very sad.

"What's happened to you?"

"I am sad because I have nothing to cook for you."

We went looking for food about a mile west of Torim. We filled our basket with edible green weeds and took it home. She quickly boiled the greens. Fortunately we still had a little salt. Bitter green weeds for breakfast too. We were so hungry.

Pancha said, "I know how we can eat. I will pawn my gold earrings," and off she went to the store, where the Mexican gave her five pesos worth of groceries. She ran all the way home, and soon had made us corn tortillas and coffee.

Tuesday morning I woke up early in order to listen for the trucks heading into the wood forest. I was lucky, catching the first trucker, and no one else was around. I sold him all thirty-two loads for sixty-four pesos. As soon as I reached home, we ate a little food and went to Vicam to pay the Mexican storekeeper his ten pesos. We bought forty pesos worth of groceries to take home. Pancha wanted some clothes, which we certainly needed, but we decided against spending more money.

We walked to Valentina Castillo's house at Compuerta and fixed a good dinner. We left her some sugar, coffee, and beans; the old lady was very happy. After we got home we rested until the sun was not so hot, then we went to see our melons. They were beautiful. They were growing so nicely, and already some of them were quite large.

"I guess it's time to build a ramada here in the field to protect our crop because the watermelons are growing so fast," I told Pancha.

We started building the ramada that very afternoon and had it ready in two days. On April 23, 1946, we closed our house in Torim and moved to the garden, about one mile south of Torim. By the end of May the watermelons were ripening. We stayed in the ramada until August 14. Our garden was in such a sandy spot that big wagons could not get in to pick up a load. As a result, I did not sell many watermelons.

On August 15, Mariano González came out to tell us that the river was coming down. A bad flood was expected. I ran to Torim to see if I could borrow a wagon, and luck was with me. When I got back to the garden, Pancha had everything packed. We loaded our belongings and a few watermelons and left. As soon as we unloaded at our adobe house, I went back to the garden because there were over two hundred big pumpkins in the field. I was only able to get out one load. Then I told all the people in the pueblo to get out what they could. The next morning the water was over my garden.

On August 18 I had to go back to the wood forest, and oh, my God, it was hot in the wood forest in August. My clothes were all gone. It's hard work chopping wood or making ties in that heat. Sometimes some dumb Yaqui boys stole the wood I had stacked for the trucks. A lot of boys slept out in the forest and if the truckers came in at night or early in the morning, these boys would sell somebody else's wood. Or else they would take your wood to make charcoal.

One night a crazy, drunk Yaqui sold twenty loads of wood I had ready for the trucker. When I got out there, I saw clean ground where I had placed my wood pile. I was so mad and sad. I went to see a poor Mexican who lives on the truck road. "Which truck driver came in for a load of wood either last night or early this morning?" I asked him.

"Marcelo."

"Where did he go to pick up a load?"

"I don't know but I saw Navór. He took Marcelo into the forest."

"Last night or this morning?"

"Oh, early this morning," he said. I went home with a sad face.

"Did you sell your wood?" asked Pancha.

"No. Somebody stole my wood this morning and sold it to a trucker."

"Do you know who it was?"

"Yes, it was Navór."

"What are you going to do now? Why don't you go see the governor? Maybe he can arrange something."

I walked over to the *guardia* to see the governor. "Good morning, Rosalio," he said.

"I came here to see you because a Yaqui boy has stolen twenty loads of wood that I cut. He sold it to a trucker early this morning."

"There is nothing I can do for you because you did not let us know when you started working in the forest," he said. I walked back home.

Pancha asked, "What did the governor say?"

"Nothing. He said he can't help me. But that is all right. We won't starve to death."

Six times some Yaquis stole my wood, and I never did anything. I stopped going to the wood forest for a while, and Pancha and I started making *petates*. We could make three or four a day. Pancha took them to the Mexican storekeeper, who only paid forty centavos apiece. She took the 1.20 or 1.60 pesos of credit in food. Now we ate only twice a day. Making *petates* all the time is hard. You have to pound up the carrizo before you can weave the mats. Our hands were sore all the time.

With so little money or credit for food, we went into the brush looking for food when we were very hungry. Sometimes we ate a meal of nopal fruit, but neither of us liked it. I decided I should try the wood forest again; no one stole my wood this time.

On December 17, 1947, Pancha had a baby boy. She was very happy, because she wanted children. I was not so happy, because I knew that children born in December have bad luck.

A few days later Pancha said, "You better go look for someone."

"Why?"

"So they can baptize this baby."

"Oh my. I forgot. I'll go today to find a *padrino*."

I walked to Vicam Switch to see Vicente Tava. "I came to see if your son can baptize our baby boy," I said to him.

"That will be fine."

I then asked Vicente's son, "Can you baptize my baby?"

"I have never liked to baptize children. You better look for someone else. So many people like to baptize children that it should be easy to find someone." I walked back to Torim.

"Did you find someone to baptize the baby?"

"No. I couldn't find anyone. I asked Vicente's son, but he says he never baptizes babies. I guess you had better look for someone tomorrow."

Pancha had better luck. Saturnino Toropochi said he would do it. He had sixteen cows. A few days later he brought a little dress for the baby, and he and the *madrina* took the baby to be baptized in the Catholic church in Obregón. Saturnino rented a truck to make the trip. Our baby was baptized Lucio, but we usually called him Nico. Sometimes we called him Lázaro, because he was born on Saint Lázaro's day. He was registered in Bacum, as Pancha was from that pueblo.

Whenever godparents baptize a child, it is the Yaqui custom for the parents to prepare a good meal for the godparents. When the godparents returned from Obregón, we had to say, "We are so sorry, but we have no food, but if we get a little money, we will have a nice dinner for you."

"Don't worry about us," said Saturnino, "because we all are very poor." We never got enough money to cook a nice dinner for Saturnino.

Our lives were very hard. Often we ate only once a day and we were always hungry.

"What are we going to do, Pancha? It is New Year's Day. The ground is too hard to plant watermelons, and raising a watermelon crop is the only thing that ever helps us get ahead for a little while."

"Only our God can help us," she said.

I kept working in the wood forest. Grocery prices went up every few weeks. When Lent began in 1948, I could not go with the *fariseos* on their procession, but kept on chopping wood. Of course, on Holy Wednesday I presented myself to the *fariseo* chief, because I made a *promesa* to Jesus

Christ, and when you make a *promesa*, you have to do whatever you have promised. I know that my American friends do not understand about the *promesa*, but it is something you have to do.

On Holy Saturday, I was running in the church with my godparents, Felipe Vega and Nacha Sewa Buanamea when Nacha fell down. She got up looking very white and scared because she knew what that meant, but she kept running with me and made the sign of the cross on my breast and put the rosaries around my neck. We knew she would die before the next Easter, and indeed she did.

My poor Pancha. She helped me in every way she could, by going up to the Mexican *guardia* and helping the soldiers' wives wash their dishes or clean their quarters. The Mexican women liked her and gave her food.

After Easter I went back to the wood forest. I could have gone up the valley to work for the Mexican farmers in the irrigated district, but they only paid three pesos a day; the mosquitoes are terrible there; and the groceries cost more in their store.

Nico was growing. But he cried all the time from hunger. Pancha would weep with him because we had nothing to feed him. Many nights I got up to toast some pumpkin seeds for him so he could sleep a little.

One day Pancha suggested that I write to my American friends to see if they had any old clothes, because our clothes were full of holes. I wrote Dr. Holden and explained what was happening to us in Torim. Pancha started praying to God over the letter I wrote, praying that Dr. Holden would answer. She prayed every night. A few days later I said, "I believe I will see if there is a letter in Vicam."

I went alone because Pancha was too weak to carry Lázaro so many miles. Dr. Holden's letter was waiting. It contained five dollars, and said that he would soon send along some clothes. I wrote him another letter, asking him to send the clothes to my daughter Marcelina in Eloy, Arizona, as any package coming through the Vicam post office would be robbed. I knew that Marcelina was coming to Torim with her brother, Salvador, in December.

With the five dollars I bought a lot of food at the Mexican store and rushed back to Pancha. Even with my load, I made it from Vicam Switch to Torim in an hour. "Oh, Rosalio. Where did you find the food?" asked Pancha.

I showed her the letter from Dr. Holden and told her about the money. She was very happy. She thanked God that her prayers were answered. Then I told her that Dr. Holden would send clothes, and she said, "Oh,

I thank God so much because he answered all my prayers, and I thank Dr. Holden, too." Nico had never seen so much food. He did not cry that night.

A few days later Guadalupe Chávez Sandoval, the Mayo who gave me the adobe house, came to see me, saying he needed a laborer for his ranch.

"I don't have a thing to do here in Torim, so I will go with you. What kind of work am I going to do?"

"I would like for you to build a new house on my ranch, and build some cow pens," he said.

"How long will the job last?"

"About a month."

"Fine, I will go with you."

"Well, I have a wagonload of cheese which I am going to sell in Vicam Switch. I'll be back to pick you up in two days, so be ready."

Pancha and I packed the things we wanted to take with us and left everything else, including all my tools, in my godfather's care. We closed our house and were ready when Guadalupe came back in his wagon. The first day we made twenty miles, camping at San Juanico. As soon as we cooked breakfast the next morning, we started on and reached the ranch at Bachomobampo about noon, December 1, 1948. Bachomobampo is a rancheria in the eastern Bacatete Mountains some three and a half miles from Torocobampo. Guadalupe Sandoval ran over two hundred head of cattle on his ranch. We met many nice people there. Every morning we were given a half gallon of milk and cheese curds (*requesón*) left from the cheese making. Our baby, Lázaro, was happy and well fed, and Pancha made friends with the women. I worked on building the house whenever I could, but the weather was bad and it rained a lot.

Guadalupe Sandoval sent me to the small town of Agua Caliente some miles to the north for provisions late one afternoon. On the way back I saw a gold flame at Roroischahue, as the Yaquis call it, or Cerro de Delores in Spanish. The flame burned for about five minutes, getting lower and lower. This flame is a *lumbre* in Spanish and *taji* in Yaqui. One can go crazy from seeing such flames. This was a famous *lumbre;* I had been told of it when I lived in Tucson. I did not tell Sandoval what I had seen, although I told Pancha. I never went back there to dig for gold.

I finished Sandoval's house, built of interlaced saplings plastered with mud, and built a calf pen. When I was through, Sandoval took us and a big load of cheese back to the Rio Yaqui; we stopped one night at Coyote, near San Juanico, so the mules could rest. The people there were very nice to us, giving us places to sleep and feeding us a good supper. It was December 30, 1948, when we returned to Torim. We had spent a nice Christmas in the mountains. Our Nico got back to Torim a fat little boy from drinking all that milk.

Pancha and I left Nico with my *fariseo padrino*, Felipe Vega, and walked over to Vicam to buy a few groceries and clothes with the money Sandoval had paid us; we hurried back to get Nico as fast as we could. We had twenty pesos, some food, and a few clothes on New Year's, so we entered the New Year in better shape than before.

Marcelina had come down with Salvador. My son Salvador was in the U.S. Army during World War II. While he was in Europe he made a *promesa* to the Virgin of Guadalupe that if nothing happened to him in the war, he would make three big fiestas in her honor. He came to Torim for the fiestas in December of 1946, 1947, and 1948. When they came in 1948, I was in the mountains building the house for Guadalupe Salvador. In 1946 and 1947, however, I had been in the village. Salvador and his family and Marcelina and her three daughters stayed with Teresa Coco-morachi. Salvador's first fiesta was equipped with plenty of food and many dancers. Everyone from the first governor of the pueblo to the poorest soul in Torim was invited. This was the first time I had seen them since they were small children. I was glad to see how they looked. Marcelina brought us a package in 1948.

Pancha said, "Marcelina came in December to deliver the clothes that Dr. Holden sent. Let's find out where she left them."

"Oh, I forgot about them. I'll ask Salome."

Salome, however, was dead drunk, it being New Year's Day. His wife was there, so I asked about a package left by Marcelina.

"Oh yes. Marcelina left a package for you with Cristina Morales."

"Thank you. That is what I wanted to know."

We went to see Cristina, who gave us the package. Few things were left in it, as Cristina had taken out nearly everything. We did not say anything to her, but we knew what she had done.

After the New Year the river started rising, and day by day it got higher. All over the Yaqui country the Yaquis knew a flood was coming, because snakes and frogs were climbing trees. This is a sign that God sends to warn the Yaquis of high water. This sign has never been wrong. Pancha and I went to gather firewood for cooking, and we saw rattlesnakes, other snakes, ants, and toads up in the mesquite trees.

"Look at that rattlesnake up in the tree."

"He must be hunting rats."

"I do not think so," I told my wife. "The Yaquis say that when snakes climb the trees, a flood is coming."

I kept showing her the animal signs, but she did not believe anything I said. We gathered our wood and went home. Valentina Castillo was waiting for us with a dozen big loaves of wheat bread and a quart of honey.

"Oh, *tia!* Where did you get all the food?"

"The bread I just baked, and friends gave me the honey."

"*Tia*, is it true about the flood? Are the Yaquis right about the animal signs?"

"A flood is coming, and I guess the Yaquis are right about the animal signs."

Pancha said, "A little while ago we saw rattlesnakes and toads up in mesquite trees."

"The animals never lie," Valentina said.

Soon the Mexican *guardia* received a telegram from Corrál, upriver, saying that the river was cresting at a high level. A lot of Yaquis living near the river waited too late to leave, and many died.

On January 12 I walked out to look at the river at a place about three miles east of Torim where there is an abandoned river channel that is always dry. But that day it was full of water. I ran home and told all the neighbors that the river was getting much higher.

Telegraph messages about the height of the water were sent from Corrál every hour, and the Mexican soldiers kept warning everyone. I told Pancha that if the water continued to rise all afternoon, we would have to leave. Pancha worried about Valentina. "She can save herself on the hill," I reassured Pancha.

We watched the river closely, and the water kept rising. By dark it was running around the old church in Torim. A Mexican soldier at the *guardia* said, "Oh, this is nothing. It will soon be much worse."

I ran home and told Pancha, "There is no reason to wait any longer, because water has reached the old church."

We quickly packed our bedroll and what little food we had, picked up Lázaro, and started walking north in the darkness. About a mile north of the pueblo is an old channel, usually dry. We waded through three feet of water to cross it. At Babu-u four houses stood empty. Leaving Pancha and Lázaro in one of them, I ran back to our house to get some more things, taking my dog along. Already water was flowing through the pueblo. I packed up a load, and the dog and I ran back toward Babu-u. Now four feet of water was running in the old channel.

"How is the water back there?" Pancha asked.

"There is plenty of it."

We sat in the old house for about two hours; Lázaro slept in Pancha's arms, but we did not close our eyes. We could hear a lot of noise from the south, from Torim. People were calling.

"I guess something is going to happen to those people," we said. In the bright moonlight we saw new water coming our way. I threw a rock out where it had been dry ground shortly before, and it splashed.

"We better get out of here."

"Where can we go now?"

"We'll go to my *padrino*'s at Corasepe."

I carried a big load; she put a load on her head and carried Lázaro in her arms. About two hundred yards from the old house we saw the ghost of Babu-u wearing a black coat. He walked across the road in front of us, scaring my dog, who ran back to us.

"What is that?" asked Pancha.

"Just a ghost." He walked down to the water and disappeared. We saw him no more.

We got to Felipe Vega's house.

"Good morning."

"Good morning. How did you get out of Torim?"

"We left about dark last evening."

Everyone at the ranch was awake and gathered around a big fire. They gave us hot coffee, for it was terribly cold.

I started down the hill to see some Yaquis at the foot of Corasepe Hill, but I met them all coming up the hill because water was coming into their houses. Running back up to the Vegas' house, I told my godfather, "*Padrino*, we better get out of here. Lots more water is coming this way."

Old Valentina and her family were there, but they decided to wait at Corasepe a little longer. Pancha pleaded with Valentina to come with us, but she refused.

Before sunrise we loaded all the wagons and left Corasepe. The cowboys drove the cows to the railroad tracks near Vicam, on somewhat higher ground. The rest of us moved out to high ground near the Indian school at Vicam. In the afternoon we saw water coming around the east side of the school. I told Pancha, "We better go to the Indian school. You run over and ask the director if we can move over there."

She left Lázaro with me and ran the half mile to the school, returning with two boys from the school. "The director says to come on, and he sent these two boys to help us. The water is still rising."

All of us who had come from Corasepe moved over to the school; the director let us have an empty house and fed us a good meal. More Yaquis came to the school, and the water continued to rise. One group came from Torim. They had taken refuge on a high hill north of the pueblo where they were safe from the water but ran out of food.

"Rosalio, can you get back to Corasepe to look for old Valentina Castillo?" asked Pancha.

The director sent six boys with me. We waded at least two feet of water most of the way. Close to Corasepe Hill, the water was four feet deep and running fast. We crossed and went up the hill, where many Yaqui were congregated. I found Valentina. "You had better come with us now. Pancha is worried about you."

"I can't get across the deep water."

"I've brought six boys from the school, and they can carry you."

Four big boys picked her up, and the other two carried her bedroll. Some of the other Yaquis decided to come with us. It took about two hours to reach the school. Pancha was very pleased to see Valentina, who was very hungry, as they had very little food left at Corasepe. This was January 14, 1949.

The water continued to rise. Loud crashes came from the brush as big saguaros fell. By this time the telephone and telegraph wires were down. On January 15 the water came up nearly to the school. By January 19 water was in all the Yaqui villages. Some little airplanes came to drop food to the stranded Yaquis. Every bag they dropped contained coffee, sugar, ten pieces of bread, ten tall cans of salmon, a half kilo of rice, one kilo of beans, cigarettes, matches, and a half-dozen Mejoral (aspirin)— all sent from Mesa City, Arizona.

I wrote to Dr. Holden telling him all about the flood. Right away he sent ten dollars, and the next day I received five dollars each from Dr. Wagner, Dr. Turner, and Mr. McMillan, making twenty-five American dollars.

So many Yaquis lost everything they owned in the flood. A big boxcar, sent from Mesa City, Arizona, arrived at Vicam Switch on January 17. It contained food and clothes for the flood victims. A large airplane flew over Vicam on January 18, dropping four large packages, each containing four hundred blankets. People in Navojoa, Obregón, Guaymas, Hermosillo, and from many places in the United States sent food, clothes, blankets, and medicine to help the poor Yaquis.

Virtually none of these supplies were ever given to the destitute Yaquis. General Ramón Rivera (a Mayo) at Vicam Switch took everything he could get his hands on. Seven Yaqui men helped him steal all the supplies. They are León Tava, Javier Lenes, José María Mayo, Emiliano Gómez, Miguel Valdes, Lorenzo Soledo, and Agustín Ybarra. Those seven *yoris* got everything they wanted because they were stealing for General Rivera.

I saw an Arizona newspaper that carried a long story about the city of Phoenix, Arizona, sending seven hundred dollars to the Yaqui tribe. The tribe did not get a cent, but the *yoris* did.

A Mexican from Guaymas came on January 22, bringing rubber rafts for rescue work. They picked up lots of people; some said they had been in the top of mesquite trees for three or four days without food. All these hungry Yaquis were brought to Vicam. They asked General Rivera for food, and he said, "Well, I have very little food, but anyhow, I will help you."

He ordered his *yoris* to hand out provisions. They gave each family one kilo of flour, a half kilo of sugar, a quarter of a kilo of coffee, and one kilo of rice and a half kilo of beans. That is all he ever distributed of the supplies. Everything else he kept to sell later. Every blanket (there had been sixteen hundred in the air drop and more sent by train) was sold through the Mexican store in Vicam or peddled by the *yoris*. Day by day more wet Yaquis came into Vicam; many had fever and everyone was hungry. The river crested on January 22; we got two feet of water in the Indian school.

Miguel Toledo came to the school. "Rosalio," he said, "your brother Manuel and most of his family were drowned. Only one boy swam to safety."

"I can't believe you."

One of my godfathers came to me, and I asked him, "Is it true that Manuel is dead?"

"I didn't see them, but I guess it is true because his son came to our house, very wet. He said that his father and mother were walking behind him with the other two children. When they got to the deep water, he didn't see them anymore. That is what the boy told me, Rosalio, so I guess Manuel and Rosa are dead."

Manuel, Rosa, and their three children had been living in their field, about a half mile south of the hill where Miguel Toledo lived. They had eight horses and a few goats there, and these were drowned too.

After the water started going down, the people started looking for relatives. Mariano González searched over Manuel's field and along the river for his brother and his family. Men went by boat, over the wide valley looking for lost people. They found one old man and his wife in a tree, where they had been for eight days. They were so weak they had to be carried out in blankets. Days later Mariano found the bodies of Manuel, Rosa, and their two children.

Two weeks after we fled from Torim, we went to see our muddy house. Yaqui thieves had broken in and stolen everything we owned. All my tools were gone. All our clothes, too. I went from house to house looking for my tools; I suppose the thieves had sold them in Vicam, because they were not to be found in Torim. Two months later I saw a man in Vicam wearing my leather jacket.

"Who sold you this jacket?" I asked him.

"I bought it from Nacho Paroy."

"What did you pay for it?"

"Half a gallon of mescal." My own good friend, Nacha's husband, had stolen my jacket.

We lived at the Indian school for a month. Thirty other families were there. The director fed us a meal a day for a while. Then he got tired of feeding so many hungry Yaquis. We spent nearly all of our twenty-five dollars on food for the thirty families. When only sixty pesos remained, I told Pancha we had better leave or all our money would be gone.

Juan Jacom, the witch from Corasepe, was camped on a hill near the school. He could not come to the school because all those Yaquis hated him. I went over to the hill to talk to him.

"Good morning."

"Good morning," he said, putting down a wooden block to sit on. His wife, Anita, brought a cup of strong, hot coffee.

"We would like to move over here with you until we can move back to Torim."

"Good. We will all stay here together until the road dries."

Pancha and I moved our bundles; Valentina carried Nico. Juan built two small jacal houses there on the hill for us. We talked about what good crops would grow in the Yaqui Valley that year.

"I would like to plant fifteen kilos of corn and fifteen kilos of beans," I said.

"Where do you plan to plant?"

"I haven't found the place yet."

"I have plenty of good wet land that you can borrow. I will even help you with the planting." he said. We walked over and looked at his fields, which were nicely cleared.

"I believe we can plow in about three days."

Pancha and I left Nico with Valentina and went to Vicam to buy the seed, which cost 41.25 pesos. We also bought a few groceries. We were left with 10.75 pesos.

"How are we going to live on this small amount of money and no prospect for more?" I asked Pancha.

"As soon as we move back to Torim, I'll begin making *petates* again."

We planted corn and beans in just two days. The land was already well fenced. "What do I owe you for your mule team and your labor?" I asked my friend.

"Nothing at all. Someday you can help me." As long as I lived in Torim I was too poor to help him, but I always remember him.

Lent had started when we moved back to Torim, February 16, 1949. My poor Pancha got sick and could not eat. Valentina made many kinds of medicine for her, but they did not seem to help. To make some money, I started making posts about five miles south of the pueblo. When I got home every night I had to cook supper for Nico and myself. Pancha could only eat fruit, so I took our little bit of money and bought her canned peaches and canned strawberries.

After three weeks of post cutting, I got paid forty pesos. Then I took Pancha to the doctor in Vicam. For five days I walked twenty-two miles a day, just to go see her in Vicam. I cared for Nico and chopped wood besides. I was awfully tired. Finally I told myself on a Friday, "Rosalio, you are crazy. You don't care about your wife. Don't walk another mile." For two days I stayed home in Torim. Sunday night Pancha walked to Torim.

"Why didn't you come see me? I've waited for you for two days."

"I'm awfully sorry. I just got so tired from walking that I had to rest. Are you a little better?"

"No. I feel the same."

Pancha had spent twenty-five pesos on medicines prescribed by the Mexican doctor, and he never did find out what was wrong with her.

Before I joined the *fariseos* for the Fiesta de Gloria, I went after Valentina and spent the rest of my money on groceries so they could bring me a lunch to the church.

As I have said before, *fariseo* members cannot go home from Holy Wednesday until Sunday. Neither can they talk to any women or girls. If they catch anyone kissing a girl, the guilty ones are taken before the *fariseo* chief. If they have any money, they get off with a fine. Otherwise they have to drag a big cross around. No one can intervene with the *fariseos*, although they can help the person carry the cross. After they have carried the heavy burden of the cross, the *fariseo* chief says to them, "Who is to blame for this? You or the *fariseo* society?"

If they answer, "I am to blame," they are turned loose. But women and girls often get mad at the *fariseos* and answer, "You are to blame. You are the one who is making me drag this cross." Then the *fariseo* chief gives them another type of punishment, such as kneeling for an hour on hard garbanzos. That is the way the *fariseos* act, according to *fariseo* society law.

Since my *fariseo madrina* had died, my *padrino* had to find me another *madrina*. This year Rita Sánchez was my *madrina;* and oh, my God, she fell down on Holy Saturday as we ran in the church, and we were so sad. Sure enough, she died later in the year.

When Easter was over, I saw that Pancha was worse. Although our money was gone, I said, "We must go see the *curandero* at Compuerta." Pancha was so weak that we went very slowly. Andreas Tayechea was gone; his daughter said he was away for several days, visiting his brother.

Another curer, an old woman, also lived in Compuerta. We went to her house. "Oh my. You look very sick. What is the matter with you?" she asked when she saw Pancha.

"I've been sick for two months. I can scarcely eat. Can you give me some medicine for my illness? I'm afraid we have no money."

"I'm sorry, but I can't help you. I have no medicine for your sickness."

We sadly returned home. That night Pancha started to pray to our God. Every night she prayed and prayed. There was so little I could do. I went out into the brush to gather wild foods. I gathered mescal hearts and baked them for twenty-four hours, buried in the ground. I could cook up to two dozen hearts at once. Lázaro liked eating the cactus, and it kept us alive.

One evening one of the boys in the pueblo brought an American to see me. "Are you Simón Palos?"

"Yes."

"My name is Mr. Green; and I have been told you speak English. I come from Berkeley, California." We shook hands.

He said, "I am very glad to know you. How are you getting along?"

"We are not doing well at all. My wife has been ill for more than two months, and I have no money to heal her. I guess only the good Lord can help her."

"Don't worry about your wife. She will be all right soon. I believe you and your wife understand about God. God does everything for us on this earth. Medicine does no good without a faith in God."

He went on to tell how he had had a hard life and had been in many dangerous places such as South Africa and Japan, but no harm befell him because he had a really strong faith in God. He had learned to speak six languages: an African one, French, German, Austrian, Italian, and English. He told us many wonderful stories about our God, and we loved to hear everything he said.

"May I eat supper with you?" he asked.

"There is nothing to eat in the house. Just two old tortillas for our baby boy."

He gave me ten pesos, saying, "Go buy some food." I bought a kilo of flour, a big can of sardines, sugar, coffee, and lard.

"The store was out of bread, but my wife can make some flour tortillas to eat with the sardines."

"Don't bother. I'll just eat the two old tortillas."

Pancha opened the sardines, heated the tortillas, and made coffee. He refused the coffee, so we drank it.

"When do you plan to go back to the United States?" he asked me.

"I guess there is no hope. Some friends from Texas used to come here to the Rio Yaqui, but it has been a long time since they came."

I showed him Dr. Holden's letters.

"I think I like this man. I may go see him sometime in Texas. Don't you worry about a thing, because I know you will have good luck. Our good Lord will help you, just as he helped me."

I piled six *petates* for his bed, to get him far enough off the ground that the bugs would not keep him awake all night. Early the next morning I went from house to house looking for eggs for Mr. Green's breakfast, because I knew that Americans like eggs for that meal. Finally I located two eggs, which Pancha cooked and he ate with tortillas.

"We are awfully sorry, but there is no more food."

"Don't worry. I'll get a good lunch at Vicam."

Before he left, he blessed our poor home and all of us so we would have good fortunes; he also gave us another ten pesos. He is the only white man who ever slept or ate in my house. "I will come back to see you soon," he said.

After he got back to California, he sent us two little Bibles, one in Spanish for Pancha and one in English for me. Pancha loved to read the Bible, because she found many wonderful words of our God.

Two days after Mr. Green left, Pancha was still very sick. We remembered what he had said about our God; I also remembered the things my grandmother told me about curing, because she was a very good *curendera*. She always said that the adobe wall remedy was the only cure for nausea and vomiting. One must scrape some adobe from an east corner of a wall and mix it with water.

"Now I remember what my grandmother always said about curing your kind of sickness, and I am going to make some medicine for you."

I scraped the adobe from the east corner of our house, filled the cup with water, and jiggled the cup until the adobe dissolved. "In the name of Our Lord, this medicine will relieve this poor lady."

"To my God," responded Pancha, as she drank it.

This was about nine o'clock in the morning. She waited for her customary morning session of vomiting, but it did not come. Our God and my grandmother's medicine cured her in just one moment. Day by day she got stronger and the sickness was gone. Soon she began making *petates* again.

We were getting some green corn and string beans out of the garden by this time. Late in June the beans and corn were ready to harvest. We closed our house in Torim and moved out to the ramada in the field. That same night it rained and we got soaked to the skin as we huddled in the ramada. The rain showed no sign of letting up, so we went back to Torim. When we got there, we found the door broken down; nearly everything we owned was gone. The only tools that had not been stolen were those hidden in the field. My hand saw, the accordian, two water canteens, and our clothes were gone.

I found a footprint in the soft floor, and I went at once to find Hilario Coronado, an expert tracker who can identify the footprints of everyone in Torim. "Can you tell who has been in my house?" I asked him.

"That is where Nacho Paroy stepped."

My old friend had done it again, for he is the same one who robbed our house during the flood. Since his wife, Nacha, died he did not care what he did.

Pancha, Nico, and I moved back to the field. "I don't know what I will do after we gather this little crop of beans and corn," I said to her.

"I believe this is your last chance. Why don't you write your friend in Texas and see if he can arrange permission for you to work a few months across the border?"

"I think you are right. I have been here in this village for seventeen years, and there is no way to make a decent living. I have suffered every one of those seventeen years. I will write Dr. Holden right away."

Dr. Holden answered my letter within a week, saying he would be glad to arrange for a six-month permit, but he did not know how long it would take to make the arrangements.

Meanwhile, Pancha and I harvested seven sacks of beans and all the corn. I borrowed a wagon to haul it into Torim; I paid the wagon owner fifty pounds of beans and fifty pounds of corn.

As soon as we finished, I left for Hermosillo to begin getting my papers ready for the labor permit. I went to the church for a baptismal record, but my name was not in the old book. I was able to get a paper certifying my birth date from a judge. On August 2 I went to the Federal Palace to arrange for a passport, which cost me 54.65 pesos. Then I went to see the United States consul in Nogales to see about my permit, hoping that I could cross the border right away. I was very disappointed to learn that it might take months to arrange. He advised me to return to Hermosillo and wait. Dr. Holden wrote that he could do nothing more until the permit was processed by the government.

Pancha wrote every few days from Torim saying that she was sick. She had been left with all the work of shucking the corn crop.

During September, October, and November, life was hard for me in Hermosillo. Every day I tried to find work, but no jobs were available. I lived with Chepa Moreno instead of my mother, because my mother's house was too crowded. Julia and all her children were living with Cecelia. Two of Julia's sons drank too much. One was a saddle maker and one worked in a flour mill. None of Julia's children speak Yaqui; they have become Mexicans. *Tia* Chepa was poor, and often we ate only once a day; she helped me, as she always has.

On November 22 I received a letter from Pancha telling me to come home and care for Nico, as she knew she would not recover. "Come as soon as you can," she said. That night I caught the train to Vicam, arriving the next morning with twelve pesos.

First I went to Vicente Tava's house; he made coffee for us. I went to the store, thinking, "What is the best thing to buy for Pancha with this twelve pesos?" I bought a can of peaches, some meat, bread, flour, sugar, and coffee, as well as some cookies for Nico. After breakfast at Vicente's, I slept for a few hours before walking to Torim. My house was empty. I went across the street to see Teodora Torre Bakasewa.

"Good evening."

"Good evening. So you have come back."

"Yes. I got a letter from Pancha saying she was very ill."

"She is extremely sick now."

"Where is Pancha?"

"Her friends have taken her to Corasepe so they can look after her." She was with old Mayo friends she had known in Bacum, Marcelo Castillo, his wife, Lupe Aldamea, and his sister Jorgina Rapida.

"Thank you. I guess I will go out there now."

When I got there, Pancha was very glad to see me, as was Nico. "I have been very sick for more than a week. I cannot eat anything," she said.

"I brought you a can of peaches. Maybe you can eat some of that. May I open it for you?"

"Let me try a little." She was able to eat a few mouthfuls of peaches.

"I guess I had better go sleep in our house. Tomorrow I have to chop wood, as we are out of money. I will be back to see you tomorrow night," I said to Pancha. The road to Torim was very dark. The house was darker still, as I had no candle. The fleas were so bad that sleep was impossible.

The next morning I called on María Hupaumea, Salome's wife. "Did you go to see Pancha?" she asked.

"Yes. I saw her last night. I'm afraid she is very sick. I have to go chop wood today so I can get a little money. There seems to be no other way to help her."

María gave us beans, tortillas, and strong coffee, and then Salome and I went to the wood forest. By early afternoon I had finished two loads of wood. The next day we went out to the wood forest again. A bad fever hit me in the afternoon and I got home very sick. María made medicine to stop the chills and fever. The following day I was able to chop wood until the fever came, just before noon. What terrible luck we had. My poor wife sick, and now I had the fever sickness. Every morning and every evening I walked to Corasepe to see Pancha.

Pancha died on December 30, 1949, after giving birth to a baby girl. Not a peso did I have when she died, but I had five loads of wood ready to sell in the wood forest. I went to the Mexican storekeeper in Torim. "Can you buy my wood? I have five loads out in the forest. I need the money right now, and I will take ten pesos for it."

"That will be fine. Let's go get it." We went immediately to load the wood on his truck, and he paid me the ten pesos.

First I bought a candle for my poor dead wife. When I got home, her funeral *madrinas* had already fixed her body very nicely. Each had placed a rosary around Pancha's neck. The three *madrinas* and the three *padrinos* brought food to make a fiesta for the *maestros*, *pascolas*, and everyone who came to see the body. The next morning they buried her in front of the church. It was so sad that my wife died. She loved her baby boy so much.

CHAPTER **14**

## *1950–1952*

On February 10, 1950, María Hupaumea and I took the baby girl, Tara, to the judge's office in Bacum, because that was Pancha's pueblo. When we entered Tara's name in the book, the judge told María to sign as Tara's mother, so she signed Francisca Valenzuela Castro.

In Torim I continued chopping wood. Nico went with me every day now, while María looked after Tara. I always caught an iguana or a rat to roast for Nico. He thought they tasted very good.

My baby girl was not getting such good care at María's house because María had two young children of her own, and they were very poor. I thought of a girl in Hermosillo, Chepa Moreno; she had the same name as my *tía* Chepa, whose namesake she was. She was an orphan. Both *tía* Chepa and my mother had known her since she was born, and she used to help both of them with their washing and ironing. Her mother died when she was three months old in Hermosillo in 1917, and her father was killed by Pancho Villa. She was raised by a relative in Hermosillo. Like so many of the Yaquis who grew up there, she spoke very little of her native language.

I wrote to Chepa explaining that I had a little boy and a baby girl whose mother had died, and asking her to come to Torim to care for my little children. She replied that she would be pleased to come if I would send her the fare, as she had no money.

By pawning a pair of scales that I had managed to hang onto since 1936, I got thirty-two pesos, twenty of which I sent to Chepa in a letter advising her to go to Vicente Tava's house in Vicam when she arrived. One morning a Mexican soldier came to tell me that Vicente Tava had called from Vicam, which meant that Chepa had arrived. I quickly walked over to Vicam.

"Good morning, everyone. When did you arrive, Chepa?"

"About five o'clock this morning."

"How much was your fare from Hermosillo?"

"Just twelve pesos."

I went over to the post office and had more good luck in the form of ten dollars in a letter from Dr. Holden and the news that my permit was arranged. I could cross the border on or after May 1.

We were very happy because of the great good fortune that this day had brought. Even though Chepa could speak little Yaqui, she could understand everything, and we had a pleasant visit, with Chepa laughing a lot and acting gay.

Chepa and I picked up a load of groceries at the Vicam store and walked to Torim, going to María Hupaumea's house, as mine was closed. Chepa was pleased to meet María and to see Nico and Tara. The baby was sixty-five days old when Chepa arrived to take care of her. Two days later we moved into my adobe house.

Tara never knew what happened to her own mother, because I have never told her. She believes Chepa to be her mother. Nico, however, remembered Pancha very well, and often asked if she would come back to him.

"Oh yes, Nico, she will come to us again."

"If my mother doesn't come back to me, I will have to go where she is," he would say.

I guess Chepa thought we lived well in Torim, because we ate well for a while.

Lent of 1950 had already started. I was too busy in the wood forest to go with the *fariseos*, but on Holy Wednesday I reported to the *fariseo* chief, staying until Sunday. Sunday morning Chepa did not bring me anything to eat at the church. When the fiesta was over, I found her sitting in a corner of the house.

"What's the matter with you? Are you sick?"

"We are all sick from not eating. The food is all gone. That's why I didn't bring your breakfast to the church."

"Don't worry. I will find something."

Elena Valdes, the Yaqui woman in charge of the Torim church

money, usually kept four hundred or five hundred pesos in her house. I went to see her.

"I came to see you because we have a great necessity. Could you do us the favor of loaning us ten pesos? I will pay you back as soon as I sell my charcoal."

"I am awfully sorry, but I cannot help you. So many Yaquis owe me money, and no one pays me back. This money belongs to the church."

"Well, thank you."

At home, I got out my hammer and machete to pawn at the Mexican store. "I need five pesos. I will leave my tools here until I sell my charcoal. I want them back when I repay you."

"Keep your tools. I will give you five pesos worth of groceries on credit, and you pay me when you sell your charcoal."

I took the groceries to Chepa, and she cooked a meal in the middle of the afternoon. I gathered some bitter green weeds near the river for supper and breakfast. Chepa made a flour and water gravy to eat with them.

Chepa and the children went with me to the wood forest the next day because I needed Chepa's help to rake the charcoal that had been smoldering for almost a week out of the oven. The charcoal was about half burned up.

"Oh my, what bad luck we are having," said Chepa.

"It's not so bad. There must be enough charcoal left to fill seventy sacks."

We worked hard raking the charcoal out one side of the oven and throwing dirt on it to stop it from burning. The next day we dug it out and filled forty old sugar sacks. Quite a lot of charcoal was left unsacked. I slept by the charcoal that night to guard it. For three days I waited for a truck. Finally Chepa came out and suggested I walk over to Chumaiumpaaku to find a trucker.

Chumaiumpaaku is a little place about three and a half miles east of Torim. Mexicans live in each of the eleven houses; every family there owns a wagon. The men make their living buying wood and charcoal from the Yaquis and selling it from house to house in Obregón. I went to see Tony Martínez.

"Well, what brings you around here? We haven't seen you for a long time. What can I do for you?"

"I've come looking for a wagon. I've forty sacks of charcoal in the forest."

"I'll be glad to buy it. I just got in last night from Obregón and I need another load. Where is your charcoal?"

I named the place; he knew exactly where it was because he knew every inch of the Yaqui wood forest. I walked back to the charcoal. As soon as he came in his wagon, we loaded the charcoal and he paid me eighty pesos. The people with trucks or wagons pay two pesos for a sack which they sell in Obregón for five pesos.

When I got home, Chepa said, "What news do you bring me?"

"I've sold the charcoal for eighty pesos."

"That's wonderful. Are you going to Vicam for sacks for the rest of the charcoal?"

"I don't think so. It would cost at least fifteen pesos for sacks and we have to leave soon for Hermosillo, as my permit to go to the United States becomes effective in four days. I guess we better keep our money."

We started closing our house. Everything of value was moved to Salome's house. I kept sleeping in the forest every night to protect the charcoal. I was hoping a Mexican would come along who was willing to buy loose charcoal, but none did. When we left I gave the charcoal to Salome.

May 2, 1950, we left Torim. After spending the night in Vicam with Vicente, we caught the eleven-thirty train for Hermosillo. I stayed with Chepa three days, and then I left for Nogales. After paying seventeen pesos for my bus ticket, I was left with fourteen pesos.

I made arrangements for a cot for the night (costing six pesos) before I went to the market for supper. Everything was so high, I said to myself, "There is no chance for a good meal here," settling for coffee and beans at two pesos. I woke up early next morning; there was nothing to do but sit around until the consul's office opened at nine-thirty, as I could not afford breakfast.

"You are Señor Valenzuela," said the consul.

"Yes, sir."

"Everything is ready for you. I have the forty dollars that Mr. Holden sent. Come back at two o'clock. Your visa will cost two dollars, and then I will give you your papers."

I thought and thought, where could I find two dollars? I remembered that Raul Zamora Díaz was living here. We had worked together on the canal in 1937. I started looking for him on the east side of town. I decided to sit in a small park and see if Raul would come by. I had seen him when I was in Nogales ten months before, and I knew that he usually walked around this part of town selling bread and small cakes. It was not long before I saw him carrying his big basket.

"Oh, hello. Here you are again."

"I came in last night. I believe that I am ready to go the United States."

"That's fine."

"Would you do me a favor? I need two dollars right now so that I can get my papers from the consul. He has forty dollars he will give me after he fixes my papers, so I will pay you back five dollars later this afternoon."

Raul looked in his pocket and counted his pesos. He had just enough to change into two dollars. He changed the money for me. I went into a restaurant and ordered a lunch for 4.80 pesos. I had just 1.25 pesos and the two dollar bills.

Back at the consul's office, it took only a short time to complete the arrangements; the consul gave me the forty dollars, saying I could cross the border any time.

Before I could cross, I had to pay back Raul. I went to a bank and got change for one of my twenty-dollar bills and returned to Raul, who was sitting in the park.

"Is everything fixed up all right for you?" he asked.

"Oh, yes. I am ready to go through the gate. Here is your five dollars."

"Thank you very much."

"I guess I better go now. See you here in six months."

That afternoon, May 8, 1950, I crossed the border. I showed my passport and my papers to the American officer, who asked me, "When did you go through here last?"

"About 1932."

He found my name on a card, and he said, "That's right. All right, you can go through."

I caught the bus to Tucson. My ticket cost $1.35. Arriving there, the first thing I did was to go to a restaurant for a good supper. I had not had food like that for years. Oh, my God, but it was good.

Walking to Pascua, everything looked different; I could not recognize any houses in the dark. Two Yaqui boys were sitting behind the Yaqui church smoking marijuana. They said they did not know my cousin, Viviana.

"Do you know that woman he is asking for?" one said to the other.

"No, I never heard of her."

I was scared because you never know what *marijuanos* will do. I asked if Gregorio still lived in front of the church, and they said yes. Then I left them because they looked awfully mean. At Gregorio's house I asked some girls where Viviana lived. They directed me to the last house on the west.

At my cousin's house, Viviana started to fix supper for me, but I said

I had eaten downtown. We sat up till eleven-thirty talking. Breakfast was early the next morning because Viviana's husband and sons worked downtown. I started out visiting all my friends and relatives. Everyone was happy to see me. Some gave me one dollar, some gave me three dollars, and Viviana gave me five dollars and bought me a new shirt. In the afternoon I went downtown to a movie. I had not seen one in eighteen years.

My sister Antonia came to see me that evening, bringing four of her daughters. She asked about all of her friends and relatives, especially her daughter Pancha Chifú, who was living in Cocorit.

For six days I stayed in Tucson, and old friends and relatives came in a steady stream to visit. I was sorry to leave, but I had to go to Lubbock, Texas. I took one bus to El Paso and another one to Lubbock, getting in about daybreak. I sat around the bus station for a couple of hours before I set out to find Dr. Holden's house. Lubbock is an easy town, and I had no trouble finding my way.

Miss Frances answered the door, and said, "Oh, Simón. Here you are." She went after her husband, and a few minutes later Dr. Holden came and invited me to breakfast. "Do you want to start working today?" he asked.

"Yes."

He introduced me to Lazarus, his other worker, and told Lazarus to fix a cot for me; we started to work building a house.

Two weeks later I sent Chepa ten dollars because I had only been able to leave her twenty-nine pesos. Soon she wrote that she was taking in washing and ironing and making a little money. Later she wrote that Salome had all the charcoal stolen that I had left for him in the forest. She had Tara baptized in Hermosillo on July 9, 1950; she had to sign Francisca Valenzuela Castro on the baptismal certificate, just as María Hupaumea had to do in Bacum. Gloria Valenzuela Chifú, who was married to a Chinese, was the baptismal *madrina* and Alfonso Tava, one of Vicente's relatives, was the *padrino*.

I spent a happy five months in Lubbock building Dr. Holden's house. When my permit was about up, Dr. Holden and Miss Frances took me back to the Rio Yaqui. We stopped to eat with Dr. Holden's friend, Peter Hurd, in New Mexico. Our first night was spent at Carrizozo, New Mexico. We reached Guadalupe Village near Phoenix on November 3. I got off at the Yaqui church to ask for my relative Severiano Hernández. A scarry old woman at his house refused to tell me where he was or when he would come home. When I went back to Dr. Holden's car, I saw an old Ford with a trailer, and Severiano was getting out of it. He was very pleased to see me and meet Dr. Holden, whom he introduced to the Yaqui governor, Juan Valencia. Juan and Severiano were brothers-in-law. The Holdens went to Phoenix to spend the night, and I stayed with Severiano.

Many friends and relatives came to see me, bringing whiskey and beer. "Why won't you drink?" they asked.

"You all know very well that I never drink." After that they left me alone. The next morning when Dr. Holden came to tell me we would stay there another day, Severiano was still drunk. Friends and relatives came to see me all day.

On our way to Tucson, we stopped in Eloy because I wanted to see my daughter, Marcelina. When we got onto the street where Marcelina lived I told Dr. Holden to drive slow while I looked for her house. Luckily, Marcelina's husband was out in front of their house.

Marcelina said, "Well, how long is Dr. Holden going to be in town?"

"He said he would be back in an hour."

"Oh, I'd better fix you some lunch right now. I'm sorry that your granddaughters are in school."

"What is your husband doing at home. Isn't he working?"

"He was so drunk yesterday that he has a bad hangover today."

Marcelina was married to Octavio Valencia, the son of my father's old friends, Eugenio Valencia, and Bela Tapia. Octavio was so hung-over that he did not say a word to me. Eugenio, who was living there, came to see me and to ask that I take a guitar to his kinsman, Lucas Valenzuela, in Torim.

When Dr. Holden returned, we left, taking the guitar. When we got into Tucson, I had a hard time finding my way around. I had to ask a Yaqui boy how to get to Pascua Village. Once there, Dr. Holden left me at Viviana's. Everyone came to visit, including her brother, Simón Valenzuela. Since I last saw him, he had left his first wife, Juana Valencia Wahuechia, for a Mexican woman named María García. This was the first time I had met her. I went to call on Juana Valencia Wahuechia, who lived with her son Cenovio. She never took another man after Simón left her.

We left early for Nogales. Dr. Holden went at once to the immigration office to complete my papers. I went to look for toys for my children. All I bought was a little yellow truck for Nico. It took only a few minutes to clear the Mexican customs; we left for Hermosillo. My *tia* Chepa said that my Chepa had gone to Vicam with the children because they had been so unhappy living with her aunt in her hillside house. I spent the night with *tia* Chepa. My mother came over to see me early the next morning. She was there when Dr. Holden came to pick me up. Miss

Frances gave nice clothes to Chepa and Cecelia; they were both very happy about that.

We got to Guaymas for lunch and to Vicam about three in the afternoon, going directly to Vicente Tava's house, where Chepa, Nico, and Tara were waiting. Everyone was in a festive mood. Chepa made hot chocolate for Dr. Holden and Miss Frances and ran to the store for some special sweet bread. Miss Frances opened her big box and began to give clothes, and clothes, and clothes, and jewelry to Chepa and all the women in Vicente's family. Such happy women you have never seen. Dr. Holden paid me off for all my work, five hundred dollars.

He wanted to go see John Dedrick, the missionary. I took him over there, and they talked for a while. This John is a nice fellow who can speak the Yaqui language better than any other white I have ever seen. He is as poor as many Yaquis, and no one minds that he lives there. Dr. Holden also wanted to see the new school, so we rode over there for a few minutes before he and Miss Frances left to go home.

That very evening the Mexican storekeeper looked me up at Vicente's house, saying, "Your Chepa owes me 240 pesos."

"Don't worry," I said, "I will pay you in the morning." The first thing we did the next day was to pay the storekeeper twenty-eight dollars, and he was pleased that Chepa's debt was paid.

We spent three days with Vicente before Chepa, the children, and I went back to Hermosillo to help my mother. As usual we stayed with *tia* Chepa. At the bank I changed two hundred dollars for 1,710 pesos. Chepa went on a spree of buying things for herself and the children. I bought a pair of shoes for my poor mother. The next day when we went downtown again, Chepa fell in love with a radio.

"We better buy this radio," she said.

"I guess it will cost too much money."

We went in the store and asked the price. Seven hundred pesos. I guess he saw we were disappointed, for he said, "Let me show you a cheaper radio. Here is a nice used radio for only six hundred pesos."

Those Mexicans are too smart, always trying to sell used things for as much as new ones. "Well, if you like it, I will make you a special price of 575 pesos."

Chepa said, "Oh, we had better take it."

So I paid the man. The salesman threw in an old used battery along with the radio. Two days later the battery was dead, and it cost me eighty pesos for another one. "We had better go back to the Rio Yaqui before we spend every cent we have," I told Chepa.

We returned to Vicam on November 13. Vicente was waiting at the station to help us carry all of our packages. We ate a fancy supper and everyone was happy except me. I kept thinking of the money we spent in Hermosillo. Over thirteen hundred pesos in less than three days. After supper they turned on the radio. Chepa and Vicente's daughter-in-law started dancing.

Salome brought his wagon over to move us home to Torim. Everyone we knew came to visit because we had money. When we were poor, no one came; then, I had no half brother, no uncle, no aunt, no one knew me

"Before we begin our store," I said to Chepa, "let's go see the wise woman in Vicam."

"That's a good idea."

On November 18 we walked over to Vicam to learn our fortune. This Yaqui woman had lived for some time in Mexico, and I believe she learned to see into the future while she was there. Whatever she says is true. We got to her house about seven in the evening. I began asking her questions about our business.

"I am willing to tell you these things. Let's go inside."

"That little business will do well for a few months. You will have good luck, but only for a few months. After that something will happen. If you want to know what is going to happen to you, I can tell you."

"No, thank you. I don't want to know," I said. "How much do we owe you?"

"Nothing."

Chepa gave her one of her new dresses, and I gave her ten pesos, even though she wanted nothing.

Chepa and I went to Obregón on a Mexican's truck to buy eighteen hundred pesos worth of provisions for our little store on November 21. When we got back to Torim, we set up the store in my adobe house, while we continued to live with Salome. Customers immediately began coming to buy. Chepa worked hard helping me. Daily she made fresh bread for the store in an oven I built for her. Meat could be cooked in the oven too.

Every four or five days I had to go back to Obregón for more supplies. Business was good. We were eating well every day. The first month no one asked for credit. Then some poor Yaquis began asking for a little credit. I always gave them whatever they asked for. Soon eighteen poor Yaquis owed me from twenty to fifty pesos each. On government payday they came to pay me; the people who owed me twenty pesos would pay me ten pesos and ask for more credit. Before long I had to change more dollars to restock the store, and on December 18 we had to close. Salome's son had been stealing candy, cigarettes, and matches every day, and there was nothing I could do about it because he was my *padrino*'s son.

Chepa and I cleaned up the adobe house and moved into it. Yaquis still came for groceries on credit, but I had to tell them that I had lost too much money by extending credit. Many people in Torim have never paid me the money for groceries they bought on credit in 1950.

Christmas and New Year's were happy. We were in our own house, a little money still remained, and we had some groceries left from the store. The children were eating well.

Bad luck came to us on January 18 or 19 when I received a telegram from Gloria Valenzuela Chifu (Tara's *madrina*) saying that my mother was very sick and I was to come to Hermosillo as soon as I could. I caught the first bus out of Vicam and reached Hermosillo in the afternoon, but my poor mother was already dead. My half sister Julia was not there either, as she had gone to Caborca with her husband. Julia's two daughters and two sons and I buried my mother that afternoon in the cemetery north of town, without a *velación* or anything.

When I got back to Torim the next day, Chepa asked, "How is your mother?"

"In the cemetery."

Chepa was so terribly sad. Over and over she said that my mother had been her best friend. "Your mother cared for me as a baby. All my life your mother helped me. That is why I came to you. I never knew my own mother, but all my life Cecelia was my friend."

I am sure that everything Chepa said is true, because I remember how Chepa helped my mother with her washing and ironing and looking after Julia's children when I was in Hermosillo in 1949. Chepa never danced to the radio again; she was always sad (*triste*).

We kept working in our little store, but business was bad. There was no reason to stock up in Obregón. We went to Obregón once to get Tara confirmed with rosaries at the church. Her confirmation *madrina* was Macaria Paderes Rubio, who lived across the road from us in Torim.

On June 12 our hen hatched seventeen baby chickens. We got up early to see them. Most were yellow or white. Three were black. I was awfully sorry to see those black chicks.

"Do you know why these three black chickens were born?"

"No, I don't know," said Chepa. She had never been around chickens in her life. "Why?"

"Bad luck is coming very near us."

"What bad luck?" she asked.

"I don't know, but we will find out very soon."

We sat watching the chickens the next morning. One of the black babies jumped all around. Chepa laughed and said, "See how happy that little chicken is."

It started trying to crow like a rooster. Its voice was little, but it was acting like a big rooster. It is a bad omen for chicks to act like roosters. Three times the baby chicken tried to crow.

"Now you see. What I told you yesterday is surely true. This baby chicken will bring us very bad luck. We just have to wait and see what will happen to us."

Two weeks later a letter came from one of Julia's daughters saying that my half sister was in the hospital and she wanted me to come to her at once. I ran all the way to Vicam to catch the first bus to Hermosillo. My niece met me at Julia's house, and we went together to see Julia. She could not talk, but she kept her eyes on me. I asked her how she was feeling, but she did not hear me. Her breath was coming fast. She just looked at me.

My niece and I left to go to their house, and Julia died a short time later. We brought her body home. The Yaquis in Hermosillo do not choose godparents for the dead any more. I sent my niece and nephew to the store with two hundred pesos for groceries to cook for the *velación*. Many people came to visit my dead sister, because she was well known in Hermosillo. Julia's two sons drank mescal all night, and every few minutes they wept like Yuma Indians. Their sisters kept telling them to stop crying; then they tried to fight everyone. They made a lot of noise all night long.

The next morning I told one of the girls to go look for some cars to take my sister's body to the cemetery. The boys were too drunk to go see their mother buried. By noon we had returned from the cemetery, and I asked the owner of the cars what I owed him. One hundred and sixty pesos.

I returned to Vicam the next day, resting for an hour at Vicente's house. "I guess we are about broke again," I told him, "because we have had a lot of bad luck. Every disaster has cost me. A lot of Yaquis owe me money that I have no hopes of collecting because they are so poor."

When I got to Torim, Chepa did not ask about Julia. She knew Julia had died. "Well, how is the luck?" I asked her.

"Much worse. I have sold almost nothing since you left. We are almost out of money. The only thing left to do is to sell the radio so we can buy some more provisions."

"Oh," I said, "Why do we have to sell the radio? The children love it so."

"You know what you can do," she said.

From July to September our business got worse. The Yaquis who owed us so much money were buying their things from the Mexican store now. Hardly anyone came to our store. At the end of September I had 160 pesos left out of all the money I earned in Texas and all the business at the store, and Chepa had only 40 pesos.

The Yaqui chief received a notice from the governor of Sonora on September 25 to the effect that all Yaquis from the eight pueblos were to have free rides to the fiesta at Magdalena.

"We better go," I said.

"Oh, we don't have enough money to go," said Chepa.

"But we don't have to pay the fare. We can go free."

Chepa was sad and did not want to go, but we went anyhow on October 1, 1951. Nico and Tara were delighted to ride the train and go to the fiesta. Chepa never did brighten up. She just stayed sad. When we got back to Vicam on October 5, I had sixty-five pesos and Chepa had twelve.

A few weeks later I had to sell the radio for sixty pesos. Chepa took the children out of the house while I took the radio away. My baby Tara looked all over the house for it. Little by little the children forgot the radio. Chepa became sadder; now she was crying every day. On October 28 everything was gone, including all the food. For a few days I tried to make chairs, but I was not any good at it.

On November 10 I got out my ax and went back to the wood forest. Poor Chepa did not want to stay alone. She and the children walked out to the wood forest with me every morning. As soon as she got there, she laid down under a tree and slept all day long. Often she refused to eat lunch with us. She became more pallid; on December 4 she was unable to walk to the wood forest with me. I was sad because there was nothing I could do. There was no money for medicine. Now that we were poor, no one came to see us. She just laid in the house alone all day while I went to the wood forest. I wanted to take her to the doctor at Vicam, but she refused to go.

"Please leave me alone. Don't do anything for me. I will never get well. The only thing I want from you now is for you to write my aunt in Hermosillo. But tell her not to come to see me, because she is very poor. Where could she get the money to come see me?"

"You will be all right. You don't look so sick." But all the same I wrote the letter.

Three days after Chepa took to her bed, Nico fell sick with chills and fever. He could not eat any more. No one came to help us.

Chepa died on December 11. At least I think that was the date. I went crazy when she died. I found four *madrinas* and four *padrinos* for her. Some Yaquis said that they had not even known she was sick.

"She has been sick for weeks. And now I have a sick boy at home by himself."

The *madrinas* and *padrinos* took care of Chepa, arranging her body, putting on the Yaqui rosaries, and bringing the *maestros* and *pascolas*. The *pascolas* dance for children who die and for people who have not been married in the church. Neither Pancha nor Chepa was married in the church, so both had *pascolas* at their funeral. My poor Chepa was laid out for twenty-five hours before they buried her in the old cemetery east of town.

I stayed with Nico, giving him water in a spoon every few minutes, day and night. My boy died about three days after Chepa. His *madrinas* and *padrinos* made a fiesta for him, and he was buried in front of the church on December 15, 1951.

My baby Tara and I went back home. Oh, my Lord, but our house was sad. Tara was as happy as ever because she did not understand what had happened. I could not stay where Chepa had lived, so we moved in with María and Salome. I wrote Dr. Holden, telling him what had happened. He answered immediately, saying that he would be in Torim by December 27.

We spent a sad Christmas. On the day Dr. Holden was to arrive I did not go to the wood forest, but waited in my house. I saw a black car pull up at the schoolhouse. It was Dr. Holden and his whole family. I went to get Tara at María's house; she was terrified of the white people.

I told them about Chepa and how happily we had lived for a few months while our store did well. I never thought we would go broke, because we started with so much money. Chepa died of *tristeza* because we lost all our money and because my mother died.

Dr. Holden said he would take me back to Texas to work. We tried to take Tara along, and in fact I took her to Guaymas, but she got sick and I was afraid for her to travel. I had to leave her with Jorge Terminal, an old friend I used to play baseball with in Tucson. He took her back to María in Torim when she was well.

# CHAPTER 15

# Since 1952

I HAVE NOT LIVED AMONG the Yaquis during most of the time since I left the Rio Yaqui in December, 1951, until the present, although I have visited Arizona and the Rio Yaqui every winter. For sixteen years I have lived alone on a farm in Lubbock County, raising cotton or doing odd jobs for the Holdens from spring till fall. I have never been hungry.

When Tara was six years old, we arranged the papers necessary to bring her to the United States. She has been raised by Simón Valenzuela and María García in Tucson. They speak no Yaqui at home, and Tara has forgotten her own language.

In the years since I have been living in Texas, I have seen Salvador and Marcelina every year. I like Salvador's wife; she treats me with respect and is good with her children. One of Salvador's sons has become a *fariseo* captain and another dances as one of the *fariseos* who carry a long lance. It is a pity that my grandchildren do not speak Yaqui. Salvador is now involved with building a new Pascua Village, and Marcelina will move there to be near him now that her husband has died in Eloy. Some crazy person told the Welfare Department she was seeing another man, so they cut off the little money she was getting.

Mariano González and Dominga Palos have kept me informed about what was happening in the Rio Yaqui, Marcelina and some of my grand-children write me from Arizona, *tia* Chepa is a regular correspondent, and my daughter Juana Valenzuela writes from Esperanza. All in all, I keep up very well with events concerning the Yaquis.

Many friends and relatives have died since I have lived in Texas. Santiago Vetem, who took part in the 1909 Pitahaya Peace Conference, died at Vicam in 1962. Tomás Kuka, the man who was married to *tia* Chepa's oldest sister, Eulalia, in Colorado, died at the ripe old age of ninety-two in Torim in 1962. Soledad Lemas died the same year. She was the mother of Felipe Vega, my Torim *fariseo padrino*.

In 1963 I had a dream that my cousin Viviana was on a ship that was leaving. This dream always means that that person will die soon. Viviana died shortly thereafter. The same dream came again in 1964 or 1965. Two people I knew were on the ship, Simón Hernández, son of Luciano at Guadalupe, and my sister Antonia. I was able to pull Antonia off the ship. Simón died within a month. Antonia had been told she had cancer, but after that she began to get better. Now she says her cancer is cured. I saved her.

My daughter Juana had a baby named Nicolasa born with the sign of the witch. When a child is born with a tightly curled strand of hair stuck to its head, it means they will grow up to be a witch. Parents wash the hair and try to make it straighten out. Little Nicolasa was born in December, 1966, and died in March, 1967, so she did not become a witch. Children born with the witch mark are never dumb.

The winter of 1967 was the first year I have missed in returning to the Rio Yaqui. I could not go because I was still suffering the effects of witch sickness in January, 1967. This is the way I was witched.

I arrived in Potam to visit my half sister Dominga Palos on January 5, 1967. We talked for a while. In the afternoon I was outside playing with the children when María Victoria Tava came over, dressed in a green and white striped skirt, pink blouse, and *rebozo*. Dominga came out to tell me she was there. "Rosalio, my *comadre* who cured you last year is here."

"I didn't bring her a gift," I said, and I stayed outside with the children until she left. You see, when she cured me the year before I gave her two dollars and told her I would bring her a real gift the next time I came. I did not have a gift and I did not want to give her money a second time, so I did not want to see her.

The next morning I woke up very sick. Dominga sent out for sweet bread at breakfast time, and I said, "This bread is very bitter." Dominga did not answer me. When she brought me a Coke later in the morning, I said, "The Coke here is bitter." Dominga did not reply.

I went to Cocorit on January 7 to visit Antonia's daughter, Pancha

Chifu, and later I spent a day with my own daughter Juana in Esperanza. Everything I ate tasted bitter, but I did not mention this to anyone else. The same thing happened to me in Hermosillo, where I visited my *tia* Chepa and Julia's son, León Gálvez.

Upon returning to my son's house in Pascua Nuevo on January 18, I told him that I was sick because someone had harmed me. On Sunday morning Salvador and I went to find a Papago *curandero* named Marques Ursua who is married to Chela Vacamea, a half sister of Simón Valenzuela. Salvador did not know exactly where Marques lived, so we asked Abato Sasueta at Marana, and he took us to Marques's house, five miles from Sasco. Marques was out working in the fields when we arrived, but he was sent for and came soon.

A small room on one side of his house contained *santos*, holy water, and other things; it was here that he and I went alone. He did not have to ask what was wrong. First he recited the rosary, then he began rubbing my chest as though he was scraping off something slimy and flinging it on the floor.

"You aren't well. A woman is doing you harm. She formed a ball of green *jariondia* leaves inside your stomach, but it will pass any day now."

Handing me a glass of holy water, he said, "Now drink this." He called to his wife, "Bring a piece of bread and butter for Rosalio." It was not bitter.

Salvador, Abato, and I ate a good dinner with Marques and Chela. Chela prepared a broth, meat with tomatoes and onions, and both corn and wheat tortillas. Every bite tasted good.

I offered to pay Marques five dollars, but he refused to touch it. "If you want to leave me some money, put it in my pocket with your own hand."

He handed me a small bottle of holy water to take along. When we got to Salvador's house, I continued to have a good appetite all afternoon; however, the bitterness returned the next day. All Monday I felt wretched. Tuesday morning I felt something working up and down in my stomach. I stepped outside and vomited a green, leafy ball.

Salvador went for a Yaqui *curandero* named Antonio Moreno on Wednesday. Antonio lit the candle in front of the saints. The first flame bent over to the south, indicating that the trouble came from that direction. Antonio recited the whole rosary, including the prayers to the Virgin Mary, the Our Father, and the Creed. It took him a long time. Then he asked for a glass of water, which Salvador's wife, Chepa, brought. Into this he broke an egg and put a few drops of holy water. A few minutes later the entire figure of a woman dressed in a green and white striped skirt, pink blouse, and *rebozo* appeared in the glass. Her face was quite clear. All four of us saw her very well. Antonio asked if I knew who she was.

"Oh, yes, that is a woman I know in Potam. I know that she killed her husband, three years ago," I said.

Later I wrote Dominga that her friend had caused me to be ill, but she did not believe it. Neither Dominga nor her son Anselmo believe in witches. I have always known about witches, but this is the only time one has harmed me personally. The effects have lasted for over a year now. Marcelina recently sent medicine (*contra yerba*) that seems to be helping.

Some people in Arizona believe that I am a witch. My aunt Camilda, when she was really mad at me, used to scream at me that I would grow up to be a witch. So many of my enemies in Tucson have died from the time of my trouble with Loreta that many believe I am a good witch. In 1955, when I was visiting Tucson, a Yaqui named Anastasia Matuz asked me if I could teach him some techniques, as his wife had left him and he wanted her back. He offered me a lot of money to teach him.

"I am sorry about your wife," I said, "but I don't know anything about such matters." Of course I am not a witch. No one in the Rio Yaqui ever thought I was.

Antonio Moreno, who showed me who was causing me to be sick, died July 12, 1967. He was the brother of Nicolás Uhllolimea, one of the Torim governors. Antonio lived in the Sierra from 1910 to 1925. In 1912 he took part in a big train robbery south of Empalme, along with some thirty other Yaquis, including Lola Posoi. Antonio buried a bag of money that he took in the robbery in a hole when he left the Sierra in 1926 to come to Tucson, where he stayed. He was a very good deer dancer. When he felt that it was finally safe to return for his bag of money, he went to look for it. He died of thirst in the Sierra, without his money. His wife, María Moreno, and a son, José Luis, still live in Tucson.

Whereas Juan Tecu Yoimere was really killed by Mexicans and came back to life, I have often dreamed I was killed, which is a good omen for a long life. The last time I had the dream was in 1967, when I dreamed that Miguel Ramíriz, a Mexican friend that works on a farm just south of the Holden farm in Texas, killed me with a knife. When I told a white lady about it the next day, she said that was bad luck, but it is not.

Two ghosts have come to see me in my little house at the farm. Bill Carter lived south of the farm. We were good friends, and I sometimes looked after his cow when he was gone. Three days after he died in 1956, he knocked on my door, and called "Hello." Miss Jane asked if I talked to him, but how do you talk to a ghost? He still comes to the door once in a while, although he has not been around for a year now. Another time a ghost I did not know got in the house and embraced me. We had quite a fight before it left.

I often think of the poor Yaquis in the Yaqui villages. While I lived there, I saw forty-eight little children die. I believe that the worst part of Yaqui life is the sickness and death of children; the parents were always sad when their babies got sick or hungry and there was nothing they could do except watch them die. Children, or anyone, could get chills and fever, rabies, or many other diseases that came and went. Many of the jobs by which Yaquis make a living end up killing them. I knew thirty-nine *petate* makers in Torim who died of lung sickness, many miners died with lung trouble, and many who do irrigation work in rubber boots die of a foot disease caused by the rubber boots.

There will always be a Yaqui tribe. The Yaqui are not like the Mayos or the Pimas, who have all become Mexicans. The Yaquis still speak their language. But I do not know what will happen to the poor Yaquis. As long as we were fighting the Mexicans in the Sierra, we were strong and the Mexicans could not take our land. Men who were brave Yaqui soldiers in the Sierra became *torocoyoris* in the valley. What the Mexicans could not take by bloody war, they may well get in the end through the banks. Since 1952 most Yaqui land has been controlled by the bank; now the banks *hire Yaquis to work on their own land* for ten pesos a day! The Yaquis cannot even plant food for themselves. They just plant wheat for the bank. Nor can a Yaqui fish or go after oysters. The fishing cooperatives run them off.

The Yaquis have always liked to have Yaqui generals, but what they need now is a general or chief of agriculture. Effective farming of land is the last hope of the Yaqui tribe. Yaqui land is good and rich. There must be a half-million acres south of the river that have never been farmed since God created the world. Many acres north of Vicam are *monte* (brush) which could be harvested of wood and carrizo or cleared for farmland. I believe a million pesos worth of wood could be cut there. The Torim lands alone are large and rich. Even General Luis Torres (who took over Torim lands under Porfirio Díaz, built a big house there, and tried to make Torim into a Mexican town) was unable to work all the Torim land. What is needed are tools and water.

If I could put in a five-inch irrigation pump and farm with tractors, as I have in Texas, the land would produce fantastic crops. I believe that shallow water underlies all the Yaqui lands. I used to dream of finding a white man to finance a modern farming operation for the Yaqui tribe.

But what's the use? As soon as something like that got going, the Mexicans or the *torocoyoris* would take it over; a few would make a little money, but most of the Yaquis would be as hungry as before. It would turn out like everything else has—the same as the time the Mexican government sent each pueblo a truck, which the pueblo governors sold for next to nothing, or the time the pueblos were given fine tractors.

Any number of businesses could profit the Yaqui tribe. A good bus service, for example. I have talked to Anselmo Romero Matos, Dominga's son and a one-time governor of Potam, about taking tourists up into the Sierra to see some of the wonderful things there like the lovely stone Corona (crown). Anselmo says it would not work. The Yaquis do not want outsiders in the Sierra.

If I had a great deal of money, I would like to buy a Santa Claus suit and go to Torim at Christmas, because the children there have never seen Santa Claus. Another thing I would like to do is make a movie of what happened in Hermosillo when I was a boy. I believe I could make such a movie, using Yaquis as actors, especially children. Mexicans would have to play Governor Izábal and Colonel Luis Medinas Varón.

No matter how much money I had, I would never buy furniture. My grandmother always cooked on an adobe fireplace; after we came to Arizona, she refused to let my father buy her a cook stove—they were an invention of the *demonio*. I would, however, like to own an organ.

Well, I told Miss Jane I would write my life story. It has been difficult. I do not write so well in English. Miss Jane said I could write in Spanish, but that would be no better. I have had so little schooling. I do not believe you can understand what I am writing in my notebooks, but anyway I have let you know about my life.

I am living, while most of the people who have harmed me are dead. I can still work hard, and that is good. I will dance again as a *fariseo*. My candle is still tall.

I thank my American friends, Mrs. Mayhugh, Miss Frances, Mr. Tom, and Miss Gladys. Dr. Holden has done everything good for me, like a good father among a family. But first of all, I thank Uncle Sam. Because of Uncle Sam, I learned a little English here in the United States of America.

THIS IS MY LIFE STORY

THE END

# Acknowledgments

BECAUSE THIS BOOK has roots that reach back into the 1930s, it is natural that many persons have contributed services, ideas, and evaluation. Many who have been concerned with Rosalio Moisés and his life story belong to those early years in Lubbock, Texas, before I was actively involved, and cannot now be isolated as individuals. When I took over the project, my father, William Curry Holden, gave me full access to his extensive diaries, notes, tapes, and photographs of the Yaquis. He had in his possession the diaries of Drs. Wagner and Studhalter written during various expeditions to the Yaqui Valley. All of these materials, as well as published sources on the Yaquis, aided me in providing a Yaqui background for my own personal use while I was working with Rosalio Moisés and his life story. Nothing from those sources actually was incorporated into the personal chronicle, which was always meant to belong to Rosalio Moisés alone, but they were invaluable in providing cross checks on his information. Mrs. W. G. MacMillan and Mrs. Winston Reeves gave me access to the photographic files of their late husbands; some of their photographs appear in this book.

Perhaps most projects have blind alleys, and if so, this one was normal. A number of people worked with great enthusiasm on facets of this project, although it was not ultimately possible to include their work in the finished version because of production considerations. Nonetheless, I feel they deserve honorable mention. Wayne Nelson copied old photographs of members of Rosalio Moisés's family. Pat Allgood of Lubbock, Texas, made the first two versions of the geneological chart, while Harley Sorrells of Calgary, Alberta, produced a third. Mr. Sorrells also created an ink sketch of Rosalio Moisés from a photograph.

Many of Rosalio Moisés's relatives allowed us to copy family photographs and clarified points for him when he wished more information. I am sure he would wish to thank Josefa Alvarez, Tula Valenzuela, Matilde Arenas, Crecensio Arenas, and Anselmo Valencia for their encouragement.

At various times over the last fifteen years, the institutions with which we were affiliated have graciously aided with secretarial help and financial assistance. I am happy to acknowledge the help of Texas Technological College, the University of Nebraska, and the University of Calgary, in the chronological order in which they extended assistance. The final typing of the manuscript was done by Charlene Vance and Donna Thomas under a research grant from the University of Nebraska. A revised introduction and the index were put into final form by Mrs. E. L. Wittig and her able assistants in the Stenographic Services of the University of Calgary.

Dr. Edward Spicer offered thoughtful and helpful suggestions. Dr. Joyce Wike and Dr. Alice Kehoe also listened and advised.

Perhaps it is unusual for a junior author to thank the senior author, but I feel my most deeply felt acknowledgment must be to Rosalio Moisés, whose patience with me was phenomenal.

JANE HOLDEN KELLEY

# Index